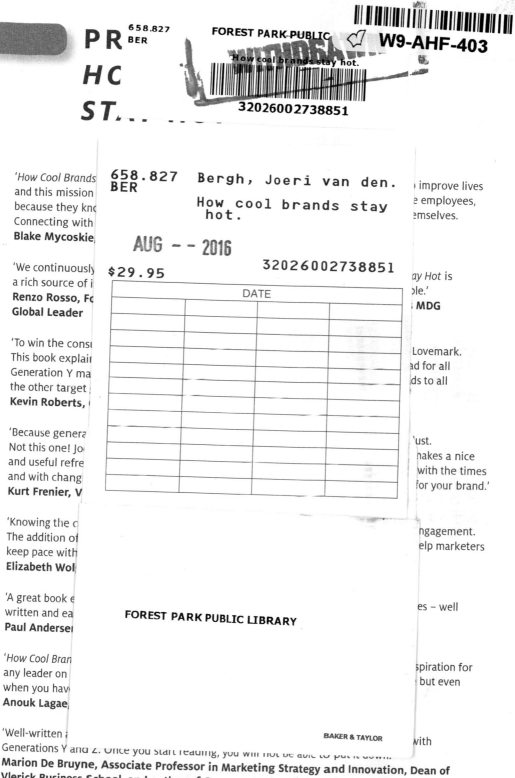

'How Cool Brands   improve lives
and this mission   e employees,
because they kno   emselves.
Connecting with
Blake Mycoskie,

'We continuously   ay Hot is
a rich source of i   ole.'
**Renzo Rosso, Fc   MDG
Global Leader**

'To win the cons   Lovemark.
This book explai   d for all
Generation Y ma   ds to all
the other target
Kevin Roberts,

'Because genera   ust.
Not this one! Jo   hakes a nice
and useful refre   with the times
and with chang   for your brand.'
Kurt Frenier, V

'Knowing the c   hgagement.
The addition of   elp marketers
keep pace with
Elizabeth Wol

'A great book e   es – well
written and ea
Paul Anderse

'How Cool Bran   spiration for
any leader on   but even
when you hav
Anouk Lagae,

'Well-written   with
Generations Y and Z. Once you start reading, you will not be able to put it down.'
**Marion De Bruyne, Associate Professor in Marketing Strategy and Innovation, Dean of
Vlerick Business School, and author of** *Customer Innovation*

'This book gives a fabulous deep dive in marketing and branding to Millennials. It is often said that the Millennials are more complex and don't follow easy, linear rules. *How Cool Brands Stay Hot* definitely reduces complexity and is a must-read for all of those who have to understand these target groups.'
Dr Alexander Linder, Vice President Corporate Brand, Consumer and Market Intelligence, Swarovski

'Van den Bergh and Behrer give an elaborate insightful view on how to reach generation Y and Z. A must-read for every marketing professional who wants to get a better understanding of young adults.'
Jean-Jacques Velkeniers, VP Marketing Europe & Business Unit President Europe West, AB InBev

'It is easily taken for granted that a hot brand stays cool forever. You continue working with what was successful in the past until one day you have become irrelevant or 'the brand of my parents'. This book helps in such an impactful way to stay in touch with Millennials and offers plenty of concrete examples to apply to your brand instantly.'
Anneleen Waterloos, Global Head of Consumer & Business Intelligence, IKEA

'One of today's challenges is having too much access to too much information. *How Cool Brands Stay Hot* focused us on key things to know about Millennials and did a great job of illustrating these themes with current marketing and advertising examples to bring them to life.'
Judith Oppenheim, Research Director, Insights & Planning, R/GA

'This and previous editions have been instrumental in bringing this generation to life for us. By introducing key elements of tangibility and insight, they're helping shape our shared journey, both as a world-class technology brand as well as a best-in-class employer brand for Gen Yers and beyond'
Anna Zanghi, Vice President Global Product, MasterCard

'Millennials – everybody is trying to understand them but very few get to both their hearts and brains. This is what Van den Bergh and Behrer do in this book, decoding young men and women who will lead the world in the coming future. For a generation famous for multitasking and lack of attention, the book helps brands in creating longer lasting bonds. The sneak peak on Gen Z is insightful too, as they are not 'younger Millennials' but a generation on its own. A great, insightful must-read.'
Marcelo Amstalden Möller, Head of Global CMI Innovation, HEINEKEN Group

'*How Cool Brands Stay Hot* holds the best and most comprehensive perspective on Generation Y marketing and I regularly recommend it in lectures on recruiting Generation Y.'
Christophe Fellinger, Talent Relationship & Recruiting Manager, Beiersdorf

'I am generally not a big fan of marketing books and particularly not when they touch so-called youth marketing. But this one was refreshing and informative, more observing and sharing a frame of thinking on the evolution of generations instead of an absolute theory on 'how to get after those young consumers'.'
Gert Kerkstoel, Partner GIMV, Investor and former Global Business Director, Nike SB

'No challenge is more pressing for today's brands than successfully connecting with Generation Y. This book offers precious insights on doing just that.'
Ricardo Marques, VP Marketing High End Imports, AB InBev

How Cool Brands Stay Hot

For my two Generation Z daughters, Vita and Jina,
who haven't lost much of their muchness yet
JOERI

For my grandmother and role model Lilly,
who had the wisdom of a 100-year-old
but the heart and mind of a teenager
MATTIAS

THIRD EDITION

How Cool Brands Stay Hot

Branding to Generation Y and Z

Joeri Van den Bergh and Mattias Behrer

With a Foreword by
Patrick De Maeseneire

KoganPage

LONDON PHILADELPHIA NEW DELHI

First published in Great Britain and the United States in 2016 by Kogan Page Limited

2nd Floor, 45 Gee Street	1518 Walnut Street, Suite 1100	4737/23 Ansari Road
London	Philadelphia PA 19102	Daryaganj
EC1V 3RS	USA	New Delhi 110002
United Kingdom		India

© Joeri Van den Bergh 2016

The right of Joeri Van den Bergh to be identified as the author of this work has been asserted by them in accordance with the Copyright, Designs and Patents Act 1988.

ISBN   978 0 7494 7717 2
E-ISBN   978 0 7494 7721 9

British Library Cataloguing-in-Publication Data

A CIP record for this book is available from the British Library.

Library of Congress Control Number

2016935538

Typeset by Graphicraft Limited, Hong Kong
Print production managed by Jellyfish
Printed and bound by CPI Group (UK) Ltd, Croydon CR0 4YY

CONTENTS

LIST OF FIGURES

LIST OF TABLES

customers a reason to put aside their mouse, and drive to that shopping mall or that street. After all, you cannot have a salad or a glass of wine with a friend online'.

Another great example, also discussed in this book, is LEGO. The company almost went under in 2003. A new management team came in, streamlined the offerings and processes, and decided to outsource – or, better, crowd-source – its design to its biggest fans, the users, as has been done with Cuusoo, one of LEGO's crowdsourcing ideas. Launched globally in 2011, Cuusoo invites users to submit – and vote for – ideas for new LEGO sets. If a design wins enough votes, LEGO reviews it for possible production, and if successful its creators will get a small part of the product's total net sales. The company therefore combines physical with digital, using social media to reach out to its communities for design, while adding to its traditional blocks, online games and movies. The result: LEGO became so successful that it was not able to fulfil all the demand for the most recent holiday season.

The second point: the purpose. Or the 'why'. Why are we here? Why are we doing what we are doing? I refer to Jim Stengel, who conducted an unprecedented, ten-year growth study and research on a global database of more than 50,000 brands. What he found was astounding: brands that are built on ideals, or companies that centered their businesses on the ideal of improving people's lives, resonate more with consumers and clearly outperform their category competitors.

Moreover, an investment in the top 50 businesses in the growth study – 'The Stengel 50' – would have been 400 per cent more profitable than an investment in the S&P 500 over that same 10 years.

Apple moved on from selling computers to creating a better world; Amazon moved on from online shopping to enabling you to discover and explore; Starbucks moved on from serving coffee to building human con-nections. They have a purpose. Akzo Nobel's paint division Dulux moved on from selling paint tins to selling tins of optimism, to colouring people's lives. It enlists volunteers and donates paint, more than half a million litres so far, to revitalize run-down urban neighbourhoods from Brazil to India.

Purpose and 'why' become more and more important and will be the vital element of any successful company and brand. In his book *Good Works!* Philip Kotler explains several cases in detail where companies do well by doing good, and proves that corporations that take this to heart, and make it a fundamental part of their strategy, receive the following benefits:

- increase sales and market share;
- strengthen their brand positioning;
- improve their image and admiration;
- have an increased ability to attract, motivate and retain employees.

A good example here, one also discussed in this book, is TOMS. I had the opportunity to meet its founder Blake Mycoskie at the World Economic Forum in Davos in 2013. Mycoskie, who calls himself Chief Shoe Giver, dropped out of Silicon Valley, went on a trip through South America, saw how many people didn't wear shoes, started to produce casual easy-going shoes with the aim of one pair sold, one pair given away around the world. Today more than 50 million pairs of shoes are given away, and he starts it all over, this time with eyeglasses. TOMS does good, and it does well.

Ladies and gentlemen, in today's world of social media, with an explosion of touch points, an overload of choice in product and service offerings, and with purposeful Millennials, people don't buy brands – they buy *into* brands. If you handle social media with engagement, the touch points with consistency, the overload with impact and the purposeful consumer with meaning and positivity, you will not only do well, but your cool brand will stay hot for a long, long time.

WHAT'S NEW
IN THIS EDITION?

Since the release of the first edition of our book, we have been positively surprised by the amount of appreciation and interest we experienced from journalists, conference organizers and CEO's and marketing and advertising practitioners from all around the world. It seems that the timing of publishing a book on the subject of branding and marketing to the new generation of consumers was plain right. We have had the unique opportunity to travel the world and present the content of the first edition from Las Vegas to Manila. Along the way of over 400 presentations and workshops in the past years, we have learned a lot from readers' feedback and obtained new insights and perspectives with every new engagement. We were honoured with great awards such as Expert Marketer's Marketing Book of the Year 2011 in Europe and the Berry-AMA Award for Best Marketing Book 2012 in the USA. And hadn't expected, or dreamed of, such wonderful praise.

When preparing this third edition, we felt that we had to do more than just update the facts and figures. We have added a more global perspective with new case studies from emerging markets as well as new global research projects we have executed ourselves in the past two years. We have inserted new up-and-coming marketing topics and consumer trends such as the maker movement, serendipity, integrity, the sharing economy, employer branding and the importance of crafts, nostalgia and local. We have placed more focus on the social media and digital parts of campaigns and social branding. Last but not least we wrote a complete new chapter on the next generation: Generation Z. Through our in-company workshops and presentations, we got in touch with many interesting marketing and advertising people. It allowed us to replace detailed academic research with the practitioner's view on the topics we deal with in our book. For the previous edition we did 24 interviews with global brand directors and CMOs of great brands in various industries. For this edition we have added four more interviews with:

Åsa Coop (CEO and Founder of Our/Vodka);

Per Hjuler (SVP Innovation & Consumer Marketing at The LEGO group) and Ward Van Duffel (VP and General Manager Direct to Consumer EMEA at the LEGO GROUP);

Jordan Casey (CEO and founder of Casey Games, TeachWare & Wrehouse);

Mark Van Iterson (Global Head of Design and Concept Development at Heineken International).

What has changed in this third edition: a small overview

In Chapter 1, we have added new data from an InSites Consulting Generation Next study in which we interviewed more than 10,000 people from four different generations: Babyboomers, Generation X, Y and Z. It gave us new insights on the generational differences. We wrote a new piece on the newborn generation alpha. The chapter also has some new cases like TOMS shoes, Pepsi Live for Now and WWF's #SaveTheAles campaign. Chapter 3 on coolness has new information on how cool brands use ephemeral media like SnapChat, Vine, Meerkat and Periscope, a new piece on toys-to-life and some new case studies: Oreo cookies, Pimkie, Powerade, and Heineken Pop-up City Lounge.

Chapter 4 on authenticity contains new parts on consumer nostalgia and on using celebrity endorsements. It has a number of new case studies like Adidas, Bud Light, Vodafone and P&G's Always. It also explains Newcastle's No Bollocks positioning and the new case study on Chipotle's integrity has replaced Levi's 501 case.

Chapter 5 on uniqueness contains the exclusive interview with DIESEL's founder Renzo Rosso, and three updated case studies: Tomorrowland, KFC and Volvo. We have also added the Nike 'better for it' campaign addressing women.

Chapter 6 on self-identification is completely revised. We have deleted the parts on teen identity construction for this edition and the section on tribal mapping of subcultures has also been erased. Instead we wrote a new part on how brands can get closer to youth by working on the five core life themes. It is based on a ten-country structural collaboration with Millennials that Viacom and InSites have worked on in the past years. We also highlight the growing importance of skills for NextGen and trends like party-cipation, serendipity and the shortcut economy. Related to a new piece on the craft culture and the importance of local involvement we have inserted an interview with the ex-innovation director of Pernod Ricard's Absolut Vodka who is now doing a roll-out of Pernod Ricard's glocal business idea Our/vodka. At the end of the self-identification chapter, you will find a new part on how subcultures are increasingly moving online through online forums and fandom pages on Tumblr and Reddit.

Chapter 7 on happiness contains new sections on haptics (touch) and music and brands. We have added a number of new case illustrations to the text: American Apparel, AllState Insurance, Apple bendgate, Nike Most Wanted, Target's pop-up stores and updated the Coca-Cola case study.

Chapter 8 is a complete new extra chapter on those born after 1996, known as Generation Z or Post-Millennials. After the introduction on their financial power and big influence on their parents' purchases, we will introduce the key DNA characteristics of Generation Z:

- They are snappy and live in the age of impatience.
- They are an emoji-onal visual generation.
- They are dreaming of creating a better world.
- They embrace imperfections.

The chapter contains valuable information on the use of YouTube video and cluster sharing, animated GIFs and SnapChat and bedroom influencers. NextGen consumer trends such as gender equality and diversity, female empowerment and world improving brand strategies such as the one-for-one business model are also explained. Case illustrations in this new chapter include LEGO, Minecraft, Always #likeagirl campaign and Intermarché's inglorious fruit and vegetables campaign.

We hope this third edition will be appreciated as much as the previous ones. Of course even readers of the other editions could benefit from refreshing their knowledge with all this new material.

ACKNOWLEDGEMENTS

We would like to thank some of the many people who have helped us along the way in writing this book. Thanks to the more than 80,000 Gen Yers who have anonymously participated in the various global research projects that gave us the inspiration for this project.

Joeri's words of thanks

In *Alice in Wonderland*, the Mad Hatter keeps confronting Alice with the riddle: 'Why is a raven like a writer's desk?' Alice sighs and answers: 'I think you might do something better with your time than wasting it on asking riddles that have no answer.'

I'm very grateful to my partners (Kristof, Niels, Tim, Christophe, Filip, Magali, Tom, Annelies and Tom), my clients and all my precious colleagues at InSites Consulting for giving me the chance to waste some time at my writer's desk. In these challenging economic times, I should probably have been using it for more profitable occupations.

I would also like to thank my best friends for taking care of me when arriving home jetlagged and feeling and behaving like Bono, and the ex-MTV Networks people for believing in this project from the very first day I spoke to Veerle Colin and Patrick Alders about the idea. Many of MTV's/Viacom International's sympathetic global staff have been extremely helpful in supporting and endorsing my work: Dan Ligtvoet, Maurice Hols, Rasmus Dige, Dora Heinkel, Mathias Wierth Heining, Simone Reitbauer, Manuela Apitz, Jin Choi, Helen Rose, Lisa Cowie, Emma Norström, Sebastian Barth, Ralf Osteroth, Emelie Wahlström, Ann Hoeree, Pascale Engelen, Anne-Elise Jardinet, Chenling Zhang, Tina Verpooten, Laura Vogelsang, Menno Wagenaar, Frank Bakker, Rogier van de Paverd, Lieselotte van der Meer, Cedric Brunings, Josine Van Der Knoop, Tobbias Dettling, Simona Sbarbaro, Christian Kurz, Nick Shore, and many more.

I would like to address a special word of thanks for the two young Millennials who have helped me to prepare the script of this third edition: Stijn Vermeulen and Eva Jult.

Mattias's words of thanks

I would like to thank all my wonderful colleagues at MTV, particularly those already mentioned by Jocri as well as the following people: Antonio

Campo Dall'Orto, Ben Richardson, Kerry Taylor, Philip Bourchier O'Ferrall, Nicolas Declercq, Hanna Hedberg, Alejandro Romero, Marta Pinilla, Benedikt von Walter, Hugo Pinto, Sofia Fernandez, Tanya Leedekerken, Mar Mayoral, Jurgen Hopfgartner, Rasmus Dige, John Jackson, Georgia Arnold, Andreas Sjövall, Kenneth Kristensen, Barbara Garcia, Willem Schelling, Karin Arner, Andrea Sahlgren and Sean Saylor.

Producing this book would certainly have been impossible if it hadn't been for the help of the following people: Patrick De Maeseneire for his original point of view in the foreword of this new edition. Anke Moerdyck for the invaluable marketing, PR and mental support and the creative promotional ideas that would easily exceed any agent's efforts – without your help over the past years I would have been totally lost; Natalie Mas for your blogging and event organizing skills and just being there when I needed you. Isabel Raes for being the Vancouver Style Reference/Figures expert; Tania Van den Bergh for proof-reading and editing; Annelies Verhaeghe for sharing the produce of her own marvellous brain cells and writing some texts on youth's brain cells; Michael Friedman for his terrific research work on the CRUSH model and the go/no go distinctive asset study, Niels Schillewaert for his valuable input to the model; Anneleen Boullart, Elias Veris and Tom De Ruyck for their input on the 'crushed ice' global community; Katia Pallini, Simona Salcudeanu, Vincent Konings, Pieter De Vuyst, Ann Renders and Tracey Jones for their quantitative research skills; Hannes Willaert and Karl Demoen for their awesome visual and video designs; the patient reviewers of the initial manuscript: Barbara Verhaegen, Sanna-Mari Salomäki, Veerle Colin, Patrick De Pelsmacker, Gaëtan Van Maldegem, Vincent Fierens, Marc Michils, Gert Kerkstoel, Dennis Hoogervorst, Dennis Claus, Steven Van Belleghem, Niels Schillewaert and Kristof De Wulf. The kind providers of new box-texts in this third edition: Maarten Lagae, Thomas Troch, and Niels Schillewaert. Herman Konings for just being Herman K. The interviewees of this edition: Åsa Caap, Jordan Casey, Mark Iterson, Ward Van Duffel and Per Hjuler. The interviewees of past editions and their colleagues and connectors: Mark Van Iterson and Mariana Suarez Carmona (Heineken), Ilse Westerik (Reckitt-Benckiser), Jörgen Andersson, Adam Vardy and Yasmin King (Esprit), Jean-Jacques Maartense (Eastpak), Michaël Werner (KFC), Christophe Fellinger (Beiersdorf), Christophe Krick (Crumpler), Francisco Bethencourt (Yildiz Holding), Peter Jung and Anna Zanghi (MasterCard International), Todd Corley (Abercrombie & Fitch), Koen Lemmens and Christophe Van den Brande (ID&T/Tomorrowland), Ishita Roy (BBC Worldwide), Luke Dowdney (LUTA), Hubert Grealish (Diageo), Mariken Kimmels (Heinz), Samantha Clarke (UCB), Clelia Morales (eBay), Anita Caras (Microsoft), Renzo Rosso, Andrea Rosso, Annalisa Turroni, Charla Caponi, Serena Pederiva (DIESEL/55DSL), Geoff Cottrill and Keith Gulla (Converse), Peter Claes and Jan Van Biesen (Studio Brussel/VRT), Wim Verbeurgt (Mini), Marc Michils and Yves Van Landeghem (Saatchi & Saatchi Brussels), Luc Rasschaert and Gunter Ooms (Belfius Insurance),

Dennis Birk Jorgensen, Anders Gam, Anja Ballegaard, Clara Buddig and Thijs Luyt (Bestseller/Jack & Jones); Saskia Neirinckx; Satu Kalliokulju, Bjorn Ulfberg, Ann Van Dessel and Jurgen Thysmans (Nokia); Jörgen Andersson and Sara Svirsky (H&M); Emelie Wahlström (MTV Sweden); Patrik Söder, Thomas Brenemark and Olle Johansson Bergholtz (DDB Stockholm); Joris Aperghis (G-Star International); Avery Baker, Sanne Krom and Jeroen Vermeer (Tommy Hilfiger); Gert Kerkstoel (former Nike); Derk Hendriksen, Cristina Bondolowski, AJ Brustein, Joanna Allen, Susan Hines, Judith Snyder and Gaëtan Van Maldegem (Coca-Cola); An Martel (Diageo); Sanna-Mari Salomäki (Kuule); Matti Rautalahti and Virve Laivisto (Cancer Society of Finland); Ellen Vermeulen (Procter & Gamble); Dirk Van Kemseke (Levi's); Joe Beek (Channel 4); Mia Venken, Kris Stevens and Peter Vandermeersch (De Standaard, Corelio); Carolijn Domensino (The Fish); Dan Hill and Joe Bockman (Sensory Logic).

Introduction

When we were young, marketing to teens and young adults was really rather easy. We, Generation Xers true to type, were eager to tune ourselves to global brands and definitely wanted to start our yuppie careers in a famous multinational. The big corporations radiated the proof of the ultimate success. Just imagine... when we were 16 we'd be able to buy those big cool brands ourselves! And that's exactly what all brands were shouting at us. Buy us and you will be so cool! And oh yes, we loved it... we even believed it. Brands were projecting cool and aspiring images in their ads. They were setting the goals we all desired to achieve. They dictated how to dress, behave, walk and talk. We didn't doubt for a minute what the marketers were telling us. We even adored TV commercials, because we were the first generation to grow up with commercial stations and it was all so new and glamorous to us. Like forbidden fruit. Our parents and grandparents gave us an allowance from time to time and we all spent it hastily on Depeche Mode or Talking Heads vinyl records, just saving enough to buy a pair of Docs or Converse All Stars and some hair gel.

Today, things have dramatically changed. This youth generation has been bombarded with commercial messages from their birth. They have learned to filter out all those loud messages and they have been empowered by their parents and teachers to have an opinion of their own and never merely believe whatever somebody is proclaiming. But the global brands are still there. So are the commercial media. And there must be countless times more choice of both. YouTube is the new TV and radio station, Facebook the new newspaper. Instead of new wave or synthpop records, Gen Yers can choose and mix dozens of music genres at streaming services such as Spotify, and what brand of gel, wax, clay, gum, spray, whip, cream-mousse, pomade, paste, texturizer, balm or lotion will they use to style their haircut tonight? To survive in the current cluttered and fragmented environment, today's teens and young adults use collective peer wisdom and social connections. They believe what their best friends and parents are telling them and self-consciously want to explore what roads they should take. They have learned to use social media to voice their opinion and not only tell brands what they expect but also strongly influence the marketing and branding of the brands they care about.

And what are brands to do now? Shouting how cool they are isn't working anymore, that's for sure. Brands have lost their role model or oracle status. Whispering might be an option, but you still need to convince the confident teen to remove his white iPod earplug and bother to listen to you instead of to all the other teen whisperers. The main point is that you have to earn youth's respect, before you can even start the conversation about your brand. This book is all about connecting with a new generation who will determine how consumer markets evolve in the next three decades. It's about staying relevant for a fickle generation that has seen it all. It's about engaging young consumers and co-creating experiences and brands with them.

Although Generation Y and Z still embrace cool brands, the ones that just claim they are cool won't even reach their radar. It takes a great deal of effort to be cool and to stay hot for this consumer group. In working with media and advertisers in our day-to-day jobs, we have often experienced some insecurity in addressing youth markets. Of course, the pressure for marketers is high when they have to deal with the most marketing-savvy generation of teenagers and young adults ever. The huge number of competitors that join them in trying to convince this age cohort heightens the stress levels and kindles the battle between brands in youth markets. Unfortunately, this rat race often ends in a brand's mere surfing on youth fads and hypes. Many research agencies seem to have limited their youth insights to trendwatching and coolhunting. Although a youth brand needs to be aware of what's hot and what's not, just to stay in touch with its environment, we believe that there's much more to the equation.

Creating brands that touch their hearts implies a true knowledge of the underlying youth drivers and needs. Something that will only be in reach when you have a long-term commitment to listen to Gen Y and Gen Z's opinion and involve them with your innovations and campaigns from the start. In this book, we will explain the five key attributes of successful youth brands to you. Together they form the acronym CRUSH:

Coolness;

Realness;

Uniqueness;

Self-identification with the brand; and

Happiness.

Each of these traits is the main topic of a chapter in this book. The CRUSH brand leverage model is based on nine years of intensive youth research and consulting grounded in a daily connection with the 4- to 18-year-old Gen Zers and the 19- to 35-year-old Gen Yers. It was validated through several global quantitative research studies and various client projects and workshops. By optimizing your brand's performance with regard to the five characteristics of engaging youth brands, your brand will enjoy an uplift in terms of satisfaction, peer-to-peer promotion (conversations about your brand) and purchase preference.

We have illustrated our youth brand vision with inspiring case stories from the past as well as the present including Sony PlayStation, Vans,

Converse, Red Bull, Levi's, Chipotle, Apple, Pernod Ricard, H&M, Trader Joe's and many more. The CRUSH model was tried and tested through new international research as well as interviews with global marketing executives of successful brands such as LEGO, Pernod Ricard, Esprit, Nike, BBC, Coca-Cola, DIESEL, Eastpak, Heineken and MasterCard and many others. If you're not working for a global and mainstream brand, it might be relatively easy to become cool for a while for parts of Gen Y or Z. But the marketers and brands we have interviewed have managed to stay relevant for the entire youth market year after year. On the other hand, we have also inserted a number of 'unusual suspects', not-for-profit organizations connecting with youth in a low-budget yet very effective way. A few examples include LUTA (from the favelas in Rio), the Ex-smokers are Unstoppable campaign and Studio Brussel's Music for Life.

We first kick off this book by debunking some youth myths and explaining how the Generation Y and Z differs from others. What are the specific characteristics of adolescents that will affect the way they connect with brands today?

The impact of our vision on youth branding is explained in the second chapter, as an introduction to the subsequent parts that will deconstruct each of the five CRUSH dimensions.

The third chapter explores what being cool means for a brand. Is it necessary to be cool and is it possible to become a cool brand in every product category?

In Chapter 4 on real brands we will prove that brand authenticity really makes a difference for the critical Generation Y. But being authentic means completely different things for Gen Yers than for other generations.

Gen Yers are on a mission to become special or unique. That's why they are also looking for unique brands that help them to stand out. But how do you make your brand unique in a post-modern world full of choice? The fifth chapter tackles this subject.

Contrary to previous generations, Gen Yers were brought up in an atmosphere of equal relationships and co-decision-making and that's exactly what they expect from brands today. This also means that brands should have a better knowledge of the values, interests and opinions of different youth lifestyle groups. The new consumer combines brands in an eclectic way to express his or her own individual identity. In Chapter 6 we will fully delve into the topics of identity development and self-identification with brands. How trendy is a hipster and what are the five core themes that are central in the lives of every youngster?

Today's youth generation is more emotional than ever. The last chapter deals with the way brands can offer them magic moments and arouse feelings of happiness.

In the completely new last chapter of this book we will focus on the next generation: Generation Z. Based on a large new study across the globe we were able to define the DNA of Generation Z and how they are different from Millennials and older generations.

Although in marketing there are never one-size-fits-all solutions, we are confident you will recognize the brand attributes that might need focus in your own market approach. Perhaps this book will even confront you with the blind spots in your current offer. By reading this summary of our findings, you will explore the Generation Y and Z world. You will understand why the five brand components are essential for the younger demographic groups and how your brand can tap into them.

We know that trying to capture the mindset of an entire generation is quite a vain endeavour. And although the world and this generation are more globalized than ever, we still feel it would be a bad idea to generalize too much. But we hope that by sharing our passion to understand and connect with these mind-blowing consumers, we will challenge you to develop relevant youth strategies and brands. Although the real difference will be made in your own creative marketing approach, we trust this book will help you to get a better grip on this fast-moving target group without losing your brand's identity in the next small trend. After all, it's all about staying true to your roots, but adapting to the changing environment and constantly finding new angles to keep this stimulus-oriented and emotional youth on board. We wish you an inspiring and exciting journey and look forward to hearing your feedback and thoughts via **www.howcoolbrandsstayhot.com**. This blog offers you frequent updates of our book with new interviews, case studies and research. You are also invited to follow our daily stream of consciousness through the Twitter addresses: **@joeri_insites**. Joeri is regularly asked to bring his vision and Gen Y & Z advice on conference stages worldwide and through in-company sessions. More info can also be found on **www.howcoolbrandsstayhot.com** or send an e-mail to joeri@insites-consulting.com.

Joeri Van den Bergh and Mattias Behrer

Defining Generation Y

Today's youth are getting the most out of their lives. Youngsters do recognize that they are raised in an affluent world flooded with choices. For most of them, the question is not how to get something but rather what to choose. In this highly competitive society, brands realized that they had to increase marketing investments to be heard above the noise of the advertising clutter. Generation Y is not only aware of being marketed to but has grown up in an environment full of brands and commercial media; it's all they have ever known. The rise of digital media allowed youth to create their own personalized world. They are able to live their lives through new online and mobile communities. Today's 19- to 35-year-olds grew up in a world where mobile phones for children and teens became commonplace and the internet was being used at school. They are so conditioned to use these internet, streaming and mobile technologies that deprivation of one of them would feel like having a limb removed. The way youth socialize, build relationships, shop and make career choices is heavily affected by the era they have been raised in. There is an ancient saying that bears much truth: 'people resemble their times more than they resemble their parents'. Gen Yers are children of the cyber revolution. Just like the industrial revolution changed lifestyle and culture by the end of the 19th century, the omnipresent connectivity and digital advancement has reshaped the social DNA of our current and future youth generations.[1]

The oldest members of Generation Y are already entering the job market, getting married and becoming the heads of households. If you haven't already targeted this cohort, now is an important time to introduce them to your brand.[2] A better understanding of what makes young consumers tick will improve your brand positioning and marketing to the target group. Whatever business you are in, this generation will make or break your market success. The long-term flourishing of your company depends on how well your brand strategy responds to the demands of this new consumer generation. Clelia Morales, Head of Social Media and PR at eBay Europe, phrases it as follows in an interview with us:

> The challenge with this generation is that your organization must be ready to act fast enough as a response to their feedback and input. Social media help you to detect their thoughts and feelings right away, but Gen Yers will expect you

to react immediately and come up with improved products or campaigns much faster than ever before.[3]

In this chapter, we will dive into the characteristics of Generation Yers. More than half of the world's population is under the age of 30. Gen Y is currently one of the largest demographic groups and will soon outnumber the Baby Boomer generation. In the United States alone, there are over 70 million Gen Yers with over $200 billion in purchasing power. Their generational impact on society, culture, business, politics and economics in the next three decades will be similar in magnitude to that of the Baby Boomer generation. 'Gen Yers are by default smart and self-aware of media and marketing', says Hubert Grealish, Global Head of Brand Communications at Diageo. 'They know how to manipulate media and play with brands. Many marketers still believe this is a threat to their profession but in fact it creates large opportunities for brands to engage with their fans. Gen Y is capable of moving an idea forward and co-creating value.'[4]

We will indicate how the arrival of this new consumer group affects branding and marketing. Of course, there are as many differences within generations as there are among generations. It's never a good idea to generalize too much, especially with a youth generation that has never been so ethnically and lifestyle diverse as today. Still, certain aspects of society and parenting will influence the way your marketing and branding campaigns are perceived by young consumers.

X, Y, Z: what's next?

Generational labels are usually the result of popular culture. Some are linked to a historic event, others are derived from drastic social or demographic changes or from a big turn in the calendar.

Millennials

Millennials belong to the third category. The term refers to those born between 1980 and 1996, although different authors use different data. It is the first generation to come of age in the new millennium. 'Y' was chosen as a popular label as they are the successors of the Generation X, but there are many synonyms such as Generation Why, Generation Search, Generation Next, the Net generation, the digital natives, the dot.com generation, the Einstein generation, Echo Boomers, etc. They are the children of the throngs of Baby Boomer parents, which explains why there are so many in spite of the declining fertility rates. Baby Boomers gave birth at a later age (average mum aged 30) and were consequently more mature in their roles as parents and tutors. They have raised their children as coaches might, with one central notion: individual empowerment. Gen Y children have been taught that all opinions are equally important. Boomers included the view of their children in every discussion or decision. Parents gave their Gen Y children the chance to learn and experience a lot of different things (in travel, sports, art, music...). The result of this upbringing is that Gen Yers are more critical and cynical and generally difficult to wow. As 'stimulus junkies' they have a shorter attention span and an irrepressible need for instant gratification. 'They use their smartphones and social media to find the information they want straight at their fingertips', says Jean-Jacques Maartense, CMO of Cartamundi, in an interview with us. 'They are very well connected and networked and value the realness, honesty and authenticity of things in life. They are looking for a more meaningful existence.'[5] If they have an idea, they will immediately want to execute it. Their parents have served them hand and foot, and that is what they will expect in life, work and relationships too.

Generation X

Generation X consists of people who were born from 1965 to 1979. Other labels for this generation include: the Baby Busters, Post-Boomers, Slacker Generation, indifferent, shadow or invisible generation, and Lost Generation. Ironically, the Generation X label was popularized by Douglas Coupland's book *Generation X: tales for an accelerated culture*, describing a generation that actually defied labels – 'just call us X'. Not only did the label stick, it has also produced labels for the next two generations – Y and Z. Xers began their career in the early 1990s when there was a recession and much downsizing of the workforce. They adopted the work ethic and focus of the Boomers but were more individualistic and pessimistic. As Gen X is trying to combine a demanding job with raising Gen Z kids, they have the highest stress levels of all generations. In their parental values they embrace laissez-faire principles allowing their Gen Z children to learn from their mistakes. Compared to the Baby Boomers, Generation X sticks more to self-reliance and personal achievement.

Baby Boomers

The Baby Boomers' label is drawn from the post-Second World War spike in fertility that began in 1946 and ended in 1964 as a result of the commercial launch of birth control pills. They grew up in an era of economic growth and full employment. The austerity of the Silent Generation was replaced by technological advancement and increasing freedom and leisure time. Boomers have lived through years of incredible change and are therefore very adaptive and flexible. They are the most confident generation. Their altruistic and open-minded thinking and never ending optimism is reflecting in the values of their Millennial children.[6]

The Silent Generation

The Silent Generation covers adults born from 1928 to 1945. They are the children of the Second World War and the Great Depression. Their 'silent' label refers to conformist instincts and contrasts with the noisy anti-establishment Boomers.

Differences between generations

Pew Research Center found that the majority of generation members believe they own a unique and distinctive identity. In Table 1.1 you will find the spontaneously uttered reasons of each generation for feeling distinctive. Although the previous youth of Generation X also cite technology as their generation's source of distinctiveness, just 12 per cent (half the amount of Gen Yers) say this. For Generation Y, technology is more than just their gadgets; they have fused their social lives into it.[7] In InSites Consulting's *NextGeneration study 2015*, 75 per cent of global Millennials are regular users of Facebook, 55 per cent visits YouTube and 48 per cent uses the Whatsapp messenger. When looking at Generation Z, Facebook usage is lower (42 per cent) but 65 per cent visits YouTube. It is clear that the youngest generation is more into visual and video communication. Already more than six out of ten 4- to 6-year-olds frequently goes to YouTube. The success of

TABLE 1.1   What makes particular generations unique?

	Generation Y	Generation X	Boomer	Silent
1	Technology use (24%)	Technology use (12%)	Work ethic (17%)	WWII/Depression (14%)
2	Music culture (11%)	Work ethic (11%)	Respectful (14%)	Smarter (13%)
3	Liberal/tolerant (7%)	Conservative (7%)	Values/morals (8%)	Honest (12%)
4	Smarter (6%)	Smarter (6%)	'Baby boom' (6%)	Work ethic (10%)
5	Clothes (5%)	Respectful (5%)	Smarter (5%)	Values/morals (10%)

SOURCE: Pew Research Center, January 2010

tablets in families with kids and teens affects the nextgen's media behaviour.[8] Technology makes life easier for Millennials and is bringing family and friends closer together. McCann Worldwide did a global study in 17 countries combining 7,000 interviews with youngsters. The report named *The Truth about Youth* states that Millennials live in a 'new social economy' in which recommending and sharing brands is front and centre in their daily lives. Laura Simpson, Global IQ Director at McCann Worldwide, said about the study: 'What we saw is that technology is the great global unifier. It is the glue that binds this generation together and fuels the motivations that define them. Young people utilize technology as a kind of 'supersense' which connects them to infinite knowledge, friends and entertainment opportunities.' Given a list of things (including cosmetics, car, passport, phone and sense of smell) and told they could only save two, 53 per cent of those aged 16–22 and 48 per cent of the 23- to 30-year-olds would give up their own sense of smell if it meant they could keep an item of technology (their phone or laptop).[9]

On the other hand, if parents join Facebook and invite their son or daughter to become friends, this might lead to uncomfortable situations. Online confrontations between generations happen, especially because older generations are often unaware of the implicit social rules (tagging, wall postings, etc). For Boomers, work ethic is the most prominent identity claim; for the Silent Generation it is the Second World War and the Depression that makes them stand apart.[10]

In an interview with Francisco Bethencourt, VP Global Marketing at Yildiz Holding, he explains that Gen Yers live in a multichannel, multimedia world with many more ways of engaging interactions with peers, companies and brands. 'They want to share their thoughts in a more active way and this has a tremendous impact on brands, advertising and companies', Bethencourt says:

'The Millennials' as a generation is much larger in number than Gen X, and is becoming the new mainstream in many developed countries. It is a much more diverse generation, with Hispanics now leading and shaping the way. Before, Hispanics, African-Americans and Asian-Americans were minorities; today they are reaching majority status in many cities and states around the United States and are profoundly influencing people's habits and traditions. In the developing world, we are seeing the rise of the middle class, which is younger and better connected to the outside world than before with much more disposable income. The new consumer is multitasking and checking stuff on his or her Facebook page and sending text messages while watching television.[11]

It's not just technology that is shaping the personality of our youth, it's actually also the other way around. If you reverse the direction of causality, it's a perspective that helps in explaining technological evolutions. The Boomers were a generation that was very much concerned with self-sufficiency and they took the mainframe computers from their parents and turned them into personal computers in the 1980s, supporting individual work on everyone's desk. Generation X took that individualism to the next level. They were interested in making money by buying low and selling high. Gen Xers introduced online auction sites such as eBay in the 1990s and they have boosted e-commerce in general. Today it is because of the social needs and the peer tethering of Generation Y as well as their high need for me-marketing that the web has turned into a network of social communities.[12] 'The ease and agility with which Gen Y absorbs content is amazing', says Ishita Roy, former Marketing Head South Asia at BBC Worldwide:

> Technology is clearly a big difference with the other generations but they're also more engaged and active and very vocal. Their ability to voice their opinion and act upon their ideas is far higher than with previous generations. One of the biggest lessons when I was working for Discovery Channel was to be very conscious about the tone of voice of anchors and on-air communication. They don't like people, channels or brands to talk down to them. So if you don't want to alienate them, you have to keep your messages very friendly and inviting. They are used to eye level communication with their parents and teachers and expect the same style from everyone.[13]

Generation Z and Gen Alpha: the new kids on the block

And what about the generations following Gen Y? Some have called these children Generation Z as the normal alphabet successors of the Y and X Generations. Generation Z was born after 1996. They are the children of Generation X and most of them are still in primary and secondary school.

You can be pretty sure we will see a bunch of new names popping up over the next years. Some simply call them post-millennials; others have dubbed the current kids and teens as 'plurals'. The latter is short for 'pluralists' and reflects the ethnic and religious diversity of the youngest as well as their openness to mix different backgrounds in their social circles. Larry Rosen of California State University, has already coined 'iGeneration' in his book *Rewired: Understanding the iGeneration and the way they learn*. The 'i' is not only referring to the popular Wii, iPods, iPads and iPhones but also to their need for customization and individualizing. Thanks to digital TV, they can watch whatever they want at any time, stop live television and fully customize their media consumption. They were born in a society in which constant connectivity and individual mobile devices are normal. They started using the computer mouse at the early age of 18 months. According to the NextGeneration InSites report 41 per cent of European Gen Zs and 59 per cent of US Gen Zs own a tablet themselves.[14] They don't see technology as an instrument, for them it is just a part of life. The way this will affect their thinking and behaviour is not clear yet, but they will certainly adopt new learning styles focusing on how to gain access to every piece of information, synthesize it and integrate it into their life.[15] In a JWT study among Gen Z in the UK and the US, they are dubbed the 'first true mobile mavens'. They take high-speed internet, available anytime anywhere, for granted and don't know what a landline is. Nine out of 10 would be reluctant to give up their mobile phone and value their connection to their friends more than allowance money, material goods or real-world activities such as going to the movies or dining out. Another conclusion from the study is that Gen Z has a high brand awareness and significant impact on household purchases. For instance, 70 per cent of parents report that their teen influences their choice of a mobile phone.[16]

GfK MRI data revealed that almost 9 out of 10 13- to 18-year-olds find it important to get good grades and 63 per cent enjoy school for the educational aspect. Teen drinking, smoking and sex along with pregnancies have fallen 44 per cent since 1991 according to the CDC's National Centre for Health. Generation Z seems to be more responsible, smart, tolerant and inclusive than the Millennial generation. Perhaps they will be dubbed 'Generation Nice'? Marketing to teens and Gen Z will have to be more informative and meaningful with much attention paid to the responsibility and especially inclusiveness of brands.[17] Gen Z makes up a quarter of the population and their spending power has been estimated to $200 billion per year when taking their influence on household purchases into account.[18] As they are entering the workforce and will become a large consumer cohort by 2020, we have dedicated an extra separate chapter to Generation Z.

After 2010 new-borns belong to another new generation named Gen Alpha. Scientists of different disciplines, such as meteorologists, tend to move to the Greek alphabet after exhausting the Latin one. Gen Alphas are the kindergarten and pre school children of Millennials. About 2.5 million of them are born around the globe each week. As the first iPad was launched in 2010 and the word of the year back then was 'app', Gen Alpha's are raised with a tablet and touch screen in their small hands. It is clear they will be even more influenced by visual and video communication. There are now 100 hours of YouTube videos uploaded every minute. Generation Alpha will be the most formally educated generation in history. They will live in a world where India and China are no longer emerging markets but dominating the world's economy.[19] Some sociologists expect this new generation to be more materialistic as they are the children of older and wealthier parents with fewer siblings. Others believe Millennial parents will react against consumerism and rather go back to basics in the hope their children will hold on to their youth for a longer time.[20]

How permanent are generational characteristics?

A question often heard during speeches on Generation Y is: aren't those youngsters just in a life stage, a mindset that they will outgrow when they age? Well, the answer is: NO! Experience with previous generations such as Gen X has shown that the mindset of youngsters won't change when they reach the age of 40. Generations do not change over time to look identical to their parents at the same adult age. A generation is a product of current times and obviously the technologies, media, social markers and events that uniquely shaped them. Values, attitudes and priorities set during youth will remain identical for the rest of their life.[21]

The Millennial consumer in the United States

The Boston Consulting Group released a report titled *The Millennial Consumer. Debunking Stereotypes.** It was based on research comparing the views, behaviour and attitudes of 4,000 Millennials (aged 18 to 34) with 1,000 non-Millennials (aged 35 to 74) in the United States. BCG concluded that the Millennial generation is actively engaged in consuming and influencing. Their influence will only increase as they mature into their peak earning and spending years.

* The original report 'American Millennials: Deciphering the Enigma Generation' can be accessed for free at **www.barkleyus.com** or contact jfromm@millennialmarketing. com for more information.

Some of the key findings of the study were:

- Millennials and non-Millennials spend roughly the same amount of time online, but Millennials are more likely to use the internet as a platform to broadcast their thoughts and experiences and to contribute user-generated content.
- Millennials are far more engaged in activities such as rating products and services (60 per cent vs 46 per cent of non-Millennials) and uploading videos, images and blog entries to the web (60 per cent vs 29 per cent).
- Millennials put a premium on speed, ease, efficiency and convenience in all their transactions. For example, they shop for groceries at convenience stores twice as often as non-Millennials.
- They are receptive to cause marketing and are more likely to choose products whose purchase supports a cause (37 per cent vs 30 per cent).
- Of Millennials who make direct donations (34 per cent), almost half donate through their mobile devices (15 per cent), compared with only 5 per cent of non-Millennials.
- When it comes to making purchases, Millennials are far more likely to favour brands that have Facebook pages and mobile websites (33 per cent vs 17 per cent). They overwhelmingly agree (47 per cent vs 28 per cent) that their lives feel richer when they're connected to people through social media.

- Millennials are far more likely than non-Millennials to be the very first or among the first to try a new technology, and they tend to own multiple devices such as smartphones, tablets, and gaming systems.
- More US Millennials than non-Millennials reported using MP3 players (72 per cent vs 44 per cent), gaming platforms (67 per cent vs 41 per cent), and smartphones (59 per cent vs 33 per cent), while more non-Millennials reported using desktop computers at home (80 per cent vs 63 per cent) and basic cellphones (66 per cent vs 46 per cent).
- As a result, US Millennials are also much more likely to multitask while online, constantly moving across platforms – mobile, social, PC and gaming.
- More Millennials than non-Millennials reported using a mobile device to read user reviews and to research products while shopping (50 per cent vs 21 per cent).
- So-called 'crowd-sourcing' – tapping into the collective intelligence of the public or one's peer group – has become particularly popular among Millennials.
- Millennials are much more likely than non-Millennials to explore brands on social networks (53 per cent vs 37 per cent).[22]

A cause without rebels: the new parent-child paradigm

Surprisingly, Pew Research Center's survey revealed that 79 per cent of the US population believes there is a 'generation gap' in society. This is 5 per cent higher than the 74 per cent that saw this gap in the roaring year 1969. But the modern gap is mostly about the different ways in which old and young are using technology. Only about a quarter of those surveyed saw conflicts between young and old in the United States. Among today's Generation Y, 52 per cent say becoming a good parent is one of the most important things in their life. That's 10 per cent higher than youth in 1997 (Generation X). Eight out of 10 youngsters applaud the classic ideal of getting married and starting a family.[23] Gen Y get along well with their parents. They report fewer fights with mum or dad than older adults say they had with their own parents when they were growing up.[24] Six out of 10 US teens say their family eats dinner together at least four nights a week. Eighty-five per cent identify a parent – rather than a peer – as their best friend. Of these, 53 per cent call Mum their best friend vs 32 per cent who say it's Dad.[25]

Little Emperor Syndrome

For many parents of Gen Yers, getting their teens' approval is the most important thing in their lives. They treat their children as friends rather than subordinates. A major explanation for this is that the average number of children per female has drastically dropped, while the divorce rates have gone up. Gen Y children get far more attention than previous latchkey-youth generations. It's the Western variant of China's 'Little Emperor Syndrome'. Parents project high hopes for a better future on their only child and turn him or her into the major focus of the family. As the family tree increasingly gets smaller (with fewer branches of brothers, sisters, cousins, aunts and uncles), the bonds between parent and child are strengthening. Moreover, Baby Boomer parents have shifted away from the traditional disciplinarian role as a reaction to their own relationship with their parents. Today's parental environment is one of open democratic dialogue and negotiation, rather than conflict, rebellion and resistance. Two-thirds of parents claim to ask the opinion of their children before making big decisions such as choosing holidays. According to parents, this openness is the glue to keep the family together and an investment in the future. Three-quarters of parents claim their relationship with their children is more open than the one their own parents had with them. Discipline has been replaced by tolerance. Today's young people simply don't need to be rebellious and difficult anymore.[26] Dove's 'campaign for real beauty' successfully connected Millennials with their mums.

Helicopter parenting

About 52 per cent of Gen Yers have daily or almost daily contact with their parents via text, e-mail, phone or in person. One third claims: 'my parents are more involved in my life than I really want them to be'.[27] According to the Q3 2014 report of Ypulse, 86% of 18- to 32-year-olds don't want to become 'helicopter parents' themselves.[28] Youngsters are often shielded from the realities of life. 'Helicopter parents' increasingly try to protect their Gen Y children from growing up too quickly. They are called 'helicopters' because they are always hovering to have a permanent view on what their children (even if they are older than 20) are doing and to manage their lives as a coach or manager. The mobile phone has become a new and indispensable body part of youth. A substantial 83 per cent of them sleep with their mobile phone turned on in their bed. The device has also received the function of an umbilical cord for their worried parents. Through texting and voice calls they are able to contact their children at any time and check on their safety. Unfortunately, in our discussion groups, the youngsters often admit they don't pick up their phones if they see it's their old folks.

The opposite of helicopter parenting is called 'free-range' parenting. Generation X parents tend to give their Gen Z children more responsibilities and more space to develop. Reflecting on the way they were raised, many Millennials in our research state that they would only change one thing in the education of their own children: give them more freedom.

Boomerang children

Parents are increasingly replacing monthly or weekly allowances with need-based money handouts. This change resulted in a 'want it now' generation that is not learning the real-world value of money and will take longer to live independently. The trend of young people delaying departure from the family home ('Hotel Mum and Dad') has been boosted by the economic recession. It has also led to an increase in 'boomerang children', returning to parental homes after a period of independent living. In 1980 in the United States, 11 per cent of the 25- to 34-year-olds were living with their parents. By 2008, this figure had risen to 20 per cent and according to the Pew survey, 10 per cent of young adults, aged 18 to 34, have moved back with their parents during 2009 because of the recession. The US Census Bureau reported that 5.9 million young adults (aged 25 to 34) were living in their parents' household in 2011, up from 4.7 million before the recession.[29] For her book *The Accordion Family: Boomerang Kids, Anxious Parents, and the Private Toll of Global Competition* Johns Hopkins University sociologist Katherine Newman interviewed college students and found out that 85 per cent will return to live with their parents after they graduate. According to her, the return to the nest is not just benefiting the cost-conscious young adults. It keeps parents young because they are not moving in the empty-nest life cycle themselves. They are enjoying the nice parts of parenting without the difficult aspects related to supervising teenagers.[30]

A consequence of Gen Y's closeness with their parents and the boomerang trend is the increasing and enduring influence of youngsters on the family purchases. In Figure 1.1 you will find the results of an InSites Consulting study on Gen Y's influence in household purchases. We interviewed 4,065 respondents, aged 15 to 25, in 16 countries around the world. The biggest influence that global Millennials report is found in the technologies that their parents are adopting (52 per cent) and the products that they are buying (44 per cent). But they also affect the programmes that Baby Boomers watch and even the holiday destinations and shops they visit. The 15- to 25-year-olds did report they only have a limited impact on their parents' music choice (37 per cent no influence at all) and political preferences (39 per cent no influence). Although the latter was different in Brazil, India and China where at least 30 per cent of Gen Yers reported they did have influence on political choices of their parents.[31]

By staying at home, Gen Yers are getting a lot of perks. Parents are covering their bills, food, toiletries, rent and travel and acting as chauffeurs, cleaners, cooks and laundry services for them. Where young adults used to leave home in search of independence, today they are quite comfortable in bedrooms that are mini-flats stuffed with their own TV, DVD and game consoles. For many important decisions in life such as a job, housing, banking or a car, Gen Y will automatically turn their heads towards their parents. HR managers and university selection committees have even reported an increased presence of parents during the interviews. It is the new paradox in

FIGURE 1.1   Gen Y's influence on parents' purchases

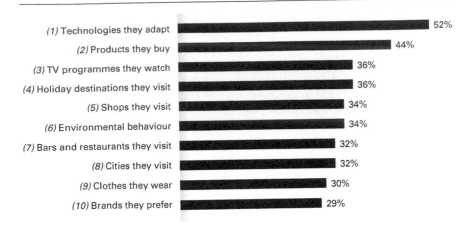

youth sociology. Kids are confronted with the adult world at an earlier age because parents want them to be stimulated to explore the world. This phenomenon is called 'KGOY' (Kids Getting Older Younger). On the other hand, they are much slower in taking independent decisions. More than 8 out of 10 youngsters report that their parents are always available for them 24 hours a day. For parents, being an adult has become dull and unattractive. Youth is everything. They want to remain youthful as long as they can. Many Gen Yers admit their parents want to wear what they are wearing, adore co-shopping and they even regularly swap clothes. The line between parents and children is increasingly blurring.

Insane in the brain: teenage neurology

Teen brains are still under construction. Their hardware is to blame for the unpredictable behaviour that is led far more often by their emotions than by their logic. Neuroscience is slowly discovering the secrets of teenage brains. Scientific studies indicate that adolescence is the period in which habits and behaviour are shaped. Two processes are responsible for this blueprint. On the one hand, we see an explosion in the creation of grey matter.[32] This boost in thinking power gives teenagers the opportunity to excel in all kinds of areas. The more they engage in certain behaviour, the better they will become at it and the more skills will be anchored in their brains. At the same time, cells that are never used are eliminated. The 'use it or lose it' theory dictates that if teenagers do not engage in certain activities during their adolescence, they will never do them at all simply because the neural connections will be absent for these activities. For example, if teenagers are not exposed to a healthy lifestyle, their brains will be built up around the famous sex, drugs and rock 'n' roll mindset.[33] Because teenage brains are still very flexible in this period, it is an important moment for brands and products to communicate to this target group. If people are consuming a certain product or brand in their young years, their brain will be programmed for similar behaviour when they are adults.

Emotional roller coasters

However, not all communication will have an equal effect on the adolescent brain. Neuroscientists have revealed that some strategies work better to connect with teenagers. Teenage brains function like an emotional roller coaster. Brain researchers have uncovered that this is a direct consequence of the brain growth. Unlike adults, their frontal lobes are still in full development. This brain area is responsible for taming the wild beast reflexes in us. It suppresses emotional and primitive reactions and makes us behave like good citizens. Frontal lobes also help us with logical reasoning. They are directly related to another brain structure called the 'amygdale', the source for emotional processing. In the adult brain, the frontal lobe is in control and triggers coming from the amygdale are largely ignored. It is only in cases of dominant emotional stimuli or when we sedate the frontal lobe, by drinking too much alcohol for instance, that emotions take the upper hand. With teenagers the amygdale is in the driving seat. Because the frontal lobes are still immature, they will show more emotional and impulsive behaviour. Research has also shown that adolescents are more eager to respond to emotional stimuli.[34] Emotional information is more likely to be noticed, processed and remembered. In terms of consumption, they are looking for stimulation of their positive emotions.[35]

Identity construction and brands

Although the amygdale and frontal lobes play different roles in teenage brains, it is exactly the interplay between them that is responsible for their most important development: the creation of an own identity. Adolescence is typically the stage in life where you start reflecting about the self. Youngsters spend a great deal of their time trying out different roles. By engaging in different activities, they try to shape their identity. Their self-concept is shaped by past experiences. Positive life experiences such as getting positive reactions to a new outfit, good grades at school or positive feedback on your guitar playing, help in building a positive self-concept. Failure or negative feedback leads to a more negative self-concept. All these experiences cause emotional reactions in the amygdale. The amygdale reinforces the positive experiences by sending a signal to the frontal lobes that will give it more importance within the self-construct. For marketers it is important to realize that consumption can play a powerful role in shaping one's identity. If young people get positive feedback when consuming your brand, it will be more likely to find an emotional connection with them. This will lead to a stronger place for your brand in a youth's self-identity.

Idealism and activism

The frontal brain lobes are also capable of going from the concrete to the abstract world. A consequence of the abstract mind is idealistic behaviour. Because abstract thinking capacities are growing, teenagers at a certain age will finally be able to understand how the world works. By reflecting on the world, they will be capable of envisioning a perfect ideal world. During that phase, youngsters can become very critical about the actions of past generations. At first, this idealism is often reflected in endless discussions with their parents and teachers. When growing up this idealism is often transferred into activism. Youngsters join animal rights movements, become members of political parties or organize social actions with their youth movements. Brands and products are not spared from their critical judgements. Company processes, origin of goods and advertising are studied and can be used as a symbol of protest. Other brands embrace this idealism by explicitly supporting good causes.[36]

TOMS Giving

TOMS is a popular brand among young people. They appreciate that the brand makes a difference by using material from responsible sources, employs fair-wage labour and gives back to communities. TOMS sells shoes, eyewear, coffee and bags. Every time a client buys a product, TOMS helps a person in need through the so-called One for One model (buy one, donate one). TOMS Giving Team works with different partners to provide products or to support the partners contributing societal services. The brand currently has more than 100 collaborators in more than 70 countries around the world. They have to fulfil different qualities. All partners are sustainable, local, neutral, and they need to have long-term goals.

Every year TOMS launches the One Day Without Shoes campaign. The non-profit Soles 4 Soles revealed that over 300 million children don't have shoes to wear which leads to discomfort, decreased access to education and diseases. For two weeks people can post their bare feet on Instagram with the hashtag #WITHOUTSHOES at @TOMS and for every picture they receive, the brand donates a pair of shoes. During the eighth edition in 2015 TOMS helped no less than 296,243 children.[37]

Risk-taking behaviour

During puberty, teenagers often involve themselves in risk-taking behaviour. Many parents can verify that they have caught their son or daughter taking drugs or secretly drinking alcohol. Boys and girls who were known as quiet kids decide to sneak out in the middle of the night, hitch a ride to a party and terrify their parents who notice their absence in the morning. Teachers are confronted with youngsters who decide to hang around in pubs rather than attend classes and principals wonder why they decide to make a small fire in the school bin. It seems that at a certain age, teenagers lose their senses and have an irresistible urge to indulge in stupid and dangerous behaviour. Again... their brains are to blame. Risk-taking behaviour is something we all indulge in on a daily basis.[38] To be successful we need to engage in new and unknown behaviour: if adults do not dare to take up responsibility for a certain job at work, they will never feel the resultant gratification. If you never start talking to unfamiliar people, you will be stuck in your small network forever. There needs to be a first time to drive a car or ride a bike. Both adults and youngsters need to take risks in order to achieve something in life.

There is, however, more than achievement alone as a reason to engage in risk-taking behaviour. We seek danger also for the thrill of it. Surviving risky behaviour leads to pleasure. Think of the feeling when you exit a rollercoaster or the kick you experience when you have successfully addressed a large crowd. There is one specific substance in the brain called dopamine that has been associated with pleasure seeking. Experiments on rats have shown that taking away the dopamine systems leads to passive and lazy behaviour. The test animals showed no intention to explore their environment. Dopamine stimulates adults as well as youngsters to take action that leads to pleasure. The more it is activated, the more you will seek out pleasure and the more you will take decisive action to find new thrills.

So far, it is clear that risk taking and pleasure seeking are human proclivities. How can neuroscience explain why youngsters seem particularly eager to undertake stupid things? Research has shown that dopamine regulation in the developing young brain is out of balance.[39] Some studies have found evidence for an overproduction of dopamine that turns youngsters into mega pleasure seekers. Other research claims rather that the risk behaviour would be caused by a sudden decrease in dopamine production in comparison with childhood output. In order to reach the same levels of reward, adolescents are condemned to undertake more risky behaviour. Again there is an important relationship with the premature development of the frontal lobes. The adult brain suppresses dangerous behaviour because its frontal lobes can make an estimation of the consequences of their actions. However, youngsters live in a physiological situation where their brains tell them to take risks but cannot stop their urge for pleasure. Risk-taking is a theme that many successful youth brands are using. In 2015, Pepsi launched the Challenge campaign (see the following box).

Pepsi Live for Now

During 2015 the new Pepsi Challenge campaign 'Live for Now' ran for a whole year. Instead of doing the usual blind test between Coke and Pepsi (which marked its 40th anniversary), Pepsi released a new campaign for the younger generations. With these campaigns, Pepsi wanted to create an emotional connection larger than just the taste of their product because sugary items aren't that appealing anymore. Celebrities like Usher, Serena Williams and Usain Bolt signed up with the brand to help motivate consumers to take on a series of challenges. Every month the influencers communicated a new task on social media. The challenges were always a combination of popular culture and social responsibility which appeals to the Millennials generation.[40] They wanted to turn everyday activities into something more exciting, full of adrenaline. 'Game of drone football' was one of them, a soccer game with a drone that suddenly descends from the sky and throws a football at a group of friends. With thirty thousand reactive LED lights, the field had illusion lines, goalposts and a scoreboard, and applauding people were projected on the surrounding walls. Pepsi also changed up its tagline 'Maximum Game. No Sugar' to 'Maximum Game. No Daylight'.[41]

Social media platforms were being used and the popular Jerome Jarre, known from Snapchat and Vine, was also included. With this campaign Pepsi wanted to change the global perspective to a local one by creating individual campaigns per region so customers feel related. As a challenge Indian residents could design their own Pepsi ads that were shown during the Indian Premier League cricket games. There was a food-challenge in Thailand and a music challenge in Latin America. This way Pepsi could regard cultural differences and behaviours. The customers could give back while attempting something challenging.

Another way to give back as a brand was by asking consumers to share the hashtag #PepsiChallenge on social media. For every hashtag Pepsi donated $1 to the Liter of Light organization that offered ecologically sustainable lighting to over 18 developing countries like Kenya.[42]

Stimulation junkies

Today, anything is media. Everything and everyone is constantly spitting out messages whether it is on Twitter, Snapchat, Whatsapp, SMS or Facebook.

Young people were raised in a cocoon with their anxious parents often being afraid to let them go out. It is no surprise this generation has embraced technologies to build new communities through tweeting, texting and friending. Equipped with a bunch of portable media, Gen Yers are never alone or out of touch with their friends. Youngsters get addicted to this constant entertainment and distraction. They can't think of a life without stimulation and variation. If they are for some reason disconnected, they feel boredom more than any generation before. Constant connection and compelling content are no luxury; they are fundamental everyday life expectations. iPhones are affecting the daily routines of youngsters, telling them when to get up, what to do, what their friends are doing, etc. The first thing many youngsters do when they get up is to switch on their computer, if they still switch it off to begin with.[43] Their mobile is always on, unless the batteries have run down.

The triumph generation

Ask a Gen Yer when adulthood begins, and chances are high he or she will answer 30. For this generation your early twenties are a time to move around, try different things and date different people.[44] This need for stimulation and instant gratification is also translated into consumer behaviour. Generation Y shows a relaxed attitude towards consumer purchasing and debts. In *Gen BuY. How tweens, teens and twenty-somethings are revolutionizing retail*, Yarrow and O'Donnell state that shopping is 'the new weather'. Talking about clothes, music, cars and the latest techno-gadgets brings Gen Yers together and keeps them engaged. Buying fashion and entertainment items are vital to leading a happy and hedonistic life and shopping is just another form of exciting entertainment to them. Shopping provides a 'mental vacation'. To de-stress from their busy lives, they will search for pure indulgence. Shopping plays an important emotional role and helps youth to calm anxiety during the many life transitions they have to cope with.[45] The large amounts of non-essential purchases are justified as 'deserved' or a 'reward'. Sometimes, buying a gift for someone else is a good reason for a 'treat' of their own.

For this reason, Gen Y is sometimes also dubbed the 'triumph' generation. It is spoiled with parental attention and expect a lot of feedback and attention at work too. This perception of 'entitlement' has changed the perception of credit card usage and lending services with this generation. After all, finances are of secondary importance to the pursuit of happiness through consumption.[46] Although Gen Yers have also suffered from the global economic downturn – the youth unemployment rates are the highest since the Second World War – they don't seem to panic. In a report of PricewaterhouseCoopers only 25 per cent of Gen Y consumers say the economy has significantly changed their spending behaviour, while 36 per cent of Generation Xers and 37 per cent of Boomers say it has changed their shopping habits.[47] Viacom's international youth culture newsletter *Sticky* reported on a study on what Gen Y in six European markets thinks about jobs, money and the economy.

Sixty-seven per cent of young people say that they never use the word 'failure' to describe how they feel and 70 per cent are positive they will get their dream career and simply ignore the crisis.[48] In an InSites Consulting study two-thirds of British and US youth expect the next year to become a better year than the previous one. In the BRIC markets of Brazil, Russia and China more than 75 per cent felt the same. Gen Yers across the globe also think the future is more important than the past.[49]

A fragmented world

Through online technology, youth get what they want without having to look too hard. They live in a culture of convenience, consuming snippets, devoid of ever seeing the entirety. There's no need to research a topic when you can just Google it to find the answer. This short-cut way of life is something they have been brought up with. Instead of knowing a few topics in depth, they have a little knowledge about everything. This affects the society more than you might think. The length of a *Time* cover story has dropped from 4,500 to 2,800 words in the past 20 years. Average news sound-bites have slipped from 42 seconds in 1965 to a present-day low of 8 seconds. We want more entertainment better and faster.

Bite-size commitment

Youngsters pick and mix individual parts of media to create their own personalized products and services that fit their individual needs. There's no need to buy a whole album on iTunes, you can create your own. Bite-size formats in a much wider variety have replaced mass and uniform media formats. Gen Yers are only bite-size committed. The good side of this is that they are much more open to hop between different styles. They listen to different music styles and festivals offer 6 to 10 different performance stages to fill in the needs of variety and style switching. RSS feeds on the internet allow you to make your own personalized multimedia news medium. But this doesn't mean that traditional media have lost their meaning to Gen Yers. When chilling out, a newspaper or TV programme caters much better for their need to de-stress and relax. In one of our studies on the use of newspapers among youngsters, we have found that a traditional daily is linked with 'pyjama moments'.

A friend's focus

Now that online tools enable youth to achieve social interactions, the broader offline community has eroded. Students listen to lectures without having to attend the sessions together with fellow students. They are less and less interested in connecting with those around them who are outside their immediate inner circle of friends, family and relatives. New forms of online communities, MMORPGs (Massively Multiplayer Online Role Playing Games such as *Runescape* and *World of Warcraft*) and belonging to groups such as those on social networks have filled the void created by this hyper-fragmented environment.

This generation has different technologies, media, brands and a number of different core friendship groups from which they select the right ones according to situation, event, time and mood. Friends are fun to be with, more understanding than anyone else and can be tribally differentiated for different needs and moments.

Various studies have illustrated how Millennials are much more likely to discover new brands or products through a friend mentioning it on his or her online profile or status update.[50] They are also more eager to post a status update when they see products they are excited about. In a JWT study about social shopping and e-commerce, half of Millennials claim to do so compared to one out of three Gen Xers and 19 per cent of Boomers. Fifty-five per cent say they are more likely to purchase something if a friend recommended it on Facebook and 53 per cent will ask Facebook friends' opinions about planned purchases. Again, this is much lower for the Gen X and Baby Boomers' generations.[51]

Implications for brands

Brands targeting Gen Y should offer the same degree of choice and allow young people to interact with the brand elements they like. Gen Yers are creating their own personal brands by combining competitors with personality traits that reflect their own identity. Youngsters are more fickle today but they tend to be selectively loyal to those elements of brands that touch their hearts and that keep their promise. It is up to brands to fit into the complex identity of youngsters today rather than the other way around. Brands aren't dictating styles or image any more.

Another result of the fragmentation is that competition for brands has surpassed the traditional category borders. Brands need to tap into the need for new cohesion and group belonging by bringing youngsters with shared passions together.[52] In 2006, Nike launched Nike+: technology that tracks data of every run and connects runners from all around the world at the Nikeplus.com website. They log on and sign up to register their running programmes and goals. The key development to bring runners together on the web was the Sport Kit sensor that synchronizes with an Apple iPod or iPhone and tracks runners' speed, distance and calories burned. When runners dock their iPod the data are automatically uploaded on the Nike+ community. On the website different tailor-made training programmes are available and members can check out the most recent activity of runners in their own neighbourhood. They can either try to achieve their own goals or be more competitive and challenge others in the community. The success of the community has also translated into sales results for the company. Before

Nike+, the brand accounted for 48 per cent of all running-shoe sales in the United States. Two years later, in 2008, the share had grown to 61 per cent. Of course, this growth cannot be reduced to the success of Nike+. Although product innovations play an important role, choosing running shoes is very much connected to habit and the Nike+ community and tools stimulate runners either to stick with Nike shoes or to buy a pair when they were used to another brand.[53] At the start of 2012, Nike introduced Nike+ FuelBand. It looks like a cool wristwatch, but at the same time the device tracks everybody's activity such as walking, running, dancing, sports and other everyday actions. As a FuelBand user, you set your daily goals and the inside accelerometer will keep track of all movements and update you via the watch's colour (from red to green) as well as a mobile and online app. Again you can compare your results with others via the motivational website.[54]

From living in a fragmented world that is giving them continuously more freedom and opportunities, Gen Y also feel more concerned and insecure. More freedom equals more responsibility and finding out what's right and what's wrong. Youngsters feel the need for more meaningful things in life: stability, harmony and authenticity. This search can really feel like a burden to them and that's why they want to be connected with their friends.[55] Brands need to acknowledge this search for authenticity. Although Gen Y favours peer-to-peer reporting (Twitter, social networks and blogs) over traditional media, they still see TV and TV commercials as the most trusted medium that is suited for brand building. They know that TV advertising is expensive and it is therefore a sign that a company or brand on TV must be stable and successful.

Lose your Facebook account in a Roulette game!

Russian Standard Vodka is stressing its 100 per cent Russian origin to target consumers in over 70 markets. The top premium vodka is produced using a Russian recipe, only Russian ingredients and it is distilled and bottled in St Petersburg. Completely in line with this DNA the brand launched a Facebook app. The app was developed by students from the Miami Ad School Europe. The video introducing the game on YouTube and Vimeo stated:

Young people spend more and more time on social networks like Facebook. For some, it's even like a real, second life. To find out how important this virtual life really is, Russian Standard Vodka created the world's first social media gaming experience where you can lose your digital life: Russian Facebook Roulette.

Continued...

Lose your Facebook account in a Roulette game!   *Continued...*

The video received more than 170,000 views in its first three weeks. It directed participants of the game to a micro-site where groups of four Facebook friends would hand over their login data in a game of virtual Russian roulette. One unlucky participant would have his or her Facebook account deleted permanently. The remaining three would be entered for a chance to win a week-long trip to Russia – 'for real, not on Facebook' as the video copy explained. The campaign was a Cannes Futures Lion finalist and was covered on over 200 blogs such as Mashable and PSFK.[56]

Crowd-sourcing and co-creation

Open source is a technique used in the development of computer code. It means that the coding allows other participants to cooperate and build better software and applications. The 'open source' idea is very much in line with the expectations of Generation Y. It has evolved much further than just software and computer code and is the backbone of many Web 2.0 applications. Wikipedia for instance is an open source encyclopaedia and dictionary that is not only constantly building better definitions but is also updated amazingly fast. Less than two hours after one of Michael Jackson's employees called 911 on 25 June 2009, Wikipedia reported Jackson's cardiac arrest. The open source site had beaten the CNNbrk Twitter stream by 18 minutes and was updated more than one hour before the first mainstream news article appeared on MSNBC.com.[57] Wikipedia servers received 1.24 million requests for the English article about Michael Jackson in the first hour only, 8.7 million in the first 24 hours and 14.4 million in the first seven days.[58]

User-generated content

Generation Yers like the idea of being in full control of everything and don't passively accept what is given to them. They embrace ownership of content and want to be able to edit and change their environment every minute. Youth marketers should adapt the same 'open source' philosophy. A brand is not what a company wants it to be; it's what Gen Y consumers want it to be.

Online tools have made it possible for youth to create their own unique support structures through interactions with friends. They have a constant open feedback channel with their peers that will help them make decisions, no matter whether they are choosing a movie to watch, a new pair of jeans to buy or a boyfriend to date. These connections are as real to Gen Yers as offline supports. They often claim they have 200 friends on Facebook whom they know personally, which would be quite difficult in the offline world. Although it is hard to understand for older generations, these new 'passive' type of friends are very valuable to them. Gen Yers around the world have 140 Facebook friends on average, compared to 91 among Gen Xers and 64 among Baby Boomers.[59]

Trusted brands become friends

Gen Yers are cynical about the way brands behave and are no longer willing to trust anything based solely on faith. They would rather trust unknown peers than brands and have the tools to undercut the authority of brands and advise each other. Word-of-mouth marketing is therefore more effective as they tend to trust their friends' opinions. Online friends don't replace traditional real-world friendships. They are an extension of existing friendship groups. An offline friend will call them on their birthday, while an online one may write a message on their online space. The online world is Gen Y's entertainment, it is not their life. Media that reach them through their peers' filter are automatically relevant. Facebook is one of the main filters for young people today. It delivers content that is almost always relevant and organizes many aspects of their lives: events, music, photos and communications. It's Gen Y's diary.

On average Gen Yers are following 12.4 brands on social networks, compared to 11.7 brands that are followed by Gen Xers and 7.5 brands that are followed by Baby Boomers.[60] Brands on social networks should behave like friends connecting with them, not just like distant brands. But they should not try to act as a friend in the traditional offline form; rather as one of the passive friendships that exist and develop in online social networks. Just as with their other passive friendships they will get to know you through watching and gaining an insight into the brand's online life. Appealing brands do not dictate but engage them by providing involvement and perceived control over the brand. Gen Y wants a less top-down and more equal relationship with brands than Generation X. Brands in social networks should offer them tangible services or sponsored utilities instead of advertising. Youngsters are turned off when a brand is seen as an uninvited intruder into their space.

When a brand's behaviour is not transparent to them, they will assume it is hiding something from them and is dishonest. The increased marketing savvyness means that they are now demanding something back from brands. Brands need to work harder to build a connection with young target groups and authenticity is key. They are not just seen as product providers but as life and lifestyle supporters. This youth generation has a much greater emotional attachment to brands which display that they really understand their lifestyles and make themselves relevant by supporting their needs. Gen Y puts much more emphasis on brand experience and brand credibility.

Don't you wish your girlfriend was hot like me?

In 2011, social psychologist Nathan DeWall, working at the University of Kentucky, published his results of a deep dive into the song lyrics of the *Billboard Hot 100 charts* between 1980 and 2007 while controlling for genre to avoid skew in urban music. He found that the song lyrics in the 1980s were more likely to stress happy togetherness and harmony. Just think of Paul McCartney and Stevie Wonder singing *Ebony and Ivory*, Kool & The Gang's *Let's all celebrate and have a good time* or Diana Ross and Lionel Ritchie bringing *Two hearts that beat as one*. If you compare that to the linguistic analysis of today's songs, for instance Fergie dedicating an entire Black Eyed Peas song to her 'humps', Justin Timberlake's *I'm bringing sexy back*, or Lady Gaga's song *Hair* that is basically about nothing else than her hair, it's clear that these are more about one person, in most cases the artist him- or herself. DeWall concludes that pop songs are reflecting the growing narcissism in society, specifically among the Gen Yers, also being dubbed the 'Me Generation'.[61]

A soap called 'ME': youth's new narcissism

Generation Y has also been dubbed 'the ME generation'. Indeed, Gen Yers sculpt, craft and storyboard their lives in social networks to present campaigns of themselves. Eyes are always on Gen Yers. They are stars of their own soap operas in which all their friends play their parts with comment boxes and status updates as the scripts of the soap. Youngsters increasingly look at their world through a journalist's lens trying to find an interesting story. With every photo taken, they wonder whether it could be their next profile picture. Youngsters who are still formulating their belief systems are attracted to well-defined and authentic brands that help them to strengthen their values and reinforce the identity they are building.[62] Jean M Twenge, Associate Professor of Psychology at San Diego State University, is convinced that narcissism is much more common in our recent youth generation. According to her studies, the average US college student in 2006 scored higher on narcissism scales than 65 per cent of students in 1987. In other words, in less than 20 years, the number of college students with a high narcissism score has risen by two-thirds. The professor mainly blames our education systems designed to raise the self-esteem of youth.[63] In her 2009 book *The Narcissism Epidemic*, she even suggests treatments for what she deems an epidemic.[64]

Celebrity worship and the 15 Mb of fame

The constant stream of media updates in youngsters' social networks and on their mobile phones means they are always aware of what their friends are doing and their friends know what they have been doing. Youngsters have never had so many live benchmarks as today. The media celebrate the young and successful whether it's sportsmen, actors or singers. In 2005, the Kaiser Family Foundation came up with a quite remarkable finding. No fewer than 31 per cent of US teenagers were convinced they would become famous one day.[65] In the same period, UK policemen had to cope with a trend of youngsters taping 'happy slapping' movies and posting them on YouTube. More recently, a 19-year-old made the global news headlines by creating a video in which he and his friends are demolishing a brand new iPad with a baseball bat. In an interview with the LA Times, the young videographer said he was a big Apple fan and bought two other iPads that he didn't pulverize. He just thought the stunt would be funny. Within less than two days, more than 765,000 people had seen the video on YouTube.[66]

Today, there are so many tools for micro-celebrity: being a studio spectator, talk-show guest, reality TV participant, appearing on YouTube or talent-scouting TV shows such as Pop Idol, etc. In his book Hello, I'm special, Hal Niedzviecki states that pop culture is creating the myth of instant stardom. TV shows such as The Osbornes demonstrate the ordinariness of celebs and in a climate where Kate Nash and Lily Allen are discovered on MySpace, everyone can elevate themselves to new heights. Psychologists at the University of Leicester have identified a mental disorder named 'celebrity worship syndrome'. Their research claims that one in three youngsters in the UK suffer from some derivative of the disease. For most of them this is luckily limited to casually following the careers and lives of certain celebrities.[67] According to Jake Halpern's theory in Fame Junkies, this interest in celebrities and the tendency to form para-social relationships with them is fuelled by loneliness and the innate desire to belong. The more lonely and under-appreciated an adolescent feels, the more he or she wants to befriend the ultimate popular guy or girl. Proximity to the famous is a way of receiving recognition and status for the self. Nothing's new. In US high schools there are two main routes for teenage girls to belong to the elite group: either become a cheerleader or become a friend of a cheerleader.[68]

However, these authors may be exaggerating the phenomenon. Recent research found that very few Gen Yers consider becoming famous an important life goal. Just 4 per cent consider it very important and this is not different from older generations. The vast majority (86 per cent) say fame is not important to them.[69] Celebrities have always had a big appeal to the general audience, whether it was Marilyn Monroe in the 1950s or Kim Kardashian today. Nevertheless, we do acknowledge that this generation has a higher self-esteem and a higher need for self-realization and uniqueness than former generations. The continuous media and peer benchmarks, as well as society and parents stimulating Gen Yers to turn their life into a success story affect their thinking and behaviour.

Status anxiety

Youth today have unrealistically high expectations of becoming millionaires before they are 30. Media often portray the successful 20-something CEOs of their own companies endorsing the 'you can be anything you want to be' mythos. The increased importance of self-esteem and self-importance also shows up in increased materialism. Back in 1967, 45 per cent of Boomer freshmen said it was important to be well off financially. By 2004, 74 per cent of Gen Y freshmen agreed.[70] This is translated into high starting salaries and working life expectations. A mere 31 per cent of employed young people say they earn enough money to lead the life they want. However, they are more optimistic than other generations about their future earning power. Among the ones who say they don't earn enough money, 88 per cent think they will be capable of earning enough in the future. Being financially secure is also a concern for 7 out of 10 teens aged 13–18 around the world.[71] In the *Generation Y around the World* report, InSites Consulting revealed that 42 per cent of British youngsters want to make enough money to retire or live off their own means as quickly as possible. In France and the US this figure climbs to 50 per cent and in Brazil and China it is even the case for more than 6 out of 10 youngsters.[72] But the negative aspect of this status anxiety is an increased self-imposed pressure and an increase in fear of failure among youth. Youngsters feel ashamed that they can't live up to their own high expectations. The midlife crisis of the current Generation X is actually already taking place, transformed into a quarter-life crisis, among Gen Yers. In an extensive quantitative European study on health, BBDO came to the conclusion that older people put less pressure on themselves than youth. More than half (53 per cent) of the 18- to 24-year-olds frequently feel stressed compared to 29 per cent of 55+. Fifty-five per cent of the young feel tired and lacking energy compared to 37 per cent among 55+.[73]

The social network voyeurism and exhibitionism has also created a more hedonistic culture. Youth problems such as binge drinking are increasingly justified as youngsters feel comforted by the fact that everyone else is doing it too. The more extremes happen in their lives, the more content they have to post on their Facebook walls. Experiences in the offline world provide content (the new social currency) for online life. They know that their behaviour is being recorded and will pose for pictures with the specific intent of uploading these on social networks.

Social networks allow Gen Yers to support many more and much deeper passive friendships than previous generations. They value social relationships and love to work, shop and date collaboratively a lot more than previous youth generations. Gen Y seems to be more loyal to people than to companies. This is not only important for HR programmes but it also urges you to put enough emphasis on the social aspects of your brand. The store personnel and your employees can really make a difference. They are the advocates of your brand's DNA.

Is your brand Pinteresting?

Pinterest is a content curation platform, which allows users to organize and share interesting content that they find on the web, that they upload themselves or that they see with other users. It is a pinboard-style bookmarking site, a social network, a gift-finder and a platform for collaboration all in one. Pinterest was founded in March 2010 and by the end of May 2012 it had become the third most visited social network in the USA after Facebook and Twitter. In September 2015 Pinterest announced it reaches 100 million monthly users.[74] The content (such as links, images, videos) is organized on different 'boards', created and named by the user himself. Popular categories are travel, cars, film, humour, home design, sports, fashion and art. Users can browse other pinboards for inspiration, they can 're-pin' (over 80% of the pins are 're-pins' of other users) images to their own collections and they can 'like' photos and comment on it. Other users or a selection of other users' boards can be followed. Pinterest allows its users to share 'pins' on both Twitter and Facebook. This integration allows users to share and interact with a broad community. More than 20 per cent of the Facebook users are using Pinterest on a daily basis.[75]

For a retailer Pinterest is interesting as a showcase for their products (and their prices). A user can even browse for gifts by clicking on the homepage on 'gifts' and filtering a price range. Pinterest is establishing itself as a huge traffic driver for online retail. Also online publishers are receiving a lot of traffic generated via Pinterest, even more than Twitter did in February 2012. Especially content from magazine websites and blogs that focus on home decor, arts and crafts, style and food are among the most frequently 'pinned' subjects on Pinterest. It is no surprise that those sites are reporting significant traffic growth from Pinterest.[76]

As Pinterest is one of the fastest growing social sites of the moment with a large user base, the site is becoming more and more interesting for brands. It should not take too long before brands are integrating Pinterest in their social media approach. Kotex claims to be the very first although Peugeot did organize a Pinterest Puzzle earlier. The 'Women's Inspiration Day' by Kotex is a sort of influencer campaign. By analysing individual pins, Kotex identified 50 influential women in Israel. Based on their individual interests, Kotex made a gift box full of individual gifts. To receive their gift box, all they needed to do was to 're-pin' the Kotex gift. The women received their gifts and posted comments about the gifts on their social pages, blogs and of course their Pinterest page. The campaign resulted in 2,284 interactions and almost 695,000 impressions.[77]

Millennial myths: debunking conceptions of Gen Y

Youth behaviour typically sets many tongues wagging; especially older generations, such as Generation X, who have many prejudices against Generation Y. We would like to challenge some of the common misunderstandings.

Gen Yers only put trust in peers

Generation Yers are allegedly only capable of trusting their own friends. It is true they do attach a lot of importance to their peers' opinions and word-of-mouth and have more real-time channels to connect with them. This doesn't mean that they only listen to peers. In a survey InSites Consulting did for Levi's Europe, we asked what would be the most trusted source to decide what new pair of jeans to buy. The results are shown in Figure 1.2. Although 74 per cent prefer the opinion of their best friends, shop personnel are trusted too. They even put a higher trust on commercial staff than on their own mum. Still, Mum remains an important source. This confirms the better relationship between Gen Yers and their parents, although Dad doesn't seem to be the fashion style specialist. Brochures and commercial websites of the jeans brands are as important as reviews and objective forums on the internet. So although they are marketing savvy, this doesn't automatically imply that they don't trust commercial media anymore.[78]

FIGURE 1.2   Most trusted opinion when buying jeans

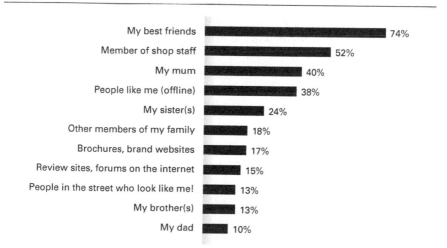

They reject global brands and mass marketing

After four years of researching 'cool brands' among Gen Yers, it is safe to conclude that they are not the 'No Logo' generation at all. Global mass advertising brands such as Coca-Cola, Nike and Nokia are still among their most beloved brands. The advertising and marketing strategies of these brands changed to appeal to the new consumer though. Coke's 'happiness' campaign, for instance, is much more emotional and on an equal level with the consumer than the 'real thing' or 'always Coca-Cola' campaigns of the past.

The global presence of brands radiates a sense of power with which Gen Y is happy to affiliate. Because they seek reassurance for what they perceive to be a chaotic world, they are looking for security. Global brands are a safe haven because they have proven to be able to survive. If they had not been delivering high quality and reliable offers then they would surely not be around today. Great brands are always one step ahead of the rest and are continually innovating and updating their products. Although some of the brands in youth's preferred list such as Levi's, Apple, Nike and Coca-Cola have a US origin, this is no longer the ultimate rule. Scandinavian brands such as H&M and Nokia, German brands such as Adidas, and Italian fashion brands such as DIESEL were able to conquer global youth's trust. As children of a media-dominated society, Gen Yers love excellent visual communication from their beloved brands. They tend to adore ads that:

- portray openness;
- express closeness, warmth, caring and harmony;
- show that a brand is natural and stays true to itself (authenticity);
- support the simplicity of the brand;
- have witty humour;
- provoke controversy.[79]

More than 7 out of 10 youngsters say they are critical towards advertising in general. In Figure 1.4 you will see some interesting results from our brand authenticity work for Levi's Europe. Most youngsters like humour and irony in advertising and they want to hear the unvarnished truth. Although Gen Yers are stimulation junkies, it remains important for brands to stay consistent in their messages. Youngsters today generally reject image-oriented advertising.[80]

They are ethical consumers

'In Japan there is a term called 'kuruma banare' (demotorization), which indicates that youngsters fall out of love with cars', says Wim Verbeurgt, Marketing Manager MINI in an interview with us.

> They prefer public transport, bikes or even skateboards to go from A to B in big congested cities. Cars are no longer relevant to them. Although this could be a reasonable threat, I think this trend is less alive in the Western world. However,

FIGURE 1.3   Gen Y's Attitude towards advertising

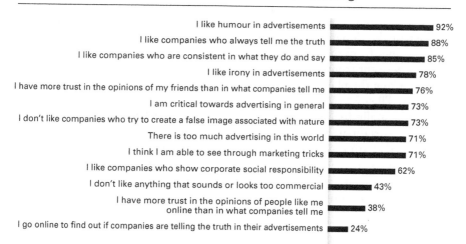

it could come here as well, as it is caused by traffic jams, environmental issues and the ever-rising cost of owning a car. Solutions are: building smaller city cars like the MINI and finding alternative fuels. Of course, the authorities have a huge responsibility in this as well, as taxes account for a considerable part of the fuel prices and they manage public roads.[81]

Ethical, green and charity issues are of growing importance for this generation. Concepts like 'voluntourism', or travel including volunteering for a charitable cause would never have grown in popularity without the caring and social Generation Y. The need to 'do something good' while at the same time discovering new places and challenges (like providing medical aid in a foreign country) is so close to the values of this generation.[82] However, the media have made Gen Yers feel numb for many of these messages. Footage from the developing world, wars, and nature disaster zones are projected on the same screens they watch movies and play games on. They have become another fiction, far away from their own real words. They only take these issues into account when they are directly affecting their immediate social circle or local world. Gen Yers transfer all ethical responsibilities to organizations. Although they will try to avoid buying unethical brands, they will rarely deliberately choose a brand because of its charity programmes. Being ethical is important to them as a principle, but it is not their utmost concern when choosing favourite brands and they will rarely compromise the convenience of their own lives to make a difference. A brand's socially responsible image will never make up for poor quality or other basic issues.

Because eco-claims became just another advertising strategy in the first decade of the 2000s, Gen Yers are cautious in really believing what a brand is saying about protecting the environment. In April 2010, sports fashion brand PUMA worked together with Yves Behar's Fuse project to design a shoebox that would reduce its environmental impact. Many Gen Yers reacted rather sceptically on blogs. PUMA claimed in a movie that using a bag instead of a box reduced the use of cardboard by 65 per cent, eventually resulting in lowered usage of paper (trees), energy, water and emission of carbon dioxides. Youngsters called it propaganda, questioned the positive impact of the design, uttering that 77 per cent of the carbon footprint in shoes comes from the raw materials (leather, rubber and cotton) and only a mere 5 per cent from packaging.[83]

Protecting the planet is not a typical Gen Yers thing, it is the result of the zeitgeist. They recycle as much as the other generations and they will buy environmentally-friendly and organic products as much as other generations.[84] More important to Gen Yers is that they don't just get bombarded with traditional charity programmes but that they can make a difference by owning the values and choosing how and where charitable contributions will go.[85]

Earth Hour, a subsidiary charity of WWF, invented a beverage that recreates beer in the future if we don't take action against global warming. The initiative was a part of the #SaveTheAles campaign that released during Earth Hour 2015. People could win different prizes if they posted a #NoBeerSelfie on Twitter, Instagram and Facebook. A report by the University of Queensland revealed that the quality and quantity of hops in Australia would negatively develop in the future. The beer, designed with GPY&R and beer experts (Willie the Boatman and Young Henrys), was called the Drought Draught and contained dried-out malts, stale hops and a lot of salt. This way, people could taste the change of climate, a poor quality beer.

Earth Hour created awareness with a different approach than other environmental campaigns. The tone of voice was more fun and engaging but the core message remained strong. Beer is a component of people's every day life so they feel personally related. It's also a social product where people talk about in a comforting setting. Earth Hour planned more tasting sessions across Australia and launched an online beer petition that gave people a chance to send a message to political leaders. The campaign led up to the UN Paris Climate Conference in November 2015.[86]

Generation Y cares

InSites Consulting conducted a research community study connecting 100 urban Millennials from 15 different cities around the world to learn about the dimensions and drivers behind cool brands, shops and places. One of the topics discussed was the social and ecological responsibility of global brands. Various aspects like green claims, fair trade, animal welfare and climate change were tackled in an online on-going discussion among 18- to 29-year-olds. One of the striking conclusions was that Gen Y seems to be more worried about people than about the rest of the environment.

Continued...

Generation Y cares   *Continued...*

To them, fair trade is a normal part of society and people deserve right treatment wherever they are working on earth. Since they want to be paid a fair amount of money for their own work, Millennials feel that if Western people need products from developing countries, the wages should be fair too. Safe working places and 'not exploiting people' are synonyms for social responsibility to them, while Gen Y's interpretation of environmental responsibility was much vaguer. To Gen Yers, eco-care means keeping the impact on the environment as low as possible and both global and local actions are much appreciated, although the more local equals the more relevant to them. Although youth root for Body Shop's policy against testing cosmetics on animals and think rare species should be protected, in the end humans are more important to most of them than animals. 'You support what you put your money in', was one of the literal quotes of the research community. This actually means that if a company like Apple has their stuff produced in China in unsafe working circumstances, Gen Y feels it is Apple's responsibility, even if it's a third-party producer.

Millennials generally don't like companies to brag about their CSR (corporate social responsibility) programmes. They appreciate those corporations that define clear company goals without big PR campaigns. When a company advocates these responsible actions and tries to push other players in the industry to follow the same path, it earns extra Gen Y respect. A brand like PUMA for instance is praised for making their eco-footprint a shareholder KPI (key performance indicator), improving working standards within the industry and sponsoring sports in emerging countries. Persistence in pursuing social and environmental goals is much appreciated. Even though Fair Trade, as a brand, went through difficult times, the consistent belief in its philosophy and core values is what matters to this generation. Cadbury and Sainsbury's, which both went down the Fair Trade route, are seen as great examples of social brands. Gen Y is frequently confronted in media with natural disasters that are often linked to the changing climate. Gen Yers do believe the concept of global warming, it's not a myth and is high on their agenda. They think we should act in the very near future to stop climate change before it's too late. Although youngsters say it's clearly an urgent matter, they feel incapable of solving the problem themselves because of the huge global proportion of the climate problem. When asked for personal efforts they mention recycling and re-using packaging. German youth especially seemed quite proud of the results of their national recycling efforts.[87]

They are lazy

Gen Yers are believed to be lazy because they mostly take the shortest way to get what's needed. But that's simply the way they were educated, attaining the objectives with the least possible effort in a smart way. Most youngsters will express a strong work/reward ethic. Nine out of 10 believe you will get your rewards in life when you work hard enough. They do know they have been spoiled by their Baby Boomer parents and realize that when they move out as adults they will have to work hard. Failure is assumed to stem from laziness. Most teenagers will only select role models and celebrities that have worked hard and really earned their success.[88] Barack Obama and Britney Spears are both often quoted as people who are admired for their work ethic and for achieving great things from humble beginnings by overcoming adversity to maintain their success.[89]

About 56 per cent of US youngsters aged 15 to 25 are considering becoming self-employed. This percentage is slightly higher than in the UK (52 per cent). People seem deeply convinced of a career as self-employed entrepreneur in the BRIC countries. More than 7 Millennials out of 10 consider making the move. Danish (39 per cent) and German (40 per cent) youngsters are less keen on being self-employed. Only 1 out of 10 USA youngsters who are currently employed consider the possibility of staying with that same employer for their entire career. This percentage is comparable to the UK. In the BRIC countries the loyalty 'for life' towards employers is as good as non-existent.[90]

'Today I am what I create', explains Tom Palmaerts, Youthwatcher at Trendwolves.

> After sharing text, pictures, video and audio found online through social networks, we are now more interested in creating something ourselves, because it is per definition more shareable. It is comparable to baking your own cake rather than buying one and then sharing it with your friends or colleagues. Creativity is a status symbol. Creative entrepreneurs are the new superstars. Their work is featured on T-shirts and bedroom walls of teenagers. Design and creation, whether it is digital, visual, video or architecture, is the new rock 'n' roll. Young people like to associate themselves with people, brands and visual formats with a creative image. It's the reason why Facebook picture trends like owling, planking, leisure diving and tilting are picked up globally. They are easy to copy formats that still give young people the idea that they belong to a creative group of people.[91]

It is also the reason why an easy-to-use photo app like Instagram is so successful. It turns every smartphone snapshot into a work of art and you can immediately share it with your friends and receive 'likes' and comments. Social networks that not only connect young people with each other but also facilitate and endorse creativity will be the winners of the next years.

Gen Y clearly has a fusion lifestyle. 'There's no clear separation between work and life, not just in terms of time management but also in motivations,' says Christopher Fellinger, talent relationship manager of Beiersdorf in an interview with us.

> They get gratifications from work and seek a way to enjoy life through their job too. Organizations need to become more flexible in their structures and processes to deal with the individualized needs of this generation of employees and spend more time to explain and sell regulations when they are in place. Gen Yers do not just accept what is said to them; they have to believe the policies and see the relevance themselves.[92]

A study by Cisco Systems among college students and young professionals between 18 and 29 years old revealed that 40 per cent of them ask their future employers about the social media policy and use of personal devices (like smartphones and tablets) in the workplace. For one quarter this policy is a key factor to decide whether or not to accept a job offer. One out of six Gen Y respondents would rather decline a job than not have access to social media at work.[93]

Gen Y's different view on the work–life balance and other expectations on flexibility, management and feedback leads to many critical questions during our presentations and in-company workshops. Gradually, companies will have to re-think their structure, motivational systems and leadership style to make their business Gen Y-proof. Nearly 10,000 Millennials turn 21 every day in the USA and by 2025, three out of every four workers globally will be Gen Y. 'Where leadership used to be direct, in command and in control, quite hierarchical, today it must be more focused on individual and group accomplishments', says Todd Corley, SVP and Global Chief Diversity Officer at Abercrombie & Fitch in an interview with us. 'They also want to push the envelope to make it better for everyone involved and around them. They didn't grow up with hierarchies and want inspiring, transparent and innovative leaders with a vision. For this generation, everything is on the table, there is no limit or taboo.'[94]

Millennials are used to immediate responses on every Facebook status update or Tweet. They expect the same degree of responsiveness in the workplace. They want to be able to ask questions and get career advice and feedback all the time. They want mentors rather than managers, because they grew up with this type of relationship with their own parents. An impressive 93 per cent of Millennials say they want a job where they can be themselves at work. That includes making their own hours at work, remote working, plenty of 'me time' on the job and dressing in a comfortable way. The vast majority (83 per cent) want a job where their creativity is valued and their opinion and insights are heard. They feel their boss can learn a lot from them.[95]

The performance generation

The current generation of youth seems to be born to perform. They are ambitious, enterprising and self-conscious and their main ambition is becoming famous. When you look around you, there are plenty of examples. Career kids... the name says it all. We see an increase in the number of children and youths who start up an adult career or activity at a younger age. The number of young (and they are really young!) entrepreneurs is growing, both nationally and internationally. Here are some examples: Lars Duursma, aged 24, appeared in *Business Week* with his training company Debatrix, and Fleur Kriegsman started her successful Hipvoordeheb.nl (an online fashion shop) when she was only 14. But it's not just about entrepreneurship. We have all heard about Laura Dekker, the 13-year-old sail girl. The new LAKS president (Action Committee of Scholars), Steven de Jong, is aged 18 and during his presidency he is working for a solid education for all youngsters. These examples are not the only ones. Data show that the number of young entrepreneurs in the Netherlands is increasing exponentially. In 2007 there were 13,421 registrations of entrepreneurs aged up to 24, in 2008 the figure rose to 28,730 and in 2009 the number of young entrepreneurs soared again to 43,095. There is a strong increase in ambition among youth. How can one explain this trend?

In the past decades, households changed into 'negotiation' modus. Youngsters are getting more and more room for discussion, and obtaining authority from hierarchy is continuing to be less acceptable. This generation of parents wants an equally matched relationship with their children. They push children to do what they like and to discover their own passions. A good relationship between parent and child is key. These changing household ratios are at the basis of the ambitious performance generation. Parents continue to push their children to excel in something. Being average is insufficient. Parents see their children as the centre of the universe, and children internalize this. The consequence is that children also think they are unique and fabulous. Recent research organized by TNS Nipo into narcissism among Dutch youngsters showed that almost half the children aged 16 to 24 think that they are 'very special', whereas this is only the case for a quarter of the 55+ group. People with a narcissistic personality show more sense for initiative, have more perseverance and often have a more positive mind. Those are the characteristics of ambitious career children. Furthermore, there are unlimited options these days to show your

Continued...

The performance generation   *Continued...*

talents and ideas to the world, which pushes the surfacing of young talent. It is mainly the arrival of social media that was a catalyser in that area. These days you can become famous or successful from your own bedroom, which is exactly what most members of this generation want. The Foundation Mijn Kind Online (my kid online) published research results in 2009 showing that 61 per cent of the youngsters aged 11 to 17 want to become famous. Becoming famous seems like a real option for this generation, thanks to the internet. A typical example is Esmée Denters, an 18-year-old girl from Oosterbeek (a village in the Netherlands) who was discovered via YouTube where she uploaded shot movies singing covers in her bedroom. She signed a contract on Justin Timberlake's label and released a couple of albums. Is this valid for all youngsters? Have we raised a generation of highflyers who are independent and ambitious? No, unfortunately we haven't. There seems to be an increasing split in the group of youth. On the one hand we have youngsters who are independent and ambitious, who follow their passion and who go through life without a care in the world. On the other side we have a large group of youngsters who struggle with all the options and the performance pressure and who actually have an increased need for clarity and structure. This group should not be forgotten about either: they are the ones who need extra attention, structure and guidance.

Judith Lieftink is Marketing Intelligence Consultant at ANWB

They are multi-tasking wizards

A common misunderstanding about Generation Yers is that they are multi-taskers.[96] With the rise of new technologies and social media they are showered with information. The ease with which youngsters follow people on Twitter, answer text messages or communicate via MSN or Facebook astonishes adults and might lead to the false conclusion that Generation Y is particularly good at processing multiple streams of conversation and information. Research, however, has evidence for the opposite: until the age of 22, youngsters are less good at multitasking. They have more difficulties than adults in distinguishing relevant from irrelevant information and have fewer abilities to park a certain chunk of information for later usage. Although they are exposed to more information channels than before, this does not lead to an increased absorption of this information. Only strong and short messages are able to pass through the stream of information. There is a limit to what our brains can actually process simultaneously. While we are able to perceive multiple stimuli in parallel, we cannot process them simultaneously. This is especially the case when the different messages are non-related. Young people are actually not attempting to process non-complementary messages simultaneously but rather switching back and forth between different activities.[97]

Steve Johnson, author of *Everything Bad Is Good For You*, calls this strategy to cope with information overload 'telescoping'.[98] Johnson claims that younger generations have got smarter in using these strategies by evolutions in popular culture: not only gaming but also soaps on television. The latter increasingly have complex narratives with, instead of one main plot, several separate alternating storylines. TV series used to have 'pointing arrows', clues in the plot that clarify what will happen next. Recent popular youth TV series such as *24*, *Heroes* or *Lost* lack these pointing arrows and there isn't even a clear distinction between good and bad characters anymore. There's a bit of the dark and white side in everyone. Leading actors unexpectedly die in the midst of the series. Youngsters have learned to analyse these series as puzzles. They don't need to study medicine to understand the rather medical scripts of *Grey's Anatomy* or *House MD*. They simply deduce the meaning of the difficult terms from the context. This is exactly what they do when they learn to master new technologies or tools. They don't read manuals, they just 'probe'. Youth master the skills of deduction, probing and telescoping. They don't multitask.[99] In April 2010, only a few days after Apple launched its iPad, MTV Networks released interactive iPad apps for *Beavis and Butt-head*, *MTV News* and *VH1 To GO*. MTV is also investing in co-browsing apps, meant to be used while youngsters are watching TV, to run on the iPhone or Android devices. The goal of these apps is to make chatting with friends more user-friendly by facilitating conversation without your eyes abandoning the on-screen action. The idea is that mobile devices are easier to use while watching TV than laptops or desktop computers, and the iPad tablet is the perfect in-between.[100]

Conclusion

Of course a number of elements of Gen Yers' behaviour are more linked to their young life stage than to their generation. The fact that their brains are still under development is one of these universal features. This explains why generation after generation of youngsters adore freedom, push their limits and are involved in risk-taking behaviour. They want to explore the world around them and discover novelties. Identity construction and the need for self-expression are also universal adolescent themes. Madonna sang: 'Music makes the people come together.' This is specifically true for youngsters. And although every lifestyle group and every generation has different genres, festivals and music carriers, music will always remain one of their main preoccupations.

You can also see Generation Y as the ultimate products of our postmodern society. Gen Yers are both individualistic and very sociable. They have traditional family values but are very tolerant and open as well. For instance, they are more sexually and ethnically permissive than former generations. They do have a strong work ethic but want a balanced life and lots of leisure time as well. They don't want to make the same mistakes as their Baby Boomer parents who traded in a fair amount of their spare time to succeed in life. They have seen the downside of their parents' success in terms of broken marriages, absentee parenting and stress-related illnesses.[101] Many youngsters take a sabbatical year after they have only been working for one or two years. They want to get rich and believe they will earn a lot, but at the same time enriching experiences are even more important. They cherish their local roots and love brands with local anchors but at the same time they think very globally, in career terms as well as in friendships and travel.[102] Generation Y is a more positive generation than Generation X with a stronger belief in a better future and a better world.

The specific characteristics of Gen Y we have discussed in this chapter will affect the way you should conceive your marketing and branding targeted at this group. Gen Yers will only stay interested in your brand if it succeeds in whetting their curiosity. Keeping your brand cool by incremental innovations is the key to winning their loyalty. Gen Yers want it right here, right now. Their need for instant gratification must be satisfied by immediate advantages. They are five times more likely to open promotional text messages on their mobile (if they did subscribe to them of course) than an e-mail. Brands like Vans and Charlotte Russe encourage their young clients to sign up for texts containing special offers and goodies.[103]

While constantly renewing your brands and products, staying real and true to your own brand DNA and unique identity is essential. Gen Y is more marketing savvy and will immediately see through fake marketing strategies. Honesty and transparency are important aspects of successful youth brands. Again, both the uniqueness and honesty Gen Yers look for in brands are nothing more than a reflection of the times they were raised in. They were born in a society that celebrated individual success and were stimulated to become unique and special. Twenge has also highlighted that the younger generation has a compulsive honesty. If you're not true to yourself and you conform to someone else's rules, you might be seen as dishonest. Gen Y appreciate directness. Instead of making image claims in advertising, brands should demonstrate what they stand for by their deeds. For Generation Xers, brands were communicating status and had to express that they were winners. For Generation Yers, brands are tools for communicating who they are.

Baby Boomers gave their children many choices and taught them to make their own choices from early childhood on. Think of pre-schoolers choosing their own clothes in the morning. Even if they ended up wearing terrible combinations, that was okay because they were expressing themselves.[104] Brands and products are seen by this generation as important in creating their own personal and unique narrative. Your brand needs to mirror the values and identity of the youngsters you are targeting. Brands that communicate a similar view of life will be more appealing.[105]

Brands provide them with a way to stand out from the mass. Brands stimulate discerning usage. At the same time, successful brands have to bring social acceptance for youngsters in their reference groups. A youth brand will only be a youth brand if Gen Y can participate, co-create and co-shape the brand identity while it receives the most important youth currency: content for offline as well as online conversations. To experience brands in exciting environments contributes to arousal. Positive emotions are one of the most important reasons why this generation of stimulation junkies will be loyal to your offer.

Those companies and marketers that adjust their branding strategies to address the needs of this emerging segment will find themselves better connected with them and thus more successful.[106]

HOT TAKEAWAYS FOR COOL BRAND BUILDERS

- Gen Yers are stimulus junkies who look for individual empowerment (control) and instant gratification in the hot brands they choose.

- Gen Yers fuse their social lives in technology, not the other way around.

- Content is the number one social currency for them.

- Hot brands continuously bring new cool content.

- Friends are the relevancy filter through which Gen Yers process brand messages. Hot brands embrace social media and peer-to-peer strategies in which they don't dictate but engage youth by offering them control.

- Gen Yers put more trust in people and social connections. Hot brands value the role of employees, shop personnel and ambassador clients to defend and spread their DNA.

- Gen Yers have a bigger influence on family purchases as a consequence of the 'hotel mum and dad' and boomerang trend.

- Gen Yers select and mix the right snippets for the right moment and need. Brands should cater for this variety of moments and needs and offer choice.

- Hot brands don't just offer products, they are the supporters of Gen Yers' lifestyles.

- Brand affection and self-identification with the brand is built during adolescence as a result of brain development.

- This consumer generation is searching for anchor brands that provide them with stability, harmony and authenticity. Brands need to have a well-defined, transparent and consistent meaning and a clear vision.

Developing a brand model for the new consumer

The idiom 'friend of a friend' or FOAF is often used when someone is not sure who the source of a certain story is and the story cannot be confirmed. 'I know it from a FOAF' or 'it happened to a FOAF.' Rodney Dale, a British writer specializing in urban legends, coined the term in his 1978 book *Tumour in the Whale*.[1] No, the Great Wall of China is not visible from the moon. Toilets and bathtubs don't drain differently in the southern hemisphere and ostriches just run away when they sense danger. They don't bury their head in the sand. These are all examples of urban myths. They perfectly illustrate the power of human narratives.

The power of word-of-mouth

As stories are so embedded in human nature, they tend to express both our rational and emotional selves.[2] From a research point of view, it is therefore interesting to analyse the stories that Generation Yers would spontaneously tell about brands. After all, brands only exist in their minds. This generation of consumers do not passively receive the brand stories told by companies, they co-create the meaning of brands.[3] 'Consumers have always been in control', says Geoff Cottrill, Chief Marketing Officer (CMO) at Converse, interviewed by us. 'But today, they have more tools to use their control. They have more and faster access to information and are able to express their feelings. Successful brands are obsessed by consumers and respect them. They add human elements like honesty in their branding', says Cottrill.[4] For marketers this means that the old trick of shouting how fantastic your brand or using your brand is, won't work anymore. Today, listening to these young consumers, understanding how they are fitting your brand into their lives and lifestyles and adding to conversations by offering services and content that is relevant and helpful to them is crucial. The good thing is that this generation are talking a lot about brands. In its TalkTrack survey among more than 2,000 US teens aged 13–17, the Keller Fay Group found that youth have on average 145 conversations a week about brands. That is twice the rate of adults. They are also talking about the advertising they observe. The number of citations from advertising and media was 10 per cent higher than in the adult population. Brands that were leading the conversation in the study were Apple, American Eagle, Dr Pepper, Chevrolet and Nintendo. The broad categories that were most talked about were: media and entertainment (mainly TV content), sports, recreation and hobbies, technology, telecom, and food and dining. Gen Yers are three times more likely to use online tools (texting, instant messaging, e-mail, social networks, chats or blogs) than adults. Most of the teen conversations (58 per cent) about brands are positive.[5]

In our own youth brand conversation research, we saw that 13- to 29-year-olds have more conversations on topics such as mobile phones and operators, games and game consoles, as well as MP3 players and cars. The 15- to 17-year-olds had more talks on portable game consoles. Girls talk more often about beauty care and chocolate, boys about beer and spirits. But both genders' chats contain on average an equal 2.5 different brand mentions. Although the net generation is indeed using online media more than the 35+ population, 86 per cent of brand conversations are still taking place in a face-to-face situation.[6] A Japanese study based on the responses from more than 1,700 teenagers between the ages of 13 and 18 years revealed that face-to-face word-of-mouth elicited stronger affective brand commitment than mobile-based.[7] About half of the Gen Y population said that peers were frequently telling them about their experiences with products and brands. The same percentage regularly share their own brand anecdotes with their friends. A substantial 43 per cent of youngsters aged 20–29 are even actively recommending certain brands.[8] For this generation, word-of-mouth, specifically through peer conversations, has a strong impact on buying preferences. Six out of 10 brand conversations between youngsters will change one of the participant's opinions. In one third of the talks, they will incite someone to try a product or brand for the first time.[9] Observing Gen Yers' talks about brands both on- and offline is therefore an important new task of youth marketers today. Word-of-mouth measured through a brand's share of conversations is increasingly replacing old-school key performance indicators (KPIs) such as share of voice (a brand's relative advertising spend).

'Brands have to be more social today and that doesn't mean just launching a Facebook page', says Peter Jung, former Senior Business Leader Consumer Marketing (youth segment) at MasterCard International in an interview with us. 'It's about building a community of consumers and establishing a relevant, credible social voice. Younger consumers expect brands to respond to comments and invite dialogue. It takes serious commitment and engagements to get people to talk about your brand or service – we constantly ask ourselves: why would they care, why would they share?'[10]

Of course social media can help to endorse this ongoing conversation with consumers. 'The buying cycle of sneakers is different compared to the daily bought FMCG products', says Geoff Cottrill, CMO of Converse. 'So, in between the moments of purchase, there should be a reason to stay in touch with our brand. Converse has almost 38 million fans on Facebook, which makes us a top five brand on that social medium after Coke, Red Bull, Nike and Oreo. Apart from being a footwear or apparel brand, we are also a network of Converse fans who want to interact with each other in an engaging and entertaining way. We bring SXSW reports (South by South West – a cool annual music, film and interactive festival in Austin, Texas) to add to the conversation. On Instagram, there are three quarters of a million pictures tagged with Converse shoes. It's all about people expressing their individuality and creativity through the lens of Instagram. It's consumers who make a brand cool, not the brand itself', concludes Converse's CMO in our interview.[11]

The research base: 5,000 brand stories can't be wrong

Because listening to Gen Y's own creation of brand meaning is the only way to learn what it takes to sustain a successful brand, we invited more than 5,000 14- to 29-year-olds across different regions of Europe – the UK, Germany, France, Spain, Sweden, the Netherlands and Belgium – to participate in our brand research. We asked them to share their most and least favourite brands with us in three different product categories:

- clothing;
- mobile phone devices;
- sweet snacks (chocolate bars or sweets).

Then we randomly showed them their most desired brand in one of the three categories and invited them to write a short story of at least 750 characters about that brand. They could write whatever they wanted about their preferred brand.

The five success factors of Gen Y brands

When examining over 5,000 stories in these categories through text-mining techniques, the five most common denominators of favourite brands that we had experienced in our years of research and practice with Generation Y were confirmed: brand coolness, realness (authenticity), uniqueness, self-identification with the brand and happiness. These five aspects of a youth brand will enhance its success in the Generation Y market. For mnemonic purposes, we have coined the acronym 'CRUSH' to describe what's important to Gen Y. Each of the subsequent chapters of this book is dedicated to one of the CRUSH elements – the basic building blocks of successful youth brands:

- Coolness: What does it mean to be a cool brand for this generation? How do you achieve a cool status and why should you bother?

- Realness: Brand authenticity is a key aspect that discerns long-term winning brands from fads. With Generation Y, authenticity is attained in another way than the traditional approach of claiming origin, heritage or history.

- Uniqueness: A clear positioning based on a sustainable brand DNA will increase impact among youngsters. This generation is craving for anchor brands in a fragmented world. But how do you assert uniqueness when most innovations are copied within only a couple of months?

- Self-identification with the brand: Gen Yers will only feel emotionally connected with your brand when it feels like a friend to them. This implies that your brand should reflect their diverse lifestyles. A better understanding of their identity will make your brand fit in with youth's lives while embracing diversity.

- Happiness: Almost 80 per cent of the 5,000 brand stories were severely coloured by emotions, with happiness being the most uttered one. Popular youth brands know how to leverage from positive emotions and avoid arousing negative ones.[12]

To validate the CRUSH elements globally, InSites Consulting executed a large-scale quantitative survey at the start of 2011. We interviewed 4,065 15- to 25-year olds in 16 countries around the globe. From the long list of 33 different characteristics that could be attributed to brands, Gen Y didn't just pick 'coolness' for its top five. It's not that coolness is not important to this generation; we will explain that in the next chapter. A brand's coolness results from a complex mixture of attributes. Gen Y will never merely buy something because it is deemed 'cool', youth is too marketing savvy to be tricked. When Gen Yers talk about their beloved brands, they universally share the same attributes. In Figure 2.1 the most important brand characteristics for Generation Y around the world are shown.

To be embraced by this new consumer generation, brands should have their own style (part of coolness as well as uniqueness), deliver a positive emotional experience (happiness) and stay up-to-date (coolness). The brands Generation Y in 16 countries favoured also have a clean reputation and real/authentic feeling (realness), are unique and something to identify with (self-identification). Although the top-ranked items were universal across different regions around the world, some attributes were more important in certain parts. Being up-to-date is of greater importance in the USA and Russia. A clean reputation scored higher in Russia and China and more Chinese youngsters were highly involved with authentic and spiritual brands. In Brazil and India brands should also provide a safe feeling and in Brazil ecological engagement is strongly approved.[13]

FIGURE 2.1   Most important brand characteristics for Generation Y around the world

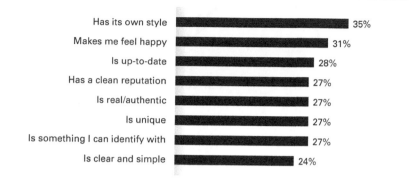

Has its own style	35%
Makes me feel happy	31%
Is up-to-date	28%
Has a clean reputation	27%
Is real/authentic	27%
Is unique	27%
Is something I can identify with	27%
Is clear and simple	24%

Brand leverage: one step beyond brand equity

In our study, we linked the individual CRUSH scores of each favourite as well as non-favourite brand to the brand strength to measure the impact of each CRUSH component. More information on how we executed these analyses can be found in Appendix 1 at the end of this book. Traditional models measuring the strength of a brand are often too focused on brand equity or brand image. They mostly take brand awareness, image and loyalty into account. More recently, the degree to which someone would recommend a brand to others (also called the Net Promoter Score or NPS) was added as a key brand metric. InSites Consulting participated with Houston University to develop its brand leverage model. As a result of the study, a clear relation was found between the extent to which consumers talk about brands and brand leverage. Brand leverage is defined as a combination of brand satisfaction, recommendation and closeness to ideal.[14] Brand leverage is the guarantee that your brand will sustain throughout time and remain hot year after year.

Figure 2.2 gives an overview of how the CRUSH elements contribute to this brand leverage among youth. The detailed impact of each CRUSH component derived from our study is shown in Appendix 1.

If Gen Yers highly rate your brand on each of the CRUSH elements, your brand's image will improve and they will talk about your brand. Both brand image and brand conversations will have a substantial positive effect on your brand strength (brand leverage), ensuring that your brand will stay hot with this fickle consumer generation for a long time. We also found a very strong direct relationship between youth's self-identification with the brand and brand leverage as indicated by the dotted arrow in Figure 2.1.

Let's illustrate the CRUSH model with a couple of cases. The first one describes Esprit's struggle to re-connect with the younger generation. While Esprit has a strong Californian heritage and unique soul, the clothing brand

FIGURE 2.2   The CRUSH components

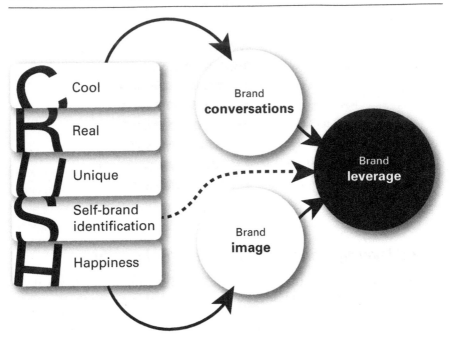

lost its mojo for the younger generation, especially when confronted with new competitors such as Forever 21, Uniqlo, Hollister, Primark and many more. The second one is perhaps a stranger in our midst. The 'Ex-smokers are Unstoppable' campaign wanted to turn young smokers into ex-smokers by using positive emotions (happiness) as the main drivers for brand conversations and behavioural change. The European Union's biggest anti-smoking campaign ever was awarded with a Gold Euro Effie and the Best Innovative Use of Print Award.

CRUSH into practice: two case studies

Esprit: finding a re-connection with Gen Y

At the end of the 1960s Susie and Doug Tompkins were selling apparel from a VW bus and their headquarters was the Tompkins' apartment in San Francisco. Susie was the creative designer of the Esprit fashion line and Doug the financial head. In 1979 John Casado developed the Esprit logo. Casado was advertising art director for Young & Rubicam and also the creative brain behind Apple's logo. In the 1980s Esprit launched the 'Real People Campaign', shot by the famous photographer Oliviero Toscani. In 1998, 'edc' (Esprit de corps) was founded as the young people's sub-label of

Esprit. In February 2012 Esprit announced that it would close all retail stores in North America because they had been losing money. 'Esprit used to be a cool brand in the 1980s and 1990s but today for Gen Y it's more a place where their moms and dads go shopping', says Jörgen Andersson, former SVP and Director Brand and New Business at Esprit.

Esprit used to be way ahead of the time. The logo, the shootings, the campaigns were cool back then. But like many other companies when the founders leave the company, the values of the founders kind of disappeared and so now we have to re-connect with these values. Design is the first thing to tackle, creating the most beautiful and inspirational collections. Design was taking place in Düsseldorf, Germany. You can have the headquarters there but you have to take design input from all over the world, so we put up design studios in London and Hong Kong. Then you have to embrace the fact that there are so many talented people outside your company that could contribute. To create the most inspirational stores in the industry, we are currently hiring the best people in the industry, architects and visual artists. Then when everything is fixed you can talk about PR, marketing and how to communicate the story in a way that young consumers start to feel something and want to share it as social currency.

When people heard that Jan Nord (creative director) and myself switched from H&M to Esprit, they thought we were going to do a fashion designer collaboration and copy-paste what we did for H&M. But of course that's not the case because every brand has its own heritage and destination. Esprit is not H&M; it's not about fashion catwalks but about contemporary clothes brought in a passionate way. It's a human brand that cares not only about the looks but also about what's happening around us. When we decided to join Esprit the ethos and DNA of the company was amazing and we were both challenged to try and reinvent or re-create Esprit not as a retro brand but as one that feels relevant and contemporary. Because there is a need for a brand that makes you look good and feel good. The campaign with Gisele Bündchen as a model (see Figure 2.3) was a very quick way of getting Esprit back on people's shopping radar because many women didn't visit our stores anymore or not to the extent they used to. So we looked for a natural beauty that could be linked to the California heritage. We wanted to show her as she is, as the women and not the model. Esprit is all about: if you feel good, you look good, not about pretentious catwalk fashion. And Gisele was the perfect match. In the TVC she talks about style, quality, about sustainability, about colour, about love like a human person would. Of course Esprit is about millions of confident women, not just Gisele, so we are slowly going to build around this portrait of confident women but for a start we wanted something powerful enough for people to see it.

I think brands need to connect more emotionally. When you buy, for instance, on the internet, you don't even have the shop experience anymore, so it's the emotional power and connection of a brand that will make it googled. You need a brand that's bigger than the product, a community, almost a religion like Apple was able to do. When Steve Jobs came back to the company, he cut the catalogue from over 200 products down to 10 and he increased focus on the core competence and products and made them perfect in terms of usage experience. So it's all about listening to your consumers and understanding their needs and dreams. They know the answers to every brand's challenges. When we started at Esprit, we did a large global survey about the brand, where they shop and why, and how they would create their own brand just

FIGURE 2.3   Esprit's campaign with Gisele Bündchen

to understand what they expected from us. Apple understood that consumers found computers and smartphones too complex and they created user-friendly products that a five-year-old can use along with aesthetic and differing designs. Part of the problem of Esprit is the lost emotion and soul. When you go inside a store you don't feel anything, it's only about the product, which is very generic. Susie Tompkins was the first to create a sustainable ecological collection in the industry and everyone was following her. Her husband Doug is an environmental activist and he also co-founded The Northface in 1965. In the 1990s Esprit did a campaign to express 'buy less', only buy what you need: instead of buying three T-shirts buy the one you really like. I have had many talks with Doug and Susie and people around them when we came on-board to understand the DNA of the brand and Doug Tompkins said: 'The financial guys told me that I was crazy with that kind of campaign so that's why I eventually decided to leave the company. They only talk about growth, but we only have one Earth, we cannot continue to grow. When growth became more important than what you do and how you do it, that's greed. Whereas if you do a product in a way that people sympathize with and you do it better than the others, the result is that you will sell and make money.'

So knowing this brand's history we will start talking about small projects that are in line with this DNA. For instance, one project in Australia with wool farmers allowed their sheep to eat fresh grass, move freely around, allowed no mulesing. Basically when you have happy sheep, you get a higher quality of wool, almost like cashmere. Esprit is buying the production from this farmer for the next five years and hopefully when that is spread in Australia other sheep farmers will adapt their sheep stations. So the market economy and environmental ambitions can go hand in hand. The product will feel better, of higher quality and the story behind the product will make you feel better about wearing it too. Step by step, in explaining this to our customers, I think they will not just like us for the collection but also for our approach, not only WHAT we do but also HOW we do it. The way we behave and care. Our job now is to take Esprit back to where it used to be. The whole company in California was built around community thinking, believing that the group is always stronger then the individual. That's where the name came from: 'Esprit de Corps'. They worked with graphic designers, fashion designers and people from around the world together on projects in California. They were way ahead of their time and thinking extremely modern. I think a local dimension is still really, really relevant. Starbucks for instance is a global chain, it looks the same everywhere, but maybe it should become a bit more Japanese in Japan, Belgian in Belgium, etc. People will get bored of global brands and shopping streets that look the same all over the world. In every city there's always a new district popping up where you can find local designers and local talent. I think people today are more and more embracing local initiatives, whether it's food related or a clothing store. When we are opening new stores with Esprit we try to integrate local elements in the design and architecture for instance. Of course we want the stores to reflect the Californian heritage so there will always be natural material, green plants but with a local touch (see Figure 2.4). We don't want salmon being fished in Norway, shipped to Thailand for processing and shipped back to Sweden to be sold. It's not a sustainable way of taking care of our Earth's resources. In fashion it could mean producing and knitting clothes in the country where it is sold. For instance 'made in Sweden' for a Swedish brand.[15]

FIGURE 2.4　Esprit's New Stores

Esprit's new approach is clearly using CRUSH elements: starting from the brand's unique DNA and building on Esprit's authenticity in every small detail from the design and production, towards the shopping experience and campaigns. Eventually Esprit wants to re-connect with Gen Y through a lost emotional connection.

The 'Ex-smokers are Unstoppable' campaign

Almost one in three Europeans (158 million or 32 per cent) smoke. Smoking continues to be the largest single cause of preventable death and disease in the European Union. Every year 650,000 Europeans die because of smoking and another 19,000 people die from passive exposure. Research shows that, on average, 31 per cent of European smokers have tried to quit at least once in the past year. On the other hand, research also indicates that the quitting efforts aren't always fruitful. The campaigning efforts for getting smokers to quit have largely been focused on prohibition and scare tactics. Years and years of anti-tobacco campaigns have taught people how bad smoking is and how their health and future might be affected negatively by smoking habits. In the meantime, people trained themselves to filter the terrifying messages out as much as possible. The European Commission has promoted smoking cessation campaigns since 2002. The first 'Feel free to say no' campaign ran from 2002 to 2004. The second campaign 'Help: for a life without tobacco' ran from 2005 to 2010. This campaign focused on smoking prevention, smoking cessation and passive smoking and targeted, in particular, young Europeans between 15 and 25 years old.

The campaign 'Ex-smokers are Unstoppable' shifts the focus from the dangers of smoking to the advantages of quitting smoking. The Ex-smokers are Unstoppable campaign was intended to run for two and a half years in all European Union countries. The campaign creates a positive message that aims at supporting long-term motivation. Instead of scaring young people with bad news, the focus is on the positive new life ex-smokers seem to discover. The campaign celebrates ex-smokers and portrays them as inspiring role models to encourage current smokers to quit. The smokers who want to quit are not only a large group to start with, but they don't need to be convinced of the necessity anymore. The challenge is to find the right motivation to actually get them to act on their desire to stop. In addition to the motivational message, practical help and guidelines on how to stop is provided. Together with leading scientists, psychologists and communication experts, the iCoach was created. The iCoach is an online tool that takes smokers through a five-stage process that provides motivation, advice, tips and a daily e-mail to help them to stay on course. Obviously, the campaign was targeting young smokers as research showed that people aged 25–34 are more likely to smoke and still have the opportunity to correct a lot of the wrongs tobacco might have caused. Gen Yers are not so open to scare tactics, as most of the negative effects like chronic diseases or cancer don't manifest themselves yet and they often believe themselves to be untouchable.

The new and positive message of the campaign was communicated in print, audiovisual (television and seeding) and online (display ads, banners, search engine, social media), national and international events and PR (see Figure 2.5). In certain countries, the positive message was adapted to specific national needs and motivators. For instance, Scandinavian women might be more sensitive to health benefits, while the Bulgarian youth could be more interested in the financial benefits of stopping smoking. All channels were aimed at generating traffic to the website, where the visitor was immediately directed to the iCoach programme to turn intention into behaviour. Rather than just having the European Commission addressing the youth, the portability of the message and material was maximized to share among themselves. Interesting material came to the surface: stories from real ex-smokers, with real dreams and real ambitions. Facebook pages provided a place to share and comment on these stories. Facebook was used as a central platform for all campaign activity through 29 pages. Facebook members were recruited for a photoshoot (with world renowned photographer Rankin) to find ambassadors willing to share their ex-smokers' stories with the rest of the world. The call for stories was shared virally and seeded via anti-smoking, health and sports bloggers. The personal stories were used in the autumn campaign wave and the winners became the face of the campaign. Print and television ads glorified ex-smokers' achievements and were on pan-regional TV channels, Eurosport and Euronews. They were also seeded online with Goviral and EBuzzing to extend the reach and enlarge conversation potential. Again, all media directed to the website where visitors could immediately register on the digital platform iCoach to become an ex-smoker. The total budget of nearly €6 million was split into print (49 per cent), television (17 per cent) and digital (34 per cent). With this budget, 19.4 million 25- to 34-year-old smokers and 347.3 million adults were reached across 27 EU member states.

Post-test results show that smokers who have seen the campaign on television, via banners or in print, indicate that they really were interested, wanted to find out more and got some new and positive motivation out of it. Television advertising performed exceptionally well. The majority of the public sees a new breath in this campaign, and smokers in particular identify new elements. More than 50 per cent of the smokers that have seen the campaign find that the campaign is saying new things about stopping smoking. A large majority (67 per cent) of the sample is convinced that this new approach will convince more people to stop, and an even larger group (80 per cent) thinks that it does a better job than the previous prevention campaigns did. The post-test clearly indicated positive results with both smokers and non-smokers, as respectively 44 per cent and 36 per cent indicated that they had talked about the campaign. Moreover, 97 per cent of all

FIGURE 2.5   The Unstoppable print campaign

**EX-SMOKERS
LOOK BETTER**
–
Out with the grey skin and yellow stains on your fingers and in with the whiter teeth and shinier hair! Quitting smoking is simply the most effective beauty treatment on earth.

**EX-SMOKERS
TRAVEL MORE**
–
When you stop smoking you start saving lots of money. If you smoke a pack a day, and each pack costs €8, you could save around €2,920 a year. That could buy you a lovely holiday, including palm trees, tropical fruit cocktails and plenty of unforgettable experiences. And the following year you will save the same amount again, and the year after that, and so on until the day you die. That means lots of holidays – especially since non-smokers live longer, too.

**EX-SMOKERS
HAVE MORE MONEY**
–
A pack of 20 cigarettes costs about €8. That's not cheap, but the average European can afford it. Now let's say you smoke a pack a day. That's €56 a week, which still doesn't hurt your wallet too badly. Now let's calculate what that comes to per year: 365 × 8 = €2,920. Wow – that's more than the average net monthly wage in the European Union. So if you quit smoking you gain an extra month's salary, every year, starting now.

**EX-
SMOKERS
ARE LESS
NERVOUS**
–
Oddly enough, smokers often light up when they are feeling nervous, which doesn't make much sense because nicotine works as a stimulant. It helps release adrenaline into your blood which makes you even more nervous. Besides that, living with an addiction is hardly ever relaxing. So wind down and put out that cigarette!

**EX-
SMOKERS
ARE MORE
CONFIDENT**
–
Quitting is anything but easy. So ex-smokers are usually proud of themselves – and rightly so. It's a big achievement so why not feel good about yourself? By quitting you have shown that you are everything but a quitter. Your friends and family will be proud, too. And, by the way, you'll smell better and look better, which is another boost for your confidence.

**EX-SMOKERS
SMELL BETTER**
–
When you stop smoking you stop smelling like a cigarette or an ashtray. And that's a great improvement. For a smoker, smelling like a cigarette or an ashtray isn't a big problem. Their houses smell like that and so do their clothes, so for them it is a comfortably familiar smell. Even your kids smell like cigarettes when you smoke indoors. But to the 71% of Europeans who don't smoke, smelling like a cigarette simply means you stink!

**EX-SMOKERS
ARE HEALTHIER**
–
Old news, agreed. But it's no secret either that each year 650,000 Europeans die of smoking-related diseases. And only a small number of them actually grows old first. The health benefits of those who quit smoking include increased lung capacity, greater stamina, and fewer respiratory infections. Those who quit smoking also decrease the risk of cancer, strokes, and cardio-vascular diseases.

**EX-SMOKERS
HAVE MORE FREEDOM**
–
It's a free world – nobody is forcing you to quit. But think about it: what else makes you bother complete strangers, frantically search for a light, slip out of restaurants between every course, become nervous on long flights, or ties you to a hospital bed for a very long time? So why not make your escape while you can?

**EX-SMOKERS
SLEEP BETTER**
–
When you are young, smoking doesn't keep you awake at night. But things change when you get older – your impaired breathing makes you feel more tired in the morning, while your evening cigarettes create too much adrenaline which means it takes you longer to fall asleep.

**BECOME AN EX-SMOKER
BECOME UNSTOPPABLE**
–
If you can beat your cigarette habit, you can do almost anything. Ex-smokers are healthier, feel younger and have more confidence. They look better, smell better, have more money and a more positive outlook. Basically, ex-smokers are unstoppable!

With help from our free health-coaching platform iCoach, you can become an ex-smoker, too.
More than 30% who start the programme quit smoking.

Go to www.exsmokers.eu and become unstoppable.

EX

SMOKERS
ARE UNSTOPPABLE

An initiative of
the European Commission

BECOME
UNSTOPPABLE ON
EXSMOKERS.EU

the conversations on the campaign were positive. On average, 18 per cent of the young smokers who have seen the campaign recommend it to someone else. An average of 28 per cent of the smokers are considering quitting smoking after seeing the campaign. Television and print were the most effective media. An average of 20 per cent of the smokers claimed that they visited the website after seeing the campaign, which indicates that they actively searched for more information. In the period 15 June to 31 October 2011, more than 1 million unique visitors went to **www.stopsmokingcoach.eu**. There were 359,545 visits to the registration page and 40 per cent of the visitors really registered on iCoach.

The Ex-smokers are Unstoppable campaign understood that communicating with Gen Y, as explained in the 'H' of the CRUSH model, is all about positive emotions and happiness instead of stressing the negative aspects of smoking. This positive approach combined with the power of word-of-mouth and peer-to-peer conversations led to a big success. 'The "Ex-smokers are Unstoppable" campaign for the European Commission is exceptional in many ways', comments Marc Michils, former chairman of Saatchi & Saatchi Brussels, the agency behind this campaign.

Not only because of its strategy, promoting the benefits of quitting rather than focusing on the dangers of smoking. But also because of its scope: the campaign was rolled out in all 27 European countries. It is also built on innovation by offering (ex-)smokers practical help and support through iCoach, a free online health coach. It's great that the campaign's creativity and proven effectiveness got acknowledged at the Euro Effie Awards. How proud can a socially engaged adman be.[16]

Conclusion

From listening to over 5,000 Gen Y stories of favourite brands, we learned that the brands with which this critical generation become engaged share five basic elements. We created the 'CRUSH' acronym to anchor these components of successful youth brands in your mind. In the subsequent chapters of this book we will explain to you in-depth how each of the CRUSH components can contribute to a better connection between your brand and the new consumer generation. Both research insights and case illustrations will give you inspiration to create cool brands. Although developing a cool brand is a first important step to being relevant for the youth market, it takes more to stay hot for a long time with this fickle consumer generation. The chapters will each highlight the steps to keep your cool brand hot for Generation Y.

HOT TAKEAWAYS FOR COOL BRAND BUILDERS

Gen Y's most favourite brands all share five key elements:

Coolness

Realness

Uniqueness

Self-identification

Happiness

These CRUSH components have an impact on brand image as well as brand conversations that will result in a substantial leverage for your brand.

To keep your cool brand hot for this fickle generation, the CRUSH model offers a proven branding approach.

What cool means to brands

Be just like the Fonz... and what is the Fonz?
He's cool... that's right... just be cool...

That's what Samuel L Jackson's character tells the robber at a diner in the final scene of Tarantino's *Pulp Fiction,* without any doubt one of the coolest crime films ever made. Arthur Herbert Fonzarelli or 'Fonzie', 'The Fonz', was the lead character of the US sitcom *Happy Days* (1974–84) played by Henry Winkler.

The Fonz's coolness is not only originating from the way he is dressed: his inevitable black leather jacket, the white T-shirt underneath and blue jeans, not forgetting his hair regularly combed and greased into style. It is also in the way he walks and talks. Fonzie is an Italian-American high school drop-out driving a motorcycle. He's notorious for his romantic experiences with all attractive women in his surroundings. But the womanizing car mechanic has some other skills too. He's able to fix the jukebox at Arnold's restaurant with a single punch of his fist. And he solves most of his friends' problems in 'his office', the Gents in Arnold's restaurant. Both acts usually end in The Fonz's iconic finger snapping, double thumbs up and the inevitable catch phrase 'Aaaaay'!

This combination of jukebox music, looks, skills, movements and language certainly contributes to the cool image of The Fonz. In fact, sociologists would immediately recognize the resemblance of these traits with the symbolic codes teenagers use to identify with peers during adolescence. In this awkward period, teenagers are extremely concerned about how they look and believe everyone is constantly observing their appearance and behaviour. The drastic physical changes they have to struggle through and the emotional crashes involved simply make symbolic codes and behaviour vital to them. To them 'cool' equals a set of discernible body movements, postures, facial expressions and voice modulations that gives them a strategic social value within the peer context.[1] Marcel Danesi, Professor of Semiotics at the University of Toronto, focused his book *Cool. The Signs and Meanings of Adolescence* on dress codes, hairstyles, language, musical tastes and other symbolic systems used to identify with peers.

In this chapter, we will question what 'being cool' means for today's youth and how brands can tap into this cool world and develop a cool identity. This is the first step of the CRUSH model that will leverage your brand's connection with Generation Y.

Gen Y's definition of 'cool'

Because of the fragmentation of media and styles, today it is harder than ever before to find one single definition of 'cool'. Although the meaning of 'cool' is subjective, it certainly signifies some sign of admiration or at least approval. Still, when MTV Networks asked us to study which brands were the coolest among youth, we were not so sure we were on the same wavelength. The one thing that worried us the most was the way Generation Y describes something cool. Could we just ask which brands were cool to them, or perhaps 'cool' wasn't the right word to track 'coolness' anymore. In fact, youth slang is continuously changing and generations tend to linguistically differentiate themselves from their predecessors. There are indeed plenty of synonyms for cool: awesome, hip, in, trendy, wicked, sick, chill, dope, hot, dry, swag, raw... Some of them are typical products of the zeitgeist, as you can see in Figure 3.1. To stay up-to-date on the newest Gen Y slang words, check out the hashtags: #millennialslang, #genYslang or #millenniallingo on Twitter. They are often used by the researchers of @ mtvinsights and based on their daily youth interviewing practice.

FIGURE 3.1   Synonyms for 'cool'

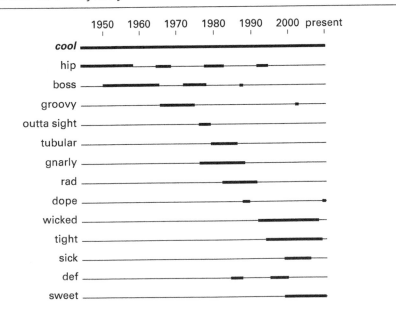

To all, seeming 'cool' has enduringly managed to resist this generational changing of the guard. We asked 500 Gen Yers to help us understand which words were in fashion to express someone or something to be cool.[2] As a first conclusion of the study, we saw that everyone was capable of explaining the concept of 'cool' in their own words. Youngsters spontaneously came up with 39 different meanings. To the majority (29 per cent) 'cool' is just a synonym for appealing or fun. Others mentioned connotations such as 'in' (15 per cent), 'renewing and innovative' (10 per cent), 'hip' (6 per cent), 'original and unique' (6 per cent), 'pleasant' (4 per cent) and 'trendy' (3 per cent). If you look at these descriptions, most are related to products, brands or events: must-haves or trendsetting stuff. Six out of 10 even agreed that advertising determines what's cool and what's not. Yet 12 per cent referred to the other sense of cool: a relaxed state or personality, which is more linked to persons and role models. In aided associations, we found that three key dimensions of 'coolness' were confirmed. Gen Yers perceive a brand as cool when it is attractive to them (51 per cent) and when it has an air of novelty and originality (55 per cent). Denotations that were the least connected with coolness were: 'arrogant' (4 per cent), 'luxurious' (8 per cent) and 'alternative' (13 per cent). The last one was particularly interesting to us, since the original use of 'cool' attitudes was clearly more edgy and alternative than Gen Y's contemporary definition. Only 11 per cent of the surveyed young people, mostly boys aged 13–19, found it a necessity to break rules or be a rebel in order to attain coolness.

These findings reassured us that 'cool' was still a good word to use to discuss cool brands with this generation. Ypulse endorsed our European results with similar research in the United States. More than 4 out of 10 teens and collegians, regardless of gender, are regular users of the word 'cool' to describe something they like or are excited about. More than half of them see it as an appearance, attitude or style. One third considers cool to be integral to a product. Most Millennials feel coolness is a personal and subjective item and therefore only mildly influenced by others. Ypulse also polled for current alternatives to the word cool. While youth came up with more than 50 synonyms, including neat, epic, badass, tight and rad, highlights included awesome, sweet, nice and amazing.[3]

Cool barometers

To be cool as a person, wearing the right clothes, adopting the latest trends and looking great might help. Yet you can't learn to be cool, it's more a personality trait. The top sources that set the youth standard for coolness are: their own friends (61 per cent), television broadcasts (32 per cent), magazines (29 per cent), advertising in general (26 per cent) and music festivals (23 per cent). For those aged 13–19, advertising, musicians and music videos are a more valuable source of cool. The least imperative cool barometers are professional sports stars and sports events. When asked unaided to name the persons they believe were the most cool, friends (23 per cent) won by a nose from music artists (20 per cent) who appear to be much cooler than actors (11 per cent). Merely 2 per cent of youngsters (most of them above the age of 20) would call themselves cool. Athletes, politicians and freedom fighters were barely mentioned. The bulk of respondents also condemned teachers and parents to the uncool league. The latter should not worry too much though. In the list of people considered as role models they are the absolute sovereigns with only close friends reaching near their position. Below the age of 20, international celebrities are also recognized as role models.[4]

Cool archetypes

From the brand stories we have received from more than 5,000 European Gen Yers we could derive 14 archetypical characteristics predicting the coolness of a brand. In order of importance, these cool ingredients were:

- trendy;
- high status;
- clean reputation;
- successful;
- creative;
- fun;
- cheerful;
- own style;
- changes a lot;
- luxurious;
- clearly stands for X (X = specific claim or positioning);
- contemporary;
- honest;
- retro.

When brands were linked to items such as cheap and impatient, they had significantly lower coolness rates.[5] This all comes back to having a clear and consistent brand vision or DNA, a unique cheerful style and constantly creating exciting and creative innovations confirming that vision. It is about reinventing yourself, not by looking at what others are doing but by developing from within the heart of the company or brand. This grassroots building has nothing to do with chasing coolness but with creating and maintaining relevance for the stimulus-addicted Generation Y. In InSites Consulting's *Coolness around the world* survey among 4,065 Millennials in 16 countries, Converse (All Star) finished in the top coolest brands on earth. An average 60 per cent of young people found the brand to be 'cool' to 'very cool'. In Brazil even 74 per cent agreed Converse is cool. The result was comparable to the 59 per cent for Nike and better than the coolness score for Adidas (54 per cent) and PUMA (47 per cent).[6] Nike Inc. bought

Converse in 2003 after it went bankrupt in early 2001 and was acquired by Footwear Acquisitions. Since its re-birth, the brand had stressed its unique brand DNA and appeal to creative people.

Converse: grassroots marketing in practice

A good example of grassroots marketing can be found at Converse, founded in February 1908 by Marquis Mills Converse in Malden, Massachusetts. The All Star basketball shoe was introduced in 1917, two years after Converse had begun to manufacture canvas basketball shoes. In 1922 basketball player Charles H. 'Chuck' Taylor complained about sore feet and Converse gave him a job as a salesman and ambassador of the brand. In 1934 his signature was added to the All Star label. Chuck Taylor worked at Converse until shortly before his death in 1969.[7] 'Chuck Taylor's All Star design is an iconic classic footwear silhouette that initially started as a performance basketball shoe and was adopted by US counterculture punk rock artists in the 1960s and 1970s', explains Geoff Cottrill, the Chief Marketing Officer of Converse in an interview with us. 'As a low-cost affordable shoe it became kind of a "uniform" of the punk rock scene. At first Converse fought this adoption, because it wanted to be an athletic sports brand. So initially the brand ignored the gravitational power of creative people, like musicians and artists who embraced the brand and used it as a symbol of self-expression.' But in the past 10 years Converse realized what it stands for and what the brand means to people. 'All cool things associated with the brand happened when it was at the feet of our consumers', says Cottrill. 'It's all about the people who wear Converse and what they are doing while wearing it.'

Of course in its more than 100 years of existence, the brand and the products have evolved but always from the same brand vision and DNA. 'All brands need to evolve and innovate; if they don't, they risk becoming nostalgic', says Geoff Cottrill.

> Just like Coca-Cola and Levi's have their iconic product, Converse has its basic iconic silhouette that hasn't changed. But we do innovate with colours, washes, fabrics, prints, styles and partnerships with artists and designers to keep the brand cool. Ten to 12 years ago Converse was basically selling the red, white, black and blue All Stars. Today we have hundreds and hundreds of new styles every season.

Think of models like the Chuck Taylor All Star, multi-tongue, double-upper, XX-Hi, Glow and many others as recent examples. Converse is selling more than 70 million sneakers a year globally in a wide variety of styles. In the summer of 2015 Converse announced the launch of an updated version with improved comfort and support and called it the Chuck Taylor All Stars II. The redesigned interior of the shoe includes Lunarlon impact-absorbing foam, a perforated micro-suede lining to improve breathability and padded tongue and collar. Apart from the extra cushioning and arch support, changes consist of monochrome latte eyelets, an embroidered logo patch and colour-matching shoelaces. Although retail prices for the II went up with $20, the update sold out in the first few days.[8] In his interview, Geoff Cottrill, CMO of Converse, explained the brand's four basic marketing principles to us.[9]

The four branding principles of Converse

1 Celebrate the audience, not ourselves. Converse should turn the camera on the brand fans and what they are doing, not on the brand itself, and facilitate fans turning the camera on themselves. In today's marketing and branding, you ought to recognize that your audience is smart and sophisticated and has the ability to make or break your brand.

2 Be useful. Use your marketing investments to help your audience and make the world a better place. Rubber Tracks, Converse's own music studio in Brooklyn, New York, is providing musicians and artists with the chance to record their tracks free of charge. It is the Converse way of connecting with creative people by helping young up-and-coming talents who cannot afford studio time. Saving the 100 Club in Oxford Street, London is another good illustration. The club is an iconic music temple where many punk rock bands like The Sex Pistols had historic gigs. When the club was close to bankruptcy, Converse agreed on a four-year partnership to help the owner to keep the place open. Converse did not ask for a name change or any big logo inside the venue but instead asked for the opportunity to host (and stream online) two or three shows a month. It allowed the brand to bring consumers into the club and have them experience gigs of, for instance, Paul Weller, Santigold, Blur and many more.

3 Own, don't rent. Instead of traditional sponsoring and buying your reputation, Converse wants to contribute to culture. The brand believes that its consumers are driving change. The 'three artists, one song' platform for instance is bringing diverse artists together who have never met before to create something new and extraordinary. Converse releases the single and supports it just like a record label would do. It has launched seven collaborations like that up till now. Artists choose themselves what they want to take as a theme of their creativity.

Continued...

The four branding principles of Converse *Continued...*

4 Bring different cultures together. Converse embraces diversity and creative spirit is the similarity to be found across age, gender, race, background, style...

In 2015, Converse's 'Made by You' campaign displayed thousands of portraits of people in their own pair of Converse sneakers in their as-worn state. Rather than spotlighting the product or celebrities wearing the brand, the campaign exhibited shots of creative street kids, amateur musicians and everyday artists in global cities like Tokyo, Berlin and São Paulo. The portraits appeared in a gallery in New York's Flat Iron district and through the social media feeds of Converse including Instagram and Facebook. 'Made by You' celebrated self-expression with the sneakers as a means of showing a part of the consumer's own personality.[10]

The magic cool formula

Some of the Coolest Brands[11]

Coolest mobile phone brand[12]
iPhone (Apple)   8.3/10
Samsung
Nokia

Coolest soft drink brand
Coca-Cola   7.7/10
Fanta
Ice Tea

Coolest energy drink brand
Red Bull   7.1/10
Burn
Nalu

Continued...

Some of the Coolest Brands   *Continued...*

Coolest make-up brand
Nivea   7.0/10
L'Oréal
Maybelline

Coolest shoe brand
Nike   7.4/10
Converse All Star
PUMA

Coolest denim brand
DIESEL   7.9/10
Replay
Levi's

Coolest game consoles
Wii   7.8/10
PlayStation 3
Xbox 360

We have learned that using the word 'cool' to investigate which brands are capable of touching the hearts of Generation Y is indeed a good option. But what is really determining coolness? Is it the attractiveness of a brand, the edginess, or originality? Is there a difference in how youth perceives the coolness of persons and brands? Is brand coolness dependent on product categories? We asked 300 leading-edge youngsters, aged 18–24, to track their cool experiences on a daily basis for an entire week. In the 'cool sneaker journal' they could classify three types of experiences themselves: a 'hit' – something or someone who wants to be cool and succeeds well; a 'fail' – something or someone who is desperately trying to be cool, but fails miserably; an 'accident' – something or someone who unintentionally and unexpectedly comes across as 'cool'.

Then we asked them to tag the experiences (people, music, sports, TV, brands, products, etc), explain why these experiences were cool or not cool to them and upload some pictures, videos or music. For us to develop metrics for a cool experience DNA, the young adults in this project had to rate their experiences on coolness, effort (the perceived intention to be cool), and five dimensions:

- originality;
- popularity (appealing to peer group);

- edginess;
- appeal (personal likeability);
- buzz value (is it something they would talk about to others).

In total about 500 experiences were logged: 42 per cent hits, 30 per cent fails and 28 per cent accidents. In Figure 3.2 you will notice that the 18- to 24-year-olds predominantly reported on people (specifically people trying too hard to be cool).

Eighteen-year-old Laura, for instance, shared with us the following 'fail' and 'hit' in the people category. FAIL: 'My mother and I, we are very close, a bit like sisters. But she has the habit of joining me for shopping. That's okay to me, but what I find annoying is that she tends to pick exactly the same clothes as me. It's like she's stealing my own identity. That's totally uncool and I think it's not for her age anymore.' HIT: 'I've been watching a broadcast on the life of Brigitte Bardot on the telly. She's really cool. All she has done to save and protect the animals.'

To develop an overall coolness formula, we made an estimation of coolness based on the attributed scores of the 500 reported experiences. Three out of the six variables had an impact on the coolness score and explained nearly 80 per cent of the cool perception.

As shown in Figure 3.3, we distilled the overall cool formula for Gen Y into 22 per cent original + 23 per cent popular + 55 per cent appeal.[13] Since

FIGURE 3.2 Types of cool hits, fails and accidents!

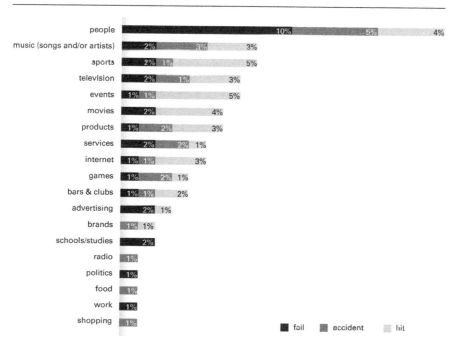

FIGURE 3.3 The magic formula of 'cool'

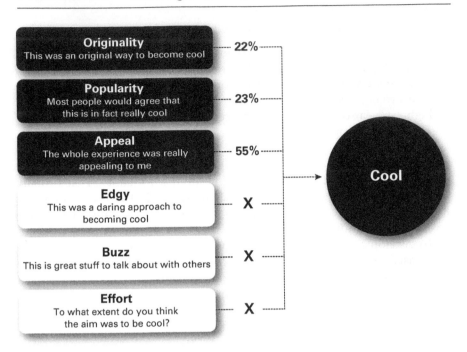

this formula was an estimate for a mix of different observations such as the coolness of people, music, events, products, brands and many more, we had to validate it for products and brands. In a large-scale follow-up survey more than 1,500 teenagers and young adults (13–29) had to judge brands they knew in 35 categories on the three determining aspects of cool.

For the 375 products and brands involved, the cool formula is slightly different: popularity remains equally important (23 per cent), but the impact of originality (38 per cent) on coolness increases, while the importance of attractiveness (43 per cent) decreases slightly. The cool formula teaches us that uncool brands with lower scores on appeal or popularity can start to strengthen their brand by first working on originality, for instance in product innovation or communication. A higher perceived originality will positively affect a brand's coolness.

'Youth buys brands to make a certain identity statement', says Jean-Jacques Maartense, former Marketing Director Eastpak EMEA.

> But, when everyone is copying that statement, a brand becomes mainstream and trendsetters will move on to other less mainstream brands. It implies that brands need to renew themselves continuously to avoid this. New products or innovations help you to build a new storyline. For Eastpak, it meant adapting our products to new needs like laptop sleeves and changing the designs with new trendy materials and colours and partnerships with artists in our Artist Studio line.

In collaboration with Designers Against Aids, Eastpak asked 130 designers around the world to make unique creations that were sold for charity. Eastpak also organized a design contest, 'Bag in Town – a bag for 24 hours', inviting young creative designers around to explore the relationship between bags and urban life and redefine the aesthetic and functional needs of a bag. Six finalists – three chosen by a jury of experts and three by the general public – will be able to create a prototype of their bag concept which will be exposed online for voting. The winner receives a $5,000 cheque and will see his or her design manufactured by Eastpak. 'Eastpak became a high school brand and that wasn't exactly what we had in mind, so the brand is aiming a bit older right now', says Maartense. To address the 20- to 28-year-olds within the Gen Y target group, Eastpak refreshed its communication campaign with the 'when was the last time you did something for the first time' theme. The idea was to stimulate people to live their dreams and think younger again. Do something crazy, explore the world and achieve something you haven't achieved yet. 'It matches perfectly with the positive spirit of Gen Y and their need to realize personal dreams', says the former marketing director of Eastpak.[14] In 2015 the brand asked Jean Paul Gaultier to design a limited edition series of seven backpacks with part of sales going to Designers Against Aids.

Not all categories are equally cool

Depending on the product category, differences were also found between the cool formula dimensions.

For example, it is clear from Table 3.1 that in categories that have a shared usage with peers (game consoles, mints, chewing gum, beer, spirits) the weight of popularity within the coolness formula is higher. The ones that are for private usage – whether it's refreshments (soft drinks, fast food, crisps), TV stations or fashion (jeans, sports and fashion brands) – derive their coolness more from a personal appeal. Product features such as taste, style or content are often the drivers of this personal appeal.

Some categories have a tougher job in creating cool brands

If you are not working in the fashion industry you will probably ask: isn't it extremely difficult for my category to be considered cool by young people? It depends. We have asked them which things (products) or people will have a more or less easy job to be cool. The results could be classified into five divisions. The figures in Table 3.2 represent the Cool Handicap Index (CHI), or the number of Gen Yers who said it is easy to be cool in this category minus the number that said it is hard to be cool. A negative CHI means that more youngsters think it is hard to be cool in a category than it is an easy

TABLE 3.1   The cool formula for different categories of product

	Appeal	Popularity	Originality
Overall average	42%	20%	38%
Game consoles	37%	29%	34%
Mints	41%	26%	33%
Chewing gum	40%	25%	35%
Beer	43%	25%	32%
Spirits	43%	23%	34%
Soft drinks	49%	22%	29%
Fast food	51%	9%	40%
Crisps	47%	18%	35%
TV stations	48%	19%	33%
Jeans	48%	14%	38%
Sports brands	45%	12%	43%
Fashion brands	45%	14%	41%

job. Sometimes something is 'cool' without working at it. For example, friends, music and musical artists, actors and actresses are 'cool' immediately. Just like people, some sectors naturally have more 'cool potential' than others. Mobile telephones, jeans, game consoles and shoes are products that have a significant cool status with young people. In contrast, banks, temp agencies, tour operators and coffee and tea brands hardly appeal to young people's imagination.

The brands that populate these industries, however, are not as easily classified. Cool brands are not just found in cool product categories. Take mints. This sector has a negative cool potential index of –15 per cent. Yet, Tic Tac, Ferrero's brand of mints, gets a fantastic individual rate of 7.5 out of 10 for coolness. On the other hand, there are brands that profit little from the coolness status their sector has built up among youth. Fila for instance is a brand in a cool category (sports brands) but not succeeding in transferring this coolness to the brands. Categories such as coffee/tea and ready-made meals however, which have more difficulty being cool with young people, can increase their score by focusing on originality, as can be inferred from Table 3.1. This refutes the preconceived notion that it is much easier to be cool as a brand of jeans or a game than as a bank or breakfast cereal brand. For categories at the bottom of Table 3.2, it might be a more difficult job to make products cool for Generation Y. For the ones at the top, it is easier because the total category radiates 'coolness' but of course competition from the other brands doing 'cool things' in that category will be greater. In 'uncool' categories, it is easier to surprise and wow the Gen Y audience with unexpected campaigns, activations or innovations. Water only scores –22% on the Cool Handicap Index so let's take this category as a challenging example. Vittel has always encouraged a healthy lifestyle and released a creative campaign in March 2015 to emphasize their idea, the Vittel Couch Converter. Consumers could send a picture and a piece of fabric of their old couch. Vittel transformed the first 50 entrees into a stylish sneaker. The brand also released a massive operational campaign for French residents. They could win 200 pairs of shoes (five different models created for the occasion), t-shirts and a backpack from recycled PET. [15]

TABLE 3.2   The Cool Handicap!

Mobile phones (devices)	65%
Jeans	56%
Game consoles	51%
Shoes	51%
Soft drinks	47%
TV programmes	44%
Fashion brands	41%
Sports brands	40%
TV channels	38%
Fashion chains	36%
Cameras	35%
Crisps	20%
Deodorant	19%

TABLE 3.2   *cont'd*

Spirits	16%
Beer	12%
Fast food chains	12%
Energy drinks	11%
Sports drinks	10%
Chocolate bars	5%
Healthy food chains	3%
Shoe chains	2%
Chewing gum	2%
Make-up	–1%
Mobile phone operators	–5%
Hair care products	–11%
Fruit juice	–12%
Mints	–15%
Breakfast cereals	–18%
Water	–22%
Shavers, razors, razor blades	–23%
Ready-made meals	–25%
Tour operators	–33%
Coffee/tea	–37%
Temporary employment agencies	–48%
Banks	–53%

The Australian insurance brand AAMI tried to make safe driving cool to attract young consumers. They designed the Safe Driver app which measured driving behaviour such as speed, braking, phone usage and the length of trips by using GPS to track your journey. Drivers earned points for performance after 10 rides over 300 kilometres and received different tips. They could look up their score on a board and compare it to their friends' and families'. One person got titled as Australia's safest driver and won A$100,000 as a reward. AAMI set up different initiatives to promote the app. Firstly there were different activities on the Safe Driver website. Visitors could use a tool to do a Driver Duel with their friends on Facebook or Twitter, testing who is the safest driver. By taking a quiz, they could see which celebrity their driving skill matched, Mr Bean or James Bond. They could also fake news stories to prank their friends. Secondly they also released different TV ads, created by Ogilvy Australia. Finally, local comedians Hamish and Andy posted their Driver Dual on YouTube. AAMI changed safe driving into something to be proud of and their tone of voice appealed to young people.[16]

Injecting coolness in an uncool category

Cooling your brand is important and a possible option for every product or service category no matter what the handicap index is. Let's take charity as a challenging example. In 2006 radio station Studio Brussel (the leading alternative youth radio station in Flanders, part of public broadcaster VRT) started 'Music for Life'. Jan Van Biesen, net manager Studio Brussel explains:

> The idea was to lock up three key hosts of the station in a glasshouse centrally dropped in student city Louvain for a week just before Christmas. The trio had to present song requests during seven consecutive days while permanently living in the house with only juices as nourishment. Listeners and corporates ordering a request paid a contribution that would be donated to a good cause in cooperation with the Flemish section of the Red Cross.[17]

The station engaged many young people to participate and support the charity and the first edition raised about €2.7 million. In the subsequent years Studio Brussel repeated the sympathetic action for various good causes in Louvain as well as other student cities Ghent and Antwerp. What started as a crazy idea grew bigger every year with increasing proceeds. Music for Life soon became a yearly celebration of solidarity in Flanders and a strong charity brand that aims to raise awareness and funds for so-called 'silent disasters'. Silent disasters are emergency situations that are not covered by the world's press and don't get the attention and the funding they deserve. For instance, the sixth edition of Music for Life at the end of 2011 broached the subject of diarrhoea, the most important cause of death among children worldwide. Although the disease is quite easy to prevent and cure, only 39 per cent of children with diarrhoea in developing countries get proper treatment. The disease kills 1.5 million children a year as a consequence of severe dehydration. A lack of safe water, general hygiene and clean sanitary

FIGURE 3.4   Studio Brussel's 'Music for Life'

facilities are main causes of the disease. Red Cross Flanders is building wells and water pumps in countries such as Namibia, Burundi, Nepal and Mozambique and promotes hygiene in those regions by role-playing. Using the typical Studio Brussel-styled slogan 'We DO give a shit', the station organized an amazing edition with glasshouses in the three visited historical student cities (see Figure 3.4). Music for Life 2011 wasn't just a radio show but also an online stream, a broadcast on national and digital TV and much more. As in previous editions a Music for Life single was recorded and sold via iTunes. Greeting cards designed by famous cartoonists contained a CD with all charity singles and were sold through news shops. The station was also selling knitted caps and again the audience could organize crazy sponsored events for life themselves. A mobile app using the Foursquare principle allowed users to check in every time they visited their lavatory and collect points for which sponsoring brand Samsung would donate money to Music for Life. The 2011 edition raised more than €7.1 million. An incredible 4 million Flemish people listened to the radio station's Music for Life broadcasting. This is about 65 per cent of the total population, whereas the station's market share is usually situated around 11 per cent. Almost half of the Flemish audience watched the TV broadcasts and 700,000 visited the stubru.be website. Nearly 2,400 crowd-initiated charity actions were registered. In an interview with Peter Claes, Content Strategy and Marketing Director at VRT (national broadcast company), he explains the three reasons for this success.

The first one is a very genuine and great involvement of our radio deejays. As mentioned above, they went beyond human efforts for a silent disaster.

Therefore they did deserve a lot of respect. Secondly, Studio Brussel has a track record of original and very emotional campaigns. Although Belgium is a rather small country, we strive for campaigns that stand out even on an international level. Thanks to our creative partners at the boutique agency Mortierbrigade we won gold, silver and bronze lions in consecutive years at the Cannes International Advertising Festival. In 2008, we even obtained the titanium lion for the 'black boy' campaign [see box]. Last but not least, it's about a format that enables the listener to become the real hero of the campaign. It's not about merely engaging with your target group, nor just connecting with them. It goes much further. It's about recognizing that they realize the greatness of your brand. It's about providing wings in putting them into the spotlight as they fly. We call it the transformational power of your brand. We believe that the transformational power of your brand is the real driver of coolness.[18]

Black boy grabs water to raise awareness

One of the Music for Life events, benefiting the Red Cross and its water programmes, aimed to raise awareness about the shortage of drinking water in Africa. 'We were looking for another way to approach this problem, not to just make an advertisement', says Jens Mortier, owner of agency Mortierbrigade in an interview with *Adweek* . 'We wanted to find a much more direct way of confronting people with this problem.' Instead of merely creating a spot asking for help, the agency had a young black boy, Gaetan, run into live broadcast studios to grab the glass of water usually unnoticed in front of newscasters or show hosts, drink it, and then run off again (see Figure 3.5). 'We thought this action would stress that it's maybe not so normal to have a glass of water, and make it clear it's not within reach for millions of other people', says Mortier. To keep the reactions of the hosts as real as possible, the agency informed only the shows' producers in advance, keeping the on-air talent in the dark. 'They didn't know this was going to happen', says Mortier. He adds that it 'wasn't so easy' keeping the project quiet, but the station owner, government-owned VRT, gave the agency access to the live broadcasts of five prime-time shows, including political, sports and entertainment programming.

The 5- to 10-second interruptions, which took place for three days over a weekend in December, were filmed and later broadcast as a commercial that explained who was behind the events and why. The work stirred the curiosity of the Belgian public, and on Monday morning the media was buzzing about the TV oddity. The radio station soon explained it was behind the stunt, as did the TV programmes, and the public service announcement ran for a few weeks after the fundraiser.[19]

FIGURE 3.5   The thirsty black boy campaign

How to make your brand cool

Ingredients of cool are heavily dependent on product category. For alcoholic drinks, for instance, cool brand ingredients include authenticity, rituals, exclusivity and understated marketing. Jack Daniels' coolness for instance is harnessed by the strong US icon heritage and authentic connotations such as masculine values, blues and cult. Absolut Vodka, without heritage, has a strong minimalist and exclusive image backed by low-key marketing, sponsorship of art events and limited edition packaging design (eg in black leather or mirror glass). Not forgetting that it is distributed in select venues. Absinthe, apart from its illegal opium-based hallucinogenic origin, has its ritual involving sugar, a spoon and a flame. Tequila has its salt and lime ritual.[20] To freeze your brand, common techniques include: creating exclusivity and scarcity, regular surprises, novelties and innovations, and advertising and selective media usage.

Exclusivity and scarcity

Being a cool brand equals consumers fervently wanting to buy your brand. In InSites Consulting's *Meaning of Cool* survey, we asked 13- to 29-year-olds what possibilities they could see to up the coolness of a product or service. Fifty-six per cent mentioned the fact that only a very few others have the same product. Only 12 per cent said the opposite: if everyone else has a certain item, it becomes cooler. The latter was higher among the 13- to 19-year-olds, affirming that in this life stage the need to belong to a peer group and for common brand usage is bigger. Forty-five per cent said the store where you buy something affects its coolness. One of the most successful ways of boosting desire is by creating exclusivity in retail channels or scarcity, for instance when launching a new product such as the Xbox 360. Depending on your sector it can be a good option to have a more trendy upscale range with a smaller-scale distribution to maintain brand appeal for the innovative cool people. DIESEL, the well-known Italian jeans brand launched StyleLab at the end of the 1990s, a laboratory of young designers' ideas sold as an upscale line in flagship stores and contributing to its image of stylistic and creative freedom. In 2008 the StyleLab offer was replaced by DIESEL Black Gold, an exclusive casual-luxury label only available in the upscale boutiques of the brand. The Converse stand-alone flagship store in Carnaby Street, in the Soho district of London, is selling the more expensive part of its collection as well as limited editions only available in that specific store.

The scarcity approach is also the basis of up-and-coming ephemeral communication tools like Snapchat and Vine or live streaming media such as Meerkat and Periscope. Content that vanishes in seconds is more valuable than thousands of likes on platforms like Instagram. If personal messages disappear, they are even more exclusive and really trigger your attention. To appeal to Millennial consumers, designer brands are offering more transparent ways to have a peak at their new collections and trends. On Skype, Twitter and Instagram you can follow the catwalk backstage. During the Fashion Weeks in February 2015 several designer brands took an innovative approach to engage with their young audience. They showed different fashion trends in real time and made the threshold smaller for younger followers. Michael Kors has a total of 25 million followers across Twitter, Facebook, Instagram, Vine and Pinterest. The brand has always been on the social trend. They were the first brand that bought an Instagram ad. Because of their popularity with the younger demographic, it is a necessity for them to be active on every new, relevant platform. They also included Kendall Jenner and Allison Williams to the brand, two Millennial-influencers. During New York Fashion Week, Michael Kors shared different content on Snapchat 'Stories': runway pictures, backstage shots and front-row pictures. Besides Snapchat they also live streamed their runway show and people could access the chat by using the hashtag @AllAccesKors. This hashtag got tweeted over 4,000 times and Socialbakers revealed that Michael Kors dominated the social media rankings at the New York Fashion Week.[21]

Burberry partnered up with the Japanese messaging app Line to livestream their runway show during London Fashion Week. The followers could watch the Autumn/Winter 2015 show by using the mobile live cast functionality 'Line Live Cast'. Burberry also made online stickers that could be shared on the chat. About 1.8 billion stickers are being send online every day. The stickers are more popular in Japan than in the Western world where emojis and texts are preferred. The Burberry stickers were Cony and Brown – the very popular bunny and bear characters online – dressed in iconic Burberry trenchcoats and scarves.[22]

Topshop created digital billboards for London Fashion Week with real-time updates about new trends. On the billboard they integrated different clothing items from the store that match the hashtags with trends on Twitter. If followers tweeted one of these hashtags to @Topshop, they received a shopping list adapted to that trend. The billboards were located in pedestrian areas in London, Birmingham, Leeds, Liverpool and Glasgow. They were only a ten-minute walk away from a Topshop store so customers could immediately visit with their list and be on trend. Only the customers that followed the billboards and the Twitter account were the first ones to buy the new trends. The Topshop models also made Vine videos before entering the runway and Topshop shared them on social media and their website. These initiatives led to an immediate and relevant approach to the brand by the Gen Y and Z audience.[23]

Innovation and novelty

Although exclusivity and scarcity can increase the cool factor for a while, it will also ruin sales revenues in the long term. Unless you have a niche strategy, in most cases substantial profits will only come in when your product is widely bought and not only adopted by innovators or early adopters. This breaking out of the product life cycle's introduction phase has been named 'crossing the chasm' by Geoffrey Moore. Brands addressing youth are often facing this balance exercise: moving into the big league and still retaining credibility. When a product or brand is more mainstream, the trendsetters – cool people – tend to leave it and move to the next thing, which will potentially lead to the brand's loss of 'cool'. To keep these innovators on board your brand simply has to be... innovative. Consistent and constant improvements, developments and variations will maintain the innovator's interest.[24]

Although Apple's iPod was a big hit from its first original design back in October 2001, the brand has introduced a range offering six different versions of its popular portable media player. The hard-drive-based Classic (discontinued at the end of 2014)), the touch-screen Touch (six updates in eight years), the video-capable Nano (eight updates in ten years) and the Shuffle (five updates in ten years). Not to mention Apple's latest success products: the tablet iPad (four updates in five years and three spin-offs: the iPad mini with four updates in only three years, the iPad Air with two updates in two years and the brand-new large iPad Pro), cellular iPhone (with more than 13 million devices sold only three days after the launch of the latest 6s and 6sPlus). Innovation is the key to keeping your brand cool As a response to the growing trend of fitness trackers and wearables, Apple launched its highly anticipated watch in 2015, immediately taking two thirds of the market.

In a US study of 524 brands in 100 consumer categories correlating annual growth rates of revenues between 1997 and 2001 with dozens of market factors, Blasberg and Vishwanath of Bain & Company came to a remarkable conclusion. Winning brands with growth rates that tripled the average rate were found in both high and low growth categories, among new and mature products, big and small, premium and value, market leaders and followers... Only two things made them stand out from the pack: innovativeness and aggressive advertising. Winning brands drew at least 10 per cent of their sales from products introduced during the study period and were 60 per cent more likely to have a share of voice that was significantly higher than the category average. Innovations varied between ranges of attributes, new product formulas, new positioning or packaging. Nabisco's Oreo cookies were one of the winners. Since its introduction in 1912 there had been only one Oreo cookie, the regular chocolate biscuit sandwich with vanilla cream filling, for more than 60 years. Between 1974 and 1996 Nabisco only introduced a few variations. But from 1997 to 2001 the company launched a never-ending follow-up of innovations including seasonal cookies, single-serve packs, etc. Nabisco heavily promoted each new launch. The result? From 1995 to 2002 Oreo sales grew at an average annual rate of 7.5 per cent, more than four times the industry's average. The global turnover of the brand kept on growing. Oreo is probably the best-selling cookie in the world with a sale of 2.5 billion dollars in 2014. The cookie is available in more than hundred different countries and more than one billion dollars were generated in developing countries like China. There is even a National Oreo day on 6 March. Besides the delicious taste and the unique design, the brand generates constant interest by introducing variants of the cookie. Examples are Oreos with different kinds of fillings: peanut butter, mint-flavoured, coffee-flavoured, watermelon and red velvet. Fans also find new ways to use the product such as Oreo churros, cheesecake and milkshakes. McDonald's launched a McFlurry with Oreo.[25] .

Advertising and media selection

Thirty-six per cent of youngsters believe good advertising has the power to cool a brand. Only 17 per cent stated endorsing celebrities as a source of cool and a very high price would only work for 12 per cent. Another noteworthy result was that just as the retailer influences cool perception, the media containing a brand's advertisements also shape the perceived cool image. Commercials on music channels such as MTV were twice as much (29 per cent) linked with cool than the ones on general youth stations (13 per cent) and five times more than on general population TV channels.[26]

The Coca-Cola Company refreshed its second-largest global brand Sprite in 2010 after a period of slowing growth. The theme of the global ad campaign, produced by Bartle Bogle Hegarty, was 'The Spark', using the brand's logo and authenticity as an inspiration. It refers to a spark of fresh thinking as well as the spark on your tongue when drinking Sprite. The first TV commercial features the young urban singer Drake who is looking foiled during a studio recording session. 'I'm just not feelin' it', he utters, until he drinks a bottle of Sprite. Special effects show the liquid transforming his body, after which he suddenly starts singing a new tune. In China and India local popular music and film stars will replace Drake. 'Given that there will be 800 million teens in the world by 2020, with 300 million in China and

India alone, we see this as a great time to be launching a global campaign for Sprite', said Joseph V Tripodi, Chief Marketing and Commercial Officer at the Coca-Cola Company, in an interview with *The New York Times*. 'Whether a teen is based in the United States, India or China', Tripodi said, 'he or she shares a passion for creativity and a love of music and films.' Coca-Cola used considerable digital and mobile elements including content on sprite.com as well as an iPhone application.[27]

The 10 rules of cool advertising

Cool brands seem to have cool ads. In an InSites Consulting study for MTV in the Netherlands, we found a high correlation (of .67) between the perceived coolness of a brand and its advertising executions. We looked into the results of 315 brands in 15 different consumer industries. The sectors with the least cool ads according to the Dutch Millennials were: banking, automotive, cosmetics, tour operators, mobile operators, jeans, fast food and fashion.

The Top 5 of brands with the coolest advertising were:

- Heineken (beer)
- Coca Cola (soft drinks)
- Centraal Beheer (insurance)
- Nike (sporting)
- Albert Heijn (retail)

When we compared the brands with the top 25 per cent coolest ads with the ones that were in the bottom 25 per cent, the former had a purchase rate that was double the rate of the uncool advertisers. From analysing the TV commercials Gen Y liked, we were able to derive the 10 rules of cool ads:

1 Stay true to your brand's DNA in every ad (= be authentic): Bacardi's commercials such as the 'Island commercial' are about nightlife, partying, socially connecting. Nike's World Cup 2010 'Write the future' commercial was about famous soccer teams and players in history.

2 Be recognizable. Stay close to the daily life of youth. Think of themes like boy meets girl (like the 'Coke Zero TVCs') or boys against girls (like the 'Heineken walk-in fridge').

Continued...

The 10 rules of cool advertising   *Continued...*

3 Humour is the key to happiness. Sentimental (warm) humour and parodies (like the 'men with talent' in Heineken's TVC) work best with the emotional Millennials.

4 Fantasy themes work well as long as they still relate to the daily routines of youth. Coke's 'Happiness Factory' commercial shows a fantasy scene but starts and ends with the real life vending machine.

5 The 'SU-SU-SU-dio' rule: cool commercials know how to build up SUspense and then have a SUdden SUrprise moment. Glad you sussed that out, didn't you? Centraal Beheer's 'Daddy Cool' commercial is a great example. And thank you Phil Collins, for inspiring me.

6 Music is the answer. But always use exciting, up-tempo, recognizable and easy-to-remember tunes. Or create your own summer hits like Coke, Bacardi, Levi's, etc have been doing in the past.

7 Load it with emotions, many emotions, BUT only positive emotions like happiness...

8 Short takes, fast editing and many different camera positions. Gen Y has a short attention span and IS used to the visual magic of 3D and SFX movies, games and videoclips. You don't want them to get bored after five seconds.

9 Recognizable gimmicks such as the 'Heineken yell' enhance your ad's recall.

10 Re-use the same lead actors and characters in successive campaigns and commercials. Recognizing the actors will induce brand familiarity and trust. The 'Albert Heijn' commercials always show the same store manager.[28]

Is Gen Y loyal to cool brands?

A comment we often hear among brand managers when giving workshops on youth marketing is that young people and specifically Generation Y members are fickle and probably not the most brand-loyal population. So why should you bother putting your money and efforts into this target group? Why should you freeze your brands until they are cool, if tomorrow this coolness will rapidly melt? Because it is clearly an important way to build and strengthen your brand's competitive advantage to this youth generation. And, as we have demonstrated in this chapter, coolness equals youth choosing and buying your product now and in the future, even at premium price levels. In the second chapter we saw that coolness is an important part of the CRUSH brand model that will leverage brand image, conversations and brand strength. As you have read in the first chapter, it is true they were raised in a world full of choice and experiences. These stimulus junkies aren't easily impressed and attaining their fidelity is not an easy job. But it's your job as a marketer. They are your next generation of consumers and for most marketers they are your current consumers. You should grab every chance today to make them stick with your brand. We do think the disloyalty among youth has been overemphasized and the lack of loyalty among other age groups is underestimated. Gen Y is moulded by the age we're living in today, just like you. When we give speeches on this topic, we tend to ask the audience who is still in a relationship with their very first love. In a company of 100 listeners, there's generally only one... Not only young adults like to experience new things. This is the age of the experience economy. Although there are regular articles stating that Gen Y is less loyal than other generations, there is hardly any empirical proof for this statement.

Being loyal to one

We interviewed 3,000 13- to 29-year-olds to get a better view on their brand loyalty.[29] The first thing we wanted to learn was for which products or services they were spontaneously convinced to choose the same single brand over and over again. The highest mono-amory (brand loyalty to one single brand) was found for the following products and top brands:

- mobile phone devices: Nokia, Samsung, iPhone, Sony Ericsson;
- soft drinks: Coca-Cola;
- fashion and sports: Nike, Adidas, G-Star, Bjorn Borg;
- computers and electronics: Apple, Sony;
- personal care: Gillette, Nivea.

You could conclude that for those sectors that are important to them, this fickle generation is capable of sticking to one favourite brand. But still we have to see this in the right perspective. Even Coca-Cola, the brand with the highest loyalty, only has 10 per cent of youngsters consuming their brand as the only soft drink. The final conclusion here seems to be that brand mono-amory is a too rigid way of examining youth's loyalty.

Being loyal to a few

As a result, we looked at it from another angle and asked for the number of brands they take into consideration when making a choice in each category.

Gen Yers undoubtedly form a serial monogamous target group. They switch between a limited set of trusted and cool brands for many categories, as shown in Figure 3.6. In customer-bonding literature this is called attitudinal loyalty, which has replaced pure behavioural loyalty among consumers of

FIGURE 3.6 The number of brands considered within each category

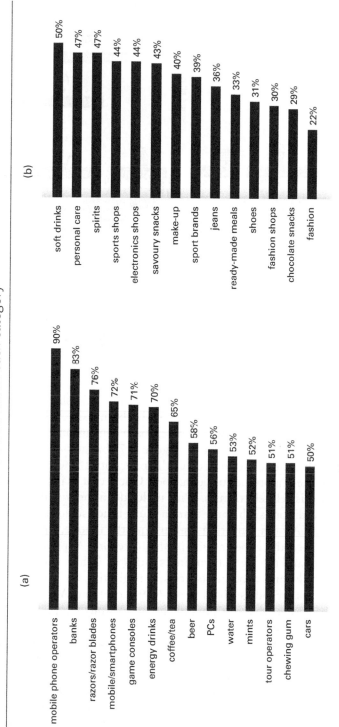

(a)

mobile phone operators — 90%
banks — 83%
razors/razor blades — 76%
mobile/smartphones — 72%
game consoles — 71%
energy drinks — 70%
coffee/tea — 65%
beer — 58%
PCs — 56%
water — 53%
mints — 52%
tour operators — 51%
chewing gum — 51%
cars — 50%

(b)

soft drinks — 50%
personal care — 47%
spirits — 47%
sports shops — 44%
electronics shops — 44%
savoury snacks — 43%
make-up — 40%
sport brands — 39%
jeans — 36%
ready-made meals — 33%
shoes — 31%
fashion shops — 30%
chocolate snacks — 29%
fashion — 22%

% who would only consider a few brands

FIGURE 3.7   Average coolness of categories

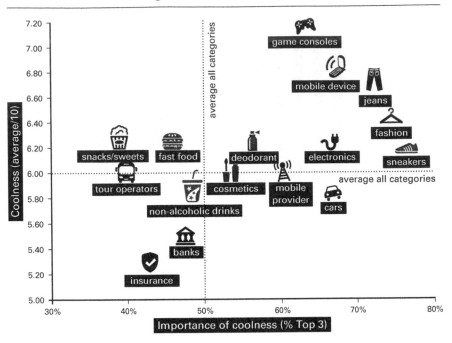

all ages. When you look at the schema in Figure 3.7, showing the relation between the average coolness scores of the brands in each sector and the importance Gen Y attaches to coolness, some conclusions can be drawn.

In the upper right quadrant of Figure 3.7, badge item products (categories that the youth use to project their identity to peers) have certainly understood the importance of being cool. One sector may be an unexpected member of this cell: electronics. With its loudly approved design and latest innovative additions such as the iPad (a multi-touch screen tablet computer), the MacBook Air (an ultra-thin laptop) and the iPhone, Apple is the brand that has pushed the expectations of this category. Apple's brand coolness rate is 7.2/10 and the highest within its industry. Other sectors such as non-alcoholic drinks and deodorants are still neglecting the power of coolness. In spite of this, brands such as Coke (7.9 score) and Axe/Lynx (7.1) have illustrated for years that it is possible to successfully adopt coolness in their marketing and branding strategy.

In the automotive industry there are only a few brands actively targeting youth, such as the MINI. Nevertheless, turning 18 and getting a driver's licence means so much in the lives of adolescents. It is a magic moment that allows for specific marketing campaigns. Fortunately, things are changing in the sector. In the UK, Mercedes is offering driving courses for kids who are at least 1.5m tall. Renault did several TV campaigns for the Twingo addressing a Gen Y target group by using the close relationship between parents and their children in a humorous way. In the United States, Toyota's off-shoot brand is aimed at the Gen Y target group. By 2020 the Millennial generation will make up nearly half of the consumer market with 62 million people. Scion is all about creating a personalized, customized car. When it was released in the US, 50 per cent of the new customers were under the age of 31.[30] In the Netherlands, VW created a branded TV programme *License to Liberty* together with music and youth TV channel TMF. It was part of a new branding strategy of Volkswagen in which they launched relevant concepts linked to important life stages. To rejuvenate VW's image, the brand claimed the driver's licence moment in the life of youth. In the *License to Liberty* TV programme, five candidates competed in driving course challenges. All five could attain their licence but only one of the candidates could win the VW Polo. Eighty per cent of the target 16–24 group saw this TV format on TMF. More than 430 driving schools joined in and 5,200 youngsters applied for the programme. The show received massive free publicity coverage. In the *Cool Brands* survey in the Netherlands, VW was the only volume make capable of reaching coolness levels across Gen Y comparable to BMW and Ferrari. VW also adapted a co-creation programme in China called 'The People's Car Project'. Volkswagen's brand name literally means the 'people's car'. So instead of just building cars for people, they invited Chinese consumers to re-invent how cars are ideated, designed and built. An online 3D creator tool on zaoche.cn allowed visitors of the website to create a custom car design which was then posted online for votes. VW's engineers regularly reviewed the submissions, gave feedback to the creator and took inspiration from the crowd-sourced ideas. The site received over 10 million unique visitors and not less than 100,000 submitted design ideas. Three concept cars were actually created from all these ideas: the Music Car, a Beetle with LEDs that change colours as a response to the driver's choice of music; the Hover Car, a zero-emissions two-seater that hovers over electromagnetic road networks; and the Smart Key that tracks the status of your car and keeps an eye on it via satellite.[31]

Coping with Gen Y's commitment phobia

Generation Y tends to suffer from commitment phobia, thus forcing companies to re-evaluate their strategies. Industries that traditionally require long-term contracts or some kind of a commitment will need to adapt their business models in order to retain their Gen Y customer base. The industries that will most likely be affected by this trend are: the gym, health and fitness clubs; cable providers; new car dealers; wireless telecom carriers; furniture stores and wedding services. All of these industries earn about one-quarter or more of their revenue from the Gen Y group in the USA and their goods and services involve some kind of commitment.

1 The Gyms, Health and Fitness Clubs industry. Many fitness clubs realize the importance of catering for the Generation Y age group, considering its members generate an estimated 24 per cent of the

industry's $25.3 billion. As a result, fitness clubs are increasingly allowing customers to pay on a monthly basis without making a year-long commitment. Some gyms will even pro-rate a member's monthly payment if the customer is going to be out of town for an extended amount of time. As gyms and fitness clubs move towards monthly contracts, IBISWorld expects more Gen Yers to join gyms.

2   Cable Providers. Cable providers are a good example of an industry that demands a commitment from its customers. Gen Y generates about 16.2 per cent of the industry's $63.5 billion. Cable providers generally require a year-long contract, which makes many commitment-phobes hesitant to purchase such services. Cable providers have been offering discounts on year-long contracts at certain times of the year. This tactic has been enticing to Gen Yers, many of whom remain price-conscious after being heavily affected by the recession. In the coming five years, IBISWorld expects cable providers to continue re-evaluating their contract terms. With the increase in online streaming of TV shows and movies to computers and WiFi-enabled TVs, many consumers will rethink their cable contracts.

3   Wireless Telecommunications Carriers. Similar to cable providers, operators in the wireless telecom carriers industry require customers to sign a long-term contract. Although many Gen Yers commit to these contracts, they cringe at the idea of not being able to change providers quickly without expensive fees. New firms with more flexible terms have entered the industry. These companies do not require long-term contracts but still provide 3G and 4G networks and plans with unlimited talk and data. Also, major companies like AT&T and Verizon in the USA offer pay-as-you-go phones for people who may want to be on larger networks but not be tied to a contract. While this $20.1 billion industry is affected by Gen Y's commitment phobia, it manages to get by relatively unscathed. This is due in part to the fact that smartphones are extremely important to this generation since it values being constantly connected to social circles and breaking news.

4   Furniture Stores. The commitment phobia of Generation Y does not stop at memberships and contracts alone. Companies that sell expensive products with long lifespans are also affected. An example is the furniture stores industry. Quality furniture is expensive and most consumers purchase it with the intention of keeping it for many years. Inhibited by the fear of committing to a style that could quickly become outdated, a residency that could quickly change, or the inability to shift one's decorating design without a large amount of money, the Gen Y group often choose to purchase inexpensive furniture. That's why IKEA is doing such a great job with Yers, and Target and Walmart in the USA are retailing more and more furniture

to cater to this trend. With Gen Y currently accounting for 14 per cent of industry revenue, furniture stores will have to change their product lines and strategies if they wish to attract more of this generation in the coming years.

5 New Car Dealers. Similar to furniture stores, the new car dealers industry is negatively affected by commitment-phobes because its products require a financial commitment (sometimes a long-term one). Gen Yers are hesitant to take the plunge of purchasing a new car, hurting the $510 billion industry. Further pressuring the industry is the move towards renting cars for short periods of time. The expansion of car sharing companies like ZipCar is helping consumers get by without owning a car. To attract more Gen Y drivers, new car dealers will need to prove why buying a car is more beneficial than public transportation or car sharing. Dealers might be able to pull customers back by increasing their leasing abilities, enabling drivers to lease cars for shorter amounts of time or selling cars at heavy discounts.

6 Wedding Services Industry. Gen Y generates about 58.2 per cent of the wedding industry's $49.4 billion in revenue. But, over the past 40 years, the marriage rate has been declining and at an accelerated rate since the start of the recession in 2008. With an increasing social acceptance of cohabitation, Gen Y will continue to put off marriage. IBISWorld expects many Gen Yers to get married in their early and mid-30s. When they do get married, they are likely to spend a significant amount of money. In 2010, for instance, the average wedding cost more than $20,000. Although Gen Y's commitment phobia will hamper the wedding services industry in the near term, growth may pick up as the group approaches its 30s and finally decides to settle down.

From the findings of our study, we can also demonstrate the importance of creating and sustaining cool brands. The graph in Figure 3.8 shows the relation between the individual coolness score of 540 brands in 30 different categories and whether that specific brand was picked as first choice or not. The bond (73 per cent) seems to be very strong, which is illustrated by the linear curve predicting the relation between both variables.

Cool brands (with a minimum score of 7.5/10) in the study were purchased twice as much as uncool brands (rates of 6.5 or less). When we asked the 13- to 29-year-olds whether they would buy those same brands in 3, 5 and 10 years from now, we discovered that their projected loyalty for cool brands was also more stable than for the uncool brands. This resulted in a self-reported projection of long-term preference that was three times higher than for uncool brands. Cool brands are also able to ask for a higher price, resulting in higher margins.

FIGURE 3.8 Relationship between coolness and brand preference

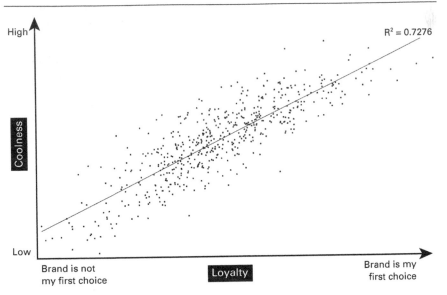

Four ways coolness affects brand loyalty

The 'cool' factor can make or break your brand as consumers increasingly use brands to define themselves and use their own perception of what's cool to differentiate products and brands and to pick the most attractive ones within the massive market choice. The role that coolness can play for your brands depends on the sector you're working in.

The mapping in Figure 3.9 combining category fidelity and the significance of coolness shows four patent situations.

1 Survival of the coolest

In the upper left quadrant, there's fierce competition between a large set of acceptable and interchangeable brands. Youngsters choose a brand based on price/quality relationship and availability but also on marketing campaigns that appeal to them. If your brands file under this situation, being a cool brand is a must to survive. Cooling your brands will aid you to make the less brand-loyal customers more faithful. For instance, if you take a look at the jeans industry, Levi Strauss was almost the single brand choice of youth until the 1990s. But the sector moved from the upper right corner of the scheme to the left when other brands like DIESEL, Replay and G-Star Raw entered the market. It became even harder to keep the market share and loyalty when designer brands such as Dolce & Gabbana, Gucci, Armani and many others saw the point of joining the denim market.

Pimkie disrupted retail by putting its clothes for sale in hotel wardrobes. The brand launched 'The Mini Fashion Bar' as a pilot project in Antwerp and later on in different boutique hotels across Europe. The selected clothes

FIGURE 3.9   The role coolness can play

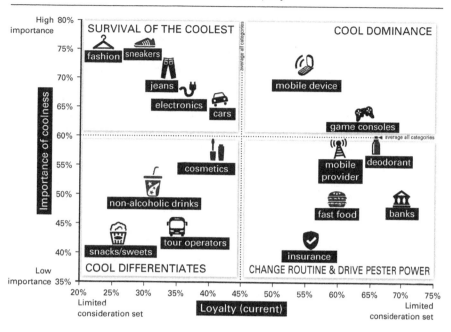

were appropriate for the country, season and weather making it very convenient for the guests. They could wear these items and easily put them on their hotel bill which increased the buying possibility. Pimkie prices are affordable. This way the guests could try out the brand and got a Plan B when they didn't bring the right bits. The clothing mini-bar was followed by a menu where the customer could see the specific items. The QR code led them to the website with the full Pimkie range.[32]

2 Cool differentiates

In the bottom left corner of the mapping, fast-moving and low-ticket items are situated. Since these are easier to buy and often based on impulsive choices, youth's loyalty is quite low. It's just easy and not so risky to experiment. Yes, they are stimulus junkies. This doesn't mean they don't have favourite brands for these categories. In these circumstances, cooling your brand differentiates you from competitors. It is crucial to offer cool and unordinary, unexpected impulses, such as new flavours or varieties, new impulses. You have to catch their attention. In the chewing gum market Stimorol launched the Senses product line, using black and silver as the main packaging colour codes together with fancy variety names like 'watermelon sunrise' and 'rainforest mint'. The brand also has the fusion-line combining two tastes (eg 'vanilla goes mint', 'strawberry goes lemon', etc). Competitor Mentos introduced the Aquakiss with a similar stylish aura as the Senses line. Mentos also launched the cubes, an attention-grabbing new chewing gum packaging and the Blast series, gums with a liquid centre.

Sportlife, a brand of mother company Leaf that has been on the market since 1981, launched Sportlife Vibes with a unique 'squeeze box'. The new packaging and 'unbox your freshness' slogan was endorsed by branded TV contests in which participating teens could win their own skate ramp, design their own sneaker line or own their own graffiti wall in the city centre.[33]

In the salty snack industry, PepsiCo owns a cool brand too. Doritos has been out-cooling competitors with campaigns that are in line with Gen Y's interests and desires. Just think of the user-generated commercials during the Super Bowl, which had more than 6,100 entries in the last edition, or the 'design your Xbox computer game' contest. Doritos and PepsiCo's sister brand Lay's understood that keeping your cool equals keeping your Gen Y customers loyal. Both brands frequently introduce new flavours; the best trick to keep things fresh is to launch varieties that will only be available for a limited time. Another way to differ from competitors is finding alternative consumption occasions or new cool ways of distributing your brands. Sports drink Powerade designed three different interactive billboards that passers-by could use for their workout: a rotating rock wall, a punching meter and a lifting pull-bar. Afterwards they received a bottle of Powerade. The brand wanted people to experience their slogan 'You have more power than you think'. Powerade also removed a pain point of runners by offering drink stations during their run. Joggers don't want a hassle with bottles or to take breaks to stay hydrated during their work-out. Via an app called NonStop Hydration you could pre-order bottles of Powerade, confirm it at least 100 metres before passing by a pop-up terminal across the popular running routes and a bottle of Powerade would come out of the vending tube. The app also included an index that calculated dehydration based on the weight, speed and the route of the runner. This way the brand could automatically dispense a drink when a runner passed by a station. A new retail channel with no competitors was born. The brand sold up to existing customers and attracted new ones. Its sales increased with 8.4 per cent in these areas.[34]

3 Cool dominates

In the top right corner of the diagram, we find products and services for which being cool is important and here youngsters show a substantial loyalty to the brands they are used to. If you're working in this business, your challenge is to break the fidelity of the prospects that are loyal to one of your competitors. In this area of the schema, being the pioneering brand gives you a clear first mover's advantage. Understanding the age entry points of your products is important. If you were not the innovator, the only way to steal a massive market share from your competitor is by changing the rules of the category. This implies either changing the target group, occasion of use or market standards.

A good example is the game console market. Microsoft released the first version of Xbox to compete with Sony's PlayStation 2, Sega's Dreamcast and Nintendo's Gamecube at the end of 2001. It had superior graphics support, Dolby Interactive Content-Encoding Technology and a hard drive. The main success factor proved to be the *Halo* game, an exclusive to Xbox FPS (First Person Shooter). It meant the end of Sega and the Gamecube was not able to compete with Sony or Microsoft. But Xbox's battle with Sony was clearly more difficult. Early Xbox games weren't using the powerful hardware. This decreased the competitive advantage of the Xbox. Sony countered the attack of Microsoft by securing exclusives for highly popular games such as *Grand Theft Auto* for a while. Nintendo struck back at the end of 2006 by launching the Nintendo Wii console. The Wii's main distinguishing feature is the wireless handheld controller – the Wii remote – which detects movement in three dimensions. The technology was based on hard-disk saving technology (sensing movements of a portable device to save the hard disk from crashing). In an interview, Nintendo's game designer Shigeru Miyamoto said: 'The consensus was that power isn't everything for a console. Too many powerful consoles can't co-exist.' In December 2006, Satoru Iwata, CEO of Nintendo added: 'We're not thinking about fighting Sony, but about how many people we can get to play games. The thing we're thinking about is not portable systems, consoles, and so forth, but that we want to get new people playing games.'[35]

As of February 2010, the Wii was leading over the PlayStation 3 and Xbox 360 in worldwide sales. Clearly inspired by this market development, Microsoft announced their Project Natal on 1 June 2009. Project Natal was the code name for a depth sensor that allows users to control and interact with the Xbox 360 without the need to touch a game controller at all. It led to the Xbox Kinect console. Sony had to follow the market trend too and came up with the PlayStation Move. Worldwide more than 96 million Wiis were sold as of June 2012, compared to about 67 million Xbox 360 consoles and 64 million PlayStation3s. Sales of the Wii for Nintendo seemed to be slowing down in 2011 and the company suffered its first loss in 30 years. A lack of new innovations as well as increased competition from smartphones and tablets is challenging the Japanese game giant. The 3DS, a 3D version of Nintendo's popular handheld DS was less successful than expected. In a response to this negative evolution, the company announced the Wii U, which is, surprisingly, targeting hardcore gamers again by re-introducing a controller that combines a touch screen with game buttons[36]. Since the end of 2010 computer game developers found a new market combining toys with games, the so-called toys-to-life. Activision was the first to enter the market with Skylanders. The toys have a near field communications radio chip (NFC) that is read by a portal you connect to the game console. It brings the figures to life in the videogame while high scores and other information of the game are saved in the toy. The more toys connected to the console, the more exciting the game. It's not a wonder that the toy-to-life industry is already worth €3.5 billion. Nintendo has launched the Amiibo-figures, and Disney entered the market with Infinity, connecting its broad catalogue of characters and storylines such as Pirates of the Caribbean, Monsters Inc, the Incredibles and Star Wars to videogames. As it is clearly a clever way to make physical toys more relevant to digital native children,

LEGO will introduce Dimensions with action figures of Batman, Lord of the Rings and Ghostbusters. [37]

4 Coolness to change routines and drive pester power

In this bottom right part of the schema, the brand loyalty of youth is strong but coolness is relatively less important to them. The products in this quadrant are either routine purchases or even stuff that is bought by parents for their adolescents. Cooling the brand will push the brand up in the chart, making it more appealing than competitors. Another effect brand coolness may produce is putting the brand on the youth's shopping list (pester power). Procter & Gamble wanted to grow the market share of its Braun brand by targeting the Braun CruZer, a male grooming (shaving) device at the youth segment. The brand solutions division of MTV created a branded TV format named *King of Snow*. During eight weeks youngsters participated in a snowboarder contest filled with tests, stunts and challenges to become the King of Snow. The Belgian champion freestyle snowboarder assisted the candidates in achieving the most spectacular results. More than 60 per cent of the youngsters who had been watching the broadcast evaluated it as original, entertaining and interesting. One-third of the viewers had talked about the programme to others. Aided brand attribution of Braun CruZer with the show was 41 per cent. By supporting the TV programme, Procter & Gamble has improved the creative, young and local image of its Braun brand. Youngsters who had seen the show significantly rated those brand personality items higher. *King of Snow* viewers also had higher brand awareness and net promoter scores. Procter & Gamble also noticed an immediate consumer sales effect after the broadcast.[38] The campaign resulted in an ongoing growth to 6.2 per cent value share (coming from 5.0 per cent) or 16 per cent of total Braun shavers business.[39]

How to find out what's cool

The main point of the previous section of this chapter is that young consumers aren't leaving your brand because they have a good reason to do so. They will switch to another brand because yours isn't giving them compelling reasons to stay with it. It happened to Reebok. It has happened to Converse and Levi's. And to many other brands that once were the coolest of their industry. And chances are that at a certain point in time, it will happen to your brand too. In the summer of 2012, Abercrombie & Fitch reported a 10 per cent decline in sales and announced the closure of 315 underperforming stores and postponing opening new international flagship stores. Superdry is also struggling to keep the brand hot. The biggest challenge of youth marketers is to keep their products and brands funky. The trick is to keep your marketing campaigns up-to-date without losing your brand's authenticity. Staying true to your own brand identity and DNA might seem patently obvious but our daily practice teaches us that it is the one golden rule that is often ignored in targeting young consumers.

Marketers are easily blinded by the glamour of sponsoring cool events or creating links with celebrities. Gen Yers are more aware of marketing spin than previous generations. If they don't see a clear fit with their perception of your brand personality, they will interpret this as a fake buying of coolness. Youngsters will find your brand isn't cool because if it were, your brand wouldn't need this image stealing. It takes a subtle approach to remain a cool and relevant brand without losing your real identity. The trainer collection of Nike introduces new styles every season. The lead times of clothing designers have decreased from 18 months to a year or even six months to be able to react faster to street trends.[40] Often, marketers feel they have to continuously demonstrate their knowledge about people, looks and music.

Coolhunters

In this urge to catch the new vibes a whole new industry of 'coolhunters' appeared in the late 1990s.[41] Sociologist Malcolm Gladwell, later famous for his books *The Tipping Point* and *Blink*, coined the term 'coolhunter' in an article in *The New Yorker* magazine in 1997. In this piece he interviews DeeDee Gordon and Baysie Wightman while they are discovering trends in the streets for trainer brand Reebok. The key to do this coolhunting is to find the cool people and not cool things. Because only cool people recognize what is cool. And because cool things are always changing, you can't look for them yourself. In fact you would only think back to what was cool before and then extrapolate this, which is of course the wrong idea.

Cool people on the other hand are more constant. In Gladwell's editorial DeeDee says she is looking for individuals who don't look like peers but are setting themselves apart from everybody else. To them 'cool' is doing something distinctive. These young hipsters are often recruited in fashionable city areas and/or occupied in certain kinds of job, for instance fashion, art, photography, media, music, film-making, design, etc. It is important to employ young and trendy recruiters and moderators who can relate to this type of research participant. Cool people want to remain ahead of the herd and disdain the uncool, especially uncool researchers.

Gladwell also comments on the circularity of coolhunting. The more hunters are bringing cutting-edge trends to the mainstream, the faster innovators move on to the next thing. Eventually, to follow these high-paced trends, companies need coolhunters.[42] Because coolhunters are constantly protecting the necessity of their work, they have received substantial critique in the past. They were the objects of contempt among anti-globalists such as Naomi Klein. Klein argues that coolhunting is a euphemism for black-culture hunting. When young black innovators are influencing white Americans, then coolhunting ensures that profits will keep flowing where they always have done. Serious researchers, both academic and in agencies, disapproved of the 'high priests of cool' too. In particular, the fuzzy nature of what defines cool and the recruitment process of cool people depending on instinct, sixth sense or gut feelings made them quite nervous. Not to mention the commercial success, status and cooler image of coolhunters. Still, we do agree with the critics on one point: it is better for your brand to find new ways that help your Gen Y consumers to express themselves than to merely copy the stuff that cool people are expressing.[43]

Cool networks

Nowadays, word-of-mouse through social network sites, blogs, e-mail and instant messaging is boosting the viral tempo of trend diffusion. The rise of these networks has made Rogers' standard work on the diffusion of innovations obsolete.[44] Other authors such as Bob Metcalfe, founder of 3Com Corporation and co-inventor of Ethernet found that a good or service increases in value to potential users depending on an increasing number of users. Think of fax machines, mobile phones, e-mail, instant messaging, chat.... This finding became known as Metcalfe's Law.[45] David Reed commented on this law in saying that it underestimates the value of adding connections to a network. This became clear with the appearance of social network sites such as LinkedIn or Facebook. When you connect to a user in a network, you also connect to a significant number of sub-networks. This phenomenon exponentially increases the value of each connection as opposed to simply summing up the two connections. Reed's Law is an improved way of looking at the diffusion of ideas, innovation and cool products and brands.[46]

Reed's ideas have also dramatically changed the business of coolhunters. Instead of talking with a few cool people in the streets of the fashionable city districts back in the 1990s, they now connect with leading-edge consumers, cultural reporters or style-runners all over the world. Rather than asking them questions about products and brands, they are now observing social networks, communities and blogs where cool people are already spontaneously discussing the cool stuff.

In an interview, Carolijn Domensino, ex-coolhunter of Carl Rohde's agency Signs of the Time, says:

> In the early days you travelled a lot but the problem is that you can't be everywhere at the same time. Nowadays it's important that you are in close contact with people who run their own fashion blogs. Actually, they replace you, because they give you all the information you need. A coolhunter nowadays needs a strong digital network with online coolhunters who share their information with you (and you with them). It's not that the way of analysing has changed but the information flow is growing bigger and bigger and is increasingly powered by the internet. The point is that everyone can be a coolhunter now.[47]

Coolmining

Since more than 71 per cent of Europeans in the 15–24 age bracket and 64 per cent of 25- to 35-year-olds are sharing their own private lives on social network sites such as Facebook[48] these sites have a wealth of information for youth watchers.

Diageo tapped into these rich data to improve the Christmas campaigns for its whisky brand Johnnie Walker to the 21+ market. Through this Christmas campaign, the brand is targeting a specific group of young men (aged 21 and older) who are ambassadors of the Johnnie Walker values. Diageo wanted deeper insights into the behaviour and lifestyles of its target group to endorse the marketing campaigns. What were their interests, attitudes and ambitions? InSites Consulting recruited 24 participants, aged 21–30, who met the target group criteria and asked them to become friends with us in all the online social networks they were actively engaged in. We followed our new friends for a week and with the aid of web-scraping software, we extracted all the information available online including conversations with other social network members, pictures, group memberships, status posts, profile information, etc. We then analysed the available data with the aid of text analytics. We were able to extract:

- role models (stand-up comedians, film-makers such as Quentin Tarantino);
- favourite music;
- preferred holiday destinations;
- the sports and games they liked;
- their online behaviour (visited websites and blogs: many newspaper sites and music sites such as last.fm for instance, but also gaming environments);
- favourite TV formats and programmes: eg *Pimp My Ride*, *Jackass*, *South Park*, *Weeds*.

We finally found that for the Johnnie Walker target group, life is not always easy and they try to escape from trouble now and then. This escapism translates into partying all night long, immersing themselves in other worlds such as movies, games or online social networks or e-commerce. They also de-stress by driving fast cars and motors, relaxing on holidays or watching many hours of TV feeds. They are quite confident about their own skills and value intelligence and knowledge.[49] The insights from following the Johnnie Walker target group online in their social networks were used for Diageo's Game Plan, a yearly strategic plan. In an interview, An Martel, Customer Marketing Director at Diageo, explains:

> What consumers tell you in usual surveys is never 100 per cent the truth. Studying and observing them in their own environment without really asking questions is much more valuable. We have used these insights to adapt our media plans. As a result of the online qualitative research, we have integrated local role models into our approach. Our classic PR plan was switched to an online plan involving local bloggers. We had observed that our target group is keen on certain blogs. By following our consumers online, we were able to find new insights and confirm existing trends.[50]

Coolfarming, co-creation or crowd-sourcing

Peter Gloor and Scott Cooper discern a second type of using collective wisdom in their book *Coolhunting*. They call it 'coolfarming' and it implies getting involved with creating new trends. Where traditional coolhunters would have rejected this idea and named it impossible, these authors claim the coolest ideas come from a collective mindset. Innovation is a result of the collaboration of people who share interests but not necessarily jobs or disciplines.[51] The success of crowd-sourcing is related to two principles. James Surowiecki described in his bestselling book *The Wisdom of Crowds* how when grouping the information from different individuals, the decision of a group will always outperform the decision made by one single member. The second principle can best be summarized as 'managers' bounded rationality'. Bounded rationality is the idea that in decision making, the rationality of individuals is limited by the information they have, the cognitive limitations of their minds, and the finite amount of time they have to make decisions.[52]

Moreover, recent research carried out at the University of Wageningen has shown that products whose packaging is labelled 'co-created with consumers' will sell significantly better than equivalent products which do not carry this label. In other words, consumers have more confidence in each other's judgement than in the judgement of professional experts within a company.[53] A couple of years ago Tropicana's new orange juice packaging developed by guru brand designer Peter Arnell failed. Sales dropped by 20 per cent because consumers didn't recognize their Tropicana in the shelves and bought another brand. After only six weeks the brand had to switch back to the old packaging and bore a cost of $35 million. This phenomenon is backed by MIT Professor Erich Von Hippel who found that the new products proposed by end-users to 3M produced eight times more revenues than those exclusively developed by 3M's internal R&D department.[54]

From our own research we know that more than 50 per cent of consumers are willing to help brands and companies they like to improve their communications, products and services but only 3 per cent of companies have experience in doing so.[55] 'The true CEO of the company is the consumer', says Jörgen Andersson, former CMO of fashion retailer UNIQLO.

> The Gen Y generation is very aware of fashion trends and quicker in their interpretation than fashion companies. They use tools like Pinterest, Polyvore or Tumblr to create very creative mood boards. Bloggers, just girls like my daughter, are suddenly sitting front row of the Marc Jacobs show. As soon as Balenciaga show trash jeans on a catwalk, young girls will take their jeans, steal their dad's razorblade and trash them to create the Balenciaga look. Everyone can get access to anything immediately and share it. It's making some people in fashion very nervous. Take Tom Ford for instance who decided to close his show for the audience stating in a *Harper's Bazaar* interview that he wouldn't make it public because it would only allow H&M and Zara to copy it faster than he gets his own collection out onto the shop floor. I think this transparency is really fun, because if you start opening it for your consumers, you are co-creating the brand together. Young consumers don't want companies pushing products to them, they want to be engaged from the beginning.[56]

Co-creating or crowd-sourcing marketing can be executed on different levels. Think of 'the big price drop' in which retailer Tesco asked clients to choose the items for the next price cuts. PepsiCo's Lay's chips brand has been running flavour-naming and -defining contests with consumers in 15 countries since 2008. In 2012 they launched the 'Do me a flavour' contest in their US home market by opening a pop-up store on New York's Times Square, showcasing all the past winning flavours from around the world including the Australian Classic Caesar Salad or the Thai Spicy Crab.[57] In China electronics retailer Media Markt co-created a sales promotion by asking their customers to get a haircut in their shop to receive a discount. No fewer than 8,500 Chinese people participated and the sales went up 60 per cent. Having a haircut at New Year is believed to bring good luck for the next year.[58]

Heinz has asked the first 57 visitors of a new website to co-develop a new cap for its iconic bottle. The number 57, also mentioned on each ketchup bottle, refers to the 57 varieties of Heinz. 'For this generation it's all about relationships and social connections', says Mariken Kimmels, former Marketing Director Heinz Continental Europe, in an interview with us. 'You have to involve them in your branding and marketing strategy and think of marketing as building relationships again.[59]' According to Ypulse 81 per cent of Millennials are keen on helping brands or companies to create new products. 87% of them say brands should ask young consumers their opinion before they design a product. Millennials want to be heard and love to support their favorite brands. Involving young people in defining the future of your company might sound daring but brands that do, book success.[60]

Unilever started The Unilever Foundry which involves start-ups or people with an innovative idea. The participants create a brand vision, a marketing plan and a product road map with a Unilever mentor. The brand funds the different initiatives.[61]

Brandy Melville is a popular Italian clothing brand with a Californian vibe which is growing rapidly amongst teens. The possible reason is that the brand follows the opinion of a group of employed teens on the clothes and the ideas and makes them post regularly on social media. They help the brand grow closer to their target group and create subtle peer-to-peer marketing. The girls mostly have a big following on social media or have a style sense similar to Brandy Melville. [62]

Taco Bell has always been making efforts to engage with Millennials and succeeds by partially including them through co-creation. The brand had already organized an intern competition to invent new innovative ideas for the brand in the 90s. The Doritos Locos taco was born, a taco with the flavor of Doritos. In 2012 Taco Bell launched the product that has since made over a billion dollars. It was the brand's most successful product so they keep on including the young fans. Recently a young team of Taco Bell executives invented a new concept with premium tacos and craft beer to appeal to customers who don't want to eat at Taco Bell.[63]

Heineken's structural consumer board

With its strapline Open Your World, Heineken is a brand that is not only preaching this type of openness, it is actively co-creating and crowdsourcing its marketing. Since the start of their Open Design Explorations programme, they have been reaching out to leading-edge consumers and young designers to develop surprising new takes on nightlife: from the launch of the Heineken Concept Club at the Milan Design Week in 2012 to their Pop-up City Lounge at the London Design Festival in 2014. These creative playgrounds of experimentation are not about developing new ideas about age-old problems, but about revealing innovative problems to solve. Even while it is uncovering insights to fuel the creative process, Heineken is collaborating with its cool consumers. InSites Consulting has been a partner of the initiative from the start, discovering nightlife insights through Instagram ethnography and online research communities. An example of such an insight is the value of conversation in a lounge bar. Lounge bars are all about sharing stories with close friends. The quality of the conversations is highly valued. So when one of your friends is looking around every few seconds to find a waiter to order a next round, it's breaking your eye contact and the quality of your conversation. The Heineken lounge features modular conversation cocoons with great acoustics. Your group is separate but not disconnected from the other guests, and the edge of the pod simply changes colour when you want to order another round of drinks – drawing the attention of the staff so you don't have to. Mark Van Iterson, Global Head of Design at Heineken International, explains how the Open Design Explorations program has evolved:

The over-arching goal has remained untouched: design is key for the Heineken brand, which is a progressive forward-looking brand. Not design on a pedestal, but social design. Each of our open design initiatives also has a specific goal, from increasing the on-premise presence of the brand in premium nightlife venues to motivating people to drink responsibly. The biggest change in the programme is the scale; to increase the impact of our design programme we have to link it to other initiatives in the organization. A great example is the Pop-up City Lounge. Not only is this concept space in itself travelling from the London Design Festival to Mexico City's Fashion Week, the concepts introduced in this space are being implemented on a wider scale. As part of the beer gardens in Bangkok, we have created an enormous roof terrace bar that seats over 1,000 people, in the exact same style as our concept space. We're also leveraging the Open Design Explorations in our 'Spectre' campaign. In this James Bond activation you'll notice the vector-style products from our Pop-up City Lounge.

Continued...

Extending the reach of the Open Design Explorations while keeping its focus on the leading-edge consumer has proved to be successful. Heineken won the prestigious Creative Marketer of the Year 2015 award at the Cannes Lions Festival of Creativity. Staying true to its nature, Heineken isn't celebrating this by looking back, but by keeping its eyes on the future. In their Talent Lab, they're providing a new blank canvas to ten up-and-coming creative talents from five countries across the globe that have never won an award at the Cannes Lions. Instead of reinventing a new occasion, they're challenging the norm and making it cool to drink responsibly. After several communication campaigns, Heineken is now approaching the topic of moderation from the design perspective. Heineken will keep on surprising us with new angles and challenges, but in order to stay cool, they will continue to do this in close collaboration with leading edge consumers and young design talent.[64]

Thomas Troch, Research Director InSites Consulting New York

FIGURE 3.10   The Heineken Popup City Lounge!

Peter Pandemonium: adults' desire to stay young and cool

Contrary to popular belief among marketers, coolness is relevant to consumers of all ages. A youthful outlook is no longer the sole preserve of the young and the essential meaning and traditional definition of 'youth' has changed. You don't have to be named Peter Pan or Michael Jackson to file under this trend. The older consumer wants to stay in touch with younger generations and is more eager than ever to stay young for as long as possible. Some brands, think of Apple as the ultimate example, allow them to keep a cooler image while not affecting their maturity. It may come as a surprise that in Europe 62 per cent and in Asia 61 per cent of the MTV viewers are more than 25 years old. In the United States and Latin America the percentage is lower but still about 49 per cent.

Viacom Brand Solutions International, MTV Networks International's advertising and marketing sales division, conducted a large-scale study named 'The Golden Age of Youth' in 18 countries worldwide among more than 25,000 26- to 46-year-olds. Findings indicated that, globally, people are staying younger longer and are connected to contemporary youth pursuits for a more extensive period of time. The fact that people are having longer lives is one major contributing factor along with the 'youthification' of culture. It has now become more acceptable for older people to indulge in youthful behaviour. While teenage youth are highly focused on material gain and employ brands to define their identity, Golden Youth (25+) own and enjoy premium and luxurious brands in order to affirm their identity. Fifty-two per cent of them agree with the statement that they still have a lot of growing up to do. Twenty-three per cent would even love to be a teenager again. Contemporary youth can now be defined more accurately as 'the absence of functional and/or emotional maturity'. This requires a completely new marketing approach. Traditional adult brands need to adopt a more youthful tone to avoid being seen as irrelevant or 'for people older than me'.[65]

Christopher Noxon wrote a brilliant book on the youth-celebrating consumer culture and coined a word for the phenomenon: *Rejuvenile*. 'They constitute a new breed of adult identified by a determination to remain playful, energetic and flexible in the face of adult responsibilities', Noxon says. For the Boomer generation, brand and youth nostalgia may be the drivers, for Generation X it is merely suspending adolescence. The book is loaded with examples, such as the trend for colourful cupcakes; 'Disnoids', obsessive adult fans (with no children) of Disney theme parks; AFOLs, adult fans of LEGO; or 'grays on trays', ski slope slang for elder, sometimes arthritic snowboarders.[66] According to ESA, the US entertainment software association, the average computer and video game player is now 39 years old. More than 25 per cent of Americans over the age of 50 play video games. In 1999, this was only 9 per cent.[67]

Flip-flop generations

William Higham, author of *The Next Big Thing*, calls this phenomenon Flip-flop Generations. The New Old are still pursuing the sex, drugs and rock 'n' roll lifestyle of their youth. According to The National Council on Aging, 61 per cent of all 60-somethings today are still sexually active. The fastest-growing group of online daters consists of singles aged 55 and older. The number of 50-somethings using drugs rose more than 70 per cent in the period 2002–08. There are more marijuana consumers among them than in any other age group. The average age of a motorcyclist is now 47. On the other hand researchers notice a growing trend of adolescents moving away from the typical hedonism and liberalism. They claim this is a result of paranoid parenting and the recent economic downturn. Today's 'conserva-teens' are more concerned about their financial future and security than ever before. Only 10 per cent of teens want to be ahead of everybody else in buying the latest technologies as soon as they become available. There is a growing emphasis on morality and family in their set of values.[68]

In our research we found that the impact of the coolness rates of favourite brands on brand image and conversations was even slightly higher for respondents older than 30 than for those below the age of 30. These findings confirm the 'adultescent' trend of the past 10 years. 'Adultescent' was accepted into the Oxford Dictionary of English and is defined as 'a middle-aged person whose clothes, interests, and activities are typically associated with youth culture'. Jay Leno reacted in his show, saying: 'Have you heard this word? It's an adult who lives and acts like a child. Or as women call that – men.'[69]

Conclusion

The first step in sustainable brand building to the Generation Y is 'cooling' your brand. Coolness today means much more than the semantic strategic value of the movements, postures, facial expressions and voice modulations made famous by The Fonz. Coolness has also surpassed its historic links with resistance or rebel attitudes. For this youth generation, cool brands are attractive and appealing brands that are popular in their immediate social circle and bring a sense of novelty, surprise or originality.

The main sources that set the standards of coolness are friends, TV, magazines, advertising and music festivals. Music artists are much cooler than movie actors. Although some product categories have a cool handicap, cool brands are found in all categories. Even in uncool sectors, brands can become cool leaders by adapting the most determining drivers of coolness in the coolness formula. Often, originality and innovation (in communication, events, packaging and varieties) are the keys to cool your brand. Other ways of freezing your brand include exclusive retailing or volume scarcity, and advertising on cool channels.

After reading this chapter, you shouldn't doubt cooling your brand anymore, it is necessary to keep your products or services relevant for the future generation of consumers, Gen Y, and it won't harm your brand in appealing to the older generations. One thing you should keep in mind is that you can't fake being cool or copy cool stuff from others. Old-school coolhunting or trendwatching doesn't make sense. You need to cool your brand while at the same time staying true to your own identity. This Gen Y need for authenticity will be elaborated in the next chapter. Coolmining and coolfarming, both involving youth, are better routes to improve your brand's connection with this generation.

HOT TAKEAWAYS FOR COOL BRAND BUILDERS

- If your brand is perceived as cool, the positive impact on your image and brand conversations will leverage it to stay hot for the long term.

- Cool brands don't only have a higher short-term preference; they also protect brands in the long term and are a guarantee of loyalty even for the fickle youth generation.

- The most important sources to know what's cool: social media, peers, TV, magazines, advertising and music festivals.

- Being cool does not equal being rebellious, edgy or alternative, at least not to the mainstream and biggest part of the youth population.

- In different consumer categories, coolness can help your brand in a different way.

- Cooling your brand includes constant innovation, exclusive offerings and advertising and promotion on cool channels or in cool environments.

- Hunting coolness doesn't make sense; it's better to use the collective wisdom of youth through coolmining of communities or coolfarming (co-creation).

The real thing: brand authenticity

04

Nostalgia. It's delicate but potent. Teddy told me that in Greek, nostalgia literally means, 'the pain from an old wound'. It's a twinge in your heart, far more powerful than memory alone.

In the final episode of the first season of the US drama series *Mad Men*, Don Draper, creative director of ad agency Sterling Cooper, uses the nostalgic value of the Kodak projector to increase its market potential. Although Kodak's new slide projector is named 'The Wheel', Don advocates a different name, 'The Carousel' in his client presentation built around slides of his own children, his wedding and other nostalgic family moments.[1] *Mad Men*, created and produced by Matthew Weiner, who also worked as a writer for *The Sopranos*, has won many awards including 16 Emmys and 4 Golden Globes. It is the first and only cable series to win the Emmy Award for Outstanding Drama Series in each of its first four seasons. The show, set in the 1960s, follows Draper's life inside and outside the Madison Avenue advertising industry. It is particularly praised for its historic authenticity. The writers are notorious for spending much time on research to include the most accurate set designs, costumes and props.[2] For the fifth season, creator Matthew Weiner paid $250,000 to use the Beatles' song *Tomorrow Never Knows*. It is very difficult to license the band's music for television, but Weiner felt the high fee was worthwhile because it was thematically and chronologically consistent with the setting of the show.[3] Viewership for the premiere on 19 July 2007 was much higher than any other AMC series to date and the fifth season's premiere in 2012 had 3.54 million viewers.[4] Don Draper's performance of the Frank O'Hara poem 'Mayakovsky' from *Meditations in an Emergency* in the second season of *Mad Men* has even led to the poet's work entering Amazon's top 50 sales chart.[5]

Fifty years after the *Mad Men* era, marketers are still fond of using the nostalgic values of their brands and products to appeal to Gen Y's desire for authenticity. Adidas turned its 1971 leather tennis shoe named after Stan Smith into a fashion hype in 2014 after it had been off the shelves for several years. The brand reignited the popularity of the shoe with a combination of celebrities (Pharrell dropping ten hand-painted Stan Smiths at hipster store Colette in Paris), online buzz (personalized sneakers for influential bloggers) and a controlled amount of supply.[6] Advertisers understood that their brands should have a purpose and point of view that is bigger than just selling stuff to the kids. The example of *Mad Men*, produced in the 21st century, also proves that you don't need an old brand to be perceived as authentic.

The nostalgia effect

According to a study published in the Journal Of Consumer Research, consumers are more likely to spend money when they feel nostalgic. They become less price sensitive when they think about the past and they also more willing to give more money to others when reflecting on a nostalgic past event. Social media have discovered how feelings of nostalgia can connect people. Twitter even has two popular hashtags stimulating users to share nostalgic moments on two weekdays: #tbt (throwback Thursday) and #fbf (flashback Friday). Travel portal Expedia tapped into this trend with their 'Back to Ocean Beach' campaign in 2015. Each week Expedia picked one winner among Instagram and Twitter users who had tagged their photos from past holidays with @Expedia and #ThrowMeBack. The winners received a travel voucher to return to the place where the picture was taken and – recreate the moment. Facebook has experimented with ways to recall old memories since 2010. The initial 'Year In Review' app received criticism when people were confronted with memories of ex-lovers, deceased friends and an apartment that caught fire, all with the text 'Here's what your year looked like!' Meanwhile Facebook has changed the app and algorithms behind the 'On This Day' to make it more accurate, taking dislikes, past relationships and so on into account. On This Day shows status updates, photos and posts you have been tagged in from exactly one, two or several years ago.[9] At the start of 2015, Nike visualized data from its apps and wearables (Nike+ and the Nike Fuelband) combined with weather and location data in personalized animated videos called 'Your Year'. Runners received a personalized e-mail that linked them to their own YouTube movie.[10]

FIGURE 4.1 Levi's back pocket label

Authenticity is defined as 'the quality of being of an established authority or being genuine, not corrupted from the original, or truthfulness of origins'.[11] Many brands tell consumers when they were established. For instance, on Levi's jeans the logo (see Figure 4.1) shows us that the use of copper rivets to strengthen the stitched pockets of the denim working pants was patented on 20 May 1873. This was the day blue jeans were invented. Kronenbourg, the brewery founded by Geronimus Hatt, is also communicating its year of birth, 1664. It is also the name of the main lager brand of the firm. The label on a Heinz tomato ketchup bottle says 'since 1869', not only indicating its date of birth but also suggesting Heinz was the first brand in the ketchup category. In 2008, The Coca-Cola Company launched a global marketing campaign under the 'secret formula' flag. It consisted of a TV commercial, a website and packaging referring to John Pemberton's invention of the secret formula for Coca-Cola in 1886. The main message of the campaign was the authentic and honest Coke recipe, containing neither preservatives nor artificial flavourings.

Academic research has demonstrated that this type of information may increase a brand's likeability by inducing a perception of originality. If you are a marketing professional, there's a big chance that the thought of using labels such as 'original', 'classic' or 'the real thing' has at least crossed your mind once. They are probably more widely used than the date of origin and have the power to convey the message that competitors are merely weak imitations.[12]

The classic view on brand authenticity, which uses an objective definition linked to origin, history, heritage, people or places, has been challenged in the last decade. Research revealed that people's perception of authenticity is of course highly subjective and socially constructed. It is derived from ongoing interactions between the brand manager or marketer, consumers and society. Studies have identified that brand authenticity is a good predictor of buying intention.[13] Authentic brands are more likely to attract bigger spenders and they are a good driver for word-of-mouth support.

In this chapter, we will explore the dos and don'ts of brand authenticity as a marketing strategy aimed at Generation Y. In our first chapter on the characteristics and behaviour of this generation, we amply demonstrated how they are critical and marketing-savvy consumers. They often consider the purely image-based strategies of brands that 'are' instead of 'do', once so successful in targeting Generation X, to be utterly inauthentic.

When a certain brand identity or campaign proves to be successful in the market, copycats awake. *Mad Men*'s success evoked some parodies too. Jon Hamm (the actor playing Don Draper) was the host on *Saturday Night Live* and parodied his constantly drinking, smoking and womanizing character. In *The Simpsons* episode 'Treehouse of Horror XIX' there's a scene in which *Mad Men*'s animated title sequence is adapted, using the theme song of the series on the soundtrack.[14] Even the children's television show *Sesame Street* ran a parody of *Mad Men* with Muppet versions of Don Draper and two other advertising guys.[15] The issue of brand identity theft will obviously have to be addressed in this chapter too.

The roots of real: why brand authenticity is the 'in' thing

James Gilmore and B Joseph Pine II dedicated an entire management book to the topic of authenticity. They claim the search for authenticity has become more prominent in the last years. The authors link this evolution to the rise of the experience economy. More people than before are looking for experiences, not only in travel and entertainment but also in important life moments such as their birthday, wedding, matchmaking, dating, etc. But service providers are automating customer interaction jobs; take online banking and voice recognition automated call centres as examples. In response, on the website GetHuman.com people are posting short cuts (immediately hitting the '0' or '#' or weird keypad combinations) to go directly to a human being working at the customer service division of hundreds of companies. Consumers are forced to interact more with machines and hence place greater value on person-to-person conversations.[16] This is unquestionably also the case for Generation Y consumers. In our authenticity survey for Levi's, we asked 13- to 29-year-olds which sources they would consult for advice when buying clothes. The number one response (75 per cent of answers) was 'my best friends' and at number two 'someone of the shop personnel' (54 per cent). Brochures, websites, review sites and magazines were chosen by less than 30 per cent.[17]

Authenticity as a driver of brand choice

In our postmodern society, we are all looking for less materialistic buying motivations. Choosing a nostalgic or authentic product or brand enables us to reduce the feeling of guilt. Instead of 'consuming', we discover new sensations and enjoy a forgotten or seemingly lost past. Generation Yers are constantly looking for new experiences or thrilling events that engage them personally and will be remembered forever. This might give the impression that 'old' or 'nostalgic' attributes aren't appealing to them. But that's not the case. The market is not only flooded with an abundance of goods and services, but also increasingly filled with deliberately staged live experiences. The distinctions between real and unreal or fake are blurring for youngsters. This has affected the choice criteria young consumers are using today. Their perception of how real, genuine or sincere a company or brand is, has become essential in doing business with them. When lacking time, trust and attention, brand authenticity plays an important role in choosing between equal alternatives. Youth seems to value authenticity in a world that is characterized by mass production and marketing. The popularity of reality shows on TV, for instance, can be seen as a quest for authenticity within the traditionally fiction-oriented entertainment industry. The vintage trend in fashion and design is a reaction to mass production and a consequence of youth's need to differentiate and stand out from others.[18] In the postmodern market, nostalgia for the 'good old one' appeals to Gen Y's demand for simplicity. Converse All-Star basketball shoes, for example, haven't changed the overall design since Charles 'Chuck' Taylor created it in the 1920s. The style consistency and its rock and art heritage made the brand a popular choice for an alternative and creative group of youngsters.[19] The key to creating brand authenticity is providing opportunities for self-expression and self-fulfilment. Consumption of products often functions as a marker of identity. We will discuss this in Chapter 6.

An ancient marketing strategy

Although authenticity gets a lot of attention in postmodern marketing books, there's nothing new under the sun. Back in the 14th century Bordeaux winemakers felt severe competition from the lower-priced Bergerac *terroirs* along the Dordogne river in the interior east. In their first reaction, the merchants convinced the English controlling the port of Bordeaux to impose heavy taxes on wine from the interior. When Italian, Spanish and Portuguese wine-growing expanded and the French couldn't cope with the lower prices anymore, Bordeaux winemakers focused on the authenticity of their products. This allowed them to charge a premium price. They unified the small *grands crus* into a few larger holdings and associated them with neighbouring country houses or chateaux such as Pétrus, Margaux, Latour and Mouton-Rothschild.[20] This marketing technique, positioning luxury wines as a natural product as opposed to industrial and mass-produced, is still employed today. French winemakers stress the historic style specific to the particular chateau, or *terroir*, and create a brand aura. Michael B Beverland examined the strategies of 26 French wineries and discovered they are outwardly downplaying their real scientific and business expertise to appear different from commercial competitors. Instead, they project their sincerity by telling a story of commitment to tradition, production excellence and passion for the daily craft.[21]

Authenticity in the music industry

Authenticity has traditionally been of high importance within cultural sectors such as the arts and music. Think of the German music project Milli Vanilli in the late 1980s/early 1990s. When producer Frank Farian confessed the recording didn't contain the voices of Fab Morvan and Rob Pilatus, their Grammy Award for Best New Artist 1990 was withdrawn. The Beatles were famous for singing their own compositions as opposed to The Monkees who sang professionally written songs. Today many pop music artists are still using their own personal roots as a sales message. It is not only often projected in rap (50 Cent, Eminem) but also in pop music. For instance in her 2003 hit *Jenny from the Block*, Jennifer Lopez stresses her authenticity singing: 'no matter where I go, I know where I came from [the Bronx].'[22]

Newcastle's No Bollocks approach

Beer brand Newcastle Brown Ale has become king of 'meta marketing', often making fun of common marketing practices in the beer industry. Its so-called 'No Bollocks' approach, created by agency Dota5, deals entirely with telling it how they think it is. 'We're selling you beer': no more, no less. For instance, they promote their Facebook page with a simple claim: 'Like us on Facebook so we can legally spam you with ads.' Their positioning compared to other beer brands is based around the promise that Newcastle will never 'bullshit' their customers. One of the most famous examples was a billboard that Newcastle put up directly below a Stella Artois billboard. The Stella poster showed one of the brand's glasses and read 'It's a chalice, not a glass'. The Newcastle Brown Ale billboard also showed one of the brand's glasses, but instead had the line 'Who uses the word "chalice"?' Another example are the coasters they distribute to bars, which have 'If this coaster doesn't make you want to order a Newcastle, then the coaster sales guy lied to us' written on it. Even the typical neon signs that get put up in bars and cafes are used in a meta way, with one of them reading 'A $400 sign to get you to buy a $6 beer'.[23]

Continued...

Newcastle's No Bollocks approach   *Continued...*

The fact that they humorously advertise about advertising creates an authentic positioning, which also resonates well with Gen Yers. Additionally, they have deliberately chosen a 'digital first' approach, with Facebook and other digital channels being the most important marketing investments. Another of their self-depreciatory campaigns showcased the importance digital has for them. In June 2014, Newcastle promised 'a millionth of a million dollars' ($1) to the next 50,000 people that followed them on Twitter. In just two weeks, they had already doubled its follower count. The reasoning was once again part of the 'no bollocks': 'Why endure the unsolicited marketing of other beer brands for free when you could endure Newcastle's unsolicited marketing and get paid?'[24]

For the Superbowl of 2014, they created a campaign called 'The Greatest Ad Never Made'. While other (beer) brands put up trailers online for the TV ads to be shown during the biggest gridiron match of the year, Newcastle created a trailer for an ad that was never actually made. They simply made fun of not being able to pay the required millions to create a Superbowl ad, showing a behind-the-scenes of the failed attempt to create a legitimate ad. Big stars such as Anna Kendrick participated in the campaign, often comically complaining about how they were asked to star in the ad (that was never made) but in fact never did. These videos only appeared online and not on TV, but created a lot of conversation. On Superbowl night itself, the Newcastle and Dota5 team also posted 'If We Made It' videos on their social media channels, explaining how they would have improved the actual ads made by competitors. This strategy worked: according to the agency brand awareness rose by 5 per cent in the two weeks after, while the consideration to purchase rose by 19% in the demographic group they target (males between 22 and 39). The brand awareness in this demographic also reached a very high 90% back in March 2014, directly after the very successful Superbowl campaign.[25] Similarly, they once again made fun of the whole advertising frenzy with their Superbowl 2015 campaign. Actress Aubrey Plaza invited other brands to join the #BandOfBrands, an opportunity for all kinds of other brands to join up and get a spot and a mention in Newcastle's Superbowl ad, which was also partly broadcast regionally on TV. The end result was a funny chaotic video in which almost 40 companies and brands were showcased in less than a minute. The different videos combined gathered almost 5 million views on YouTube.[26]

Authenticity in advertising

In advertising, the use of authenticity is prevalent too. Although the authentic stereotypes such as Marlboro cowboys, genius artists and outlaws had been parodied a lot by the end of the 20th century and hence lost their mythical aura, the underlying values of freedom, autonomy and individuality are still relevant in youth marketing today. In an extensive study, 1,000 print and television advertisements for trainer and jeans brands directed at 18- to 25-year-olds between 1999 and 2005, were analysed. Only 15 per cent of the ads had no link with authenticity at all. The jeans sample was especially striking. Escape, challenge and relaxation from formal rules were depicted in scenes straight from the desert, a rooftop, the edge of town, the street or the everyday. Quite often the ads ended with an open road representing a path of authentic self-discovery. Models were travelling across wide landscapes on dirty motorcycles or in worn and dusty vintage cars. Designer jeans were modelled on the street, not a catwalk, and showed people engaged in ordinary, mundane acts (eg drinking coffee, eating yoghurt). Interior locations in the ad scenes were mostly downmarket, dirty places. Long-haired, bohemian characters frequently appeared in music studios or were involved in creative arts such as painting or sculpting. Creative people are often regarded as being authentic because they are authors of their properly created art. The trainer advertisements often related to the hip-hop street culture including creative acts such as break-dancing, graffiti and dj-ing. Adidas ads were referring to nostalgic footage of Muhammad Ali, combining the artistry of Reebok with the athleticism and achievement appeals that Nike has been claiming consistently throughout the years.[27]

True tales and crafted cult: how brands portray authenticity

Michael B Beverland, an Australian professor of marketing, has dedicated much of his academic career to the subject of authenticity. According to his work published in *Building Brand Authenticity*, iconic brands can portray their 'realness' through seven habits. We have used his structured knowledge to illustrate how youth brands can tap into authenticity too.

Authentic habit 1: storytelling

Authentic brands are collections of stories that provide an emotional connection with the consumers. They create stories from the consumers' circumstances, take advantage of lucky events and allow and stimulate others (both ordinary consumers and celebrities) to tell their own stories about the brand for them. Nike appointed its corporate director of education as the Chief Storyteller. Nelson Farris has been working for the company for 40 years so he has experienced the evolution and growth from the early days. Today he is responsible for training Nike staff members and the so-called 'ekins' (nike in reverse), the brand ambassadors. Farris's stories are about the spirit of innovation and Nike's commitment to helping athletes.[28] Beverland suggested multiple possible story themes that authentic brands can use. Often they are connecting companies and brands to real people. Some examples of themes include:

- Creation and creativity: brands that lack creativity are usually me-too or follower brands. Authentic brands are obsessed with innovating. Think of Quiksilver continuously investing in wetsuit and board technology. These stories reinforce the perception of the brand's sincerity because the people behind the brand are viewed as lovers of their craft and merely motivated by the pursuit of perfection rather than money.

- History: many brands are linked to history. Vans and Quiksilver, for instance, originate from the early days of surf and skateboarding.

- Community: consumers forming offline and online communities around brands. For instance, Coca-Cola has more than 30,000 groups on Facebook; one fan page even counts more than 93 million fans today and was started by two friends who had no relationship at all with the company.

- Place: links to geographical locations are often used by food and beverage brands but are also common in the fashion (Italy), hi-tech (Japan) and car (Germany) industries.

- Consumers: own stories of consumers showing their affection and commitment and expressing their own identity. Red Bull's Facebook page reaches 30 million people and one of the successful apps is the 'drunkish dials' section that let fans rate the hilarious phone calls of people dialing the brand's 1-800 number.

Authentic habit 2: appearing as artisanal amateurs

Mainstream brands will often emphasize quality and production efficiency. Authentic brands often stress their craft traditions, combining the passion of the amateur with the skill of an artisan. They will downplay behind-the-scenes and state-of-the-art R&D and production processes, as well as market research and marketing budgets. Common techniques include illustrating the lack of training of the founders. Remember how Ben and Jerry, two hippies who weren't able to get into medical school, followed a $5 correspondence course on ice cream making? Or the young founders of Innocent Drinks whose future depended on the two bins at a music festival labelled 'yes, we want you to start a company' or 'no, we don't'? Ralph Lauren never had any fashion training and Steve Jobs couldn't write code.

Authentic habit 3: sticking to your roots

This is not the same as simply repeating past practices. Although authentic brands have to evolve and be creative, the novelties always have to reflect the roots of the brand and the original spirit of the founders.[29] We think the story of Vans is a good illustration of this. The roots of the US manufacturer of trainers that primarily targets boarders and surfers go back to 16 March 1966. Paul Van Doren and his three partners started The Van Doren Rubber Company to produce shoes and start selling them directly to the public. The sticky soles and rugged colourful designs made the Vans popular among skateboarders and BMX riders in the 1970s. In an effort to compete with large athletic shoe companies at the start of the 1980s, Vans made the decision to produce more mainstream football, baseball, basketball and even wrestling and skydiving shoes. Although Sean Penn made Vans Slip-Ons internationally popular when wearing them in the youth movie *Fast Times at Ridgemont High*, the core action sports lovers turned their back on their once beloved brand. The wide range of products had drained the companies' resources and when Vans didn't manage to overcome its debt, it had to file for bankruptcy in 1984.

In 2004, Vans was acquired for $396 million by VF Corp, home of brands such as Eastpak, The North Face, Lee and Wrangler. Vans then learned its lesson to stay true to its authentic roots when addressing their core target group of 10- to 25-year-olds. According to the VP of Marketing, Doug Palladini, the four pillars of Vans culture are: action sports, music, street culture and art. Since 1995 Vans has been the primary sponsor of the Warped Tour music festivals. The brand is also co-sponsor of Mountain Dew's action sports tour. In 2012 Vans announced plans to open a nearly three-acre skate park in Huntington Beach, aka Surf City. In an interview with *Brandweek*, Palladini said: 'The biggest challenge now is to maintain the energy that we have. We want this to last for the long term, not ride the trend while it's hot and then figure out what the next cool thing is. It's about continually reinforcing who we are as a company, always going back to our action sports heritage and DNA to find new opportunities instead of trying to blow something out for the moment.' To keep their cool, Vans shifted to a segmented offering. The high-end assortment, named Vault by Vans, is only sold in limited editions through boutiques with higher pricing. The Classics line, targeting a core group of boarding youth, is sold at skate- and snowboard shops. Another line for the masses is sold at bigger retail outlets. Vans sells different styles that appeal to different personalities, ages and gender.[30]

Authentic habit 4: love for the craft

The people behind authentic brands radiate their love for their craft. This reflects the desire of consumers to get paid for doing what they love. It involves product-orientation with an eye for detail, involvement of senior management in the core activities, and a never-ending quest for excellence or perfection. Authentic brands are often design-led and they let consumers experience the production, their own craft, as opposed to co-creation and co-design approaches. In 1952 Jack O'Neill opened the world's first surf shop in his garage in San Francisco. Jack is seen as the inventor of modern wetsuits because of his many improvements to the design and quality of the surfer's equipment including creating a prototype with neoprene. His son Pat O'Neill, who was appointed as CEO of the company in the late 1980s, invented the leash, a cord connected to the surfer that prevents his board from crashing into cliffs and breaking. In the process of testing the leash, father Jack lost an eye and has worn an eye-patch since then. Today O'Neill is still a leading surf brand with a global market share of 60 per cent in wetsuits.[31]

Southwestern Distillery in the UK promoted their Tarquin's Gin by launching an Apple FaceTime video chat with the founder, Tarquin Leadbetter. Tarquin's Gin is hand-crafted in batches of a maximum of 300 bottles and the distillery really wanted to emphasize this craft element. Every consumer got invited to open up FaceTime and have a chat with the founder and distiller. Using the interactive label of their own bottle, they also had the chance to get a completely personalized story behind the actual bottle they were holding in their hands. In its first month, the 'Taste with Tarquin' campaign activated over 600 customers (18% of sold bottles) to make a FaceTime call.[32]

Authentic habit 5: consumer immersion

Authentic brands absorb their surroundings to inspire breakthrough innovations. Companies such as Nike hire staff who are engaged in amateur or professional sports and are in fact Nike customers. The Chinese sports brand Li Ning developed inner soles uniquely adapted to Chinese feet after its staff immersed themselves in running and found that most global brands did not comfortably fit Chinese feet. DVV Insurance, part of the Belfius company, learned from an online research community among Gen Y that most of their products were too complicated, too expensive and not relevant for the daily frustrations of students. Asking advice from an insurance agent also seemed too difficult a step for them. DVV co-created a new insurance package tailored to the needs of youngsters leaving home for their studies or to start their professional life. The insurance, dubbed Cocoon Start, is targeting young people up to the age of 30. It kept coverage of theft and fire incidents but removed some other ingredients because young people rent flats or small houses without gardens. Next to the civil liability and legal expenses insurance, DVV added specific features suggested by the crowd. The Home Computer service, for instance, covers accidents with laptops, computers or tablets. Home Emergency ensures 24-hours assistance for sudden unforeseen urgencies that need an intervention, such as problems with heating or sanitation. Girls' magazine *Flair*, owned by the Finnish media group Sanoma, added augmented reality to its magazine after listening to their young target group. The Layar mobile app pointed readers directly to web shops where they could see fashion outfits in different colours, or hear and see behind-the-scenes footage of the editorial staff.

Authentic habit 6: be at one with the community

Apart from stressing their national and regional roots, authentic brands also play a significant role in the development of their industry, not only by introducing innovations but also in a broader perspective. For example, Chuck Taylor, the originator of Converse All Star basketball shoes, wrote books on basketball strategy. Authentic brands are also sensitive to culture and gaining legitimacy in subcultures. Levi's made sincere commitments to gay rights. It was one of the first brands to advertise in gay publications and the Levi Strauss Company extended its employee benefits to same-sex couples. It even ended its relationship with the American Boy Scouts because the organization banned gay scout leaders.

P&G and their feminine hygiene brand Always collaborated with Leo Burnett Mexico to try to help specific local communities in and around Mexico City. Thousands of women die because of cervical cancer, and Always found that this is likely in part because talking about the female reproductive organs is considered taboo in these regions and communities. The local languages of these groups actually contain no words for uterus or womb; this often resulted in bad communication with doctors and subsequently subpar diagnoses. Together with several linguists, cultural experts and doctors they decided to create their own descriptive names for the organs (eg 'baby's house' for uterus). Local women were encouraged to start using these words when talking to medical personnel as means to better explain their symptoms. To help the next generations, these words were also collected and distributed in a book called *Palabras Íntimas* (Intimate Words). This campaign was one of the winners at the Cannes Lions in 2015.[33]

Domestic violence is still a social issue requiring much attention. Vodafone collaborated with Y&R Istanbul to help Turkish women in cases of emergency. Disguised as a regular flashlight application, the Red Light app enabled women to enter phone details of three trusted people. When they felt threatened or aggravated, they could simply shake their phone and the application would send a text message plus their exact location to the three trusted people. Because this 'secret' application was not supposed to be known about by men, there were no TV, radio or outdoor campaigns at all. The only promotion was done via YouTube tutorials. Turkish video bloggers uploaded random tutorials for very mundane 'female' things (eg how to put on make-up) that would make most men click away after a few minutes. Instead of fully completing the tutorial, however, about halfway through the video they would start talking about the application and how women could use it. According to the agency, over 250,000 Turkish women downloaded the app (24 per cent of female Turkish smartphone users) and the 'emergency' function was activated over 103,000 times. The campaign also won the Media Grand Prix and a gold Lion during the 2015 Cannes Lions advertising awards.[34]

Authentic habit 7: indoctrinate staff into the brand cult

Authentic brands are backed by fanatical and devoted staff that share the same brand values and are both passionate about the company's cause as well as open to new ways of thinking and doing. This requires a specific HR approach. Applicants at Virgin were requested to perform, sing, mime or dance. It's a way of recruiting people who will want to go the extra mile to satisfy customers.[35]

Authenticity axioms

To conclude, Gilmore and Pine have formulated a simple but interesting set of 'axioms of authenticity' in their book *Authenticity. What consumers really want*:

- If you are authentic, then you don't have to say you're authentic.
- If you say you're authentic, then you'd better be authentic.
- It's easier to be authentic, if you don't say you're authentic.[36]

The first, the last, my everything: using indicators of origin

Have you ever wondered what happens to the sales revenues of an original song when a cover song hits the charts? What do you expect? In 2009, Lisa Hordijk won the TV format *X Factor* in the Netherlands with a cover of the song *Hallelujah*. One week later, her version of the song was leading the Dutch Singles Top 100. It was in that first position for 10 consecutive weeks. Jeff Buckley's interpretation, released back in 1993, entered the charts immediately at number three. The original version by Leonard Cohen, a song from 1984, also managed to get into the Top 100 of 2009, in 27th spot.

A similar phenomenon had happened six months earlier in the UK when Alexandra Burke won the same talent scouting TV show... with the same song. Now, you might think it's the *Hallelujah* that incites a spiritual mysterious effect on people, but there's no sixth sense involved in these statistics. Apparently, whenever a cover song enters the charts, in 60 per cent of cases it will cause an immediate positive effect on the revenues of the song it originates from. The original song climbs on average 240 places in the sales charts compared to the year before. It is only a temporary effect because one year later the original song will drop 190 spots in the list.

Of course, this is partly linked to a mere reactivation in people's memory. Experiments have shown that the top five preferred songs of people are susceptible to recent exposure. For instance, if you let them evaluate a number of ABBA songs, and then ask them what their all-time favourite tunes are, the chance the list will contain at least one ABBA song is significantly higher.[37]

The first = better intuition

On the other hand, it's not just a mere exposure effect. People favour stimuli they encounter first. When they were asked to listen to similar fragments of an original and its corresponding cover song, without knowing the songs or which one was the original, 96 per cent preferred the version that was heard first, no matter if it was the original one or the cover song. If the songs used in the experiment were known to them, they preferred the one that they indicated to have heard first, prior to the study, and which was released before their birth. This phenomenon seems analogous to the process of 'imprinting'. A young animal develops an attachment for the first object it encounters. It is somehow stamped upon the nervous system. Although this imprinting only occurs once in a critical life period, it seems that the first exposure effect can happen time after time. People believe that being first has many advantages. After all, we live in a society where the winner (sports, school, etc) is celebrated with a gold medal, flowers and champagne.[38]

When we translate this human trait to a business context, the phenomenon is also known as the 'first mover's advantage'. Customers attach meanings of innovativeness and superior quality to the (perceived) first company in an industry. The positive effects of perceived originality on attractiveness and consumer choice for pioneers have been confirmed in various researches. In experiments with youngsters, participants preferred the song version labelled 1964 to the 1967 version when the third version they heard was labelled 1969, but not when the third version was labelled 1962.

Indicators of origin

Since Gen Y customers are mostly not able to distinguish the original first brand on the market from copycats, the potential power of originality indicators is huge. However, if your brand is not the pioneer in the market it would be the wrong strategy to try posing as the original one. This could undermine your credibility when the truth becomes clear and then it would only stress your dependence on the real innovator. Non-comparative indicators such as 'since 1869' on the other hand can influence Gen Y's perception but still have the danger of the pioneer competitor's reaction with explicit expressions such as 'first on the market'.[39] We will show you later in this chapter that although dates of origin do appeal to a nostalgic feeling with Gen Y, it will not be the most successful way to adopt authenticity in this market.

These labels of being 'the original', 'the first', 'the creator', are obviously tightly related to the concept of brand authenticity. Young consumers, with limited product and brand buying experiences, are looking for cues that decrease purchase risks and indicate that a brand offers good value for money. Origin, history and heritage of a brand are cues that support this brand positioning and can be seen as the traditional definition of brand authenticity.

The 'origin', as illustrated in the examples of Levi's and Kronenbourg, is the invention, the starting point or beginning of a company or brand.

'History' is what happened since the origin of a brand until now, such as new product launches, new identities, advertising campaigns, etc. In the case of the Levi's brand, this is a bucketful of iconic advertising memories. Nick Kamen undressing in the laundrette commercial of the 1980s. The motorcyclist who enters an office building in his cool The Fonz style to the tune of 'The Joker' in the early 1990s. The ADHD-style head-banging yellow puppet Flat Eric used for Levi's Sta-Prest at the end of the 1990s. Adidas is communicating the history of its brand through legendary models and the athletes who were wearing them displayed in old lockers in the interior of their shops. The difference with 'heritage' is that the latter is also a collection or collective memory of things that happened with a brand without the involved company or brand having a deliberate influence on this. Examples of heritage are: celebrities who consume or use a certain product or brand in public, for instance movie stars such as Ben Stiller and Cameron Diaz wearing PUMA sneakers in the box-office hit *There's Something About Mary*. It could also be leading edge or even mainstream consumers that pick up brands and make them fashionable or cool.[40]

Irony killed authenticity: Gen Y's perception of authentic claims

Little is known about how the critical Generation Y perceives and values brand strategies based on authentic claims. Therefore, we collaborated with the Levi Strauss Company to verify youth's perception of authenticity. The classic way of looking at the concept of 'brand authenticity' is defined by components such as origin, history and heritage of a brand. Levi Strauss & Co are known as the inventors of the denim jeans with their Levi's 501 jeans model positioned as the ultimate original jeans. They were interested in finding out what the modern interpretations of authenticity for youth are today.[41]

Origin and history

Youngsters are seldom aware of the origin of their favourite brands. For instance, in the beer category where the date of origin is often an integral part of the brand logo (eg Kronenbourg, Stella Artois) the recognition and recall of these packaging or logo items is very low. Although they believe Levi's is an authentic brand, less than 25 per cent really know the origin of the brand. Despite the label on the back of each pair of jeans clearly mentioning the date of origin, youngsters have never noticed it. When the age or history of a product or brand is concerned, youngsters tend to think more in relative and comparative terms. A brand such as Apple seems to have the same association of quality and 'being around for a while' even if it is in fact a rather recent brand. In their limited years of being conscious consumers, youngsters have always known the presence of Apple. The fact that parents or grandparents are using a certain brand is also a proof to youngsters that the brand is 'old'. They tend to think that if a product has been on the market for a long time, this is a secure proof of good quality. They also associate dates of origin with feelings of cheerfulness and nostalgia. 'Cool! My grandmother may have used it too.' But again, they don't tend to go too far back in time when considering brand history. When a brand has existed for 10 years or longer, it truly is an aged brand.

Concerning the country of origin, the critical Generation Y makes a distinction between the real origin and the country in which a brand or product is produced. Most youngsters don't know the country of origin of their favourite brands, but the awareness of where it is manufactured is higher since this is often indicated in a label 'made in...'. For certain product categories the country of origin can evoke good as well as bad quality associations. Some countries spontaneously evoke connotations of labour mistreatment or animal abuse. Japanese brands nowadays seem to have the halo of being technologically advanced, for instance, as opposed to Chinese ones, which equal bad quality for Gen Yers. Gilmore and Pine have correctly emphasized that some regions that were once known for junk, like Japan, are today symbols of quality. China currently possesses the image of 'ManuFAKEture', a term coined by Ted Fishman in *The New York Times*,[42] but may one day be known for its authenticity. Country of origin plays a more important role for the quality perception among young target groups in certain industries such as food, health and beauty, technology (durables), cars and clothing. In contrast to what we had expected from these savvy consumers, youngsters don't mind too much when brands fake a certain origin. For instance, they automatically link Häagen-Dazs ice cream to Switzerland or a Scandinavian country. When confronted with the fact that it is actually a US brand using foreign branding as a marketing technique, and the digraphs 'ää' and 'zs' are actually invalid in all Scandinavian languages, they consider this to be funny and cunning.

Authentic Bronx ice cream sold with an umlaut

Häagen-Dazs is a brand of super-premium (dense, high butterfat) ice cream that was created by Polish immigrants Reuben and Rose Mattus in the Bronx, New York in 1961. The first retail store was opened in Brooklyn in 1976. Today Häagen-Dazs is sold in 55 countries around the world. The brand name was meant to look Scandinavian for Americans. The Häagen-Dazs name gives European cachet and radiates craftsmanship and tradition, justifying the premium retail price. On early labels Mattus used an outline of Denmark, although the umlaut is never used in Danish. He also added some Scandinavian capital cities on the packaging:

Continued...

Authentic Bronx ice cream sold with an umlaut *Continued...*

Oslo, Copenhagen and Stockholm. The font type of the logo was set in bold Futura, adding a muscular Germanic effect to the name.

This marketing technique is named 'foreign branding'. It implies the use of foreign-sounding or foreign names to create a superior or authentic image. Many cosmetics and fashion brands for example use French or Italian names to make the connection with the fashion shows and designers of Paris and Milan. Other product categories have discovered foreign branding techniques too. Although the Mars' brand Dolmio sounds Italian, the pasta sauce is not made or sold in Italy. The Chinese retailer of home appliances Haier uses the German-sounding brand Liebherr to convey a message of quality. The UK manufacturer of Moben Kitchens trademarked 'Möben' in 1977 to use the German and Scandinavian quality image.
The oldest known usage of foreign branding goes back to the 1910s: the day 'Soupe Vichyssoise' was invented... at the Ritz-Carlton Hotel in New York.[43] The umlaut also became popular in the heavy metal and punk rock music scene to stress their toughness and macho image. In 1972, the American rock band Blue Öyster Cult set the scene. Since then, rock groups like Motörhead, Mötley Crüe, Hüsker Dü and Queensrÿche have followed the example. There's even a Finnish punk rock band called Umlaut.

The success of Häagen-Dazs invited copycat companies to implement the same strategy on the ice cream market. Richard Smith, an American, created Frusen Glädjé, using an almost Swedish name to position his products. Without the accent on the final e, frusen glädje means 'frozen joy' or 'frozen delight' in Swedish. Häagen-Dazs was quite unhappy with this copycat and sued the company unsuccessfully in 1980 to stop them from using a Scandinavian marketing theme. In 1985 Smith sold the brand to Kraft General Foods. What has happened to the brand since then is a marketing mystery. Kraft states that Frusen Glädjé was sold to Unilever in 1993, but a spokesman for Unilever denied this. The association of frozen milk with Scandinavia hasn't disappeared though. Canada has its very successful Yogen Früz, a frozen yoghurt brand, and there's also Freshëns frozen yoghurt selling Smoöthies.[44]

Heritage

Youngsters are not aware of the heritage of brands and it is not something they are really interested in. The history of a brand and how it was affected by acts of external people have very little importance to them. Although they seem to have respect for brands with a heritage, they are hard to convince that certain stories are true. When we confronted Gen Y with a global TV commercial of Adidas picturing the brand origin (Adi Dassler), history and heritage (including Muhammed Ali), 93 per cent of the 13- to 29-year-olds thought the story was invented. It just sounded too good to be true. Being bombarded by many made-up brand stories, adolescents generally consider these types of story to be fake and marketing tricks. Advertisers that want to claim brand heritage such as Adidas face a difficult challenge to persuade the Generation Y consumers that their brand stories are genuine and real. It is a bad idea to use large advertising and marketing campaigns to convey messages of authenticity. Their mass media connotations undermine the authentic claims. Advertising strategies to Gen Y have been using a lot of humour and irony. Typical youth advertising strategies included stressing the fact that 'it's only advertising, baby', and 'yes, we ARE trying to sell you something and you know it!' As a consequence, using heritage or authenticity claims in advertising will be considered to be 'only another advertising trick'. Brand origin, history and heritage should be whispered when you use them.

Only seven monastery brew-houses in the world are authorized to produce authentic Trappist beer. Trappist monks are part of the Order of the Cistercians. Armand de Rancé founded one of the two great Cistercian orders in 1662 in the French Normandy town of La Trappe. The name 'Trappist' was derived from this abbey. The Trappist monks originally brewed their beer to cater for the needs of the community. Nowadays they are allowed to sell their production in order to fund their works and good causes. When Trappist breweries expanded their market to an international level, commercial breweries such as AB InBev (using the Leffe brand) saw potential in mass-producing a copycat alternative: abbey beers. During the 1980s and 1990s the difference between Trappist and abbey beers became less clear to consumers. Commercial breweries used names from abbeys that no longer existed, such as Grimbergen, an abbey beer produced by Alken-Maes, part of the Heineken Group. This gave them the chance to use images of monks and abbeys in packaging, merchandise and advertising. In 1997, the International Trappist Association created a label 'Authentic Trappist Product' that can only be used by the seven authentic Trappist abbeys.

Michael B Beverland researched the perception of 40 marketing visuals (advertisements, bottle labels and packaging) from both abbey and authentic Trappist brewers. His conclusion: advertising may reinforce an image of authenticity but only in an indirect way. Generation Y in particular seemed to have trouble distinguishing the real thing from the copy. When youngsters looked at the bottle label saying 'Authentic Trappist Product', they considered it proof that the beer was probably not really the authentic one. The clever abbey advertising however, using indirect cues such as historical font types and colours (brown, yellow), simple packaging and images of monks, abbeys and cellars, supported the authentic image of the commercial copycats.[45]

If you want to use your brand's origin, history or heritage, to connect with youth, you should not do this with 'in-your-face' labels or campaigns literally telling the stories behind your brand. The critical Gen Y will not believe the story is true. Instead, you can either use indirect subtle cues of authenticity. Facebook's Timeline application is a wonderful tool to take your brand fans on a journey through your history and heritage without really shouting them in a commercial way. Instead, it encourages brands to tell their own stories and illustrate them with images and video footage. Leading newspaper *The New York Times* is making great use of this feature with its 'Inside *The Times*' section on Facebook. The timeline starts from 1851 and includes clippings of some major historical events such as Lincoln's assassination as well as unique pictures from inside the newsroom, such as a 1959 snapshot of Marilyn Monroe inspecting *New York Times* clippings in the archives.[46]

Consistency is an important aspect of authenticity. If youth see a clear fit between your brand DNA and your brand's action, they will be perceived as real.

If you really want to stand out from the copycat inauthentic competitors, let your consumers experience first-hand how authentic your products are. If your brand authenticity is linked to the production process or location, you can achieve this with guided or behind-the-scenes tours. If your brand heritage is linked to leading-edge consumers or celebrities (eg athletes or musicians) this is often done by sponsoring certain events or people. Think of Converse and music artists for instance.

Celebrity endorsements

Using celebrity endorsements for branding to Gen Y isn't without its complications. Youngsters are very critical about this marketing strategy. To them, celebrity endorsement implies that a brand is not confident enough to have an image of its own and hence it is interpreted as a weak moment of a brand. It shows that a brand has no real personality on its own and needs to buy coolness by using cool persons. Therefore celebrity endorsement only pays off in certain circumstances; for instance if the product sector is related to the natural environment and the skills of the celebrity. Real athletes such as Michael Jordan or Tiger Woods supporting the Nike brand or a real designer, Philippe Starck designing the bottle, glass and can for the 1664 beer brand, do create an added value for the brand. On the other hand Gordon Ramsay, the Michelin-starred celebrity chef, endorsing Gordon's gin – only based on the similarity with his famous first name – is not linked to the gin brand's heritage. The date of origin of Gordon's gin goes back 200 years before Ramsay was born. Youngsters will reject this kind of celebrity endorsement. The fact that Gordon Ramsay is simultaneously supporting about 400 other products is of course also undermining the credibility of this celebrity endorsement.[47]

With the launch of the Sport 15 campaign Adidas proved that celebrity endorsement can still be successfully applied when you stay true to your brand. During 2015 different stories were being shared on videos to motivate and inspire young athletes to be the best they can be at any level or at any sport around the world. The first 60- and 30-second commercials, 'Take It' and 'Takers', already started with a strong message. A voiceover said: 'The last goal? Doesn't matter. The last victory? Already forgotten. Yesterday is gone. Lost in the record books. But today is up for grabs. Unpredictable. Unwritten. Undecided. Now is ours. Do something, and be remembered. Or do nothing, and be forgotten. No one owns today. Take it.' The video included Lionel Messi, James Rodriguez and Derrick Rose, all popular athletes in different sports. Adidas wanted to address that every moment in sports is a chance for the athlete to redefine himself and his team. Besides the physical skills and talent, a great mental mindset is necessary.[48] After the launch the video 'Take It' gained over 21.9 million views in only one week and got over 2,800 Facebook shares.[49]

Some brands, however, have reversed the idea of celebrity endorsement by turning the consumer themselves into the star of the campaign. Brazilian beauty brand Natura got tired of the usual airbrushed celebrities that appear in regular campaigns of cosmetic brands. So they connected several vending machines to Facebook. Buyers could 'like' the Facebook page of the brand, and in return their own profile picture got printed on the shampoo bottle coming out of the machine. In total, the campaign resulted in about 50,000 customized bottles.[50]

Similarly, the Taiwanese coffee chain Let's Café allowed customers to take a selfie while they were waiting for their delicious latte, which then got 'printed' on the foam of the coffee using brown powder. These brands didn't need the usual celebrities to endorse, but instead turned to the customers.[51]

Another alternative twist to celebrity endorsement was used by the 'Dallas Pets Alive!' animal organization. The Texas animal shelter launched the hashtag #muttbombing on Instagram, Photoshopping dogs in need of a new home in to celebrities' Instagram pictures. For example, the famous Oscar selfie made by host Ellen DeGeneres and stars like Bradley Cooper and Jennifer Lawrence was edited to show 'Sandy the dog' among the stars, with the caption: 'I'm Sandy and I'm #muttbombing you in hopes of finding a home.' The animal shelter did the same with pictures from Ryan Gosling, Miley Cyrus and Jimmy Fallon. Eventually, even movie company Dreamworks used #muttbombing in the marketing campaign for their movie 'Mr Peabody & Sherman'. The campaign resulted in a staggering 700 per cent increase in traffic to the site of the animal shelter. Even more, dog adoptions rose by 55 per cent while various other shelters around the United States copied the same idea.[52]

In a survey by InSites Consulting among 900 13- to 29-year-olds, their new definition of authenticity was confirmed. Items such as 'years of presence on the market' and 'like in the past' were only mentioned by less than 2 per cent of youth, indicating that these connotations are less relevant to them. For almost 6 out of 10 young people authenticity is primarily detected by the brand values – social responsibility, what the brand propagates and what it stands for. Thirty per cent link authenticity with the history of a brand and only 2 out of 10 make the link with the brand's origin or heritage.[53]

How Gen Y values honesty

Honesty as a concept is much more diverse and complex for youth than the upfront interpretation of just avoiding telling lies. It is also about being respectful to youngsters, to society, to the environment, to children, animals, etc. Honesty to Gen Y includes being open and transparent. It is about not being afraid to listen to youngsters, to discuss topics with them and to stay constructive when receiving negative comments. Youngsters want to feel respected and valued in their opinion. Generation Y was raised by Baby Boomer parents, who gave birth at an older age (average age of having first child was 30). This resulted in a more mature and democratic way of taking up the role of educator, coach or teacher. As a result, Generation Yers seem to value authenticity in many more aspects of life than just in the products they buy. They would be unwilling to take a pill that would enhance their traits but at the same time fundamentally change who they are. Sometimes Gen Yers might even prefer an inferior but authentic product to another that is superior but not authentic.[54]

In September 2012 Nokia announced a new flagship phone, the Lumia 920, with a camera technology called Pure View. That innovation is supposed to allow users to shoot better pictures at night and record stabilized video thanks to the Optical Image Stabilization (OIS) function. The ad launching the new phone was showing a boy and a girl bicycling together. In the commercial it appears that the man is capturing the girl on video using his Lumia 920. On the same day, technology news site *The Verge* found out that at least some portions of the video were not shot with the Lumia 920. At a certain point in the video the couple is passing by a trailer with a window and in the reflection of the window you can see a van with a big camera that is certainly not the advertised phone. Nokia promptly reacted by posting an apology on its official blog stating that the commercial wasn't shot with the Lumia 920 but only simulating what the phone would be able to deliver.[55] Almost at the same time a photographer posted a picture of the model that was used in the still images allegedly taken with the use of Pure View. In the picture, shot in downtown Helsinki, you can see the model in the same clothing but with a set-up of professional lighting, a tripod and a large camera lens. Again John Pope, Director of Communications at Nokia, had to admit that the pictures were not taken with the Lumia 920 and that the company regrets the errors made.[56] 'You can never block negative feedback from your consumers for instance on Facebook', says Francisco Bethencourt, VP Global Marketing Yildiz Holding, in an interview with us.

> People will notice if you try to hide and there is no way to hide in the hyperconnected world. Being authentic means being honest, recognizing and admitting your mistakes openly. The other piece of authenticity is sustainability in an ample way. It's not just about an environmental point of view but also a societal point of view. Companies like Apple and Nike will need to be much more active in addressing the issues with their vendors and child labour in

China for instance. They need to be more proactive in communicating what they are doing about it and showing how they have reversed the situation. Hiding and downplaying today is not a viable strategy anymore because with a mobile everything can be easily photographed or videotaped and put online in only a few seconds. And it will be viewed and shared by millions of people around the world.[57]

In 2015, Anheuser-Busch ran a campaign called '#UpForWhatever' to promote its Bud Light brand. The idea was to print various light-hearted messages on the beer cans, explaining various scenarios that make Bud Light 'the perfect beer for whatever happens'. For example, one of the 140 slogans read: 'The perfect beer for turning up the old air guitar'. Social media users noticed a scroll that seemed completely out of line, however: 'The perfect beer for removing "no" from your vocabulary for the night'. Shocked customers quickly drew parallels with sexual violence, and promptly dubbed Bud Light 'the date rape beer'. Anheuser-Busch could do only apologize, which they did by acknowledging that the ad had 'missed the mark'.[58]

In a less well handled case, the Indonesian sports apparel company Salvo Sports failed to properly apologize for a subpar attempt at humour. The washing instructions tag on the inside of soccer shirts produced by Salvo read: 'Washing instructions. Give this to your woman; IT'S HER JOB.' Tweets containing photographic proof of the 'instructions' went viral, and prompted Salvo to explain how they only wanted to make fun of men not being as good at doing laundry compared to women and did not intend to make fun of women at all, which in the end did not really manage to appease angered consumers. Trying to justify the message only seemed to make things worse, and has resulted in the news about the sexist label dominating Google when you look up the name of Salvo Sports.[59]

For youngsters it is quite difficult to recognize honesty in people when they do not really know them. When discussing honest people with them, they will refer to people in their close neighbourhood (parents, friends, teachers) because they have known them for a longer period and have experienced whether they are honest or not. Interestingly enough, lying is not a definite no-no for this generation. People can admit their mistakes, explain everything and win back their credibility. Bill Clinton and the Oval Room confession concerning his relationship with Monica Lewinsky is a good illustration of this. The Bill Clinton 'brand' actually became suddenly more like them: accessible, human, fragile, imperfect and thus forgivable.[60] 'Gen Y appreciates real human contact with real people behind the company or brand', says Christoph Fellinger, Talent Relationship Manager at Beiersdorf in an interview with us.

> We organize one-on-one contacts between trainees and young employees as well as senior management. We don't want them to prepare a fancy presentation, but stimulate them to just speak as a person, a manager and present his or her experiences. Don't try to sell Gen Yers stories that just aren't true, because they will outsmart you and you will lose their respect and loyalty. Your credibility as an employer will be gone forever not just with them, but with their entire network.[61]

Another aspect of realness and authenticity is being democratic and open, available for everybody, not just for elites. In InSites Consulting global youth community, we have asked 150 carefully selected urban recruits aged 18 to 29 and living in 15 cities around the world for the most authentic places in their neighbourhood. One participant in Rio de Janeiro compared Copacabana beach with Ipanema beach. The first is world-famous and featured in many songs and movies portrayed as 'the perfect beach'. But the latter, located just around the corner, is definitely more real. It gathers people from all social classes, all sexual orientations and everywhere around the world.[62]

Brand honesty

The same conclusion can be made with relation to the honesty and inclusiveness of brands. 'I believe integrity is a very big success factor of cool brands today', says Christoph Krick, Head of Marketing at Crumpler (an Australian bag company) when interviewed by us. 'Gen Y doesn't just believe in marketing and mass media anymore. Brands should act like persons. You can judge people on their integrity and this is exactly how brands are judged by the new consumer generation.'[63]

It is quite difficult for a brand to claim honesty with youngsters today. Although they want to believe that some brands are honest, they feel they are never really sure. Being 'honest' as a brand means that you are worth the youngsters' money, and you never disappoint them. This reliability is detected by 'trial and error' choice strategies. In 2001 Heinz ketchup released a limited edition of numbered bottles called 'first harvest'. 'We realized that we needed to keep everything clear and transparent. A claim like 'first harvest' will only stick when you make it real by showing how it is made from the planting of the seeds to the arrival of the bottles in the shop', says Mariken Kimmels, Marketing Director Heinz Continental Europe in an interview with us.[64]

Apart from reliability, brand honesty also means staying true to your own identity. Supreme opened its first shop in 1994 on Lafayette Street in downtown Manhattan. It quickly became one of the iconic brands and shops for the New York skate scene. It grew from a number of creative skaters and artists and managed to keep that authenticity in its 19 years of existence. Although the skate brand has other shops in Los Angeles and four Japanese cities, today it is still high on the wish list of skaters. Literally hundreds of brand enthusiasts are queuing outside the Manhattan shop to get the latest cool arrivals on a typical Saturday. It is the typical youth market paradox of focusing on the authentic core businesses on one hand while also being innovative enough to stay interesting, thrilling, not boring and relevant to this fickle generation of 'stimulus junkies' on the other. Strong brands should balance their actions, reinterpreting their symbolic brand stories in response to changing tastes.[65] Considering this paradox, line extensions are often more credible than brand extensions. McDonald's can easily start serving breakfast, salads or ice cream but mobile phone cards would be too far-fetched.

In the older age group, the 18- to 29-year-olds and specifically above the age of 25, honesty is closely linked to Corporate Social Responsibility (CSR) programmes of companies and their position towards child labour, animal testing, ecology (carbon footprint) and charity. 'CSR became more important because Gen Y is smarter and will carefully spend and invest their money in a way that it actually reflects their value system', says Hubert Grealish, Global Head of Brand Communications at Diageo, interviewed by us. 'They will challenge companies to use their money in a conscious and social way.'[66] In March 2009, InSites Consulting organized online group discussions in 12 time zones across the world. The discussions focused on CSR programmes. More than 80 consumers in 63 countries took part. As a result, we defined the critical success factors of CSR programmes:

- Recognizable: Gen Y feels involved and recognizes situations covered in the CSR programme.
- Close: local programmes and actions have more chance of success.
- Credible: use and maximize your own sector's competence and expertise, do what you're good at. For example, Philips has the 'simple switch' green programme reducing the environmental impact of their products by energy-saving developments, clearly part of the brand's expertise.
- Transparency: youngsters should understand what the CSR programme is about and understand how it works.

In Hungary, you can donate 1 per cent of your tax to any charity organization. When WWF in Hungary wanted to collect donations for its green cause, they felt they couldn't just print promotional leaflets since that would imply an ecological footprint not in line with their own goals. So, instead, they made the greenest leaflet campaign ever. Only one copy of the leaflet was printed with the message: 'help to save the forests'. They asked volunteers to dress up as a panda (the mascot of the WWF) and go to a big mall. One of them took up position at the bottom of an escalator in the mall and gave the one leaflet to someone going one floor up. The other volunteer was waiting at the top of the escalator to collect the leaflet again and distribute it back to someone going one floor down. In this way, the one printed leaflet went from hand to hand and together with the YouTube views of the video demonstrating this case, no fewer than 285,142 people were reached.[67]

Corporate honesty

Youth link an honest brand to certain people working or representing that company or brand; for instance, celebrity CEOs Steve Jobs, Richard Branson, Ben Cohen and Jerry Greenfield.

For multinationals like Coca-Cola or Nike it is much more difficult to be honest, according to youngsters. The reasoning behind this is that multinationals employ more people, and the more people involved with businesses, the bigger the chance that someone within the organization could do something dishonest and ruin the company's image. In this digital age where consumers have more power using social networks, blogs or discussion boards to discuss brands, advertising or customer experiences, they have all the tools at their disposal to detect what is real, honest and true. This new reality of transparency has put an even higher premium on authenticity, making it an important driver of brand credibility.[68] This does not automatically imply that a company or brand that gets negative comments on the internet is immediately perceived as inauthentic since 'authenticity' is a combination of several dimensions and 'honesty' is just one of them. In general, the favourite brands of this generation of youngsters need to be more human, more honest and more real than brands used to be. Especially in image-oriented product categories such as clothing, fashion and jeans, a brand should be like a real friend to youngsters.

The more your products concentrate on honesty as a core brand value, the more media will be closely watching your moves. Innocent Smoothies was accused of misleading claims about its environmental credentials in the summer of 2008. *The Daily Telegraph* revealed that although the Innocent website stated that their fruit always travels by boat or rail to reduce the use of fossil fuel, the drinks are blended in Rotterdam and then transported by trucks across Europe before they are bottled in the UK. Founder Richard Reed had to admit that the website had not been updated on the new production situation. 'We are attempting to get the best quality drinks to our customers while generating the least amount of carbon', Reed commented to the *Telegraph*. 'Rotterdam is the port which all the fruit comes into, so it makes sense to blend our drinks there. It had been our policy not to talk about where our drinks are made for commercial reasons but we now seek to tell our customers everything about the drinks and be completely open with them.'[69] Innocent Drinks tries balancing ethics and business. Its products are sold in 11 countries. The company sources fruit from ethically-aware farms, uses 100 per cent recyclable bottles and donates 10 per cent of its profits to charity. The Innocent Foundation gives grants to NGOs and other charities through three-year partnerships. The company has faced some other criticisms in its past.[70] In 2007 a deal with McDonald's inserting Innocent drinks into kids' Happy Meals was heavily criticized. More recently, the sales of a small stake of the company to Coca-Cola in spring 2009 led to a tsunami of unhappy website and social networking messages.[71]

Chipotle Mexican Grill: cultivating fast food with integrity

Specializing in Mexican fast food such as burritos and tacos, Chipotle Mexican Grill has grown from one restaurant in 1993 to 1,700 spread across the USA, Canada, the UK, Germany and France in 2015. In 2014 alone they managed to add 192 new locations to its roster. The key reason for this staggering success? An integer mission statement that resonates with Generation Y. Chipotle strives to create a 'sustainable, healthful and equitable food future'. Its 'Food With Integrity' statement declares a commitment to the use of ingredients from small local farms rather than factories, the use of non-GMO (genetically modified) ingredients and making sure animals are not being treated with hormones and are able to roam freely.[72]

Chipotle's integrity and authenticity are crucial parts of the brand strategy, and the brand is not afraid to act upon it, even if this means running against its own business. In January 2015, Chipotle temporarily stopped selling carnitas burritos at more than 500 of its restaurants because a primary pork supplier did not meet its strict guidelines regarding animal welfare. This supplier was pulled immediately, eventually resulting in a shortage of pork while a replacement was being sought. Signs had to be put up in stores around the USA to explain the reason why carnitas was not in stock. Even though some customers took to the social media pages to voice disappointment at their favourite food not being available, most of them respected the decision because it aligned with Chipotle's clear-cut mission.[73]

Chipotle has seemingly raised the bar in the fast food industry, as described on their own website: 'Using high-quality raw ingredients, classic cooking techniques, and distinctive interior design, we brought features from the realm of fine dining to the world of quick-service restaurants'. The results are clear: in a 2014 survey, almost 50 per cent of US Generation Yers declared Chipotle as their favourite fast food restaurant. Gen Y youngsters appreciate the new 'fast-casual' restaurants with fresh, healthy and customizable food. Because of the strict rules and guidelines that Chipotle's suppliers have to live by, costs tend to rise higher than in any other fast food chain. This means that price increases are put through quite often, yet this does not seem to stop Chipotle from continuously gaining popularity with youngsters. Because the brand always explains why they raise prices or take something off the menu, Gen Y customers remain loyal due to the consistency in decision-making. Everything consistently fits in the 'Food With Integrity' stance. [74]

This is equally true for the various 'Chipotle Cultivate' campaigns that it has used to cut through the noise. In 2013 'The Scarecrow' won a Grand Prix in PR at the annual Cannes Lions advertising awards.[75] The campaign consisted of a three-minute movie and an app-based game. The central figure in the campaign is a scarecrow who lives in a world ruled by a massive corporation that produces '100 per cent beef-ish' food by injecting chickens with hormones and machine-milking confined cows. In the video, The Scarecrow eventually strives to bring fresh food back to the world and starts selling with the Chipotle-tagline 'Cultivate A Better World'. Overlaying this was a sombre cover of the song 'Pure Imagination' from the 1971 movie *Willie Wonka and The Chocolate Factory*. Players of the free companion app could take control of The Scarecrow and try to free confined animals and produce healthy food. Additionally, players also automatically qualified for a special two-for-one promotion in their Chipotle restaurant of choice. The campaign video gathered over 5 million views in the first week, running up to a total of 14 million after a year. In the iTunes store, almost 2,000 players gave the companion app an average 4-star rating. Both these campaigns were also strongly connected to the 'Chipotle Cultivate Foundation', a non-profit organization committed to creating a more sustainable future. Since its inception in 2011, this brand-related foundation has already contributed more than $2.5 million to various other organizations that strive towards a better world through food. The same year, Chipotle also launched an annual series of free music concerts and cooking demonstrations throughout the US under the line 'Cultivate Festival – food, music and ideas'.[76]

Another example of Chipotle-branded 'Cultivate' content appeared in 2014 when they collaborated with streaming service Hulu to launch a four-part television series called 'Farmed and Dangerous'. This comedy starred Ray Wise (*Twin Peaks*, *Mad Men*) and revolved around Animoil, a fictional company trying to increase cattle production by directly feeding 'petroleum pellets' to cows. The goal they wanted to achieve was to make viewers think about the way food is farmed, while the Chipotle brand itself deliberately played no role in the story whatsoever. According to the Mexican grill restaurant, the show at one point attained the spot of second-highest rated show on Hulu.[77]

In-store marketing regularly gets the 'Cultivate' treatment as well. Carry-out bags and drink cups cite various authors and poets, often talking about a 'better world'. For instance, a line contributed by writer George Saunders read: 'Hope that, in future, all is well, everyone eats free, no one must work, all just sit around feeling love for one another'. Furthermore, in 2015 they invited students aged 13–18 to write an original story about 'a time when food created a memory'. Ten winners saw their story published on cups and bags, and also received $20,000 to help them get to college. [78]

In an interview with Fortune, CEO Steve Heller said: 'Millennials are more concerned with how food is raised and prepared than previous generations, and they are willing to seek out and pay a little more for something they recognize as better.'[79] Chipotle takes that mission very seriously, and this pays off with a Gen Y consumer that loves authentic and honest brands. Once you become a Chipotle customer, you know that the brand will continue to walk the walk, making this a great example of how you can get Generation Yers to become loyal brand supporters.

Arwa's #PriceofWater campaign

Since 2011, Syria has been embroiled in constant conflict, causing refugees to flee to neighbouring countries like Lebanon and Egypt. One of the biggest problems in refugee camps is the lack of clean water. The Coca-Cola-owned Middle Eastern bottled water brand Arwa strived to help in this crisis. They first launched a touching campaign video to make people think about what clean water can mean to human life, reaching a view count of over 1.5 million. Then, they turned to action. Customers in-store were invited to pay absolutely nothing for water, and price tags were consequently re-printed to read 'priceless'. Instead, they could donate whatever amount they wanted to charity. Additionally, Arwa created a 'Twitter Tap'. For every (re-)tweet of a specifically sent out tweet, Arwa promised to donate money in a mission to cleanse Syrian refugee camps from contaminated water. Followers could track the success thanks to the use of a 'dynamic header', which showed water being cleansed in real-time as retweets and replies flooded in. This action eventually resulted in almost 10,000 retweets and replies, enabling the brand to donate over 200,000 litres of water to refugees and the installation of two permanent water filtration systems. [80]

Conclusion

In the experience economy, the authenticity of brands becomes more important. Not only because its uniqueness helps them to differentiate from the many alternatives but also because consumers value 'reality' in a world flooded with imitations and staged experiences. To the new Generation Y consumers the old interpretation of authenticity (origin, history and heritage) is less appealing and less relevant. Often they are not aware of these brand claims and it is not the most enticing strategy to win their hearts. The concept of 'perceived authenticity' seems to be quite interesting for advertisers. Considering the limited time frame and brand context of youngsters as well as their consumer cynicism, subtle cues suggesting authenticity (for instance in advertising or packaging) will often connect much better with them than stressing the old authenticity claims through mass advertising or labels of origin. The latter will evoke doubts of their truthfulness, while the former support an image of reliability and credibility. The modern interpretation of authenticity: being honest to yourself (the brand DNA), to youngsters (transparency) and to society (CSR) relates better to the current consumer climate as well as to specific Generation Yers' expectations fed by their education.

Being honest as a brand (or 'authenticity new-style', if you want) truly differentiates your brand from its competitors. In this digital age, honesty, as opposed to the old definition of authenticity, cannot be faked and is therefore of much bigger value to the young generation.[81] In the next chapter, we will discuss creating unique brand assets.

Generation Y consumers make purchase choices based on how well they reflect their own self-image – who they are and who they aspire to be. For instance, for many Apple lovers the brand reflects a sense of creativity and design-led innovativeness that equals their own desired personality. This will affect the degree to which they see brands as authentic. We will address this topic in the sixth chapter.

HOT TAKEWAYS FOR COOL BRAND BUILDERS

- The second step in keeping your cool brand hot is keeping it real.

- Brand authenticity drives Gen Y's choice.

- Don't underestimate the power of face-to-face personal contact with Gen Y.

- Brand origin, history and heritage are often not relevant or even not credible for the critical youth.

- This classic interpretation of authenticity should never be shouted (no mass media) but only be whispered and even better: be experienced.

- Authenticity is all about staying true to yourself; not imitating, not faking.

- Keep your brand's vision central but reinterpret the meaning of your brand following changes in tastes, interests or values.

- Honesty means more for a brand than CSR programmes or 'not lying'; it's about being respectful to youth and youth's life, about listening and discussing with them on the same level, and about sticking to your own ideas.

- Real brands are transparent, open and human: like a friend.

We all want unique brands

When we say 'Moonwalk', what do you think of?

Perhaps the Apollo 11 will immediately flash through your mind, or Neil Armstrong or even the Grand Marnier cocktail that Joe Gilmore invented to celebrate the event. But there's a good chance that most of you will rather think of Michael Jackson. Ever since Jackson performed the popping dance technique during the *Motown 25* TV special in 1983, it became his signature move for his song *Billie Jean*. Michael Jackson's 1988 autobiography was titled *Moonwalk* and he starred in the movie *Moonwalker*. Michael claimed the dance move and made it popular around the world, but he certainly did not invent the 'moonwalk'. He was inspired by David Bowie's strange moves after attending Bowie's Los Angeles show during the 1974 Diamond Dogs Tour. Bowie had studied mime under Etienne Decroux, Marcel Marceau's teacher. The latter, one of the most famous French mime artists, had been using the 'backslide' (later called 'moonwalk') throughout his career from the 1940s to the 1980s. In his famous 'Walking Against the Wind' routine, Marceau pretended to be pushed backwards by the wind.[1] In spite of all these predecessors, most people deem the moonwalk to be Michael's uniquely distinctive move.

How unique is your unique selling proposition?

The 'USP', or 'unique selling proposition' must be one of the oldest core marketing principles. Rosser Reeves, a very successful US advertising executive and chairman of the Ted Bates agency, is the father of the concept and coined 'USP' in his 1961 book *Reality in Advertising*. His three principles were:

- each advertisement must make a benefit proposition to the consumer;
- the proposition must be a unique one that the competition either cannot, or does not, offer;
- the proposition must be so strong that it can move the mass millions.[2]

Reeves' views led to dozens of strong slogans, many of which, like M&M's 'melt in your mouth, not in your hand' are still known today. But already in the 1960s, the claim-based differentiation strategy became obsolete when consumers got more marketing-savvy and were saturated with ad claims. The more creative and image-based campaigns proved to be more successful and Reeves retired. Today, the critical youth generation is not so easily wowed with image-driven campaigns either.

Perception of uniqueness

Michael Jackson's moonwalk illustrates that there's much wisdom in the words of Ecclesiastes in the Old Testament:

> The thing that hath been, it is that which shall be; and that which is done is that which shall be done: and there is no new thing under the Sun.
>
> Ecclesiastes 1: 9–10[3]

'Good products get copied very fast', says Wim Verbeurgt, Marketing Manager MINI in an interview with us. 'Personalization of the car – for instance the roof, mirror caps, or interior – was typical for MINI and was new when MINI launched it, but in the meantime several competitors offer it. We do try to communicate differently. We talk the language of the people who, although they may have a certain age, remain rock'n'roll in their heads.'[4]

We do believe however that even in connecting with the extremely marketing-wise Generation Y, a brand's unique positioning is still one of the drivers of choice. But brand image definitely lies in the eye of the beholder. In other words, it is youth's perception of a brand's uniqueness that is more important than reality. For Gen Yers, and for most of us, moonwalk equals Michael Jackson. The extent to which Gen Y perceives your brand as unique therefore matters. After all, a brand's main function is to express its difference from its competitors. Due to the overload of choice that Generation Y is confronted with, it is more sceptical of new products than ever. More than 6 out of 10 think new products are not really different. In the chapter on brand coolness, we have stressed that in high frequency categories with more competition, youth brands need to build on coolness, novelty and uniqueness to create interest and preference. In our research for this book, the perceived uniqueness of a brand improved brand image and stimulated brand conversations or buzz among Gen Y. This word-of-mouth is crucial since a quarter of 16- to 24-year-olds will only buy a product if someone recommends it to them.[5]

The uniqueness of DIESEL

With the previous edition of this book we were invited to present it to the global staff of DIESEL in their beautiful headquarters in Breganze. Renzo Rosso, founder and CEO of DIESEL, and one of the most inspiring men we have ever met, took the time to have a chat with us. 'First of all, to stay cool you have to keep the attention of your audience', says Renzo Rosso.

I believe you need to do something different from the others. I spend so much time travelling the world to find new creative people, designers and select the best of them to bring in novelty and creativity in our company. This is important because these new guys and girls, they are virgins, not contaminated by business or by any previous experiences or relations. They fuel our brand and company with their fresh views and creativity. I mean, we know the industry from our side. Our job is to adapt the creative concepts to the market, to industrialize their talent. But the first way to be cool and stay hot is to have a nice and differing product. Today you cannot build a brand just by marketing. You need a great product and adapt all the marketing to the core strengths of the product, not the other way around. Secondly, I think to stay cool, you have to live the values of your company and brand. We never buy market research figures and facts. We don't want to run our business like that. Of course we do a lot of research: we travel a lot, visit the stores, cities, watch how young people are wearing their clothes in the street, in bars, in discos. When you watch people continuously, you learn a lot.

Another success factor, according to the founder of DIESEL is to work in creative teams. 'It wouldn't work if I ran DIESEL as a dictator', explains Rosso.

In a team you make less mistakes and it enables us to have more fresh ideas. I also want our employees to be the first consumers of what we are producing. Of course, you cannot force people to wear DIESEL clothes all the time, but we [encourage] them by giving good discounts on our clothes. If you are actually wearing the clothes you are selling, you experience the product, you feel when a certain pocket is perhaps too long or the fit is not like it should be. At DIESEL we are specialized in finding new treatments, new little details in design and production. I think that is one of our core unique strengths in the industry.

The DNA of the DIESEL brand is the way in which the clothes are created, with so much effort and a meticulous eye for detail. 'I don't think other companies have it to the same extent', says Renzo Rosso.

We want to go in new materials, new designs, new details and new seasonal themes again and again. And that's exactly why you continuously need to find new fresh blood, new creative designer teams who feel the spirit of the company and the passion for details. To me that's the core success factor of the DIESEL company. I like it very much when everyone is fond of the DIESEL brand: from the poor to the richest ones. That's fantastic. Sometimes when I'm jogging, parents stop me and say: hey Mr Rosso, I hate you, you know, because my son only wants your jeans and here in Brazil it costs me one month's salary to buy a pair of DIESEL jeans. But what can I say; to create our products with this amount of research and design and detail, we cannot sell it cheaper. But it's great to see how many young people are still in love with our brand. All around the world people admire me because to them I represent a simple guy, born in a farm in Italy who created a successful company.

In one of the articles we have read, Renzo Rosso stated that young people are more into old things than into novelties. 'When I said that, I was actually talking about myself', laughs the founder of DIESEL. 'I prefer an old house to a new one, because it has a soul, a certain smell of wood perhaps. A new house: that's purely cement. I think our clothing is prettier because it looks vintage even if it is a new fabric. We treat it so that it becomes more alive. This is also DIESEL's core philosophy: to bring this kind of product to the market.' DIESEL's DNA is to do something different from the others. And it's about innovation and freshness. 'We are a group of people that try to do something six months or a year before the others', says Rosso. 'We want to stay fresh and modern. It's an attitude.'[6]

Brands that present themselves in a sustainable, unique way will reinforce their value propositions. A brand's perceived uniqueness is mainly the result of executing a consistent positioning strategy. For Gen Y consumers, it is only when a brand begins to merge with their own identity and becomes self-expressive, that they will feel a bond with the brand. In Chapter 6, we will dive into the topics of self-image and brand identification.

In this chapter, we will highlight several views on how a brand can differentiate itself from competitors. We will explain the concepts of brand DNA, battlefield analysis and brand distinctive assets or memes. A number of recent Gen Y case stories illustrate how a youth brand can build on uniqueness.

Brand DNA

Suppose we asserted that the iPod design (with its frontal round selection wheel and several distinctive colours such as black, white, red, olive green and pearlescent blue) is a copycat of a transistor radio invented by Dr Heinz De Koster, a Dutch PhD of physics, back in 1954. Would you believe us? Perhaps, after reading the chapter intro and Jackson's moonwalk story, you would. The point is, when we ask the same question in our discussion groups with Gen Yers, they think we are out of our mind. Nevertheless, it is a fact that the Regency TR-1 was the first commercial transistor radio sold in the United States, for $49.95, and it looked pretty much like the iPod. It was even launched using a punchy slogan: 'See it! Hear it! Get it!' in November 1954 by a company based in Indianapolis named I.D.E.A.[7] So, the idea of the iPod design suspiciously descends from a 1950s' transistor radio. Actually, Sony developed the iPod's long-life battery and Toshiba perfected the hard drive...[8] The fact that the iPod is from Apple Inc and is so embedded in the daily life of youngsters makes it an unbelievable story to them. Although Apple's slogan 'Think Different' hasn't been used for a few years, it is still part of the brand's deoxyribonucleic acid.

Every living organism owns unique deoxyribonucleic acid ('DNA' to friends) molecules that contain the genetic instructions of how the organism should develop and function. DNA is the basis of our own unique identity. Similarly, a brand's DNA is the unique identity that defines a brand's functioning. Apple's DNA for Generation Y includes: convenient, easy-to-use and innovative products, with an aesthetic, distinctive design for creative young people. If you look at Apple's last decade backtrack: the iPod with iTunes, Apple TV, the iPhone with the Appstore and lately the iPad tablet computer and the Apple watch... it's no wonder that youngsters believe that the brand is different – that Apple is unique. And it's not only youth of course. The company has so many brand devotees and advocates that *Fortune* magazine selected Apple as the world's most admired company in 2015, for the eighth year in a row. In the summer of 2010, Apple devotees created Cupidtino. com, a dating site exclusively for diehard fans of Apple products. The site's name is referring to Cupertino, a suburban city in California and home to the global headquarters of Apple, Inc.

Yet, Apple's design genius Jonathan Ive is heavily influenced by designs from the 1950s and 1960s. Apart from the Regency radio, bloggers found a striking resemblance between Ive's designs for Apple and the work of Dieter Rams, the German designer of Braun. Many of these designs are exhibited in New York's Museum of Modern Art.[9] Just as our own genes are partly copies of our creators, a brand's DNA can be based on earlier work. Apple definitely understood that the honest, simple and aesthetic designs of the 1960s would very much appeal to today's young consumer generation. By investing in innovative products and staying true to its own DNA in every detail, including packaging and retail interiors, Apple succeeded in claiming a unique positioning. As Alex Bogusky and John Winsor of Crispin Porter & Bogusky advise in *Baked In*, differences have to look different. The Apple iPod didn't just have a different colour from black, but it boasted the opposite of every other MP3 player cord and earbud.[10] In an interview with *London Evening Standard* Jony Ive said:

> Our goals are very simple: to design and make better products. If we can't make something that is better, we won't do it. Most of our competitors are interested in doing something different, or want to appear new – I think those are completely the wrong goals. A product has to be genuinely better. This requires real discipline, and that's what drives us – a sincere, genuine appetite to do something that is better. Committees just don't work, and it's not about price, schedule or a bizarre marketing goal to appear different – they are corporate goals with scant regard for people who use the product.[11]

In *The Narcissism Epidemic*, Dr Twenge linked the increased importance of product design to our image-obsessed culture. According to her, today's desire for physical beauty springs from self-admiration. This pursuit of beauty, illustrated for instance in the teeth-whitening trend in toothpaste, is a way to seek status and attention from others.[12] In a recent survey carried out by InSites Consulting in 16 countries, about 9 out of 10 girls aged 15 to 25 would like to change something about their body. A substantial number (23 per cent) of girls would consider plastic surgery.[13]

Volvo diverges from its DNA

It isn't always easy to stay close to your own brand DNA though. And sometimes, it isn't wise to implement it rigidly. If we say Volvo, what kinds of association come to your mind? We're pretty sure you will first think of safety. It's the core of Volvo's DNA. Now, if you want to target Generation Yers, who are currently buying more than a quarter of all new cars, and by 2020 will account for almost half of them, stressing safety is probably not the most enticing strategy.[14]

In 2004, the brand shifted away from its conservative image for the first time to promote the S40 model. Performance and excitement were the desired different associations in positioning towards youth. One of the TV commercials was executed in video game style using the S40 in Xbox's *RalliSport Challenge* setting. The other one used a music video style featuring rap celebrity LL Cool J. The S40 was also promoted in retail environments other than the traditional car dealers, such as Virgin Megastores and Bloomingdales. Volvo created an online mock-documentary, 'The Mystery of Dalaro' in which 32 people from the small Swedish town Dalaro mysteriously buy the S40 on the same day. The online movie attained 1 million visits to the website in Europe and in a few months' time the brand experienced a 105 per cent sales increase for the S40 segment.

Although the video game setting was criticized for ruining both the safety and responsibility image, Volvo attempted to stay close to its DNA by ending every commercial with the tagline, 'it's still built like a Volvo'.[15] When Volvo introduced its C30 model in the United Kingdom at the end of 2008, the creative design of the model was the core aspect of the youth positioning. Volvo initiated an online contest, 'creative30', looking for young creative talent in Britain. More than 30,000 participants signed in to compete for the people's and expert panel's prizes.

In 2015 Volvo created LifePaint to affirm their safety positioning. Cyclists can spray this paint on their clothes, shoes, bags and other things without damaging it. The fabric starts glowing in the dark in combination with the light of headlights. Volvo created this product to improve the visibility of cyclists at night. This way the brand went beyond the car industry to prove their commitment to road safety. Albedo100 and Grey London helped designing the paint. In six cycling shops in London and Kent you could get the product for free and if the LifePaint is a success, Volvo will launch it internationally.[16]

It wasn't the first time Volvo looked beyond the traditional paths of the automotive industry to keep the brand up-to-date. Today consumers, especially youngsters, have a new definition for on-demand: as soon as and also whenever required. Jonas Ronnkvist, the director of business development and strategy from Volvo car group, created several 'smart car ideas'. Volvo Roam, a delivery service to your car, is one of them. The service can unlock the Volvo and drop the package in the car. The brand has a global control over their key infrastructure and are working with engineers to reprogram the keys. 50 different keys will work for one car and the duration is adaptable. Volvo can also see where the car is parked by using a GPS function. Teradata is one of the key tech partners that analyses and tracks all the data. In this manner Volvo will offer an exceptional customer experience to their clients. The consumers don't need to be at home to receive their package or don't need to go to the post office. With this launch, Volvo will introduce the on-demand economy in the automotive industry. Volvo revealed that 92% of the participants said they found the Roam program more convenient than receiving their package at home.[17]

Tomorrowland's incredible growth

Tomorrowland is a huge outdoor dance event organized by ID&T in a park in Belgium since 2005. In 2012 it was elected as the 'best international dance music festival in the world', and it continued to win this for 3 years in a row, rising above festivals such as Ultra Music Festival Miami and Coachella. For the 10th edition in 2014, the festival expanded to 2 consecutive weekends to make sure as many dance music lovers as possible could experience the 'magic' of Tomorrowland. In total almost 400,000 visitors from 220 countries managed to score tickets for an event that was sold out within the hour, despite the additional second weekend. About 16.8 million not-so-lucky dance fans watched an official livestream on YouTube to still be able to enjoy almost 400 DJ-sets from acts like Tiësto, David Guetta, Hardwell, Carl Cox or Eric Prydz. The festival is not only known for its great DJ line-up but also for the most amazing fairy-tale decors.[18] The continuous beats and fabulous park environment create a unique atmosphere that is loved by youth from over 200 nationalities. The dancing crowd spends three days of harmony, friendship and happiness together in a fantasy world of fountains, ponds, fireworks, lightshows and helicopters dispersing flower petals above their heads. 'We try to bring something refreshing and new every year', says Koen Lemmens, Marketing Manager ID&T in an interview with us.

> We want to surprise our audience with the line-up, the design of the stages, the location (a park with a hill and a valley and ponds), the packaging and the food. We work on exceeding the expectations. We create an atmosphere of fantasy, a separate imaginative world. Everything must be part of that experience: from high quality food (Michelin-starred chefs, fresh vegetables and good meat even at the burger booth), to comfortable entrances, showers and luxury chalets for overnight stay. Some of them even have a jacuzzi, sauna and butler service.
>
> This youth generation is demanding. They want to be treated in an extraordinary way but are also prepared to pay for it. We build an experience that is comparable to the good feeling after a long holiday with memories to cherish for life and the ability to get in touch with people and start a relationship. It's more than just people watching a good show and then leaving again, we want to bring them a creative and sexy unique experience.
>
> The after-movies on YouTube have become special events all on their own. The 30-minute compilation for 2014 had almost 40 million views less than 10 months after the event, while the ones for 2013 and 2012 attracted more than 100 million views on the site. When the product is good, people want to be part of it, share movies and pictures on YouTube and Facebook and start the campaign for you. And we have of course DJs from all around the world that have their own blogs or webpages and fans. They are the ambassadors of our event too. We try to surprise our visitors. For instance the people flying in from Barcelona experienced a party flight with DJs and dancers. You know after such an unexpected event that they will talk about that to their friends.[19]

The popularity of this massive event has even inspired political and humanitarian organizations to cite the festival as an example. United Nations

Secretary-General Ban Ki-moon visited the festival grounds to praise the unity it creates between a widely differing range of cultures. To symbolize this he encarved a message in the 'OneWorld Bridge', a permanent structure that was built in the park to celebrate the 10th edition and contains thousands of messages of visitors. The message read: 'Let's work as one towards dignity for all.'[20]

ID&T added two more festivals apart from the Belgian edition: TomorrowWorld in Atlanta, USA and Tomorrowland Brazil in São Paulo. For 2015, dance music fans in Mexico and India had the chance to attend 'live events' in Mexico City and Mumbai respectively. Using a satellite link, a live video connection was made from Belgium to Mexico and India so that Mexican and Indian party people could 'live' Tomorrowland from an idyllic location in their own country. People present at the festival itself were also able to see their counterparts party together with them on the other sides of the world. Unsurprisingly, the campaign title for these events fitted perfectly in the Tomorrowland idea: 'UNITE'. [21]

Love is a battlefield: identifying market drivers

How do you claim a certain identity in a market full of competitors? Of course, your brand's strengths, and the way you succeed in endorsing your competitive edge through product innovations or smart marketing will make the difference. However, competitors will often use the same kind of brand associations and meanings if they seem to be the most salient in a certain market.

Let's take the example of the denim category again. In Figure 5.1, you will see a 'battlefield analysis' of two brands: Levi's and DIESEL. On the horizontal axis, we have plotted the number of times that Gen Yers who prefer Levi's for their next purchase have attributed certain brand image items to the Levi's brand. On the vertical axis, we did the same for the DIESEL brand (items linked to DIESEL by DIESEL-lovers). This technique allows us to map the real battlefields in the jeans market. To be preferred, a jeans brand should be well known, respected and associated with cool people. Both DIESEL and Levi's are competing with each other on these image items. If you were to look at the results for G-Star Raw or Replay, you would notice that the same items form the real battlefield. The upper left zone of the mapping depicts those image items that are currently more associated with DIESEL than with Levi's. DIESEL is more progressive and radiates prestige. From Levi's point of view, these could be items they could try to focus on if they want to gain back market share from current DIESEL buyers. But Levi's shouldn't try to stretch its brand DNA too far because then the brand risks losing its credibility for the critical Generation Y. When you take a look at the lower right area, you can identify the unique Levi's brand image items. Levi's fascinating history is the most important one.

FIGURE 5.1   Battlefield Analysis for Levi's vs DIESEL

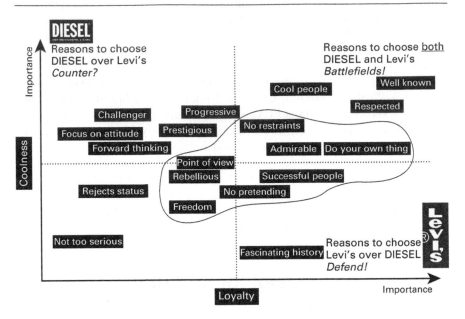

Nevertheless, in the previous chapter on brand authenticity we have learned that stressing the origin and history of a brand in advertising will have the wrong effect on this youth generation. Moreover, a regression analysis on Levi's brand coolness score revealed a negative effect of history on coolness. So, what could Levi's possibly do to cope with the DIESEL competition then? They could concentrate their marketing approach on those brand items that are both associated with Levi's and equally important to DIESEL buyers. Statements such as 'do your own thing', 'no restraints' and 'no pretending'. As illustrated in the previous chapter, this was exactly the main message in the 2008 'Live Unbuttoned' campaign for the Levi's 501.[22]

Choosing new battlefields for your brand

History has evidenced that David can take on Goliath. Think of brands such as Virgin, Apple or MINI. Sometimes, when the combat with your competitors is head on, it can be a good branding strategy to push yourself away from the battlefield by changing the environment you're working in. In the coolness chapter, we already gave a few examples of brands such as Nintendo Wii that have changed the category definition. EE, the biggest mobile network in The UK, struggled selling their pay-as-you-go subscriptions. The 16- to 30-year-olds signed up to competitors because EE didn't position itself as a pay-as-you-go provider. Although the brand offered 4G, their target group was concerned about how much data they would actually need. This young generation watches a lot of YouTube on their mobile phones so EE partnered up with YouTube celebrities Dan & Phil and Ali-A. The brand launched a Limited Edition Sim with unlimited data for two months. Customers could try out 4G, decide which data package suited them the best and could watch their favorite YouTubers for free. Together with EARN Media London and the influencers EE created the marketing such as the design of the SIM pack. The influencers also sent different personalized messages and rewards to their audience. By creating scarcity and implementing personality, EE appealed to Millennials. After the launch, EE gained more than 25,000 SIM requests. The videos on YouTube obtained more than 3 million views. After two months, the Limited Edition network engaged 60,000 subscribers.[23]

To support its positioning in the female sportswear market, Nike is motivating women during the development of their sport performances with the 2015 campaign #BetterForIt. Instead of encouraging trained athletes Nike also wanted to help challenging women who just started. The spot, designed with Wieden+Kennedy, involved different women who feel insecure when they go out doing sports. As an example, there was a woman in a spinning class having an insecure dialogue in her head because of the 'models' sitting in front of her. The tone of voice was more fun and light than other motivational Nike videos which appeal to the average athlete. With the hashtag #BetterForIt, women could post their sport experiences. Nike also launched a "90-day better for it challenge" that offered workouts from the Nike+ Running App and the Nike+ Training Club App. This campaign was the biggest initiative of Nike in motivating women's athletic progress. The female community is growing rapidly. The brand estimated to add 2 billion of extra sales by 2017 when they focus on its women's line.[24]

Brand mascots, somatic markers and memes

In an effort to reduce complexity, Gen Yers, like any consumer, group products together in a so-called 'consideration set'. Brand salience or uniqueness is the most important factor to be part of the consideration set. Through brand evaluation they choose between the brands evoked in their consideration set. Although brands within the consideration set are typically similar in terms of their product attributes, it will be the brand image that will ultimately create perceived differences between the competing brands. This brand image is, of course, more than the desired positioning of a brand. It is the collection of all brand associations held in consumer memory.[25]

Gen Y's brand choice is at least partially determined by representations of brands in its memory. According to associative network theories, these representations are never isolated in the brain but linked by connections that vary in strength. The stronger the association strength of brand representations, the more they will influence youth's purchase behaviour. Many kinds of brand or product association might be relevant to consumer behaviour of Gen Yers. Brand representations can be product attributes, such as the shape and colour of packaging or the brand logo, but also usage situations and occasions, previous first-hand brand experiences, word-of-mouth or even marketing campaigns. The most successful youth brands focus on constant innovation, heavy advertising and promotional support, quality and a visually distinctive identity.

Sometimes iconic brand identities arise by coincidence. In 1997, Larry Page and Sergey Brin decided to dump their search engine's working name 'BackRub' for something shorter and simpler. They eventually chose 'googol' (a math term for 10 to the 100th power) but misspelled the word while checking whether that internet domain was unregistered. Google.com was available and googol.com was not.[26] Google is now one of the world's best-known brand names, and its ever-changing homepage doodles to celebrate holidays, anniversaries and the lives of famous artists, pioneers and scientists keep the brand cool. This idea was born in 1998 when the two founders Larry and Sergey played with the logo to indicate their attendance at the Burning Man festival. They placed a stick figure after the second O, intended as a kind of comical 'out of office' message. Today a team of illustrators and engineers is responsible for enlivening the Google homepage and over 1,000 doodles have been created. The team receives hundreds of requests and ideas from users every day. In the summer of 2010 Google organized its first global 'Doodle4Google' contest asking youth aged 4–17 to send in their 'I love football' designs. The winning one was used on 11 July, the day of the World Cup Final. For Halloween 2011, the Doodle team carved their logo into gigantic pumpkins and produced a time-lapsed video.[27]

Logos that are distinctive often become memorable. Think of the Perrier, Kellogg or Carlsberg logos. A distinctive tone-of-voice reflected in every text or ad of, for instance, Innocent Drinks, Skittles or Ben & Jerry's, contributes to the perception of brand uniqueness as well. Other tactics include claiming a colour, such as Cadbury's purple or Heineken's green. Or memorable packaging shapes such as the Heinz ketchup bottle, Toblerone's pyramids, or the Absolut and Coca-Cola bottles.[28] In October 2012 Absolut Vodka launched a limited edition of 4 million uniquely designed and numbered colourful bottles. To produce the series of 'Absolut Unique' bottles, the company had to re-engineer its production process using splash guns and programmed algorithms combining 35 colours and 51 patterns in a unique non-repeated way. Each bottle in the shop is different from the others.[29]

A couple of years ago McDonald's replaced the red colour in its logo with green to express care for the environment. 'But, we are the only fast-food chain with a face, not just an M or logo like Subway, McDonald's or Burger King', says Michael Th. Werner, Chief Marketing Officer of KFC:

> The face in Kentucky Fried Chicken's logo is Colonel Harland Sanders, the founder of KFC. He was a cook and invented the 11 herbs and spices Original Recipe. Today we're still cooking like the Colonel did in his first restaurant. So we have a strong human history and USP that is more authentic than our competitors. We want to have a meaning in the lives of the young target group, not just sell products. It starts with the KFC philosophy. We're selling

convenient chicken products but you also get a smile, the friendly hospitality in a clean place – a restaurant experience. We serve ISP [in-store prepared] chicken, not heated-up frozen food like in many other fast food chains. We basically cook our fresh meat for 2.5 hours (including marinating in-store for 2 hours) so the product quality is better. And the food preparation and ingredients are natural not artificial. But KFC is all about having 'so good' moments in your life, so it's a higher value and meaning than just the product. To play a role in their lives you need to understand their passions like meeting friends, doing sports, listening to music and then you try and combine these passions with your offer. For instance our KFC bucket is a group offer meant to share the experience with your friends. Eating is more fun when you do it with at least one other person. And we call it the 'KFC friends bucket', we have the 'Facebook fans bucket' etc. So we position it as a lifestyle thing not just a lot of chicken for a bargain price.[30]

KFC brought back the past to honor its 75th anniversary and in an attempt to revitalize its image. The brand wanted to attract Millennials who appreciate vintage and did not see the famous ads of 20 years ago. Restaurants were redesigned, new items were added to the menu and a huge campaign was released with 'The Colonel' Harland Sanders. He is still present on the iconic buckets but disappeared in advertising for over 20 years. Three TV ads aired May 25 where he even used the brand's original name containing the word 'fried'. The old Colonel compared his world to the new world of the Millennials with a goofy undertone. On the website ColonelSanders.com fans could see Colonel's story in the interactive 'Hall of Colonels'. Visitors could also play a funny game called ColonelQuest where you play adventures loosely based on his life. One level, for instance, ordered the player to catch flying babies off a trampoline 'so the Colonel won't get sued for malpractice'.[31] He also took over KFC's Twitter account for an afternoon and posted a total of 18 tweets. The Colonel even managed to get into your car, as KFC partnered with the Google-linked traffic app 'Waze' and provided its GPS function with the voice of Colonel Sanders. The voice used various so-called 'Colonel-isms', such as "Pothole on the road ahead. I'd fill it with gravy."[32]

Brand mascots are powerful association builders too, like the puppy to advertise how soft Andrex toilet paper is or Bacardi's bat that originally symbolized good fortune and is now associated with nightlife. In his book *Buyology*, Martin Lindstrom calls these brain short-cuts 'somatic markers'. They serve to connect experiences or emotions with a reaction and help us to narrow down possibilities in a buying situation.[33] The strength of somatic markers is built by repetition and will only change slowly in time. This process, called evaluative conditioning – related to Pavlov's classical conditioning – allows our brain to link stimuli and form brand attitudes even if there's no causal or meaningful relationship between them. In other words, if Gen Yers repetitively noticed a brand at a cheerful youth happening, they would transfer the positive emotions to their attitude towards the brand.[34] The Canadian mobile telecom company Fido redesigned its flagship stores to appeal to Fido's Gen Y market. The shops display prominent pictures of people with their dogs throughout its interior to link the idea of warmth, trust and companionship to their brand. The somatic marker Fido wants to create is: 'a dog is a man's best friend, and it's always there for you, just like a mobile phone can be'.[35]

Mapping your brand's distinctive assets

Your unique competitive edge will mostly be larger than just your product or category. 'Our unique sales proposition is the entire "sexperience"', says Ilse Westerik, Senior Brand Manager Personal Care at Reckitt Benckiser.

> Durex creates products that give more pleasure and fun, like ultra-thin, ribbed or flavoured condoms, massage oil, or vibrators... We try to make protection pleasurable and remove the old taboo category of erotic attributes that used to be sold in sex shops more approachable by selling our products in normal selling points like grocery stores. Our products add value to the experience and we endorse that with apps like, for instance, the spice-dice app, a dice with sex positions for playful lovemaking. The app was in the top 10 most downloaded.[36]

To map what parts of your brand are truly unique for your consumers, brand distinctive asset research can help. The associative strength of brand representations is tested implicitly by giving respondents the online task to match visual stimuli with a target brand.[37] Let's illustrate this by a study we did in the energy drink category. We confronted 1,000 16- to 29-year-olds, all non-rejecters of the energy drink category, in five European countries (France, Spain, Sweden, Italy and Belgium) with three randomized blocks of 36 visuals. The set of visuals contained six stimuli for each energy drink brand involved in the test: Red Bull, Burn (of The Coca-Cola Company) and Rock Star (of PepsiCo). The six stimuli used were:

- a blinded can (picture of a can with brand name removed but logo kept);
- the main brand colours;
- the logo (without the brand name present);
- an advertisement;
- a picture of a brand event (sponsored or organized by the brand: Flugtag for Red Bull, a dance show in a nightclub for Burn, a mixed martial arts event for Rock Star);
- a generic activity (congruent with the brand values but not taken from the brand's website: skateboarders for both Red Bull and Rock Star, nightlife for Burn).

We first asked them to look at a set containing six blinded (unbranded) visuals of Red Bull, each shown three times throughout the randomized block, combined with 18 noise visuals of competing brands Burn and Rock Star. They then had merely 750 milliseconds to decide each time whether a displayed visual matched with Red Bull (hit space bar) or not (do nothing). The same exercise was then repeated for Burn and Rock Star.

FIGURE 5.2   Unique identifier index for three energy drinks

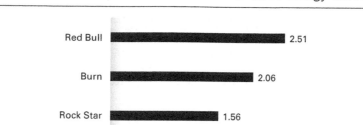

Red Bull   2.51

Burn   2.06

Rock Star   1.56

In the analysis, we first calculated a 'unique identifier' index, a score calculating the difference between hits (correct match) and false alarm rates (perceived yet incorrect match). Each of the 1,000 youngsters had a 'unique identifier' score for each of the three brands. As you can see in Figure 5.2 Red Bull came out as the clear winner – its 'unique identifier' index is significantly higher than either Burn or Rock Star. This means that Gen Yers made more correct associations and fewer mistakes in identifying all visuals in relation to Red Bull. This result is all about Red Bull's uniqueness since the youngsters had to discriminate between images of a target brand (eg Red Bull) and images from the competitor brands (eg Burn and Rock Star). The more the visuals are uniquely attributed to a brand, the more correct responses and the fewer mistakes, resulting in a higher 'unique identifier' score for that brand.

To test this method for implicit measurement of uniqueness, we also asked Gen Yers explicitly to what extent they agreed with the statement 'this is a unique brand' for each of the three energy drink brands. About 46 per cent of the 16- to 29-year-olds in the five countries found Red Bull unique, compared to 23 per cent for Burn and 12 per cent for Rock Star. This confirmed the implicit uniqueness findings.

It was even more interesting to dive into the specific visual results. In Table 5.1 you will find the average percentage of correct hits per person for each image. This reveals the brand representations that are most identifiable with a brand. As they were displayed in combination with competitor images, they are a clear indication for the strength of brand assets.

The most distinctive brand asset of Red Bull seems to be the colours of the packaging since this brand representation attains the biggest difference in hits with the two competitors. The cold colours of Red Bull, blue and silver, represent the intellect or mind, while the hot ones, red and gold, symbolize emotion and the body.[38] Burn and Rock Star are both using black as their dominant brand colour, which explains the brand confusion. Both Burn and Red Bull clearly have a very strong brand logo. The bull, part of the brand name, embodies strength, courage and stamina. The flame in Burn's logo is also perfectly visualizing the brand name as well as its energizing

TABLE 5.1   Percentage hits for specific brand assets

Brand asset	Red Bull	Burn	Rock Star
Can (packaging)	89%	82%	66%
Colours	54%	31%	26%
Logo	78%	82%	70%
Advertising	74%	71%	64%
Brand event	27%	39%	10%
Generic activity	14%	9%	8%

powers. For Burn the flame logo seems to be the most distinctive brand asset together with its own nightlife brand event.

From the figures in Table 5.1 we can also deduce that Red Bull should reconsider its advertising strategy. Not that it isn't recognized by most youngsters, but the difference from Burn is rather small. When we take a look at the average reaction time, which is another indicator of association strength between a brand and its assets, we learn that the average reaction time to the Red Bull advertising visual was 589 milliseconds compared to a lower 575 milliseconds for the Burn ad. The reason for this is clear. Burn makes use of the flames in its ads whereas Red Bull visualizes the sign-off slogan of the brand ('Red Bull gives you wings') but is not endorsing it with the red bulls of the logo, or its dominant packaging colours. From the analysis above, we could advise Red Bull to increase the use of its blue and silver colours in advertising, since that is currently their biggest distinctive brand asset. Although both Red Bull and Rock Star are endorsing skate events, the former is better at claiming the activity and associating the skate lifestyle with its brand in Gen Y's memory chunks.[39]

Trader Joe's unique grocery stores

Trader Joe's is a chain of specialty grocery stores founded by Joe Coulombe in 1967 in Southern California. Today it has over 365 stores in 25 states and is owned by a family trust set up by the late German Theo Albrecht, one of the two Aldi brothers. The chain is known for not following what their competitors do. Its specific product selection (only 4,000 items

Continued...

Trader Joe's unique grocery stores *Continued…*

from all regions around the world, of which 80 per cent are sold under its own label), store layout and graphics, and high shelves rotation are part of the store's uniqueness. Not to mention staff wearing Hawaiian shirts to stress the fun and adventure of shopping in their store. Employees create the point-of-sales signage explaining the non-branded product selection on the shelves in a non-conventional way. Trader Joe's has no coupons, membership cards or discounts. It has an everyday, low-price strategy. Many products are organic and environmentally friendly. Its limited assortment is expansive in cultural variety and attracting a growing multicultural audience in the United States. According to *Fortune* magazine the chain sells an estimated $1,750 per square foot, more than double the sales generated by Whole Foods Market. The latter is also attracting Millennials with its organic upscale premium-priced goods, diverse personnel and chalkboards featuring store employees' names and sketches. Whole Foods Market gives detailed and transparent information on where they got the food, how it was made and so on.[40] As organic and natural food are becoming more mainstream, Whole Foods wants to differentiate itself by opening new stores in 2016 that are more adapted to Millennials. The young consumers want fresh food and their financial force is growing but Whole Foods is too expensive for them. The complementary brand will create open stores with a modern design, innovative technology and lower prices. This way Whole Foods can appeal to a young audience by offering a high-tech experience at lower prices.[41]

A memetic approach to branding

In recent brand research, the brand representations and associations in our memory, or 'somatic markers', have been linked to 'memes'. Memes are the cultural equivalent of biological genes. Just like genes, they are replicators and jump from brain to brain. Everything we have learned from someone else, whether it's a story, fashions, ideas, tunes, a brand or a product is a meme. Our own brand associations are constantly infected by the associations of other people and we infect the memes of others. Memes can propagate themselves and are passed on by replication or imitation.[42] In the next chapter on self-identification, we will give some examples of youth subculture lifestyles and tribal behaviour that is also influenced by spreading memes.

But let's illustrate brand memetics with an example of Coca-Cola's Vitaminwater. Coke bought the brand in 2007, but in 2009 Vitaminwater's sales volume slipped 22 per cent as a consequence of recession. Price-conscious college students and Gen Y's young professionals traded down to tap water or sodas. To respond to this market situation, Vitaminwater used the memes 'nutrients' and replenishing fluids or 'hydration' in their campaigns. The TV commercial 'Epic Night', featured a young male getting knocked on the head with a hammer, while a voice-over asks, 'Have you ever woken up on the wrong side of the bed? Your brain's throbbing and your face is in a pile of nachos?... Vitaminwater's purple "Revive" has B vitamins and potassium that will help rehydrate after epic nights.' The use of these memes will increase the differentiation and uniqueness of Vitaminwater compared to tap water or sodas. The new metallic bottle label with a nutrient matrix, an enlarged box highlighting the vitamins and minerals inside Vitaminwater, will also have a memetic effect. Competitor Gatorade (a brand of PepsiCo) is using completely different memes that are not associated with hangover relief. They focus on 'athletic performance'.[43]

In Charles Darwin's description of evolution the process of 'natural selection' indicates that the fittest species will have the most progeny and become more prominent in future generations. The idea in memetic theories is that both genes and memes have a direct relation to brands and brand management. Memes that eventually dominate will be the ones that were reproduced the most, because they express traits that are 'the fittest' for the environment. Successful brands will ensure their existence through possessing winning memes. Brands that satisfy more customers will tend to increase their presence in a competitive market. Sometimes this requires product development and differentiation. To enhance further growth in China, Sprite's biggest market in the world, the brand launched Spritea. The tea-flavoured carbonated beverage is only sold in Asian markets where both Sprite and green tea are very popular drinks. Sprite is the leading carbonated soft drink brand in China, outselling even the Coke brand. The ready-to-drink tea consumption in China has increased by more than 30 per cent annually in recent years. To fit with this environment Sprite needed to adapt the green tea meme. To support the spreading of the meme, Spritea will be sampled across China, providing 15 million free drinks to domestic consumers. Jay Chou, a popular Taiwanese musician and actor stars in the new TV commercial for Spritea.[44]

Brands targeting Gen Yers often have to adapt to a changing environment, because youth's consumer behaviour is more affected by trends. In the denim market, for instance, the premium designer jeans trend changed the environment for the more democratic labels such as Levi's. Levi Strauss & Co has recently hired executives from competing designer labels such as Ralph Lauren and 7 For All Mankind to improve its fashion credibility. In 2009, the brand created a super-premium division called Levi's XX. It also offers a premium denim line with better fabrics and fit called Made & Crafted which is sold through upscale retail outlets such as Saks Fifth Avenue and Barneys New York. Another premium sub-brand is Levi's Vintage clothing, offering reproductions of the brand's historical archives. Although the expensive jeans will only take up a very small part of Levi's business, investing in the premium meme is important to fit with the new denim environment and radiate a credible halo over Levi's brand name.[45]

When brands miss out on changing memes in the environment, this might lead to dramatic business results. For example, in the second half of the 1970s market leader Adidas neglected the running and jogging meme among casual users although they had a strong presence in running among athletes. Nike was more sensitive to the growing interests and needs of jogging participants and surpassed Adidas. Ten years later the highly successful brand Nike failed to recognize another meme, the fitness and aerobics craze among women. Competitor Reebok introduced comfortable athletic footwear in soft, pliable leather and a variety of fashionable colours. Style-conscious consumers suddenly switched to Reebok whose sales went up from $35 million in 1982 to $300 million in 1985.[46]

Just as errors happen during DNA replication, meme mutations can also appear during reproduction. The theory of brands acting as memes gained attention during the first decade of the new millennium following the rise of viral marketing. New technologies such as the internet and mobile phones facilitate meme reproduction at a much faster pace. But they can also create the so-called 'doppelganger image' when consumers spread off-strategy brand messages. The many spoof movies and parodies on YouTube can be seen as meme mutations.[47]

Conclusion

In this chapter we have dealt with the questions every Gen Yer will certainly ask about any brand, including yours. If it isn't made explicitly, it will happen at least implicitly:

- Who are you?
- What is your unique brand DNA; your identity that makes you stand out from competition?
- What are you?
- What 'brand meaning' do you offer me? What's your brand's vision? These brand assets are structured in youth's memory in associative networks, somatic markers or memes.

In order to make your brand really relevant to youth target groups, and to create this long-lasting CRUSH, two more Generation Y questions remain unanswered:

- What do I have in common with the brand? Only when Gen Yers share values and interests with your brand, will they identify with it. In the next chapter, we will address this self-identification process and how brands can play a role in it.
- What do I feel about you? The role of emotions in branding has increased in the first decade of the 2000s and youngsters especially are more emotional in their brand choice than ever before. In Chapter 7, we will explain how happiness and emotional branding contribute to bonding with Gen Y consumers.

HOT TAKEAWAYS FOR COOL BRAND BUILDERS

- Gen Y is sceptical about product novelty or a brand's uniqueness.

- But it's all about how youth perceive a brand's major claims as consistent.

- Youth talk about the brands they perceive as unique and buys brands on recommendation.

- The positive perception of your brand's uniqueness will thus lever your brand's preference and recommendation.

- Claiming your brand's DNA in all details (including retail, packaging and so on) will support a consistent positioning.

- Choose the right battlefields to stress in communication: those close to your DNA that are of importance to the buyers of your competitors as well.

- Brand identities act as somatic markers or memes.

- Marketing situations and environments are continuously evolving; specifically in youth markets, brands need to adapt to changing memes.

Self-identification with the brand

The word 'tattoo' is derived from the Tahitian word 'tatau', meaning 'from Tahiti'. West European explorers in the 18th century such as Thomas Cook discovered the tribal tattoo practices among Polynesian people. This explains why tattoos in Europe were initially popular among sailors before spreading to broader society. The skin marks are much older than this discovery though. Even Ötzi, the Iceman who was found in the Ötz valley in the Alps and is believed to have lived in the fourth to fifth millennium BC, had approximately 57 carbon tattoos on his lower spine, knees and ankle. Some mummies (second millennium BC) from Ancient Egypt have tattoos too.[1]

Although many youngsters bear tattoos as a fashion style statement or to connect to their lifestyle subculture, many tattoo designs are originally related to gangs. The three dots in a triangle, illustrated in Figure 6.1, usually found between the thumb and forefinger, is such a 'generic' tattoo and is popular among Hispanic teenagers. The three dots have different meanings.

FIGURE 6.1 The three dots tattoo

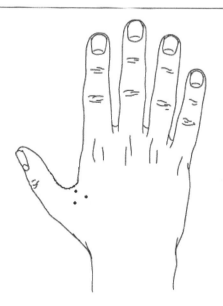

The mark is said to have its origin in gang members affiliated with the Surenos or Sur 13. They place three dots on one wrist and a single dot on the other to indicate the number '13'. 'Tres Puntos' refers to the 13th letter of the alphabet, 'La Eme', or 'the M' for Mexican Mafia. They also stand for 'mi vida loca' ('my crazy life').[2]

Tattoo marks have always been used to identify with people belonging to the same culture. From the Maori tribes to the Harley-Davidson riders, the skin marks embody affiliation with other like-minded souls. Identity is always about the body, the bodily states and desires of being, becoming, belonging and behaving.[3]

We know that the brands and products youth buy become one of the central building blocks of their identity. This is clearly the case for what we have called 'badge items' in the chapter on coolness. Youth use product categories such as clothing, sneakers and mobiles to show they belong to certain peer groups. Youngsters choose those brands that are relevant to their individual selves and that represent those aspects of their identity they want to accentuate. Products have a symbolic value and are not solely used as a tool and means but rather as signs representing their thinking and values.

In the CRUSH brand model, youth's self-identification with the brand has a very strong direct effect on brand leverage. Next to that, identification is also influencing brand image and conversations about the brand. Together with the other CRUSH factors, self-identification is crucial to obtaining a good connection with Generation Y and keeping your cool brand hot for the long term.

Self-identification can be defined as the extent to which a brand is seen as a mirror of one's own passions, interests and lifestyle. In other words: when a brand or company is capable of getting closer to the lives of youth, in a way that Millennials feel it is part of their lives, it will improve both its short- and long-term market success.

We kick off this chapter by looking at different tribes and lifestyles with some studies from the UK and the US. We will conclude that Millennials as multi-viduals tend to pick-and-mix from different styles. It is clear that brands that want to stay hot with Millennials need to find a connection with the major passion points in their lives. We will give you an overview of the five key themes in Generation Y's daily endeavours.

A quest called tribe: teens' search for a fitting lifestyle

Teens develop relationships with peer groups. These groups consist of similarly aged, fairly close friends. They are critical in puberty because they help teens to learn how to interact socially and become more independent from parents or other adults. Peer groups also give the necessary feedback during the search for identity and personality. They offer instrumental and emotional support.

Cliques and crowds

Basically, there are two types of peer group: 'cliques' and 'crowds'. Cliques are small groups with an average of five to six adolescents. Their smaller size allows teens to know each other well and appreciate one another better than others outside the clique. Cliques are the groups within which adolescents hang out and form friendships. They can be activity cliques formed by circumstance, for instance in sport clubs or music schools, or friendship cliques, which a teen chooses deliberately. In early adolescence, most cliques are single gender. Later, clique leaders start to get interested in the other sex and eventually couples will replace cliques as the new social structure.

The second type of peer group is called a crowd. Crowds are much bigger in size and not based on friendship but on common lifestyles, reputation and stereotypes. These reference groups contribute less to exercising social skills but are necessary to develop a sense of identity and self-concept. During early adolescence, a crowd provides self-definition before a teen is capable of creating an own self.[4]

When crowds or tribes are not considered mainstream, sociologists tend to call them 'subcultures'. We feel this term is a bit outdated since *sub*culture implies a reaction to a mainstream culture. Large oppositions like the punk movement or the hippie culture, all reacting against a materialistic consuming world, are less prevalent today. As discussed in the first chapter on Generation Y, youngsters are not in an opposition movement against their parents either. This doesn't mean that today's crowds are all sharing the same ideas and preferences. The traditional approach of subcultures, however, is less relevant today. The French sociologist Pierre Bourdieu coined the concept of 'cultural capital'. It is defined as the knowledge that is accumulated through upbringing and education or social status. His theoretical scheme includes social capital: you don't just get your identity from what you own or know, but also from who you know and who knows you.[5] In her study on club culture, Sarah Thornton elaborated on this concept and coined 'subcultural capital', emphasizing that subcultures today are formed more on the basis of musical tastes, fashion styles and slang rather than on values or as a response to the dominant mainstream culture. Haircuts, record collections and media usage are all identified as 'subcultural' capital.[6]

The multi-vidual

The traditional sources of 'youth authenticity' described in previous chapters have severely changed in the Gen Y society. 'Multi-vidual' youngsters like to pick and mix different fashion styles. Carrie Bradshaw, played by Sarah Jessica Parker in *Sex and the City* for instance, is depicting a postmodern reality. She wears an eclectic bohemian patchwork of trends. Yes, she's totally into Jimmy Choo shoes, but she combines them with vintage dresses. *Sleazenation* and *The Face*, two style-dictating magazines, both went bankrupt in 2004. One of the reasons for them dissolving was that Gen Y was no longer into following the fashion police.[7]

It is not only difficult but also dangerous to find authenticity in the clothes you wear. Styles become mainstream faster than ever and brands are hijacked out of subcultures within one single year. Lonsdale, which was once a popular brand among mod revivalists such as Paul Weller, got hijacked by neo-Nazi kids in the mid-2000s. Von Dutch, an authentic US fashion label, was a mainstream lower-class brand in no time. The London riots of 2011 were fired up by the usage of BlackBerry's BBM messenger service. Not exactly the ideal brand association that marketing managers would have in mind. Abercrombie & Fitch even offered a payment to one of the members of MTV's *Jersey Shore* if he would stop wearing the brand's clothes.

Similarly, during riots in Milan in 2015, the Italian government blamed the clashes on 'spoilt brats with Rolexes'. Not liking this association, the watch brand put up advertisements in newspapers to explain how they had been misrepresented because it was unclear whether the rioters actually did wear Rolex watches. Still, their brand was already linked with a negative connotation, and these advertisements probably did not make that association go away entirely.[8]

In 2013, a stuffed wolf sold by Ikea became the symbol of protests in Hong Kong. The little wolf toy was named Lufsig all over the world, but in Chinese it translated into something that sounded similar to an insult. To protest against the actions of Hong Kong's leader C Y Leung, nicknamed 'the Wolf', the stuffed toy was used everywhere, causing it to sell out in Chinese Ikea stores. The Swedish brand decided not to respond to the political connotations attributed to its product.[9]

How mainstream is a hipster?

The modern day hipster originated in the late 1990s, mainly with New York (more specifically Brooklyn) young creatives deliberately trying to go against the mainstream. They were recognizable by their metrosexual appearance which contained such things as aviator sunglasses, skinny rolled-up jeans, trucker caps and shirts as well as the right amount of facial hair in the case of men.[10] Gradually, it became more and more connected to features of the Gen Y generation themselves, as hipsters also took a liking to craft and the artisanal as well as all things sustainable and environmental.[11] Because of their attitude of 'not caring about the mainstream', tension occurred in the late 2000s when the movement gained a lot of traction on the internet and in the press with anti-hipster blogs and opinion pieces. Slowly, being 'a hipster' turned into an insulting stereotype and sort of meant you were an elitist that disliked everything popular. Conversely, however, the whole hipster appearance actually started appearing more and more in the streets. Youngsters still liked the clothing style and the way of appearing, but calling them a 'hipster' was definitely a no-go.

It is not surprising, then, that recently more voices have been raised saying that the hipster as it originated no longer exists. Because the main idea of the subculture was being alternative vis-à-vis the mainstream, the fact that the appearance of this subculture itself became mainstream inherently spelled the end of 'the hipster'. For example, big retail brands like Target offered hipster styles, dating sites portrayed a typical hipster couple, etc. All of this pointed to the fact that 'hipster' got swallowed by the mainstream to the point that the whole cultural style was no longer considered 'hip' because it had become so common.[12] Originally, clothing brands like American Apparel and Urban Outfitters saw their profits soar during the heydays of the hipster. As signs of the decline of the popularity, American Apparel hasn't made a profit since 2009, while Urban Outfitters' sales have been declining since 2011. 'Once a fashion statement becomes mainstream, it alienates the original core of people that were doing it in the first place,' explained fashion watcher Eila Mell in 2015 in an interview with fashion blog Racked.[13]

Every youngster is a subculture

In our global village, fashion designers are copied by the time their designs move from the catwalk to the shops. But this doesn't mean style differences among youngsters are non-existent. In fact, as a consequence of the 'multi-vidual' trend, there are more different lifestyle groups than ever before. Some sociologists would even claim that every youngster is a subculture on his or her own.[14] The emerging diversity and increased individuality in our postmodern society has led to microscopic mappings of youth tribes. Channel 4 in the UK for instance started tracking British youth culture in 2005. Since then, they have issued several versions of the *Find Your Tribe* survey. The results are frequently updated on uktribes.com. The large-scale research gathering data across more than 250 brands and media found not less than 23 different tribes in the UK scene. All 23 lifestyles are based on five key groups: mainstream, aspirant mainstream, urban style, alternative style and leading-edge:[15]

- Mainstream tribes respond to inclusivity. They want brands to demonstrate an easy-going, 'join us' approach.
- Aspirant mainstream tribes prefer brands that focus on exclusivity both through creative approaches and field brand activity like parties and events.
- Urban tribes love brands that help them to achieve something or do something they have never done before like exclusive travel or sponsorship of their sports activities.
- Much of the alternatives' social currency is linked with music. Brands that give them free or exclusive access to gigs, parties and festivals will connect well with them.
- The leading-edge tribes are hardest to impress. They like and value brands that show them something they don't know yet.[16]

In her book *Chasing Youth Culture and Getting It Right*, Tina Wells uses four tribes to describe the different lifestyles of US youth: the wired techie, the conformist but somewhat paradoxical preppy, the always-mellow alternative and the cutting-edge independent (see box for more info).[17]

Youth culture and tribes in the US

The Wired Techie

To the Millennial generation, The Wired Techie is the trendsetter for how modern things work. Techies are constantly coming up with new ideas to make life easier and they've turned technology into their own fashion! Known as nerds in previous generations, Techies have now become popular, have sex appeal and start companies overnight. They are now the front-runners for fame and notoriety. Techies interact with brands that respect their knowledge, challenge their skills and provide them with a cutting-edge, high-quality product. After all, this tribe embraces innovation and the future.

The Conformist Yet Somewhat Paradoxical Preppy

Preppies are easily identifiable and consider themselves popular. This tribe needs to conform, obey the rules and play the game. Preppies want the expected outcome and actively seek acceptance in brands that make them feel part of a larger group or movement. The need for inclusion makes Preppies effective communicators. Essentially, this group serves as megaphones that bring messages to the masses. Preppies gravitate towards products with style, trendiness and a brand experience that resonates with their need to 'fit in'. As conformists, Preppies will not be the first to try something new, but they will embrace brands that provide the necessary tools to make them feel trendy and part of the group.

The Always Mellow Alternative

Dubbed by *The New York Times* the 'Why-Worry Generation', Alternatives are relaxed, laid back and contemplative. What makes this tribe so alluring is their disregard for social conformity and need for independence. They have no fear in trying new things and effortlessly adopt trends and ideas into their lifestyles. It's important to pay close attention to this group. After all, Alternatives are the future. Because they crave independence, businesses that target this tribe must respect their space and allow them to adapt products to their own individual use. Alternatives discover their values independently through their own journey and become loyal to brands that correlate with their beliefs.

Continued...

Youth culture and tribes in the US   *Continued...*

The Cutting-Edge Independent

Independents align themselves with brands and concepts that are new and cutting-edge. They deviate for the sake of deviating and find trends through blogs and by word-of-mouth from their friends. Independents like to help brands break into the mainstream but will abandon a trend once it reaches the masses. This tribe thrives in indie environments that are exclusive and provide a creative outlet. By definition, Independents need to be autonomous, passionate thinkers and their need for self-expression comes to fruition in what they wear. Fashion is the extension of their passion. Independents consistently want to make a statement about who they are and what they stand for. This plays a major role in the brands they choose. Independents gravitate towards brands that reflect their rebellious, selective nature and provide them with value for their money.

Tina Wells is CEO of Buzz Marketing Group and author of *Chasing Youth Culture and Getting it Right*.

Getting closer to youth

In the summer of 2013 InSites Consulting and VIMN Northern Europe (part of Viacom International Media Networks) set up the 'Close to Youth' programme. It aimed to keep the brands and departments of VIMN Northern Europe Gen-Y-proof. In collaboration with an international task force of VIMN Ambassadors and the insight department in Berlin, the 'Celebrating Youth' research community was launched to generate a deeper understanding of the Northern European Generation Y and explore life themes to be used as building blocks for VIMN's channel brands, programming and sales approach. Ten European countries were represented by a selected group of 149 active Gen Y (aged 16 to 32) participants. During three weeks, these GenYers shared their hopes, fears and dreams and gave us insights in their daily life challenges and preoccupations. Based on this input and internal exercises, VIMN Northern Europe's sales and marketing approach was evaluated. The five crucial themes in the lives of Gen Y youth are at the core of this approach, each manifesting in a specific way.

By engaging for three weeks in a row instead off one-evening focus groups, we gained a much deeper understanding about what the key life themes actually mean. In what follows we will discuss the meaning of each of these themes for Generation Y, based on their comments in the 'Celebrating Youth'-research community. When analysing the five key themes in the lives of Millennials, it became clear to us that they are not just driving their everyday choices but also clearly influence Generation Y's consumer behavior. Each of the themes can be linked to current evolutions in Gen Y's media usage and broader lifestyle trends.[18]

Celebrating youth and party-cipation

Just like previous generations, this generation really wants to celebrate youth, enjoying it while they can and getting the maximum out of it. What sets it apart from previous generations, however, is that they are more positive (less about rebellion, more about enjoyment and happiness) and they have more freedom to celebrate their youth the way they want to. Youngsters these days can be who they want to be and be happy about it. Being young means for them that you can dream about the future, change your goals, make mistakes and try again: endless possibilities are lying ahead. Living once (YOLO) means enjoying life to the fullest, getting everything possible out of it.

Youth is a period with reduced responsibilities – until you move out, a safety net is protecting you and providing for you. It gives structure to your life while leaving room to experiment. The more responsibilities you get, the faster the feeling of being young decreases. On the other hand, if there is no feeling of independence, enjoying youth also becomes more difficult. There is a thin line between being independent and not having too many responsibilities. Celebrating Youth can be something very individual (exercising, listening to music etc). This depends on individual preferences and interests. It can be about hedonistic pleasures (being occupied with interests like music and games) but also about 'proceeding in life' (fantasizing about the future, graduating.). But 'Celebrating Youth' is not only about the individual; it is something Millennials will typically often do together. Connections with others make the experience more relevant and memorable. The experience is shared at the very moment but also afterwards: bringing up memories and evaluating all the things encountered together with someone else. These experiences often evolve around laughing, doing random things, going out together, traveling together or simply having the same interests.

Millennials increasingly want to go to events where the excitement originates from feeling part of the crowd. They want to feel part of something greater and, in an age where they are often separated by screens, they value the moments where they can come together and connect with peers. Not only connections with digital communities, but first and foremost with people in real units – and not exclusively age or gender peers. As our social and professional lives are configured more and more by bits and bytes, we see an increase in Generation Y's longing for material substance and corporality. Conviviality is gaining in interest in our sporting activities; people share challenges and experiences. We are on the eve of a breakthrough of 'sportainment' and 'party-cipation'.

Some examples

- **Run Dem Crew:** a movement founded by Charlie Dark in 2007 as an alternative to traditional stuffy running clubs. Runners start with a hug and then run together without any competitive goal. The Run Dem Crew is now sponsored by Nike.

- **Tough Mudder:** a boot camp for everyone, not only for the most sporting types. It started in the US in 2010 and immediately had 20,000 participants. The general philosophy is group thinking and participating implies you are to help and motivate others. In the meanwhile Tough Mudder organizes 52 different events on a yearly basis and no less than two million people worldwide (25 per cent women) already took part.

- **Naked Run for Freedom:** originated from the Danish Roskilde festival. The festival encourages guests to get naked and race for charity. Runners are only allowed to wear a helmet and shoes. The annual recurrent attraction at Roskilde is the naked run around the campsite. Whether motivation comes from the free ticket to the next year's festival given to the male and female winners, a desire to contribute to a worthy cause or the wish to experience a feeling of freedom, dozens of participants try their hand at nude running every year.

- **Colour run:** 5 km of running while being sprayed with paint powder. A contest without competition, figures or statistics, it is simply about enjoying the mutual activity, also called party-cipation.

- **Tomorrowland:** the biggest global EDM (Electronic Dance Music) festival in Belgium attracting 360,000 GenYers from 212 countries during two weekends of celebrating youth in the amazing surroundings of a fantasy world consisting of dancing elves, fountains and magical decorations.

Killing 'boring' & serendipity

'Celebrating Youth' is (in the eyes of Millennials) often about deleting dullness, which in many ways is more about avoiding a boring life than about killing moments of boredom. As a result, this generation is always on the lookout for new and unique experiences. Being bored, or perhaps even more being boring, is one of the biggest fears of Millennials. There's even a medical term for it: 'Thaasophobia'. Generation Y constantly want to be stimulated and does not want to end up in a routine. Their hunger for new (and unique) experiences is clearly present.

Having a boring life means:

- being stuck in a routine: not doing anything new;
- not having an opinion, no dreams, no goals;
- not being passionate about anything.

Getting rid of 'boring' means looking for anything that breaks the routine of daily life. They do this passively, actively and interactively:

- Distraction: just looking around and finding something which catches their eye;
- Action: looking actively for interesting things;
- Connection: searching and contacting others to help them to kill boring.

Youngsters are looking for things to avoid leading this boring life. This happens on different levels:

- Kill those short moments in everyday life when boredom is just around the corner (waiting for the bus, boring classes, coming home after work, having to do something you're not interested in etc.)
- Killing the BIG BORING: at some point, even all these short moments of avoiding boring get boring, so they start to search for 'bigger ways' to kill 'boring'. To really overcome a boring life they have to overcome the pyjama feeling: leave their own comfort zone and challenge themselves. This can be done alone or together with others, eg studying abroad, looking for a job, switching styles, meeting new people...

As a reaction to our behaviour which is predicted by algorithms, the over-personalization of products, services and ad messages, too many suggested links or purchases in our social media, on e-commerce sites or even in shops, we are fighting a harder battle against boredom. We feel an increasing need for unexpected, coincidental, fun discoveries and surprises in a society in which everything is becoming too predictable. It has been scientifically proven that a sandwich is better when prepared by someone else, because otherwise we anticipate too much on the taste (based on the fact that we know the ingredients), which kills the appetite. Many inventions and discoveries are the consequence of sheer luck, as serendipity could be described. Think about X-rays, Kellogg's cornflakes, 3M's Post-its, the HP inkjet printer, Viagra, the teabag, penicillin or the discovery of America. So the notion of serendipity is also important in a way that it could be at the start of a new economy, the Serendipity Economy, where other less fixed methods of collaboration increase the chances of coincidental discoveries. Collaborative social networks for companies such as Yammer and more open-ended research methods such as Consumer Consulting Boards are supporting this new way of business thinking.

Even the number one algorithm company, Google, still shows the 'I'm feeling lucky' button which immediately takes you to the first search result based on your search words. This is possibly costing Google a yearly 110 million dollars in missed income from advertising. And how about Google's famous Doodles? They regularly intrigue us and make a boring search job more fun. But it is also business *an sich*, such as the lovely surprise boxes on notanotherbill.com or the Belgian deauty.be (which stands for Discover Beauty) or the 'Pochette surprise' for €20 at the fashionable Paris retailer

Colette. Panera bread, the American bakery-and-cafe chain, has also included a healthy portion of serendipity in its MyPanera loyalty card.

Talking about playing with cards... board games, which traditionally have strict rules, now also give more room to coincidences. Examples are Cards Against Humanity – immensely popular in the US – and Shut you Mao, new and recently sponsored by Kickstarter.

Computer games such as Minecraft are very popular with the youngest generation. Minecraft is an open-world game that has no specific goals for players to accomplish, allowing them a large amount of freedom in choosing how to play the game. Since its release at the end of 2011, it has sold over 70 million copies. 22tracks.com is a curated jukebox which contains 22 playlists of 22 tracks each. All tracks are selected by DJs from four cities. The idea is that you get surprised, that you discover new genres and new music, without registering. In the travel sector there is getgoing.com where you get a discount because they choose your destination, so you are rewarded for your flexibility.

Renault introduced serendipity in the 2013 prankvertising campaign with the 'Va va voom' button on YouTube. Jeep introduced the 'Get lost' button on their GPS system. Jeep drivers can select it and choose their terrain from options like mountain, sand or woods. The GPS will then take them to one of 28 off-road destinations in the middle of nowhere. It led to almost 1.5 million views.

And last but not least, Heineken has been using serendipity since 2013 as the core of its positioning and viral marketing. From the departure roulette through the #dropped campaign all the way to the most recent Christmas carol karaoke which has already attained more than 2.5 million views since its launch.

Sharing stories and the shortcut economy

As seen, Celebrating Youth is often (not always) a WE-activity and this uber-connected generation is very WE-oriented. They share stories and experiences with a huge circle of (real and virtual) friends because they want to learn from each other and get social approval. Everything they do will only get value when shared with or by others. The fact that they're so interconnected makes sharing extremely important.

- **We share what we love** – a kind of altruism: 'I thought this story was funny/ interesting/ shocking and I think you might feel the same'.
- **We share to vent and get support:** 'When something goes wrong we share it with those around us: pain shared is pain halved'.
- **To express ourselves:** we are what we share: 'The stories that we tell also tell a story about us and this is managed consciously'.

The stories Millennials share often go beyond mere stories; they are also experiences. These experiences are being shared in the heat of the moment: 'Look what I'm doing now'.

Elements of a story worth sharing are:

- **Humour:** if something makes us laugh, we want to share this with others. A shareable story doesn't have to be funny, but it helps.

- **Unpredictability:** if a story has something unexpected it can surprise your audience and make them curious to hear more. There is no point in sharing a story that your audience can predict from A to Z.

- **Relatability:** the personal touch in a story – 'Could this happen to me?'. We are more likely to be interested in a story if it is something that we can personally relate to.

- **Emotions:** if something truly affected you, it is more likely to affect or at least interest others.

Millennials have been taught all their lives to make as little effort as possible yet to find and reach what they want when they want it in a way that suits them best. They have grown up with a rather natural 'shortcut reflex'. Older generations sometimes wrongfully mistake them for being idle. However there is not one single reason why we should make a detour. Yet we do so every day, because we were taught wrongly, because we have been conditioned differently. So we do it out of habit or because there are rules, trainings and legislations which keep us from taking shortcuts.

The access to information, technology, money and peers has been largely facilitated by social media and sharing. Just think about how peer-to-peer P2P networks have done damage to the music, TV and movie business. We will see an endless flow of new (P2P) and shortcut initiatives which – based on the Millennials' passion – will rock the boat of several classic sectors. Existing business models will get under pressure as a result of the Gen Y consumers' urge to take a quicker, easier, cheaper and less strenuous shortcut to the solution.

A few examples of this shortcut economy:

- **In the education sector:** the so-called MOOCs (= Massive Online Open Courses) such as Khan Academy, a non-profit educational website providing free world-class education for anyone anywhere through a video library and over 100,000 practical exercises. Other examples include: eDX, Coursera and Coderdojo, coaching youngsters aged 7 to 18 to learn how to code in a cosy club context, stressing the usage of open-source free software.

- **In the mobility sector:** Lyft is a cellphone application which allows users to 'order' a driver to their location in minutes. During their ride, passengers can play their own music and charge their mobile devices. All drivers are subjected to a criminal background check as well as a vehicle inspection and a two-hour training session. At the end of the trip, passengers pay the driver the amount of their choice in the form of a (technically optional) donation. Because Lyft facilitates pre-arranged travel instead of on-the-street taxi-hailing and operates on a donation system, its drivers do not need a taxi license.

Although payment is not guaranteed, the majority of Lyft users are willing to pay the drivers a satisfactory rate.

- **In the travel sector:** Gen Y is the fastest growing customer segment in the travel industry. They are expected to finance half of all travel spending by 2020. Millennials are adventure seekers. Millennials want a great place to stay and an experience which fits with them, not an impersonal treatment in an anonymous environment. The industry has already created some new travel experiences that tap into this trend, such as portable container hotels that allow guests to stay in more off-the-beaten-track locations (e.g. Sleeping Around, Sleepbox Hotel...). Peer-to-peer lodging companies like AirBNB are challenging traditional hotels. Generation Y is simply more accustomed to networking with and trusting peers.

Whenever, wherever and touchpoints

The always-on Generation Y is actively experiencing the previous life themes through all their available personal media. Millennials are using several channels: they are constantly connected online on laptop or mobile, they are looking for inspiration on television or on YouTube and events are the perfect way to make everything about the experiences. It's not an 'or' story, but an 'and' story.

- **Celebrating Youth, Wherever, whenever:** when they are listening to music while on the bus, when they are talking on Whatsapp about last night, when they are posting on Facebook about how great their trip was: Gen Y has no boundaries of time and place at all.

- **Sharing stories, Wherever, whenever:** Sharing and connecting happens all the time through all kinds of different channels with different kinds of people. Between all those different types of connections, youngsters still want to be heard. They have clear preferences for certain channels depending on the content. The moment when a story is shared also depends on the type of content.

- **Kill boring, Wherever, whenever:** Youngsters kill 'boring' wherever they are: at school, at work, when waiting for the bus, when in a club, on the street, in their bed or in the bath: every place where they may possibly feel bored. Youngsters want to be stimulated all the time, everywhere and will search for ways to avoid boredom.

Youngsters aren't only going to school and returning home, a lot of other places are also relevant to them. There is a difference between Generation Y's everyday context (e.g. practicing hobbies) and special occasions (milestones, special events). The expression, content and channel depend on this context.

Accessing TV content through VOD and other options has generated some worry in the industry that it would steal time from live TV viewing. What Viacom found is that live TV remains the dominant way to access video content. Even in Europe, where new forms of access are becoming increasingly more prevalent, the frequency of watching live TV still soars above the rest. Passion for TV content is driving consumers to seek out new ways to watch on other devices, creating new TV-watching occasions and allowing TV content to fill more time slots during the day. As device ownership grows, Viacom is seeing a trend towards multi-screen homes. Additionally, access to time-shifted options doesn't compete with live TV viewing, it actually supports it. 74 per cent of all the Millennials who participated in Viacom's European study watches live TV daily. When looking at the daily live TV consumption amongst those who have the ability to connect to the Internet, it actually went up to 81 per cent.[19]

Connecting with Millennials is not about being there all the time. It's not about figuring out what the most popular spot is and just setting up a presence there. It's not about just having a Facebook fan page or a Twitter feed. Brands like MTV and Comedy Central connect with Millennials everywhere and at the right time. Music, events, parties, reality television, cellphone services. Whether it is online or offline, through TV or through a smartphone, whether it's in New York or in Frankfurt... Millennials don't care about where MTV hangs out. They expect brands to follow them and only when they do, Millennials will return the favor. Although watching television continues to be a social experience, the traditional 'everyone sit down and watch a show together' has gradually been replaced by, 'let's sit down separately and watch a show together.' Viacom strives to create programming that people talk about and social media is one of the channels that it uses. By building engagement through social media channels, it enhances the TV-viewing experience for its audience. In 2013 Viacom held the top three top-tweeted TV shows in the US – at the same time: Catfish: The TV Show (MTV) – 511,226 tweets, Love & Hip Hop: Atlanta (VH1) – 504,301 tweets and Teen Wolf (MTV) – 283,490 tweets.[20]

Live & learn & mono-tasking

The 'why' question is very relevant to Millennials – who are often referred to as Generation (WH)Y. This fifth theme evolved around 'live/life inspiration': why do Millennials do what they do? What's their bigger goal in life? When being young there is always something new to see, do or experience for the first time – there is an entire world out there to explore and facing the world with open arms is vital. At the same time youth is also the time of self-discovery: getting to know who you are by looking back at past experiences. For every decision, youngsters have to figure out what they really want. It's an on-going quest where it's not only about today but also about the future. Youngsters are enjoying the ride, but they do not forget about the destination. They see being young as a time of 'live and learn': exploring new domains, making mistakes, trying again and developing an own identity along the way. It's not because YOLO (you only live once) that YOLT (you only live today)!

Youngsters learn to fall and to stand up again and take away some individual lessons. However, they also need people around them to help them develop: friends and family are 'life benchmarks'; other peers (celebrities, schoolmates, colleagues etc.) are also used to create an own preference pallet. Feedback from others is also necessary in the quest to make the right decisions and develop one's own identity.

As a result of the recession, the youngest of the Millennials are experiencing more difficulties in finding a job than their older peers. Since they graduated, they have experienced the consequences of the global crisis. They can no longer save money and are obliged more than ever to make choices when it comes to leisure expenses. One out of three Millennials is dissatisfied with his buying power and the number of young students with debts is rising

According to the American Psychological Association Millennials are the most stressed generation ever. Youth unemployment and social media peer pressure are the main sources of stress for Gen Y. Even those who were lucky enough to find a job, have less prosperous future outlooks. The starting salary – when corrected for inflation – has dramatically decreased since 2000 and half of all graduates started in a function they actually didn't need their degree for.[21] As a direct consequence of these augmented stress levels, the youngest Millennials and the next Generation Z have a more realistic and down to-earth attitude when compared to the 'Yes, We Can' – older part. In a recent Viacom study, survival girl Katniss Everdeen from The Hunger Games is defined as the new icon of the young generation. In the same study a substantial 84 per cent of youngsters state 'You always have to be prepare and need to have an exit plan for every possible emergency situation'. Almost half of the youngest Millennials is afraid of school violence and many of them are still referring to the destructive forces of nature (e.g. hurricane Sandy). In a very competitive and unstable working environment, it has become crucial to Millennials and post-Millennials to hyper-differentiate and to stand out from the masses. The youth has adapted a mono-tasking attitude and wants to learn and develop skills up to expert levels. Millennials are DIY YouTube pupils who are on the look-out for the best tutorials and are dedicated to keep working and improving their skills until they are the very best. This specific focus on one task or skill allows them to have a better control of their own lives and to escape from a society full of overstimulation and stress.[22] In a global study by InSites Consulting among Millennials, half of them found it very important to outdo their peers in a certain hobby or skill. Almost 8 out of 10 (78%) claims their friends would consider them to be an expert in at least one domain. Niche expertise is the new social currency. The more obscure, super-niche or nerdy, the cooler. Especially if you can build an online fan base or even commerce from your own expertise.[23]

Global citizens with a local identity

Gen Y is certainly the most globally connected generation ever. Internet, social media, Skype, FaceTime, instant and text messaging, cheap airline tickets, couch surfing... . They have all the tools and opportunities to explore the world and be in touch with a diversity of multicultural influences. Many of them will spend at least one or two years studying or working abroad. To them the world is a global village with no borders. On the other hand, we know from our research that youth care most about their immediate social circle. Their friends and family are key, and they tend to largely identify with their own village or city, and their own country. That national feeling of pride and the need to be in touch with the local community may not be underestimated. Successful global youth brands understand that they need to have a local relevance and connection. 'Part of our shift in evolution has meant that we're more locally focused', says Peter Jung, former Senior Business Leader at MasterCard International.

> The needs of youth in Turkey are fundamentally different from those in Sweden, Mexico or India. So it forces us to tailor our products and services to the region we're addressing. Turkey is an enormous youth market; 60 per cent of the population is under 30. What they need is a safe way to buy things online, so we've developed a product that addresses this need. In some BRIC markets, shops don't accept cards, so instead of swiping or entering a PIN, we are delivering ways to pay with a smartphone since the penetration of mobile devices is much higher than the penetration of card devices. In Mexico for instance social status is a major driver of behaviour – Gen Y in Mexico see value in being able to access fashion brands or experience something that their peers may not.

Peter Jung calls this 'social credibility'.[24] Francisco Bethencourt, VP Global Marketing Yildiz Holding, agrees. 'Brand execution and activation, and ultimately sales, are always done in a local communities'.

> So you need to be relevant and authentic in that local setting and be aware of local issues that are important to your consumers. It is a balance between keeping brand strategy and positioning but allowing flexibility in local execution to develop authentic and relevant solutions for your consumers locally. A common building platform in your communication and brand strategy to prevent fragmentation of your positioning is required, but you also have to activate through different cultural cuesto to stay relevant with a particular audience or community. Location-based and mobile marketing allows you to interact with your consumer depending on where he is, like a sport's venue or movie theatre or shopping centre so that you can customize promotional activities and introductions to new products. Big companies like McDonald's and Coca-Cola create a global emotional connection with the brand through their campaigns but they understand that the local activation is key to connect with Millennials today. If you look at music festivals or independent film festivals, the local flavours became much more important. So hyper-localization is a trend in society and brands need to understand that and come up with new ideas that cater for that new trend.[25]

Romanian candy bar challenges patriotism

Romanian chocolate bar ROM was launched in 1964. Its packaging is designed in the colours of the Romanian flag. But due to economic and political crises in the past years, youth in Romania were losing their national pride. They also preferred hipper US brands of chocolate candy and ROM's market share was falling. McCann Erickson, Bucharest, wanted to challenge young people's patriotism and national ego by changing ROM's packaging into the US flag. Provocative English TV commercials and billboards were stating slogans such as 'Patriotism won't feed you', 'The taste of coolness' and 'Let's build America here'.

Thousands of Romanian people were irritated and voiced their opinion through Facebook, blogs and YouTube. After one week, the original ROM candy bar was re-launched and the brand revealed that it was a joke. The campaign reached 67 per cent of the Romanian target group in only two weeks and it led to about $300,000 of free publicity in the Romanian media. In the first week of the campaign over 20,000 people joined a Facebook group asking for the return of the original patriotic packaging. ROM's Facebook page saw an increase of 300 per cent in terms of fans or likes. Sales of the ROM candy bar skyrocketed with an impressive 79 per cent increase. The American version immediately sold out as a collector's item. The campaign won the Grand Prix in Cannes for two categories: Promo and Activation and Direct[26].

More recently, ROM launched a new international campaign to affirm its patriotism by convincing their civilians to return home. Four million Romanians, of a population of 18 million people, work or study abroad. The European Commission confirmed that Romania has the highest percentage of citizens working elsewhere. ROM created a website in cooperation with McCann Bucharest where residents could persuade emigrants to return to their homeland by creating videos. These contained emotionally loaded content such as music, pictures from their childhood and traditional Romanian dishes. The videos were linked to a HR specialist who helped the emigrants find a job in Romania and the companies who sent their vacancies valued international experience. The campaign was active in countries where the Romanian rate was high.[27]

Craft culture & the maker movement

Generation Z loves the craft. Large, multinational companies struggle to sell their big story. Gen Zers try to find real value with a product, something that's unique and has a real tangible process and story behind it. It's no surprise that this trend is best noticed in the realm of food and drinks. Research has found that Gen Zers prefer fresh, home-cooked meals over prepared food so much that the fresh food consumption is projected to grow by 11 per cent in just five years.[28] For instance, 'Generation Salad', as some writers call them, seem to like cooked, home-made breakfasts such as French toast or omelettes more than the pre-prepared cereals. Similarly, microwaved food is losing popularity because these Gen Zers want to use fresh ingredients and additives to create their own personal plate of food.[29] Gen Z's interest in cooking is predicted to rise almost 10 per cent towards 2018, making them a real group of 'foodies' compared to their predecessors.[30] The fact that over 57 per cent of all 'pins' on Pinterest are somehow related to food demonstrates this foodie culture.

Etsy : the crafts commerce site

Founded in 2005, Etsy has grown to become one of the largest online platforms for hand-craft, going from jewellery over clothing to sculptures or art. After only 10 years, the platform consisted of 1.4 million active sellers selling 32 million items worldwide to 20.8 million active buyers, for a total worth of $1.93 billion. The company itself receives 20 cents upon the listing of an item and takes 3.5% of the transaction when something gets sold. The craft culture is booming. [31]

Etsy also allows certain crafters to step into the spotlights. Using curated shopping pages with some partner brands, the platform regularly puts small independent business to the front. For example, upscale retail store West Elm curated a page full of houseware items and the likes from different Etsy contributors in different cities such as New York or Chicago. This way, very local and independent Etsy sellers can gain a lot of traction by using the power of more established brands embracing the Etsy craftmanship. [32]

Large food and drink companies have been scratching their head to find a solution for the craft trend, because being large and international automatically turns you into a less attractive option for the Gen Zer that's looking for something local, fresh and unique. PepsiCo started Caleb's Kola, a small batch craft cola and the French multinational distillery Pernod Ricard (owner of the Swedish brand Absolut vodka) is fighting the craft trend by joining it. In 2014 they created the Our/ brand, utilizing several local distilleries all over the world to independently manufacture, sell and promote vodka. The only thing that Pernod Ricard contributed was equipment and recipes. Each individual distillery can handle about 50,000 cases per year, which makes it a lot more exclusive compared to the over 11 million cases of Absolut vodka produced yearly. For example, located in old Berlin docks, the Our/Berlin brand sold their Pernod Ricard franchised, locally brewed vodka to over 150 bars and stores. The price? Almost double that of Absolut, but the new generation thinks it's worth it. Because it is a very interesting and unique case we wanted to interview Åsa Caap, the very sympathetic founder and CEO of the Our/Vodka brand.

Our/Vodka: Pernod Ricard goes glocal

Joeri: Could you explain why Pernod Ricard as a mother company started with this Our/Vodka concept and idea, when did it start, how did it grow and what were the reasons for starting up this idea?

Åsa: Five years ago, when I was the Innovation Director for Absolut Vodka, one trend that kept coming back to me was the craft movement. Now, we all know that it's not a trend any more. It's here to stay and I don't think it will ever go away. People are more aware of their local community and what it means to support local businesses and local products, but back then it was not at all as established as now. It kept coming back on my table. It was just something that we had to put away since Absolut can only be local here in Sweden. I couldn't help starting to think about it though and I realized that all big players in this industry have to put it aside because it's really hard to be relevant in a local context, if you're global. I started to look around in the industry but I couldn't find anything, so I looked outside the industry and I must admit that I still have not come across one single brand that has cracked how to be both local and global. I'm sure there are brands, but I just haven't come across them yet.

If I buy local, it is an emotional choice and I don't really look at the price tag. As a mother of three, I am very price conscious but every time I choose organic or local products, it becomes an emotional choice and I just don't see the price tag anymore. I pick them for other reasons. When you call upon people's emotions like that, it's dangerous stuff, because people get very protective and you definitely don't want to be cheated. I think this is where most brands go wrong and why there is nobody who has cracked this before. I got obsessed with the fact that there weren't any brands that were both global and local, so I started working on this idea. The global part is the easy part but the local part is tougher. I wanted to find a solution for a big corporation or brand to be relevant in a local context and that is how I came up with the idea of partnering with local entrepreneurs. The business model works like this; we build the distillery in each city, we make the whole capital investment, we set up the business and then we find local entrepreneurs who run the business for us. These entrepreneurs are successful in other areas outside the spirit industry. We come from the spirit industry so we think it's much more interesting if they come from outside and bring something new to the table. They also have to have the experience of starting, building and running a successful business. We sign an agreement, we teach them everything we know about vodka and how to run the local unit, then we hand over the keys and leave them alone to run the local brand.

Joeri: **If you say 'We leave them alone', you mean you build the distillery with all the tools and then give them entrepreneurial freedom?**

Åsa: Yes, we build the distillery, we set up the business, the legal entity, the bank account, the business enterprise tools, we teach them how to produce the vodka, we help them recruit a production manager and a sales manager, we pay for all the operational costs, but we let them run the business and the brand in the way they feel best suited for their city. We just give them brand building blocks.

We use a metaphor, and that is that we have 9 siblings, identical kids, that you can easily see that they are siblings, and we wanted one to grow up as a Berliner, one as a Seattleite, one as a New Yorker and one as an Amsterdammer. Since we are from Stockholm we don't necessarily know how to raise an Amsterdammer so this is why we look for adoptive parents to raise each city version.

Joeri: **So it's in 9 cities now, you mentioned Berlin, Seattle, New York, Amsterdam, Detroit, ...?**

Åsa: There is Our/Berlin, which has been open for two years now, Our/Detroit, for one year, Our/Seattle opened in January 2015, Our/Amsterdam opened on October 1st 2015; and Our/London opened in November 2015. Then we have Our/Los Angeles which will open in March 2016. Our/Houston, Our/Miami and Our/New York will be open in a year from now.

Joeri: **How difficult was it to sell your idea to the multinational Pernod Ricard?**

Åsa: When I and my co-founders Mattias Nyström and Kalle Söderquist had formalized the idea and the business model, I turned to the company and said 'I have an idea that I know is out of my scope but I would really like you to see it', and the first reaction internally was 'Wow, great idea, but how could we pull this off, it's just impossible'. Since the deal is that we make the entrepreneurs partners and share profit with them, we basically let them run our business without being employed. That is quite a controversial business model for a big corporation like Pernod Ricard. My husband thought I would get fired and begged me not to present the idea.

It took me a little bit more than 1.5 years to convince the company to invest in a pilot in Berlin, so it was not an easy thing to do. It was complicated, controversial and also a quite heavy investment from the beginning before return on investment, but here we are. Berlin was doing good from the beginning and I think we were only open for 2 months before I got an e-mail saying 'Can you put together a team and accelerate a global roll-out'?

Joeri: **So Berlin has been running for 2 years now, since 2013? Why did you choose Berlin as the first one?**

Åsa: We did a lot of research and everything pointed at Berlin. It turned out to be a good match in many aspects.

Joeri: **So was it the combination of hipster city combined with vodka consumption and the epic centre of the craft movement?**

Åsa: Yes, also Berlin has a big start-up and entrepreneurial scene. There is also a great sense of pride for the city. One of the few things that our partners are obliged to do, is to use our space to support the local community and the neighbourhood. This can be something of their own choice, but we don't donate money, that's making it too easy for ourselves. We have a 50 m² space in each city, that the businesses use as a bar, store or an event space (depending what the local law allows) but the partners create a program where this space gets used to the benefit of others as well. It could be anything, from supporting local entrepreneurs to music events or art exhibitions. In Detroit we support a non profit called 'Detroit soup'. When they use our space, people come and pay for a soup lunch while entrepreneurs present their business idea. Then everybody votes, and the best idea gets the money that was paid for lunch. In Berlin they do a free music festival etc.

What Our/Vodka also does, is that we're not so product focused, we are more about the people and what we do. We act a lot as a family and the local people, like Pauline and Jon in Berlin, are very present and it's all about them and their network. This is why selecting the partners is so important to us. Our number one criteria, apart from them being successful entrepreneurs already, is that we could see ourselves spending holidays with them. In a corporate world, this could sound like nonsense but if you're going to put your kids up for adoption, you really want these guys to share your values, and you want to be sure that they are good people.

Joeri: **Every city vodka you're launching is different, right? If you would taste the different vodkas, would it taste like different vodkas?**

Åsa: Yes, it would, but I don't know if you could sense it in a drink on your own. If I guided you though and if we did it in a proper way, with only vodka in the glass, then you could definitely sense it. 99 per cent of the ingredients are sourced locally but we have one global ingredient that comes from us, which is an ingredient that has a fruity note to it and this is something that you could recognize the family by. However, the city vodkas are still very different from each other since Our/Berlin is made of wheat, Our/Detroit it made of corn and in LA it will be made of grapes and so forth.

Joeri: Perhaps one of the reasons why it took you almost two years to convince Pernod-Ricard, is the whole cannibalizing question? Aren't you just taking some market share of the Absolut brand, by doing this?

Åsa: Yes, this was part of the discussion. It was not a big deal since we, internally, know the brand quite well and we know exactly what the Absolut target is but of course there are touch points in the middle somewhere. With a brand as big as Absolut, it is almost impossible not to have touch points but we do target another group of people. The people we target, are not really interested in global mass-marketing brands. If these people knew the story behind Absolut, I'm sure they would like it, but they'd rather go for local brands. So it was a discussion back then but it ended quite fast since the Our/Vodka idea has such good potential that if we were not to do it, somebody else would. We decided that they are good siblings. Absolut is the handsome big brother and Our/Vodka is the cheeky little brother. They have a lot of substance in common but they are very different at the same time.

Joeri: Are there any results of the Our/Vodka approach that you can share?

Åsa: We are a start-up, with no more than two years on the market, so it is too early to predict the future but we did have our first month of break-even last December 2014, which was way ahead of schedule. Our target for this fiscal – ending June 2015 – is to become break even in Berlin. Which is a quite aggressive target, given that the global average for start-ups to break even is around three to five years.

Joeri: Why do you think the Our/Vodka concept works with the Millennial generation?

Åsa: We created Our/Vodka with the belief that there are new types of brands that the market is missing. Brands that are value based, that are personal in a sense that you can go and see them locally. Brands that are 100 per cent transparent and real. We also believe that this generation see themselves as global citizens. Our/Vodka is both. We are local (not so craft – more urban), personal, transparent and value based AND we are also global and embrace the diversity in our global family. Very similar to how the Millennials see the world.[33]

FIGURE 6.2 Our/Vodka

SOURCE: Used with permission of Our/Vodka

Gen Y's favoured brand personalities

The key to obtaining self-identification with your brand is to reflect the values, interests and opinions of your target group. For the critical Generation Y, this doesn't mean just saying what your brand stands for but proving it every day in the way your brand acts. The first step to do this is to understand the values and interests of your young target groups. From the previous section, you know that Gen Y isn't a big homogeneous group. Youth target groups are composed of a number of different lifestyles. So, you should be aware of the brand preferences and interests of the tribes that are within your target group. Next, it is important to understand that the various lifestyles are looking for different aspects of a brand personality before they will identify with your brands.

In Figure 6.3, you will find the brand personality items that the overall Millennial population wants to see reflected. Product reliability, which means that your products always deliver the same expected quality level, is the absolute number one. The rest of the top five most-wanted personalities include components of our CRUSH brand model. Authenticity or realness, for instance, is well-represented in the need for genuine and honest brands. A youth brand should have its own unique style. It should also be up-to-date and fun. When youngsters talk about their close friends, it's striking that

FIGURE 6.3   Brand Personality features

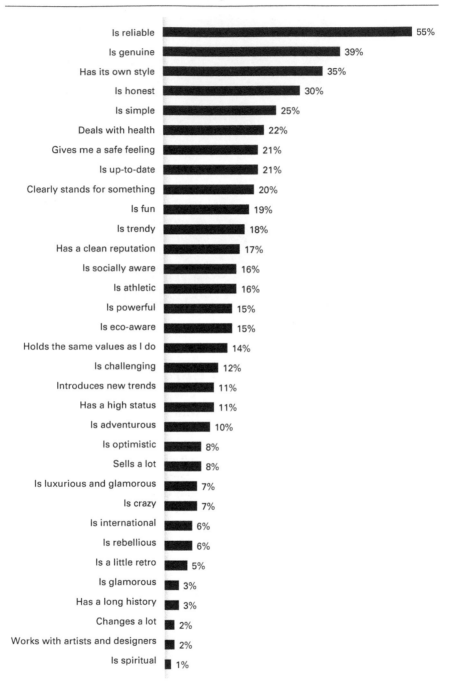

Is reliable	55%
Is genuine	39%
Has its own style	35%
Is honest	30%
Is simple	25%
Deals with health	22%
Gives me a safe feeling	21%
Is up-to-date	21%
Clearly stands for something	20%
Is fun	19%
Is trendy	18%
Has a clean reputation	17%
Is socially aware	16%
Is athletic	16%
Is powerful	15%
Is eco-aware	15%
Holds the same values as I do	14%
Is challenging	12%
Introduces new trends	11%
Has a high status	11%
Is adventurous	10%
Is optimistic	8%
Sells a lot	8%
Is luxurious and glamorous	7%
Is crazy	7%
Is international	6%
Is rebellious	6%
Is a little retro	5%
Is glamorous	3%
Has a long history	3%
Changes a lot	2%
Works with artists and designers	2%
Is spiritual	1%

they use the same traits they are looking for in a brand. A friend is someone you can always count on. He or she is honest and authentic, shares the same values and styles and is fun to have around. Gen Yers also appreciate simplicity in brands. What a brand stands for should be clear and if the product use is simple too, that's a real trump card. Apple, for instance, is a good example of a brand that combines its unique design claims with a reputation for user friendliness and simplicity.

Subcultures moving online: Reddit, Tumblr and fandoms

The continuously evolving and growing internet may have changed the way in which subcultures are formed. Most subcultures have always had a physical element to it, either due to revolving around a certain appearance or because there was a geographical aspect. Recently, the internet has made it possible to fit inside a certain subculture while living across the globe from each other and without having to go through the trouble of publicly showcasing (eg via clothing) one's membership. Dr. Ruth Evans, Lecturer in Cultural & Creative Industries at King's College London, declared in an interview with The Guardian: 'It's not necessarily happening on the street corners any more, but it's certainly happening online. It's a lot easier to adopt personas online that cost you absolutely nothing apart from demonstrating certain types of arcane knowledge. You don't have to invest in a teddy boy's drape suit or a T-shirt from Seditionaries.'[34]

Academic research in 2012 found that adolescents' formation of social roles is increasingly being influenced by interactions mediated by technology, specifically social networks.[35] This means the usual suspects like Facebook and Twitter, but two other platforms seem to fit the description of 'online subcultures' even better: Reddit and Tumblr. Both of these platforms are home to countless groups of like-minded people. As described by digital media site Mashable in 2013, 'some of these groups are so big and so active they become subcultures in their own right'.[36]

Reddit is a massive site founded in 2005, consisting of many, many different subsites, conveniently called 'subReddits'. These range from broads topics such as '/r/funny', '/r/gaming' or '/r/jokes' to very specific subReddits like '/r/Sneakers', which simply discusses all kinds of sneaker shoes and has no less than 50,000 subscribers or so-called 'Sneakerheads'. Similarly, there is also a subReddit made entirely for lovers of the fantasy cards game 'Magic: The Gathering', gathering almost 133,000 fans of the game together. All of these subReddits are little separate hubs from the main portal with a group of like-minded people sharing a deep interest of the same topic. For instance, on the 'Sneakers' page, there are discussions about new releases of shoes as well as threads about DIY-projects. The interesting part about these subReddits is that it's almost impossible to grasp the concepts in the different threads unless you belong to the in-group. For example, a thread on the Magic: The Gathering subReddit read: 'Now that it's been a week: Those who have been testing out the new mulligan rule, do you like it?' This post received 243 responses in less than eight hours, full of 'Planeswalker Cards', as the members call themselves, discussing this issue in detail.[37]

Everyone on Reddit can post anything on any page, and the different posts are peer-rated by 'up- or downvotes'. It's possible for a very small subReddit to get attention on the main page when one of the posts becomes so 'hot' on the subpage that it automatically gets featured on the main page. It's no surprise, then, that a lot of the viral messages, pictures or activities on the internet originate from Reddit, before crossing over to other platforms like Twitter, Facebook or mainstream media outlets. A lot of the typical 'internet lingo' can be attributed to the site as well. Digital media website Mashable even created a list for the uninitiated, explaining what concepts like TL; DR, OP, Troll, Karma or AMA exactly mean.

Similar to Reddit, Tumblr is a microblogging platform that allows users to post anything they want, from dumb jokes to .gif images to deep stories. According to Tumblr themselves, there are around 244 million different blogs, 'filled with literally whatever'.[38] A reblog function makes it possible to literally repost something you like on your own blog, much like retweeting on Twitter. In 2015, a survey conducted with 15,900 British and American internet users found that 13 per cent of surveyed teenagers (aged 16 to 19) considered Tumblr to be 'the coolest' social media platform, ahead of Snapchat, Pinterest and Twitter and only just behind Facebook, Instagram and YouTube. Conversely, when looking at the overall sample (age 16-64) just 2 per cent cite Tumblr as 'coolest'. Tumblr also saw a 95 per cent rise in number of active users between 2014 and 2015, making it one of the quickest growing social platforms.[39] Tumblr definitely is a platform for youngsters.

What differs the most between Tumblr and Reddit is the fact that the former has no real main portal, and thus is much more fragmented. There are a lot of blogs tied together using tags (like hashtags on Twitter) because they deal with similar topics, but you usually only get to see a certain blog in case you are actually interested in the topic and are looking for it. Therefore, it's also on Tumblr that you are able to see youngsters calling each other 'friends', even though they likely have never even seen the face of persons they are talking to. The fact that the Q&A site Yahoo! Answers has several questions of people asking 'How to make friends on Tumblr?' is an indication of how important friendship is on Tumblr.[40]

A specific part of both Reddit and Tumblr are the so-called fandoms. These groups of tightly knit crowds of fans have their specific 'digital areas' (subReddits, Tumblr blogs and tags) as well as specific language habits, often only understood by the in-crowd. These fandoms often also cross over into many other social networks such as Twitter, but their home usually lies in either Reddit or Tumblr. A fandom can be about any given part of popular culture, going from famous actors to television series. Members of a fandom often give themselves a nickname to make sure everybody knows that they belong to that group. For instance, fans of the BBC show Doctor Who like to call themselves 'Whovians', while 'Browncoats' are those who still love to discuss the TV show Firefly, which was cancelled way back in 2003. Fans of popular boy band One Direction are 'Directioners', Lady Gaga addresses her fans as 'Little Monsters' and some fans of British actor Benedict Cumberbatch like to group themselves with the flattering term 'Cumberbitches'. The list goes on. When someone not into a certain type of popular culture stumbles upon a Tumblr thread it may look like the strangest thing, as it is often filled with inside jokes and character pictures conveying an emotion. For instance, a popular Tumblr tag called 'SuperWhoLock' combines three TV shows: Supernatural, Doctor Who and Sherlock. Most of the posts consist of images taken from the different shows or deal with art or stories created by fans. The only way to understand them is if you are completely up to date with the most recent episodes or storylines of each of these TV series, yet several of the posts have been re-blogged more than 55,000 times, which means that there are 55,000 people that are in on the subject and feel some kind of connection to it.

More recently, even fashion trends have seen its inception on these platforms. For instance, a rehash of the popular 90s 'grunge' movement called 'Soft Grunge' started off on Tumblr around 2010 and quickly rose to popularity, inspiring female pop stars like Charli XCX and Sky Ferreira, whose music sounds like anything but grunge. The look usually combines band shirts from early 90s bands like Nirvana and Doc Martens shoes with colour-dyed hair and headbands. Clothing brands such as Urban Outfitters have already seized on the trend to launch clothing lines in the same vein.[41]

One thing to note is that none of these groups are very rigid structural phenomena, which makes them different compared to the old-school subcultures like metalheads or skaters. As The Guardian described in 2014: 'The internet doesn't spawn mass movements, bonded together by a shared taste in music, fashion and ownership of subcultural capital: it spawns brief, microcosmic ones.'[42] Because the internet continuously spawns new ideas and hypes, the hunt for 'next big thing' to fit in is bigger than ever. This also means that the 'next big thing' can also very quickly become 'so last month'.

Conclusion

In this chapter we have demonstrated that Gen Y is engaging with brands that know how to reflect their self-identity. Since youth is not one big homogeneous population, this implies that youth marketers need to identify the different crowds for which their brand has relevance and salience. Next, they have to understand the (brand) personality traits that these crowds of young people are identifying with. Youth brands should never pretend or scream they have the same values or characteristics but prove this by offering valuable products, campaigns, events and utilities that support this positioning both on- and offline. Considering the diversity of Gen Yers, sometimes more than one brand is needed to fit with the entire population. At least a mix of marketing tactics and communication strategies will make sure that no one rejects the brand. Although we have stressed the differences within this generation of consumers, they do of course have a lot in common too. We have talked about the five central themes in the life of Millennials and some consumer trends related to these such as hyper-personalization, glocal, the share-economy, serendipity and party-cipation. In Chapter 7 we will emphasize the most common denominator of Gen Y: the need for hedonism and escapism that is translated into the dominance of positive emotions such as happiness in brand choice.

HOT TAKEAWAYS FOR COOL BRAND BUILDERS

- Gen Y's self-identification with the brand is essential to lever your brand in terms of preference and recommendation.

- Youth choose those brands that both represent the identity aspects they want to accentuate and fit in with the crowd behaviour of the collective identities they aspire to.

- Tribal marketing is not about creating products for segments but about supporting brands that keep youngsters together as a group of enthusiasts.

- As hipsters get swallowed by mainstream, every youngster is a subculture on its own.

- To increase Millennials' identification with your brands, working on the central themes in the lives of youth helps:
  - celebrating youth: enjoying a period of reduced responsibilities and getting the maximum out of it;
  - killing boring: avoiding routines, status quo and lack of passion;
  - wherever whenever;
  - live and learn: the importance of a purpose in life and possessing skills.

- Embrace consumer trends such as party-cipation, serendipity, the sharing economy and mono-tasking.

- While youth is living in a global village, they stress the importance of local and craft.

- Subcultures have moved online.

Happiness: Gen Y's adoration for branded emotions

" _ _ _ ·· _ _ _ ··

In any type of communication that lacks the ability to convey emotions, people have always found a way to compensate. The Morse code on top of this page represents the figure 88 and was used in the 19th century to express 'love and kisses'. We could consider this code to be the ancestor of the currently widespread emoticons and emoji in texting. Generation Y in particular is seeding chat and SMS messages with these textual versions of facial and emotional expressions. Typographical emoticons, as we use today, were not invented by Gen Yers but were first published in 1881 in the US satirical magazine *Puck*.

Freelance artist Harvey Ball designed the well-known 'smiley face' in 1963. The yellow button with two black dots representing eyes and an up-turned curve representing a mouth became the universal symbol of happiness. Ball created it for a large insurance company as part of a campaign to boost employee morale. Scott Fahlman was the first to propose the use of :-) 'for jokes' in e-mails and :-(for 'things that are no joke' in a message to the Carnegie Mellon university computer science general board on 19 September 1982. Meanwhile there are probably hundreds of smiley emoticon variants. Some are more popular in certain countries because of keyboard layouts. For example, an equal sign for the eyes in place of the colon, as in =) is common in Scandinavia where the keys for = and) are placed right beside each other.

It's interesting to see that emoticons also differ between cultures. For instance, East Asians read facial expressions by looking mainly at the eyes, whereas Western cultures emote mainly with the mouth. This is reflected in

East Asian-style emoticons that can be understood without tilting one's head and in which emotions are stressed by variations in the eyes and not in the mouth. For instance (*-*) depicts a neutral face, and (T-T) symbolizes crying eyes or sadness.[1]

How do you get Gen Yers to feel ☺ and not ☹ with your brand? How do you really make a difference with your brand for this target group? It's all about evoking the right emotions with your marketing strategy. In our CRUSH model, happiness seems to be the emotion that has the largest impact on brand leverage. But what makes Gen Y happy? Generation Y grew up in a world full of choice. We know from psychologists such as Barry Schwartz that although we value choice and love to put ourselves in situations of choice, it often undercuts our happiness. The more choice there is, the more we expect to find the perfect fit, but at the same time the less likely we are to pick the best item.[2] In this chapter, we will explore the role of emotions in shaping a successful Gen Y brand. We will show you examples of using positive and negative emotions and zoom in on what makes Gen Yers happy. If you make them happy, they will feel a stronger emotional attachment to your brand.

We think less than we think: the central role of emotions

Emotions are pivotal drivers of our buying behaviour. YouTube is loaded with youngsters unpacking their newly bought game console or mobile phone in an agitated way. Whenever Apple launches a new product, hundreds of people will happily spend more than 30 hours camping in front of the stores to be among the first in line to get one. And you don't have to be a fanatic to get emotional about the things you buy. Just have a look at the products that are present around you. Now think back to why you bought these products. For some of them you might find a very reasonable explanation. For a large group, however, we're sure you cannot bring the exact purpose back to mind. You might remember the occasion or context in which you bought the product. Undoubtedly, you will recall how you felt at that moment. Rational buying is increasingly replaced by emotional shopping. As stressed in the introductory chapter, for Gen Yers shopping is top entertainment, it's all about emotions and experiences. Have a look at the story below. One of the UK boys in our storytelling research shared these lines with us when describing his favourite chocolate brand Cadbury:

> That familiar purple wrapper. It's almost like a member of my family, something which has been there since childhood. I rely on it for comfort, a treat and a motivator. Cadburys chocolate has seen me through exams, stress and heartache. It's been there when I have a celebration and I hope it will be there for some time to come.

When you read this brand story, it's immediately clear that this boy is not merely talking about the functional features of Cadbury chocolates. You do notice a great deal of emotional references, such as being part of the family, helping through stressful moments and being there when celebrating. Gen Y consumers are definitely emotional consumers. When we analysed over 5,000 stories about favourite Gen Y brands, 72 per cent contained positive emotions such as happiness, surprise, excitement, peacefulness, etc. Compare that figure to the poor 29 per cent of stories that referred to functional product characteristics, and you'll understand our point.

Neuropsychology and emotions

Although the importance of emotions in consumer behaviour is certainly not a new topic, there is still a feeling that marketers have minimized them in their market approach in the past. Of course, it is easier to change the packaging of your product or add a different ingredient than to make your brand 'less sad' or more 'passionate'. However, recent neuro-research illustrates that we have been underestimating the impact of emotions on decision making for a long time. There are three different levels in our brain:[3]

- The first layer is called the **'visceral brain'** or 'automatic brain'. These are the type of brain cells we have in common with the most primitive animals. For simple animals like lizards, life is a continuing set of threats and opportunities and an animal has to learn how to react appropriately to all of them. The visceral level is fast. It compares information from the senses with pre-wired patterns of information. Based on this judgement, it swiftly gives instructions for routine deeds: running away, freezing, fighting or relaxing. This part of the brain is therefore responsible for instinctive behaviour.

- The second part is the **limbic system**. This brain adds emotions to the sensory information from the visceral brain. It is the base of the amygdale, a brain structure that is responsible for experiencing positive and negative emotions. Based on the emotional evaluation of a stimulus, the limbic system decides to continue or stop certain performances. We have this brain in common with other mammals. This limbic level is not conscious. It is responsible for so called automatic acts. Think of the way you drive your car or how a skilled piano player seems to do cerebral activities without much effort.

- The limbic system interacts closely with the neocortex, the brain part that developed in the last stage of human evolution, called the **'rational brain'** or the 'reflective brain'. It reflects back on our acts and links sensory information to existing memory structures. Based on these reflections, it tries to alter behaviour. This leads to informed decisions and is therefore often called 'the ratio'.

The actions we undertake are the results of co-processing done by all three layers in our brain. However, research by Joseph LeDoux has shown that the impact of our limbic system is the biggest.[4] Contrary to long-held beliefs, it is not our rational brain that is in the driver's seat. Consumer behaviour is largely controlled by emotions and only sporadically overruled by our ratio.

Yes lollies

A research by the Institute of Psychiatry in London revealed that ice cream has an instant positive effect on the orbitofrontal cortex in the brain. Tip Top, an ice cream company in New Zealand, organized different experiments to validate the positive psychological effects of this sugary goodness. The company launched a campaign that gave consumers a chance to put a personal question they wanted to ask someone on a lolly stick. They could write it down on the Facebook app along with the desired addressee and the reason. Tip Top chose 24 winners and sent the personalized 'Yes Stick' to the person in question. When these people are in a good mood after eating the ice cream they are more likely to say yes. This way the brand creates an extra experience on top of the delicious ice cream taste. All the participants could also win a year's supply of ice cream. Radio station ZM did the giveaways and created online content.

Tip Top had its best summer sales in 80 years, an increase of 14 per cent on the previous summer. During the promotion, Tip Top's market share grew 7 per cent and the brand gained one million social media engagements. Last but not least, 97 per cent of the people who got a Yes Stick gave the right answer.[5]

Implications for branding and marketing to Gen Y

What do these neuropsychology findings teach us as marketers? It is crucial to re-evaluate the role of emotions in our marketing approach for a couple of reasons. First, they have a direct impact on consumer decision making. Emotional thinking works much faster than rational thinking. Our gut feeling directs very quick reactions.[6] The emotional brain processes sensory information in one fifth of the time our cognitive brain takes to assimilate the same input.[7]

Second, emotions have always had an important evolutionary meaning. Our capabilities for detecting anger, fear or disgust have served as powerful indicators for dangerous situations. Similarly, positive emotions have reassured us that we could safely engage in certain activities. Emotions are therefore important attention grabbers. We are wired to pay attention to emotions. Using emotions in communication will therefore draw your customer's attention.[8]

In the middle of our limbic system we find the hippocampus, a brain structure responsible for memory. Together with the emotion centre, the amygdale, it helps us capture new memories. Whenever a new stimulus contains emotions it will trigger the amygdale, which will then create a new memory connection in the hippocampus.[9] Every time we recall the stored information, the accompanying emotion will be revealed again. Thinking back to the exercise at the beginning of this chapter, you can now understand why it is very hard to think of the rational reasons for buying a product while we have no difficulties in recalling our feelings related to the purchase. The limbic system is therefore the seat of emotional branding. Whenever we are confronted with a brand, we will experience these emotions. We do not only consume a product, we are also emotion consumers. We eat chocolates or drink warm drinks such as coffee when we feel sad. We drink tea to relax and take away our agitation. Because of our typical memory structures, our perceptions are constantly coloured by our emotions.

What the heart thinks, the mind speaks. People who experience an emotion tend to start a communication process to share this emotion with others. Research found that only 10 per cent of the emotional experiences are kept secret and never socially shared with anyone.[10] The more disruptive the event, the sooner and more frequently it will be shared.[11] Social sharing of emotions is also positively related to the intensity of emotions. Emotions do not only appear to be an important element in stimulating word-of-mouth but also in creating online buzz. Successful viral movies trigger an emotional response in the recipients' brains.[12]

You're not the only one with mixed emotions: emotions related to brands

Emotions play a central role in understanding youngsters' attitudes towards brands. We know from previous chapters that the adolescent brain is less capable of suppressing emotional triggers. Because the frontal lobe is still

FIGURE 7.1   Emotionality of age groups (sum of all emotions)

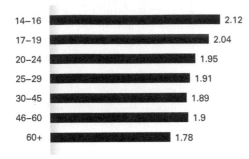

underdeveloped, it cannot sufficiently integrate the more rational informa-tion coming from the neocortex for decision making. Hence, Gen Y behaviour is even more based on emotional decisions. The developing adolescent and young adult brain is less capable of reflecting. Instead of thinking things over, their emotional centre dictates them to take immediate actions. Every parent of adolescents will recall scenes where they seemed unreasonable or unexpectedly burst into tears. Well, they can't help it. It has nothing to do with a bad character or bad intentions; it's in their brains.

These emotional reactions do not limit themselves to everyday life. In our research, we interviewed Gen Yers and older generations about the emotions that were evoked by their most and least favourite brands. When we com-pared the number of emotions that both groups feel when thinking about their favourite and least favourite brand, we noticed that youngsters gener-ally experience more emotions than adults. In Figure 7.1 you will see that adolescents (younger than 20) are not only more emotional in general, their interaction with brands is also more coloured by their feelings.

The scores are averages on a 5-point scale of answers to the question: when thinking about your most favourite brand, to what extent do you feel each of the following:

- Happy
- Disgusted
- Sad
- Angry
- Surprised
- Afraid

So how do emotions influence teenage brand perceptions? What type of emotions do they experience? There are six basic emotions that are univer-sally recognized: happiness, sadness, anger, fear, disgust and surprise. They can be distributed into two groups: the positive emotions and the negative

FIGURE 7.2 Levels of positive and negative emotions

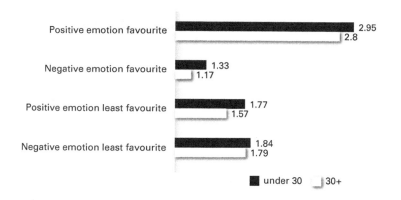

emotions.[13] In our study, we also investigated the tonality of the stories when youngsters were speaking about their favourite brand. As expected, we found that consumers expressed far more positive emotions in their stories than negative ones. The results also showed that youngsters expressed up to 20 per cent more positive emotions for clothing and mobile brands than older generations.

The same exercise was conducted for negative emotions where we found a striking result. We observed a higher intensity of negative emotions for youngsters even when they were talking about their favourite brand (see Figure 7.2). It seems that Generation Y sees the world more in black and white than the older generations. Given the fact that the emotional regulations systems of this target group are still in full expansion, this was no surprise. They simply do not have the cognitive power yet to put emotions into context.

We have been explaining why emotions for Gen Y are extremely important and that successful youth brands will arouse these emotions. But not all emotions are equally important. In Figure 7.3 you will see the frequency of expressed emotions for favourite and least favourite brands. It's clear on the whole that a feeling of happiness is most aroused by brands that touch the heart. Again, this is even more the case for Gen Yers. 'Surprise' is the second most expressed emotion for these stimulation addicts. Youngsters are triggered by new things and are more likely to take risks. They want to explore new things in order to find a new kick. Surprise is an emotion that has been successfully applied in communication. By incorporating humour caused by a surprising element or other unexpected executions, advertisers have successfully drawn attention in their campaigns.[14]

In the following paragraphs, we will discuss how brands can appeal to positive emotions and how they can suffer from arousing negative emotions or benefit from removing the negatives.

FIGURE 7.3   The 6 basic emotions associated with favourite and least favourite brands

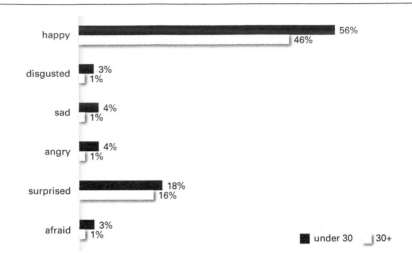

How brands can tap into emotions

Because of the central role of emotions in youth behaviour, hot brands incorporate them in their marketing and communication strategy. Youngsters become emotionally attached to those that do well. Which types of emotions are most effective in creating this sense of attachment? As mentioned before, emotions are broadly categorized in two big groups: positive and negative emotions. In order to boost their general well-being, people try to increase positive emotions and minimize negative emotions. For brands this means that two strategies are possible: you can ensure that your brand is connected with positive feelings or create a brand that is powerful in taking away negative feelings.

Studies on emotional attachment to brands have found that evoking positive emotions is crucial for brand engagement.[15] Brands should induce affection or warm feelings like love, joy or happiness and peacefulness. They should also arouse passion. Gen Yers need to feel excited, delighted or captivated by the brand.

Using the five senses

How do you pave the way for this emotional attachment? One important strategy is transmitting emotions through the five senses, as Martin Lindstrom has stressed in his book *Brand Sense*.[16] Remember, the limbic brain system is adding emotions based on the sensory observations of the visceral brain.

Scents

Special attention needs to be paid to smell. There is a direct connection between our emotion brain centre (the amygdale-hippocampus) and the olfactory region of the brain. Scent is never filtered out: it is instinctive and involuntary. The Gen Yers' nose is therefore always directly pushed into evoked emotions and memories. For many products they can easily recall how they smell and re-experience the stimulated emotion. Think of the artificial scents of Play-Doh modelling compound that bring back childhood memories. Certain perfumes or deodorant scents remind us of the girls we have loved or dad shaving to go to work. Giving your brand a scent that is linked to a positive emotion can enforce your emotional branding.[17] Sony Style stores have a vanilla and mandarin orange scent that was specially designed for them and is supposed to relax shoppers and make them feel more comfortable in the store. The scents used in Abercrombie & Fitch stores to connect with teenage girls are even available at the checkout and actively sold by the store personnel[18].

Fast-food chain KFC recently introduced coffee on its menu. Because the addition of coffee might not be seen as a logical extension of a brand based on fried chicken, the Kentucky-based chain did something extra to draw attention to this event: edible coffee cups. 'Scoff-ee Cups' are branded KFC cups consisting of a combination of sugar paper, cookies and heat-resistant white chocolate. This means that the cup is perfectly capable of keeping your coffee warm while drinking, but it also offers you a little dessert when you have finished your drink. Additionally, the designers also added a wide range of aromas such as 'freshly cut grass', 'coconut sun cream' and 'wild flowers' to the cups. These scents are specifically added to improve the mood of the drinkers, as well as stimulating 'happy summer memories'.[19]

Sound

Another sense that is particularly useful in addressing adolescents is sound. Youngsters use music as powerful emotion regulators. Music creates emotions. Movie soundtracks are the best proof of this. A thriller or romantic movie without the music score creating the required atmosphere and emotions would lead to bad box office. Response to rhythm and rhyme, melody and tune is so basic and so constant across all cultures that they must be part of our evolutionary heritage. Although the neuroscience and psychology effects of music are widely studied, they are still little understood. We do know that the affective states produced through music are universal. By incorporating music in advertising or directly into the product (think of a mobile phone with MP3 function but also a water boiler that whispers at a certain tone), an emotional state can be evoked. Teenage-clothing retailers such as Hollister play loud rhythmic thumping music to get the shoppers' hearts pumping faster. A faster heartbeat will stimulate our brain to survey the environment in order to find out where the excitement comes from. Since the emotional brain dominates in teenagers' behaviour, they will link the arousal to the clothes surrounding them and automatically feel more

TABLE 7.1   Sounds & Emotions

TEMPO	slow	sadness, boredom, disgust
	fast	activity, surprise, happiness, pleasantness potency, fear, anger
PITCH LEVEL	low	boredom, pleasantness, sadness
	high	surprise, potency, anger, fear, activity
AMPLITUDE MODULATION	small	disgust, anger, fear, boredom
	large	happiness, pleasantness, activity, surprise

Source: Gardner MP, Mood states and consumer behaviour: a critical review. *Journal of Consumer Research* 1985 Dec; 12. featured in: Gobé M, *Emotional Branding. The new paradigm for connecting brands to people.* 2nd rev edn (1st edn 2002). Allworth Press, New York, 2009.

attracted to them.[20] In the 1970s Scherer and Oshinsky tested different sounds on subjects and even then had found that apart from tempo, even pitch level and amplitude modulations of sounds can evoke other emotions (see Table 7.1).

Would like some music with your coffee?

Music has always had a special place in Starbucks' strategy. For example, the coffee chain purchased the 'Hear Music' brand back in 1999 and turned it into a concept for in-store music, in-store CD sales, branded CD retail stores and a music label. In March 2015 the company decided to stop selling physical CDs in their coffee houses due to declining sales. Completely reflecting the new ways of the music industry, it did not take very long before they announced a new relevant partner to continue their focus on a musically enhanced retail experience: Spotify.[21]

The Swedish music streaming service will be powering the music played inside the Starbucks stores, but the partnership goes further than that. Baristas and members of Starbucks' loyalty programme alike get access to curated 'Starbucks Spotify playlists', meaning that they are able to directly influence what is being played while they purchase and consume their Frappucino. These playlists are also made available publicly on Spotify itself as well as the Starbucks MobileApp, meaning the musical in-store experience can be continued outside. Additionally, Starbucks customers are able to gather points 'Stars' for the 'My Starbucks Rewards' loyalty programme by signing up for a Spotify Premium account. Starbucks continues its special connection to music but evolves in the 21st century, just as its trendy clients are doing.[22]

Visual appeal: shape and colours

Emotions can more easily be triggered by visuals than by text. The saying 'a picture is worth a thousand words' illustrates this beautifully. Gillette razors convey the efficiency of their innovative blades not by verbally explaining but by using the handle as a messenger for the blade. The Mach 3 handle had three grips symbolizing the blades, the Fusion razor (using five blades) has... five ribbed grips on top of the handle. Emotions are often difficult to express in words. On the other hand, making a simple drawing like an emoticon can be so much more meaningful than a written text. Therefore it is better to use one strong visual than a larger text in your communication to youngsters.

Clothing retailers targeting Gen Y are often masters in creating emotions visually because they immediately witness sales effect for every effort they make. Urban Outfitters, for example, practically rebuild their stores every few months to remain a shopping adventure for youth. H&M regularly change the billboard-sized graphics in the store. Both Abercrombie & Fitch and sister store for teens Hollister create visually engaging worlds with, for instance, a real-time camera showing the waves crashing on Huntington Beach with California time ticking on the screen.[23] Just like sounds and scents, colours trigger very specific automatic responses in the cerebral cortex. They can activate thoughts, memories and particular behaviour. Yellow, for instance, is right in the mid-range of wavelengths that our eyes can detect. It is the brightest colour and thus the one that most easily attracts our attention. It is no coincidence that road signs and police scene-markers often use the colour and it's also how the Yellow Pages got colour marked. Generally, colours with long wavelengths (such as red) are arousing and stimulating and those with short wavelengths (like blue) lower blood pressure, pulse and respiration rates.[24] If you have often wondered why so many global brands at the top of Gen Y's wish list (Coca-Cola, Levi's, Vodafone, H&M, Mars, DIESEL, the list goes on...) use the dominant colour red in their logo, now you know.

Even product design affects emotions. The Gillette handle described above was a good example. Think of the Apple designs. The fact that their designers take inspiration from previous decades, as illustrated in the chapter on brand uniqueness, is addressing the needs of Gen Y consumers to anchor themselves with authentic designs that transpose cultural values into the 2010s.

Touch haptics and taptics

Our sense of feeling is the first one we develop, long before the sense of hearing or seeing. 'The sense of touch is the basis of our self-awareness and worldy wisdom,' declares haptic research psychologist Martin Grunwald in an interview with *Eppi* Magazine.[25] Yet, the use of the power of touch predominantly remains focused on product design, for example Coca-Cola's iconic bottles. Research has shown that the haptic elements of packaging can indeed result in more positive brand evaluations, but the use of haptics has rarely gone beyond this. Over the past few years haptic marketing has gained more traction, likely thanks to evolutions in technology, specifically in the area of mobile devices. Recently, research has shown that a technique based on bursts of hair being blown on your hand 'Ultrahaptics' is able to evoke a whole range of emotions, from happiness to excitement or sadness. In a sense, this technique makes it possible to create the sense of touch without having a physical element in place.[26]

The Brazilian restaurant chain Outback used an early application of innovative touch-based marketing back in 2013. Customers celebrating their birthday could sit in a Facebook-connected chair that was fitted with moving arms capable of hugging the person sitting down. Every birthday message on the Facebook timeline of the party animal made the chair 'hug' that person.[27] More recently and on a larger scale, American TV channel Showtime promoted the fourth season of their hit show *Homeland* by enhancing its trailer with a touch-based experience. Watching the trailer on the Showtime app on your phone resulted in the device vibrating concurrently with an explosion on the screen, producing an immersive experience.[28]

Similarly, the Apple Watch released in 2015 has a special 'Taptic Engine' that provides haptic feedback to the wearer. Upon receiving a notification or an alert, or when a button on the touch screen is pressed, the Watch sends out a slight vibration to the wrist. This mechanism also enables the user to communicate with other wearers at a very discreet level, for example by sending vibration cues to get someone's attention or by sending your own heartbeat to someone else.[29]

Branding on negative emotions

Capitalizing on negative emotions seems a less suitable brand strategy for Generation Y. There are some common practices of using negative emotions in branding towards youngsters. A first is within the context of controversial advertising where negative emotions or shock tactics have widely been used as a legitimate creative technique to grab attention. Controversial advertising is generally created by transgressing a certain moral code or by showing things that outrage the moral or physical senses such as in the case of provocation or disgust. Arousing the negative emotions would then stimulate cognitive processing which would result in better ad recall. Especially when looking at the negative emotion 'disgust' we notice that a lot of ad executions use this emotion to reach youngsters, thinking it has a different and more positive effect on this age group.[30] But in studies of De Pelsmacker and Van den Bergh provocation seems to be an emotion that occurs to the same extent in all consumer segments. Provocation in advertising actually leads to less product category and brand name recognition and to a more negative attitude towards the advertisement. Nevertheless, it does not seem to affect the attitude towards the brand, nor the intention to buy the product. Still, although it's not hurting the brand, it won't help the brand's impact on Gen Y either.[31] This was confirmed in a study among young females in which

90 emotional fashion advertisements representing 56 different clothing brands were tested. Two emotional dimensions had a positive effect on ad attitude: hypo-activation (restful, soothed, drowsy) and pleasure (social affection, desire). The third dimension consisting of negative emotions such as anger, fear, irritation or tension had no effect at all on evaluation of the ads[32].

For their 2014 'Back To School'-campaign, clothing retailer American Apparel used up-skirt pictures of models seemingly wearing typical school uniform skirts. The company received a lot of negative buzz, and eventually the Advertising Standards Authority (ASA) decided to ban the ads.[33] American Apparel have already had their fair share of controversies in the past but they seem to embrace that provocative image. The fact that they put up billboards saying 'We're not politically correct. But we have good ethics' only strengthens that embrace. CEO Dov Charney was seen as the main reason for these controversial elements. AA's board decided to downgrade him from president of the company to 'consultant' after the release of a long list of personal offences, ranging from sexual harassment of employees and models to racist comments. In December 2014, Charney got fired altogether.[34] The new CEO, Paula Schneider, immediately promised to pull back on the sexual undertones of American Apparel's campaigns. One of the first moves was airbrushing the clearly visible nipples and pubic hair that their online lingerie store had become famous for. This in itself, however, caused puzzled public response as well, with certain critics accusing American Apparel of disrespecting the female body. Additionally, casting calls for new models asked for 'real models, not Instagram hoes or thots'. As one blog out it: 'American Apparel plans to fall back into line with the rest of the fashion industry's standards of beauty.' It seems that the campaigns under Charney's reign left American Apparel with a certain controversial identity that hit the mark with some customers, and the radical switch towards a cleaner, more 'positive' image could backfire.[35]

During the 2014 World Cup, the Hispanic department of American insurance company AllState Insurance utilized Mr Bad Luck, a kind of brand mascot they had already been using for four years. This slick-looking man in a suit was the 'personification of misfortune' and was the living proof that nobody is safe from 'Bad Luck', even in soccer. The idea was to encourage fans to send bad luck to the opposing team via a tweet with the hashtag #sendbadluck (#EnviaLaMalaSuerte). Both Spanish and English tweets were taken into account, despite the actual hashtag originating in Spanish. During the game, real-time videos had Mr Bad Luck explaining how he caused one of the tweets to actually happen. For example, during the opening match between Brazil and Croatia, someone asked for an own goal by the Brazilians. This wish came true as Brazilian player Marcelo did exactly what was asked. Mr Bad Luck quickly put up a video on Twitter explaining how he threw Marcelo's contact lenses in the trash before the game, causing the player to look at the wrong goal. During the whole tournament and its 64 games, over 300 videos like this one were put up responding to tweets in a clever way. The hashtag #sendbadluck became the top trending Twitter topic in the

US five times, while Mr Bad Luck's Twitter account saw a 75 per cent growth in followers and a staggering 1265 per cent growth in engagement. The effects were similar on Facebook, where the campaign page grew 20 per cent in likes and had an increased engagement of 569 per cent. Despite branding on the inherent negative emotions of wishing ill upon opponents, AllState used this idea to great effect.[36]

Removing negative feelings

When negative emotions for the young have a clear link with your products or brand, removing the bad feelings can be a much better emotional brand strategy. Trying to study for finals is hard these days, with all kinds of distractions keeping students from focusing on their material. Streaming service Netflix knows that their service is one of the bigger issues students face while trying to study. To acknowledge this problem, they launched a livestream on Periscope with a camera pointed at a guinea pig. The animal could sit in a part of its rectangular box called either 'Study' or 'Netflix'. The Twitter-hashtag #studyornetflix quickly started buzzing and whether by chance or not, Professor Fuzzlepants as the guinea pig was called spent most its time in the 'Study' area. In a light-hearted way, Netflix tackled an issue that a lot of Gen Yers are able to relate to.[37]

Another frequent usage of negative emotions can be found in health care and prevention campaigns targeting Gen Yers. Although this is one of the more successful applications, advertising in this area often comes across as 'too moralizing'. Youngsters are already confronted all day with information on what's good and not good for them and too often this information is not turned into behaviour.

Hijacks, hate and videotapes: when negative buzz takes over

For most brands and products, association with positive emotions clearly is the favourable strategy. However, this is not always completely within the span of control of a marketer or brand manager. Sometimes your brand evokes negative feelings that weren't intended. The Walmart example in this chapter is a good illustration. Like all evoked emotions, the negative ones will certainly lead to negative buzz. We only need to look at the numerous hate groups on Facebook or other social networks to understand how negative feelings stimulate consumers to spread the word. Predicting what will lead to negative emotions is hard. There are three main reasons why consumers start disliking a brand.[38]

A first source of negative feelings is a **physical characteristic** of the brand. Think of youngsters who get angry because their mobile phone is refusing to make a connection to the internet or who are disappointed because their expensive beauty product did not have the desired effect. Brands have few other options in this case than listening to the criticisms and learning from them for later product development. When Apple released the new iPhone 6 Plus, it did not take very long before complaints appeared on the internet about the aluminium phone bending under pressure, for example while in the pockets of tight trousers. Several videos surfaced of people trying (and succeeding) to bend the phone with their bare hands. The issue was quickly dubbed 'Bendgate' and caused rivalling smartphone designers and online commentators alike to poke fun at the company. Even though Apple tried to cross off the issue as 'extremely rare', future iPhones will most likely get stronger materials to prevent the same type of buzz arising yet again.[39]

Brand hate can also have a more symbolic cause. In the chapter on self-identification we discussed how youngsters build their identities by connecting with brands that are associated with their social or aspired lifestyle group. Similarly, they will reject brands that are **connected with their non-groups**. This often results in strong negative feelings towards the brand. The British sportswear label Lonsdale inadvertently became the victim of such a symbolic rejection. A couple of years ago the brand became very popular among European extreme-right-supporting teenagers. A carefully placed bomber jacket could leave the letters 'nsda' visible in the Lonsdale logo on sweaters. NSDA is an acronym standing for National-Sozialistische Deutsche Arbeiter and one letter short of NSDAP, Hitler's Nazi party.[40] Soon, the brand became a symbol of neo-Nazism in Europe. In the Netherlands, Belgium, France and Germany, Lonsdale was associated with teenagers of extreme-right sympathies. The brand was even banned in certain schools and nightclubs because of this reason.

Lonsdale reacted to this development by sponsoring anti-racist events and campaigns and by refusing to deliver products to known neo-Nazi retailers. In 2003, the 'Lonsdale Loves All Colours' campaign was launched, emphasizing non-white fashion models, along with increased support for initiatives that combat racism.[41] These moves to distance the brand from neo-Nazi associations, combined with the police's increased awareness of the fashion and symbols used by neo-Nazis, have made the brand less popular in far-right crowds. Although brands are seldom hijacked by a certain subculture, this example shows that it is important to keep track of your brand's role in identity formation. Extreme-right youth are brand sensitive since they are also far right on the 'me (I'm better)' axis in our tribal mapping. Brands help them to stand out from others and often they find symbolic links with your brands you haven't even noticed yourself. New Balance sneakers for instance, with a large N on the side, appealed to them because the N was seen as shorthand for 'Nazi'. The German brand Thor Steinar, founded in 2002, was an immediate hit in the right-wing scene due to its connection with Nordic mythology, which is an important element in Nazi ideas on racial purity. In 2009, when the label was sold to International Brands General Trading a company based in... Dubai neo-Nazi groups suddenly called for a boycott of the brand.[42]

Brand hijacking through social media

Brand hijacking happens when Gen Yers appropriate the brand for themselves and add meaning to it. Social media such as Facebook, YouTube and Twitter in combination with the marketing savvyness of Gen Y have fuelled this trend. Many companies are completely out of touch with these kinds of online conversation and have no online reputation management at all. Brand hijacks don't always have to be a negative thing. Greggs is the largest bakery chain in the UK with a heritage dating back to the 1930s. In 2014, the company discovered the power of the internet the hard way, but they turned it into a great opportunity. Due to an algorithm hiccup, searching for 'Greggs' on Google brought up not the actual logo of the brand, but one saying: 'Greggs Providing sh*t to scum for over 70 years'. Once this mistake was discovered, social media did the rest. People were responding saying how they agreed with the sentiment of the 'new' tagline, while poking fun and creating a lot of negative buzz. For many people the brand comes across as old-fashioned and this opportunity was perfect to showcase that. Greggs' social media team, however, did not resort to the usual dry press release that was probably expected, but instead joined in on the social media fun. They did not hide their desperation in their tweets, ultimately offering the main culprit Google a pack of freshly baked doughnuts if they would fix the mistake as quickly as possible: 'Hey @GoogleUK, fix it and they're yours! #FixGreggs'. The hashtag #FixGreggs quickly started trending inside and outside the UK, and suddenly the topic shifted from laughing at the brand towards laughing with them, while claims such as 'leave Greggs alone' appeared on bigger news outlets as well. The day of the mishap, the Greggs Twitter account saw a 553 per cent increase in mentions, with barely any of the messages attributing any blame to the brand. In fact, almost a quarter of all the posts about the brand concerned the great way in which they handled the whole deal. In a brave move, the company even referred back to the 'crisis' a day later when they asked Google to create a special 'Google doodle' for them on the search engine's homepage. That, however, was left without result. Greggs almost had its reputation tarnished due to an unfortunate social media hijacking, but it turned that whole problem around and actually came out of it with an improved and renewed positive image.[43]

The Malaysian branch of Watsons, the biggest health and beauty care chain in Asia, took a completely different approach. Adam Minter, a writer for Bloomberg and a customer of Watsons', noticed that the security seal on a bottle of medicine had been broken and reattached, which is in violation of several safety guidelines. On returning to his store to get a refund, he noticed that quite a few other packages had the same issue, but the shop assistant did not seem to care much about his complaints. So he turned to Twitter, and pointed out the unsafe behaviour to an account that was seemingly the official Watsons account: @watsonsmalaysia. The account sporting fewer than 100 followers quickly responded, accusing him of 'provoking', while also posting unfriendly comments towards users supporting Adam's original tweet. Minter then took to his blog and wrote an entry about his experience, also explaining that he tried to contact Watsons directly about whether or not the Twitter account was official, without success. His post went viral throughout Malaysia about two days later, triggering an official response from the Watsons marketing department both to Minter himself and via their official Facebook page. Even though they tried to rectify the issues with the tampered-with bottles and claimed that the police had been notified about the unauthorized Twitter account, the situation had already spiralled out of control. Other Watsons customers jumped in on the subject and complained about the same issues they had encountered shopping there. Ignoring the social media buzz and consequently not noticing that someone had taken over the brand's presence there suddenly resulted in a crisis for Watsons.[44]

Sometimes brand hijacks can even bring a new start for brands. Dr Martens shoes, initially intended as a gardening shoe for senior women, was hijacked by punk teenagers with ideological purposes and this made the brand a success.[45] Corona beer was a Mexican beer for Mexican people until it was discovered by US surfers on a surf trip who gave it a cool beach lifestyle connotation. It can now be found in 150 countries.[46]

Corporate hate affecting brands

A third reason for Gen Y to hate a brand involves the company and corporate cultures and policies behind the brand. Brands are not solely intangible. They act in the real world through the actions of the company behind the brands, such as the everyday execution of marketing strategies and overall activity related to social, ethical or political issues. Consumers do not make a distinction between a brand and the parent company. Negative feelings towards the company are easily transmitted to the brand.

In 2014 LEGO discovered the effects of making unpopular corporate deals. The Danish toy manufacturer has a long-standing collaborative history with Anglo-Dutch oil and gas company Shell, dating back to the 1960s. This includes for example the sale of branded LEGO toys in Shell petrol stations. However, fighting against Shell's oil drilling activities in the Arctic, environmental organisation Greenpeace directed its actions towards LEGO. Referring to the massively popular 'The LEGO Movie' (2014) and the accompanying song 'Everything is awesome', Greenpeace launched their own version on YouTube: 'LEGO: Everything is NOT awesome'. The campaign video pointed out that Shell is 'polluting children's imagination' and asked viewers to sign a petition asking LEGO to end their deal with Shell. Over seven million people watched the video, and equally as many signed the petition. Even though LEGO tried to resist by pointing out that Greenpeace should act towards Shell and not them, the company decided in late 2014 not to renew the running deal with Shell.[47]

Similarly, various FIFA partners came under scrutiny for supporting the poor conditions of workers preparing the 2022 football World Cup in Qatar, as well as for having ties to an organization that has increasingly been accused of corruption and shady business practices. Graphic designers on the creative community platform BoredPanda redesigned logos of companies such as Coca-Cola, McDonald's and Adidas to portray aspects of the human rights abuses they are supporting by sponsoring the FIFA tournament. For instance, McDonald's logo has two whips forming the iconic M, with the message 'Proud sponsor of human rights abuses in Qatar' underneath. These viral 'anti-logos' did not result in corporations reducing or ceasing their monetary support for FIFA, but did cause public statements from Adidas and Visa urging the organization to be more transparent.[48]

Don't worry, be happy: arousing happiness through experiences

As we have discussed earlier in this chapter, brands that are capable of evoking feelings of happiness for Gen Y will definitely benefit from this strategy. Brands that arouse happiness help Gen Yers to forget about their daily stress. In InSites Consulting's *Generation Y Around the World* survey among 4,000 Millennials in 16 countries, more than half of Millennials were expressing they feel happy. In particular, Dutch (65 per cent), Swedish (66 per cent), Brazilian (69 per cent), Chinese (66 per cent) and Indian (68 per cent) Millennials are the most happy youth groups. A relatively larger proportion of UK youth (almost 1 out of 5) is feeling unhappy. Together with Italian and French Gen Yers, they are the most unhappy nations.

To most GenYers around the world, holidays, having sex and being challenged and achieving something are the top three sources of happiness. Connecting with friends and family and listening to music are also frequently mentioned. Graduating, getting a driver's licence, meeting the love of your life are all remarkable moments in youth's life leading to happiness. Divorcing parents, diseases and broken relationships make them sad. For many Millennials cool brands know how to tap into the emotion of happiness. Coca-Cola and technology brands like Apple, Microsoft, Samsung and Nintendo especially are connecting with this generation's emotional mindset.[49] 'There are so many life stages between the ages of 12 and 30', says Peter Jung, Senior Business Leader at MasterCard International interviewed by us.

> It's filled with milestones and firsts; a first job, date, car, going to a concert or travelling without their parents, going off to university. Each of these is meaningful and of course presents both an opportunity and a challenge for a company like MasterCard. The needs of our customers are shifting during these life stages and we need to stay relevant or they'll move on. University students and young professionals are likely to become affluent families or small businesses, so they're high value to brands in an industry like financial services. Historically we've had a functional approach like delivering products that offer convenience and safety. Today we're striving for emotional engagement and relevance.[50]

In consumer research, academics have only just started to develop frameworks and scales to study the effects of brands on happiness. So the whole domain is still fairly unknown territory for marketers and researchers. Although some research found that consumption with a social or high-status impact such as car ownership correlates moderately positively with happiness, it tells us little about the role of brands.[51] From our own 5,000 brand stories, we have learned that Gen Yers develop extreme devotional relationships with brands and feelings of happiness are certainly associated with their favourite brands. Religions and philosophies such as Buddhism and Stoicism, however, taught us that striving for external goods or to make the world conform to your wishes is merely striving after wind. According to this view, happiness can only be found within, especially by breaking our attachments to external things.

Can't get no satisfaction: a formula to find happiness

In *The Happiness Hypothesis*, Jonathan Haidt lists a number of principles from ancient wisdom as well as modern neuroscience that could be helpful to our understanding of what will affect Gen Yers' feelings of happiness. The first one is called 'the progress principle', which basically means that pleasure comes more from making progress towards goals than from achieving them. That big promotion you anticipated, finishing a big project, dreaming of the printed version of this book during nocturnal writing... The moment we finally succeed won't make us happier in the end. This is again related to the functioning of our brains. The front left cortex gives us a pleasurable feeling whenever we make progress towards a goal but we will only feel a short-term effect when the left prefrontal cortex reduces its activity after the goals have been achieved. In other words, it really is the journey that counts, not the destination.

The second notion is 'the adaptation principle'. If you only have 10 seconds to name the very best and very worst things that could ever happen to you, you will probably think of winning the lottery jackpot and becoming paralyzed from the neck down. Wrong again. We are very bad at forecasting emotions. We tend to overestimate the intensity and the duration of our emotional reactions. Within a year lottery winners and paraplegics have both returned most of the way to their baseline levels of happiness. Adaptation is partly linked to our neurons. Nerve cells respond to new stimuli but gradually they habituate, firing less to stimuli they have become used to. It's why Seth Godin got bored of seeing cows in the French landscape and started writing a book on the *Purple Cow*. It is change that contains vital information to preserve our bodies and life. Human beings not only habituate, they also recalibrate. Each time we hit a new target, we replace it with another. We always want more than we have, which will always bring us back to our brain's default level of happiness. Good fortune or bad; in the long run, both will bring you back to the same feeling of happiness.

Based on studying identical twins, some researchers found that about half of our happiness is determined by our genes. It might surprise you that the elderly are happier than the young even though the old have so many more health problems. But they adapt to most chronic health problems. Another finding in happiness research is that most environmental and demographic factors influence happiness very little. This results in a real formula for happiness:

Happiness = 50% S + 10% C + 40% V

where:

S = your biological set point, predefined in your genes.

C = life conditions that you don't have under control, circumstances such as socio-economic status, health, income, sex and others.

V = voluntary activities you do yourself.

Pleasures versus gratifications

Knowing this, you will understand that with our brands and products, we will only be able to influence 40 per cent of Gen Y's feelings of happiness. Of course this makes it even more important to know what kind of activities will have the biggest impact on the 40 per cent. The tool that helped psychologists to find the answer to this conundrum is known as the 'experience sampling method', and was invented by the Hungarian-born co-founder of positive psychology, Csikszentmihalyi.

In his studies, subjects carried a pager that beeped several times a day. At every beep thousands of people wrote down what they were doing and how much they were enjoying it. In this way he found out what people really enjoy doing, not just what they remember having enjoyed. The first one is physical or bodily pleasure: mostly eating and sex. But there was one thing that people valued even more than eating chocolate after sex: total immersion in a task that is challenging yet closely matched to one's abilities. This can be reached during physical movements such as skiing, driving fast or playing team sports. The state of 'flow' can also happen during solitary creative activities such as painting, writing or photography. The key aspects of getting into this flow are: a clear challenge that fully engages your attention; you have the required skills to meet the challenge; and you get immediate feedback on how you are doing at each step (compare with 'the progress principle' above).[52]

These findings explain why Gen Yers are so addicted to computer and video games. The three conditions to get into a mental state of flow are clearly present in most video games. If you want this generation to connect with your brands and products, keep this in mind. Two things make them happy: pleasures and gratifications (see Table 7.2).

TABLE 7.2   What makes Gen Y Happy?

PLEASURES:	delights that have clear sensory and strong emotional components (as we have described in the section about using the five senses to arouse emotions)
	they feel good in the moment BUT sensual memories fade quickly
GRATIFICATIONS:	engaging activities that relate to Gen Y's interests and strengths and allow them to lose self-consciousness
	accomplish something/learn something/improve something/strengthen connections between people which can lead to 'flow'

SOURCE: Gardner MP, Mood states and consumer behaviour: a critical review. *Journal of Consumer Research* 1985 Dec; 12. featured in: Gobé M, *Emotional Branding. The new paradigm for connecting brands to people*. 2nd rev edn (1st edn 2002). Allworth Press, New York, 2009.

Gratifications will often take place as 'experiences' and Gen Yers will have higher levels of happiness when experiencing something. This is not only thanks to the state of flow but also because experiences are mostly social happenings or activities connecting them with other people. A study from 2008 published in the *British Medical Journal* reported that happiness in social networks spread from person to person like a virus. The happiness memes of even complete strangers will cheer us up. In the last part of this chapter we will discuss how these experiences can be supported by brands. 'Self-development and self-actualization are both key terms to describe what Gen Y is all about', says Mariken Kimmels, Marketing Director Heinz Continental Europe in an interview with us. 'For the previous generation material symbols like a BMW represented status. Today having an influence on what's happening is providing status: the fact that you are able to design a brand, to be part of the ones deciding the strategy of your employer, or to change politics. This generation shows its face by realizing and changing stuff, whereas the previous one was more occupied with showing off their status.'[53]

Nike Most Wanted helps young soccer players to succeed

'Nike Most Wanted' is a competition that gives amateur soccer players from around the world the chance to join the Nike Academy, a special soccer academy funded and run by Nike purely to help and guide talented players to a professional team. Starting in August 2014, players in more than 30 countries could sign up using the Nike Football app. Initially they were able to register for local try-outs held throughout October and November, where coaches and professional soccer players evaluated them. Eventually 38 players from 23 different nations successfully completed these trials and proceeded to a 'Global Showcase', which took place at St George's Park, home of both the English national team and the Nike Academy itself. Before they went through the final tests, they had the opportunity to meet Belgian star Eden Hazard to talk about various aspects of life as a professional player. In the end, eight players remained and became officially part of the Nike Academy. Since the foundation of the Nike Academy back in 2009 the brand has launched various initiatives to find raw talent for their school, including the 'Most Wanted' campaign. So far, 39 alumni have proceeded to tie up professional contracts for well-known teams such as Celtic and Hamburg, proving that Nike can help future stars to become actual stars.[54]

Magic moments: brand activation and the gamification of marketing

Events can make a powerful contribution to an emotional branding strategy because they connect the social Gen Yers with peers and let them experience gratifications. 'The shortest distance between strangers is fun and laughter', says Hubert Grealish, Global Head of Brand Communications at Diageo, interviewed by us. 'It is linked to celebrations: which is happiness related to a certain occasion, releasing energy in a shared experience.'[55] Events give brands an opportunity to showcase their strengths in a festive and emotionally charged atmosphere. The fun and happiness that youth experience at events can create a bond with the brand. Brands that are able to fulfil Gen Yers' need of fun and entertainment and understand how to cater for their pursuit of happiness will enjoy a better connection with them. When youth engage with brands at events, products and brands are often featured as part of the experience through product trials. Brands will leave a memorable understanding of the brand values, resulting in youth affiliating the product with the created atmosphere. Experiential and emotional marketing creates brand advocacy and drives word-of-mouth communication.[56] The strengths of event marketing are derived from four features:

- the personal live and multi-sensory experience of brand values;
- the interactive and personal dialogues between participants, spectators and brand representatives;
- self-initiation: voluntary participation and thus higher involvement;
- dramaturgy bringing the brand image to life and capturing the imagination of consumers.[57]

Events have been known to increase Gen Y's emotional attachment to the brand and that's why many youth brands engage in them. Think of the Red Bull Flugtag, DIESEL-U-Music Tour, Microsoft Xbox championship, etc. Since music is still one of the most universal youth passions, many youth event activities are linked to music events. Merely sponsoring an event is old-school and wouldn't work with the critical Gen Y target group anymore. If the brand owns the event, then the experience becomes a reflection of the brand.[58]

Chewing gum brand Trident sponsored a rock festival in Rio de Janeiro To create conversations about the brand, it initiated two different activations. The first one made use of Gigapan that takes huge panoramic pictures. Capturing a panoramic picture of youth waiting for the shows on main stage, it automatically took count of the number of people smiling by using facial recognition software. Once uploaded on the Facebook fan page, people could tag themselves on the pictures. Over 2,200 smiles were identified during the festival. The second activation was the Trident Cabin powered by YouTube. In a red cabin UK phone box style youth could play air guitar and technology tracked hand movements and translated them into real sounds. The performance was taped and immediately placed on YouTube to share through social media.[59]

PayPal also took to the festival scene to show how they can help festival-goers in various ways. Using a mobile app, visitors to the San Francisco festival Outside Lands could pay for their food or drinks without having to use a wallet. While you were waiting in line, you could check in to the specific food or drink vendor you were waiting to purchase from. Once you ordered, the cashier could check the system and see your name and photo on a screen. They could then send you the charge, and the only thing that you had to do was accept this to finish the payment. Apart from this, they also provided the festival with branded utilities such as photobooths, a booth to charge phones and lockers to store your valuables.[60]

Pedro Suárez-Vértiz was dubbed the most iconic singer in Peruvian history, until a motor speech disorder made him permanently lose the ability to talk back in 2011. Singing became impossible, so the bank BBVA wanted to help. Using an online petition they asked fans to sing as loudly as possible.

If 1 million fans fulfilled this request, Suárez-Vértiz would do one more show with the help of the audience. In total more than 1.4 million people participated, which also meant that BBVA also suddenly had access to personal details of 1.4 million people as everyone was asked to willingly fill in their details. The reasoning for the campaign was exactly this: gathering data without being intrusive. The eventual concert turned into a very emotional affair as 40,000 people sang their lungs out to replace the voice of their idol as he was playing the guitar. Using 800 microphones, the audience became the singer. The concert was eventually also voted as 'concert of the year' by a Peruvian newspaper, beating massive names like Metallica and One Direction.[61]

The gamification of marketing

As a consequence of what marketers have learned from positive psychology and Haidt's happiness theory, we have recently noticed a growing trend of gamification in marketing. In her book *Reality Is Broken* Jane McGonical claims that gaming is probably the healthiest and most productive activity humans can carry out. In her opinion, games are not an escape from reality but rather the most optimal way to tackle reality and find a gateway to a balanced ideal mood.[62] By using gaming techniques, obesity, abuse of authority, and other behavioural problems can be solved. The appeal and power of gaming mechanisms became quite clear with the success of 'stupid games' on smartphones or tablets such as *Plants vs Zombies*, Rovio's *Angry Birds* of which all players together would represent 200 million daily gaming minutes, or Zynga's *Farmville* hype on Facebook with almost 85 million players in 2010.[63]

Gamification can be defined as the use of game thinking and mechanisms to engage users in a certain behaviour. The most used gamification techniques include rewarding people virtually with status symbols like badges or levels, or with real awards: money, vouchers, exclusive experiences or content and extra features. In general, gamification is marketing's answer to the fact that getting the attention of Generation Y is the hardest part today. Traditionally advertisers would pay (rent media space, GRPs) to get the attention of their audience; with gamification they let them play to earn their response. Developing so-called online or mobile 'advergames' is of course the most literal way to use gaming for marketing purposes.

In April 2011, Unilever launched 'The Magnum Pleasure Hunt across the internet' to market the new Magnum ice cream, Temptation Fruit. It was the most tweeted web address in the world after just one week of launch. At first when visiting the site, you are guided to move a Magnum girl with the arrow keys, as in a computer game. Then the action takes off. The girl runs along different websites and brand pages (Samsung, Dove, some tourist sites, jewellery, Bed Head hair products, Spotify, Saab ...) where she is interacting with things on the pages while you have to get her to collect cranberries. A professional ballet dancer was chosen to get all the moves right.[64]

Following the success (an impressive 7 million players took part) Unilever launched a follow-up in April 2012, 'Magnum Pleasure Hunt 2 across the globe' to support the launch of its new variety Magnum Infinity. Again, you have to control the female character but this time the journey travels through New York, Paris and Rio collecting 'bonbons' and cocoa nibs along the way using Bing maps Streetside view interface. She passes famous brands such as luxury Italian jeweller Bvlgari, on-trend surf manufacturer Quicksilver, KLM Royal Dutch Airlines, and the exclusive Hotel Fasano in Rio de Janeiro. From street lamps to road signs, each backdrop featured within the game was built to perfection from a staggering 6,500 photographs and 3D recreation, ensuring the game boasts an astoundingly life-like look and feel.[65] In Amsterdam, they took this campaign a little further and extended it into a real-time mobile augmented reality game for one day. There were 150 chocolate bonbons hidden across the '9 straatjes' ('nine streets': a trendy district) of Amsterdam. The aim was to collect them first through the augmented reality app, and win a trip to New York.[66]

In Stockholm McDonald's installed a large interactive billboard challenging people for a digital Pong game against the computer. They could control the game via their mobile phones and if they were able to last for more than 30 seconds, they won a coupon (sent to their mobile) for free fast food at a nearby store.[67]

But gamification techniques can be used in all types of marketing actions and brand activations.

International pastry chain Cinnabon launched a low calorie cinnamon roll in Russia by installing shelves full of rolls on top of the escalators in shopping malls. To receive a free treat, people first had to burn calories by climbing the escalator in the opposite direction. The campaign increased brand awareness by 43 per cent and traffic to Cinnabon stores grew by 7 per cent during the event.[68]

Nike encouraged their runner audience to do something in return for exclusive offers. To launch the new Air Zoom 18 Structure line, Polish users of the Nike+ app could join an event called 'Plan the Unexpected'. Those who signed up then received push notifications throughout the following week with surprise running challenges. These challenges were designed to make runners go out during cold, dreary weather rather than the usual sunny afternoon run, and contained time limits or distances to run. Participants that were quickest to accept, ran the fastest or covered the most distance received thermo-active letters, informing them that they had won limited editions of the new Air Zoom shoes.[69]

Magic spaces: pop-up stores

Apart from magic moments on events, Gen Yers can also experience gratification in a special retail environment. Attitudes towards fashion retailers are mainly influenced by youth's shopping experience. During consumer interactions with the store's physical environment and atmosphere, its employees and its offerings, bonds are created between the brand and Generation Y consumers.[70] Pop-up stores, bars or restaurants that promote a brand or product line for a short time are one of the latest ways of creating an environment that is highly experiential for Gen Y consumers. Upscale fashion brand Comme des Garçons was the first to discover that it sparks off excitement and surprise through its temporary nature, intentionally springing up and disappearing quickly. Martini opened bars selling Martini-based cocktails for two weeks on one spot before popping up in another secret place. Promotion often depends solely on word-of-mouth and viral marketing. Pop-up concepts appeal to the stimulation junkie characteristic of Gen Yers and it's no surprise that they are the demographic group that shows the biggest interest in this guerrilla marketing approach.[71]

In *Brand Lands, Hot Spots and Cool Spaces* Christian Mikunda demonstrates the power of mood management in building strong brands. All Nike Towns, the flagship stores of the US sports brand, have a system of futuristic mini-lifts in a prominent central position. They transport Nike T-shirts and shoes from the underground storage to the different store floors. The see-through acrylic glass capsules float through the store and then theatrically slide open, providing a visual attraction to everyone who is visiting the store.[72]

Target often applies the power of the pop-up to showcase the wide range of items they have on sale. In 2013, the retailer set up a gigantic doll's house in Grand Central Station in New York as a way of promoting a new line in home decorating. Apart from the presence of various items in-stock at Target, the house also featured make-up artists in the bathroom and Target staff assisting 'visitors' to guide them through the house and its contents. Earlier in the chapter, we described how Target focused on helping students getting rid of their college worries.[73]

This was also executed in 'Bullseye University Live', a 360° campaign that an interwoven set of offline and online events. They first set up a 'dormitory' at the University of California in LA, consisting of five 'dorm rooms' completely decorated with Target-items. Five YouTube celebrities (Chester See, Tessa Violet, Magic of Rahat, Brooke Leigh and Jenn Imm) inhabited the different rooms, with internet users being able to livestream the inhabitants 24/7 over the course of the four days of the event. Additionally, the stream provided mouseovers that enabled viewers to instantly shop for items they liked on screen. Target consequently took this idea in smaller form to various other campuses in the USA by putting up small pop-up stores with a 'student' living in the makeshift dorm room for 48 hours. These 'Live Dorm Rooms' featured large touchscreens that made it possible for students passing by to play games or interact. Several brands, both in-house Target brands and partners such as Coca-Cola, took part in the experience by offering challenges throughout the 48 hours that the dorm room was set up. Target wanted to let students live the idea that their stores are the only ones you need to get stuff for your life in college. Therefore, they allowed students to immediately order dorm room items they liked by having them scan QR codes for the different products on one of the side walls. Shuttle buses between the location and the nearest Target store were also used in case students absolutely needed an item on the spot.[74]

In 2015, the retailer put up an art gallery in New York consisting entirely of Target items. To show off their focus on design, visitors of 'Target Too' could for example check out a large mosaic of lips, entirely made out of Eos lip balms that are sold in the retailer's store. Unlike the usual pop-up store, it was not possible to buy items. Instead, Target built up the brand experience by handing out gifts to visitors.[75]

With the rise of online shopping and mobile internet, some brands have stretched the idea of pop-up stores to a more digital level. Swedish brand Peak Performance specializes in outdoor clothing and focused on this adventurous identity with their Magic Hour campaign. Throughout 11 different countries ranging from Sweden to Japan, the brand opened up 15 'mobile pop-up shops'. The catch? These virtual shops only opened during the magic hours: the hour before sunset and sunrise. Customers could check out the map on the campaign website to find the remote locations, including mountain tops and a lighthouse on a tiny island. They had to trek to their location of choice, then open up the online shop using the web browser on their smartphone or tablet. Using the GPS function of their devices to check the location, the shops unlocked themselves during 'magic hour'. Each of the shops contained between two and four items, of which customers were able to claim just one for free. Having made their choice, participants finally got instructed to take a selfie with the background visible as to prove that they were at the correct location. This way, they claimed their prize and consequently received a voucher redeemable online. The 56 claimable items scattered between the various shops quickly sold out. Peak Performance customers not living close enough to a location, or simply not fussed about making a late-night or early-morning hiking trip, could participate in an Instagram contest. The only thing they had to do was take a picture of a sunrise or a sunset and tag this with the #catchmagichour hashtag. A Peak Performance jury picked a winner, who received a voucher worth €1,000.[76]

Coca-Cola's focus on happiness

Coca-Cola, the world's most valuable brand, is of course targeting a broader consumer group than only Generation Y. 'But the 13–30 age group certainly is a core target group for us', says Cristina Bondolowski, Senior Global Brand Director for Coke, in an interview with us. 'For Coke Red, global teenagers are very important. What's hot for them tends to change a lot and they are difficult to track. The complex variety of teen lifestyles is actually a rather recent phenomenon. They were never so individually expressed in the way they dress, communicate, shop and relate to brands as today.' Coca-Cola has its own permanent global teen research community, which allows

Coke's marketers to follow 400 of them around the world. 'One of the things we have learned, is that socially connecting with other people is what really makes teens happy.' The 'Open Happiness' campaign taps into this concept of happiness in the 206 countries where Coke is sold.

'The notion of happiness is actually nothing new for Coke', says Derk Hendriksen, Senior Global Brand Director for Coke Zero and Light. 'The brand has always been grounded in the core value of optimism and positive thinking in its history of 125 years.' To the brand, the 'Open Happiness' focus is just a contemporary way of expressing its identity. Coca-Cola's enduring positioning as the icon of universal happiness has certainly received successful responses from each new youth generation. 'Every five years a new teenage generation enters our brand franchise', explains Hendriksen. 'It is important to connect with them and teach them what our DNA stands for.' The 'Open Happiness' theme is giving the brand a more specific point of view when compared to its predecessor 'Coke's side of life'. 'It's a real call to action', says Hendriksen, 'we are inviting young people all over the world to be part of this movement.'

When monitoring teens around the world, Coke found that they have to face a lot of uncertainty today, such as big climate disasters and economic crises. Next to that, they feel quite a lot of pressure to achieve in life: finding the right job, earning money, looking great, forming a relationship, dressing properly, getting good grades at school... 'That's why we wanted this new angle on positivism to be much more direct than the 'Coke side of life' campaign', explains Bondolowski. 'We want teens to learn how to enjoy the small everyday things in life. Coke fits naturally in this busy life: drink a Coke and feel uplifted to look at life in the positive and overcome the little challenges you daily face.' It's interesting that Coca-Cola had never used the word 'happiness' before although its campaigns have always been built around optimism and historically portray plenty of smiling people.

In 2010, Coke was spreading the optimist message and searching the globe for happiness with its Expedition 206 campaign. On New Year's Day, three youngsters, 'the Happiness Ambassadors', kicked off a 275,000-mile voyage to the 206 countries and territories where Coca-Cola is sold to seek and report on what makes people happy. Their stories could be followed in real-time on **www.expedition206.com** and a variety of social networks such as Facebook and Twitter. Fans could also interact with the team members and helped to decide where they would go next and what they would do. On every stop participants designed a special Coke bottle, which at the end of the expedition was displayed at the World of Coca-Cola in Atlanta. The team visited the Shanghai World Expo along with other marquee events that Coca-Cola sponsored throughout the year, such as the FIFA World Cup 2010 in South Africa. In May 2010, print, broadcast and online media coverage of Expedition 206 resulted in about 443 million media impressions and over 1,000 media stories in all corners of the world. The blog reached more than 50,000 page views per month and 78 per cent of the visitors were from outside the United States.

In late 2009, Coca-Cola aggressively used digital media for the first time. The company placed a vending machine at St John's University in Queens, New York during exam season. The idea was to bring a little bit of happiness to a woeful time such as the winter exams. The Happiness Machine delivered small moments of happiness for unsuspecting students including flowers, a pizza, balloon animals, free drinks, etc. Several hidden cameras captured the reactions. The video was released on the internet without any media support apart from just one Facebook status update to the Coke fans (more than 3 million at that time) and one tweet to Coke's 20,000 followers. Coke spent very little money on the execution in an attempt to prove they can make compelling content regardless of the budget. The video hit 1 million views in its second week and was ranked number 1 on viralvideo.com, which tracks buzz on online videos. The video was post-tested and scored in the top 1 per cent of all ads in Millward Brown's global database and was the highest scoring English commercial ever tested by Coke in the United States. The scenes of real emotion were what drove the likeability of the ad. In the next phase the video was cut down into TV-sized portions and rolled out in other markets. Coke aroused excitement with a series of 'where will happiness strike next?' follow-up experiments.

In comparing the brand performance of Coca-Cola in its top 37 markets with the year before the launch of the 'Open Happiness' campaign, the company found a significant growth in 'exclusive love' for the brand among teens. One in three teens said Coca-Cola was their favourite brand and over 50 per cent of teens stated Coke was a brand they love.

Coca-Cola has been using the key element of music a lot in its long past but had lately been rather inactive on that front. With the 'Open Happiness' anthem and the song created for the World Cup in South Africa, Coke has regained interest in music as one of the tools to inject coolness into the brand. 'Other cool brands often use product innovation to stay hot', says Cristina Bonolowski, 'but at Coke the product is never going to change, so we have to find other ways of staying cool. Innovation in the way we communicate and emotions are both important for our brand to remain relevant for today's youth. We always say to our agencies: 'We want something that only Coke can do.' Coca-Cola certainly has the power to put a song in play in a massive global way.

They also put much focus on local brand activations and events around the world. 'We want to let youth experience our products and brand on magic moments for them,' amplifies Derk Hendriksen. 'These can be music-related events, for example the Coke Emergency Refreshment Nurses in the Benelux countries, but also other occasions like Carnival in Brazil or the NCAA Basketball events in the United States.' During the dark Christmas days, the Coca-Cola train of trucks brings happiness and light around the world and the brand is doing the same in other parts of the world with Ramadan or Chinese New Year.[77]

Contagious Magazine describes in its Coca-Cola case study how early in 2011, 40 global execs gathered at Coke's Atlanta HQ to create Content

2020, a 10-step manifesto reinventing the brand's marketing approach. The big goal behind this change was to double the revenue generated worldwide to $200 billion by 2020. In a very transparent 20-minute animated YouTube video, Jonathan Mildenhall, Coke's VP Global Advertising and Creative Excellence explains to the viewer what 'content excellence' means for Coke and how to create campaigns that are 'Liquid and Linked'. It means that they are able to communicate the brand's values successfully in the current fast-evolving digital and social landscape. 'We want to create ideas that are so contagious we actually lose control of where they go', Mildenhall explains. 'We want to inspire conversation that goes into places we couldn't even imagine. We moved away from old-fashioned brand propositions and created bigger brand spaces. Fanta is all about play, Coke Zero is all about possibilities and Coke is all about happiness. We don't want to tell people a story, but give people a story to tell. Coming out of real tangible human experiences, these consumer stories are far more authentic.'

Many campaigns of Coke around the world are built on these fundamentals. Think of the 'Share a Coke' campaign with the personalized cans in Australia as described in the previous chapter. On the beaches of Rio de Janeiro a giant Sprite dispenser brought the concept of 'refreshment' to life. In Argentina Coke's 'Cheering Truck' travelled from football stadium to stadium to record a million cheers later played out to root for the national team during Copa America. In Columbia, music fans had to bring a popular local band suspended 50 metres above the crowd down to ground level by downloading tracks through Coke FM's mobile site. Sixteen million people were reached through earned media and songs were downloaded 50,000 times. In the Philippines Coke's happiness project reunited a group of OFWs (Overseas Filipino Workers) with their families in time to celebrate Christmas together for the first time. Coke's Security Cam clip summarized random acts of kindness from all around the world. In seven countries of Latin America, Coke installed special 3.5 metre-tall vending machine offering two Cokes for the price of one if two friends would cooperate to slip the coins into the machine slot. 'Move to the Beat', the 2012 Olympics campaign with Mark Ronson, was shot with a green screen behind, so that over 100 participating local markets would be able to insert their own local athletes into the action. In terms of tweets volume, sentiment, engagement and reach, Coca-Cola was the highest-rated of all 25 sponsors of the Olympic Games. 'Today's culture demands a continual dialogue with consumers, meaning more content, more often to feed the conversations that are always on', says David Campbell, a global creative for The Coca-Cola Company in an interview with *Contagious Magazine*. Coke commits 70 per cent of marketing spend to traditional marketing, 20 per cent to local campaigns and 10 per cent to innovative ideas to ignite conversations[78].

Recently, the brand has focused on bringing happiness in Asia and the Emirates, often with a political or humanitarian message in mind. 'Small World Machines' provided a digital portal between India and Pakistan, historically two rival countries. Coke vending machines in Indian and Pakistani malls instructed participants to perform actions together with their counterpart visible on the machine's screen under the line 'make a friend in India/Pakistan'. To receive a can of Coke, some for instance had to join hands or draw peace symbols together with the Indian or Pakistani on the other side.[79]

In Bangladesh the drinks company installed six arcade machines in the city of Dhaka. Rather than accepting coins, the machines only started a game of 'Pong' when an empty Coke bottle was inserted. This encouraged the idea of recycling and caring about the environment by making the experience fun. In the first week of the campaign, 1860 bottles were collected. These bottles initially turned into a live art installation during World Environment Day, before they were recycled.[80]

During the Christmas period of 2014, Coca-Cola wanted to provide Singaporeans with a white Christmas, despite the country never actually having the chance to see snow around that time. A machine installed in both Finland and Singapore showed footage of the other country, and invited passers-by to exchange smiles and waves to each other. After this first meeting, the viewers in Lapland could shovel actual snow into the machine, which in turn caused the unit located in Singapore to spout snow. Eventually, both sides of the machine even started a virtual snowball fight. Coke managed to bring together two cultures almost 6,000 miles apart.[81]

To show appreciation towards the countless migrant workers in Singapore, customized drones dropped boxes containing Coke cans at various construction sites. These boxes also contained 2,700 photos and handwritten signs of Singaporeans as a way of thanking the workers for building the city.

Using the help of agency Y&R, migrant workers in Dubai also received attention from Coca-Cola. Most of these workers arrive in the UAE with one goal in mind: helping their family. Striving to bring happiness to these low-wage workers from across the Asian continent, Coca-Cola provided them with an opportunity to call their loved ones back home, something that is not always possible because of the high cost of calling internationally.[82] Coke-branded phone booths were placed in so-called labour camps across the UAE, but instead of using coins workers could make a phone call by simply inserting a Coca-Cola bottle cap. Each cap gave callers the chance to make a three-minute phone call. The video reached over 3 million views on YouTube in just a year, and sparked a real debate about the conditions of the workers in countries such as the Emirates.[83]

This campaign received an extension in 2015 during the #WishUponACoke campaign. People on their way home from Dubai regularly take too many presents because it has often been a long time since they have visited their families, resulting in expensive excess baggage. Persons suffering from this problem were provided with a special Coca-Cola excess baggage tag, providing travellers with 'extra five kilos of happiness'.[84] Similarly, Coke installed several 'Wishing Booths' in Dubai, allowing UAE immigrants to make a wish for their families back home in exchange for a bottle cap.

Coca-Cola picked four of these wishes at random and made them become reality. For example, the company helped set up a functioning irrigation system for the Pakistani farmer parents of one wisher. This campaign video was seen over 4 million times in less than three months.[85]

Conclusion

As experience shows, Gen Yers love campaigns that are capable of triggering positive emotions or relieving stress or other negative feelings. If your brand is capable of arousing happiness through its offer, marketing or communication, it will definitely touch the hearts of the youth generation. The key to emotional branding is maximizing the sensory appeal as well as bringing your brand alive through experiences in events or retail environments. Since emotions and happiness spread like a virus, an intelligent use of social media marketing will boost the feelings of Generation Y. Still, never forget that this is Gen Yers' medium in the first place, so it should be used with care by keeping the three steps in mind: observing, facilitating and participating.

HOT TAKEAWAYS FOR COOL BRAND BUILDERS

- Gen Y is an emotional consumer generation, which is reflected in their shopping behaviour and brand preference.

- Brands have two routes to tap into emotional branding: connecting with and arousing positive emotions or taking away negative ones.

- By addressing youth's five senses, and especially scent, sound and design, a brand puts EQ (emotional quotient) in its offer to Generation Y.

- Happiness is the most important emotion evoked by hot brands because this emotion caters for youths' needs of hedonism and escapism.

- Hot brands know how to deliver gratifications instead of pleasures.

- Gratifications are challenging experiences fuelled by gamification, through different touch points (in-store, online, mobile or at events) that require one's full attention and socially connect Gen Yers to peers.

Generation Z

Born after 1996, Gen Zers are the next kids arriving on the block. It's a given that this generation is going to become highly influential, as there are already over 2 billion of them globally[1], while they already possess an estimated $44 billion of annual purchasing power in the United States.[2] As with every generation, they have several umbrella names that are used to cover the same group: iGens, 2Ks, dot.com kids[3], Digital Natives or the Pluralist Generation[4] are just a few of them. Most of these terms already hint at what sets them apart from their predecessors, namely being brought up in a digital age while having a global mindset that makes them highly social and tolerant of diversity.

But first, it's important to understand where these digi-social kids come from. While Gen Yers were raised by group-minded Baby Boomers, these Gen Zers have been nurtured by the more individual Gen Xers. This has made for a drastic difference in parenting styles. When comparing the qualities that parents deem most important, Gen X parents tend to rate inner-focused qualities like 'hard-working', 'confidence', 'independence' and 'organized' higher compared to their Baby Boomer counterparts. On the other hand, outer-focused qualities such as 'honesty', 'respectfulness', 'trustworthiness' or 'ethical' are rated less important by Gen Xers compared with their predecessors in parenting. The individual-focused qualities carry over to the Gen Zers themselves as well, with them citing qualities like 'creative' and 'independent' as important to develop, rather than 'dependable' and 'respectful'.[5] Gen X parents experienced a significant rise in the number of divorces and therefore try to focus strongly on family values, while they also strive to teach their children about classic concepts like 'work ethic', 'etiquette' and 'resilience'.[6]

Is Gen Z ready for the world?

One of the biggest influencing features has been the highly protective nature of Gen Xers towards their children.[7] Because of the individualistic nature of Gen X parents they only want the best for their own children, which means that they would do anything to help prepare their child for the 'real world'. Added to this is the fact that Gen Zers grew up during the mid to late 2000s, years characterized by severe economic recession and banking crises, while also experiencing 9/11 and 'the war on terror' in the middle of their child-hood. These financially and societal lesser times often directly affected their parents, who therefore tried to protect their children from the 'real world out there' as long as possible. The biggest question asked by Gen X parents was: 'Is my child ready for the world?' rather than 'Is the world ready for my child?' which characterized the thinking of Baby Boomers. Similarly, Gen X parents also fed their Gen Z children with a harder sense of realism. While Gen Yers were always encouraged to follow their dreams and aspire to become anything they wanted, Gen Zers got the advice to focus on becoming great in something you're actually good at. Closely related to this is the idea that nowadays, you have to be the best in something to be considered a winner, rather than the 'everyone wins' attitude that was taught to Gen Yers.[8]

The 'make it' attitude that has trickled down via their parents is only reinforced when looking at the financial independence Gen Zers already experience from a young age. Even though they have experienced the hard-ship of recessions and financial crisis, they have also experienced the eco-nomic recovery that followed. Gen Zers have the highest disposable income of all generations, providing them with a lot of financial power that they are able to use freely. As seen in Table 8.1, Gen Z kids from four-through 17-year-olds received on average between $2 and $4 more than their Gen Y predecessors.

Additionally, in a 2015 global study by InSites Consulting, it seems that this financial power also gets used almost immediately. The Generation Z members are not of the saving kind, possibly influenced by the lack of trust in the banking system that caused their parents a lot of issues. Under-12-year-olds spend no less than 75 per cent of their allowances, mostly on video-games (22 per cent), hobbies (20 per cent) and food (20 per cent). It's no surprise that mall-based brands like Abercrombie & Fitch have seen sales declining because Gen Zers' purchase habits have shifted away from clothing, compared with their predecessors. According to a survey from Piper Jaffray, teenage mall visits have declined with 30 per cent over a decade.[9]

TABLE 8.1   The financial power of Generation Z

Age	Weekly Gen Z allowance (Gen X parents)	Weekly Gen Y allowance (Baby Boomer parents)
4–9	$5.40	$3.10
10–13	$10.10	$7.30
14–17	$18.80	$14

SOURCE: www.mainstreet.com/article/are-you-paying-your-child-much-allowance

FIGURE 8.1   What Gen Z below 12 is doing with its weekly allowance

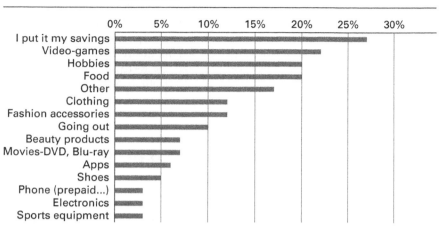

SOURCE: Joeri Van den Bergh – Who's Up NXT? presentation

The fully digitalized generation

Generation Z is the first generation to grow up in an almost fully digitalized and globally connected world. They cannot imagine a life before computers and basically live online.[10] Research in 2013 found that internet use is prevalent from a remarkably young age. In the UK, a third of three- to four-year-olds were cited as going online via a desktop PC or a laptop. This trend was echoed in other countries, with 70 per cent of Flemish and Swedish pre-schoolers going online several times a month, an activity often already started while they were three or four years old. Similarly, half of Swedish kids aged three and four already used a tablet.[11]

Toys have turned into technology, with smartphones, tablets and other connected devices ruling over daily lives. For Christmas 2010, 31 per cent of American children aged six–12 wanted an iPad, followed by a computer (29 per cent) and an iPod Touch (29 per cent).[12] Research in Australia also found that when looking at the total amount of money spent on 'toys', the largest amount is spent on electronic devices (computers, mobile phones, digital cameras etc) followed by gaming devices (PlayStation, Xbox etc).[13] In an interview with us, Per Hjuler, SVP Innovation & Consumer Marketing for the LEGO Group, says: 'We are expanding our portfolio with new digital offerings still based on the idea of bringing system-in-play. These can be standalone like LEGO Worlds, a new game available on Steam or digital experiences connected to our physical bricks like for instance LEGO Fusion and LEGO Dimensions.[14]

Surveys conducted by JWT Intelligence have shown that 86 per cent of Gen Zers use their smartphone multiple times per day, being online almost all the time. Seventy per cent of surveyed teenagers declared watching at least two hours of YouTube content each day, with 36 per cent of them actually spending over four hours per day on the video platform.[15] Even conversations inside the same house tend to go over highways of bits and bytes with the Zers, sometimes making the smartphone look like a body extension rather than a separate device.[16] This desire for the 'always on' feeling affects professional decisions as well, as research has shown that over 50 per cent of surveyed Gen Zers would decline a job offer if the company did not allow access to social media.[17]

Generation Z's influence on parents' purchases

With strong financial power, constant connectedness to the newest trends and a tight relationship with their elders, it should not come as a surprise that Gen Z kids also have quite a lot of influence on their parents' purchasing decisions. After all, research has shown that children are now able to recognize brands from the age of only 18 months.[18] Almost all of the parents let their children decide when the purchase deals with something for the children themselves, but over 75 per cent of parents also value the opinion of their children concerning family purchases. In our InSites NXTGEN research Food (54 per cent) and holiday destinations (48 per cent) are influenced the most by Gen Zers. When compared to the older Gen Y, the four- to 18-year-old Gen Z influence the adoption of technology only slightly less (38 per cent versus 42 per cent).

FIGURE 8.2   Generation Z's and Gen Y's influence on parents' buying behaviour

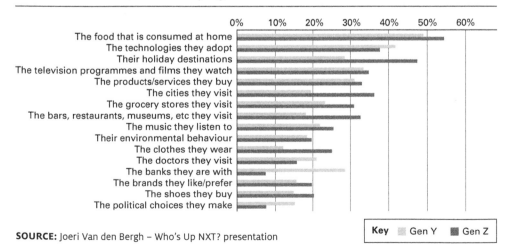

SOURCE: Joeri Van den Bergh – Who's Up NXT? presentation

To illustrate that their influencing power isn't limited to small purchases, nearly three out of five parents say they let the opinion of their kids weigh in when buying a car.[19] This trend has not escaped the car manufacturers, causing them to increasingly target young children in their campaigns.[20] In 2011 Volkswagen famously featured a young Darth Vader trying to use The Force on the new Passat family car.[21] Toyota meanwhile partnered with The Muppets in 2014, showing the puppet gang driving around in a Toyota Highlander while singing the song 'No Room for Boring'.[22] Increasingly, brands are adopting a 'catch them young' approach because of the early affinity towards brands that these Gen Zers show.[23]

Several of these trends have influenced Gen Zers in such a way that they have gotten accustomed to pressure and stress from a remarkably young age.[24] The digital and interconnected nature of their lives for instance also caused them to experience the uprising of cyber bullying first-hand, only adding to the stressful nature of their childhood.[25] In fact, they have grown up so fast that in various ways they seem to have behaved like 'mini-adults' rather than kids.[26]

As generational research has shown, the individualistic and 'I have to make it' features shown by Gen Z are not entirely unique to them. In fact, these upcoming kids fit in recurring generational archetypes and show similarities to the Silent generation that grew up, not coincidentally, during The Great Depression of the 1930s and of course to their Generation X parents, who became of age during the recession at the end of the 80s and start of the 90s.

The snappy generation

Generation Z is probably the first generation where you are almost required to make an appointment with six year olds, because they might not have five minutes of time today. From a young age, these kids' schedules have been filled to the brim with music lessons, extra tuition, language camps and several sports activities. One of the main characteristics of this generation is directly related to this: they are all about instant gratification[27].

Research in the United States has shown that the attention span of the average American has been reduced to just eight seconds,[28] which is just two seconds more than the maximum length of a video on the popular short video platform Vine.[29] Some campaigns deliberately address this phenomenon. In 2015 American insurance company GEICO launched an award-winning ad titled 'Unskippable', featuring a regular family at the dinner table. The main message of the advertisement ('Don't thank me, thank the savings!') lasts just five seconds, finishing off with the witty line 'You can't skip this GEICO ad because it's already over.' Hoping to have caught the attention, they also put up an extended cut on YouTube lasting over a minute, showing the whole family frozen in picture while the dog goes on the rampage on the dinner table. The fact that this extended video was checked out 7.5 million times in less than six months shows that grabbing the attention in that span lasting just eight seconds can really turn into a more sustained form of interest.[30]

This shorter attention span has also influenced the way in which Gen Zers look for information. In comparison with other generations, the Zers appear to be the quickest in searching relevant information. Growing up with Google has taught them to perfect their online searching skills, making them visit fewer pages, fewer websites and conduct fewer searches overall. This in turn results in them spending the least amount of time in finding an answer to a question. This 'cut and paste' way of looking for information also has some drawbacks however, as Zers tend to be less confident about their answers compared to others.[31]

The snappy way in which Gen Zers approach life consequently means that companies have to compete for a spot in that short attention span, even more so than in other generations. This attention clearly needs to be caught on the internet rather than offline. Gen Zer have financial power, and they love to shop, but mainly online. In 2013, the average share of income spent online attained 8.75 per cent for Gen Zers, while this was only 5.33 per cent for Gen Yers and 3.85 per cent for Gen X, the parents of Generation Z. Twenty per cent of girls under the age 12 already occasionally visited online shopping sites, meaning that e-commerce is centred in the shopping experience of these Zers.[32] Surveys with Generation Z have shown that the preference of shopping online over offline remains when segmenting different shopping categories such as sports equipment (60 per cent), fashion accessories (57 per cent), games (56 per cent), clothing (55 per cent), shoes (55 per cent), toys (54 per cent), books (53 per cent), electronics (53 per cent), beauty products (51 per cent) or music (50 per cent).[33]

The age of impatience

Another influence of the Gen X parents on this generation is the love for convenience. Because of their filled schedules and the high amount of pressure in their lives, any product, service or experience that makes this life simpler is great.[34] For example, several popular brands use mobile technology to let the snappy Generation Z save as much time as possible. There are the well-known voice applications for mobile phones and watches like Siri on the Apple iOS platform or Google Now for Android, but increasingly companies have dipped their toes in the realm of the 'phy-gital'. Connecting both the digital and the physical into a single flawless experience caters to the needs of Generation Z. Domino's Pizza launched a voice ordering platform in 2014 via their mobile app. Using voice commands, you could talk to 'Dom', the virtual voice of Domino's to order the pizza you want or just to have some chitchat. By lowering the barrier to order pizza, Domino's saw its sales figures rise with 11 per cent.[35] Coffee chain Starbucks launched a Mobile Order & Pay functionality in 2015, allowing users to order their favorite frapuccino without having to stand in line anymore. With a simple tap in the Starbucks application, your coffee gets ordered and you can pick it up quickly when you pass by your favorite Starbucks down the street.[36] KFC did almost exactly the same by launching an ordering application that allows users to order and pay before picking up their bucket of chicken.[37] Clothing brand Gap meanwhile provides customers with the opportunity to reserve clothes online, which they can then try on in-store in a pre-reserved fitting room and eventually buy if they like them.[38]

YouTube and clustersharing

Generation Z loves to snack on different, little pieces of entertainment. They enjoy quick bursts of communication. Popular platforms of these tech-savvy consumers only allow very short-length content to be posted, in some cases simply disappearing after a certain amount of time or views. This renders the communication short, ephemeral and exciting to Gen Zers. Posted content can contain creative relevance for this generation as they also use these platforms as a form of self-expression. Ideally, content is not longer than two minutes, but long videos shouldn't be totally excluded when trying to tell the background of the brand. A good balance between short and long videos is the perfect way to engage with Generation Z, but it's of vital importance to get their attention as quickly as possible.

This new sharing activity also creates a form of 'dark social' because traditional analytics don't work here anymore. It is difficult to measure value or engagement on these platforms. Google Analytics is a convenient tool that can help tracking to a certain extent. Some apps have their own available data and analytics. These experimental, new programmes are becoming a more integral part in the marketing mix, making it important to understand how they work.[39]

Compared to older generations who prefer text-based videos, Generation Z prefers videos with real images. Visual is key. The popularity of YouTube indicates how important visual media are to them. Research from 2014 showed that nine per cent of 'tweens' (aged 8–11) claimed to use YouTube, with 69 per cent of them apparently also having an account despite YouTube restricting use to people above 13 years old. Additionally, these kids like watching YouTube videos together rather than simply sharing them over the internet. This trend of 'clustersharing' means that YouTube videos often enter the realm of meetings with friends or family, rendering them important media moments.[40] Gen Zers prefer a personal, human connection and video represents that with a more natural form of communication. Marketers therefore need to develop a thorough video content strategy to feed the hungry video-consumers of Generation Z.[41]

#Foodporn #Sorrynotsorry

In October 2010 Kevin Systrom and Mike Krieger launched their free app: Instagram. Their unique social network met with an unequalled success. Two months after its launch they attained two million visitors. Two years later Facebook bought the company for the price of 1 billion dollars, which is still the third biggest acquisition for Marc Zuckerberg's empire (after Whatsapp and Oculus VR).[42] The initiation of Instagram (the name is actually a contraction of 'instant camera' and 'telegram') doesn't have to do with any technological ingenuity, but with ingenuous insight into the way in which youngsters use digital technology to share their experiences with others. The new status symbols.

Thanks to the increasing quality of front and back cameras on smartphones and the use of simple colour filters in Instagram's user experience, users of the world's first exclusively mobile and visual social network were able to turn every event into an upgraded picture, worth sharing and getting reactions from. I am convinced that as a result, Instagram has a much stronger impact on our consumption behaviour than whichever other social network. Twitter changed our ways of discussion with our mobile operator and other companies. Facebook changed our ways of communication with friends and family as well as how we share what's new and organize events. But Instagram is something else entirely. It makes us do things we normally wouldn't do a spend money we normally wouldn't spend.

A 2014 survey by the American market research agency Ypulse shows us how food has become a status symbol for Millennials, just like other new, attainable luxury items. Half of the 1,000 Millennials from the US who participated indicated that he or she likes to share a picture of food or drinks on social media. What's more: one fifth of people in their early twenties admitted that they had shared at least one picture of someone else's plate![43] The long queues in the streets of New York for every new foodhype (Cronuts, anyone?) or in the streets of London and Tokyo for strawberries covered with Godiva chocolate are an indication of how food has become an experience that Millennials like to share with others. Not necessarily in order to enjoy something together, but also as proof and confirmation of your status. Usually, this isn't the traditional luxury purchases anymore, but everyday stuff that create a sense of luxury and status.

By Maarten Lagae, Senior Research Manager Landor

The emoji-onal generation

Emoji (plural) is Japanese for 'picture' (*e*) and 'letter, character' (*moji*). The communication style was created by a Japanese employee (Shigetaka Kurita) at a telecom company with the goal of distinguishing the company from competitors. The (almost) second native language of the young generation is dominating online communication: it's ubiquitous.[44] Emoji are invading the internet, infiltrating in marketing campaigns and are being heavily used on social platforms. It's not a coincidence that the heart emoji was the most popular 'word' of 2014. Emojis are appealing because of their positive character and broad meaning. Emoji-only social networks such as Emojicate are booming and websites like Emojinalysis are able to show your emotional state by analysing the emoji you have used.[45]

WWF (the World Wide Fund For Nature) wanted to increase awareness for endangered animals by launching the campaign #EndangeredEmoji just before Endangered Species Day on 15 May 2015. With Wieden+Kennedy the non-profit created 17 emoji characters that represented these threatened species: spider monkey, giant panda, Asian elephant, Galapagos penguin, Antiguan racer snake, Bactrian camel, tiger, Sumatran tiger, green turtle, Amur leopard, Siamese crocodile, Bluefin tuna, blue whale, western grey whale, African wild dog, lemur leaf frog and Maui's dolphin. These symbols had already been used over 202 million times on Twitter since its launch in April 2014. WWF wanted to use this popularity to create awareness for their cause: endangered species. A user could register via the microsite endangerdemoji.com or on Twitter by retweeting the campaign message. Automatically they received a tweet back from the organization with more info. Each month participants received an emoji bill that told them how many times they had used an endangered emoji and suggested an amount of donation. Each animal had a value of 10p that was converted to the local currency of the tweeter. Participants were free to donate higher or lower than the suggested amount. Less than three months after the launch of the campaign, more than 32,000 people had already retweeted the original message, essentially signing up for the action.[46]

Animated GIFs and Vines

GIF is the abbreviation for 'Graphics Interchange Format'. A GIF file consists of different images in a specific order that move endlessly in a loop. GIFs originally started being used as moving ad banners on a web page, but increasingly youngsters use them in their messaging to convey emotions or show something funny.

Toyota launched the campaign 'Gifony' during the New York International Auto Show press event where users were encouraged to make a symphony of GIFs with sounds and images of the manufacturing process. For example, some of the 45 GIFs showed the drilling of car doors or steel being stamped into objects. Via the site for the campaign, participants and other internet

FIGURE 8.3   WWF #EndangeredEmoji!

users could make various other variations, then download their remix and share it on social media. In partnership with DJ SoNevable Toyota created a music video that was promoted on social media accompanied with a teaser video and live interactive DJ booths events. To target a broad group, the brand also used targeted search and display. With this campaign, Toyota is applying a transparent approach by showing its behind-the-scenes while concurrently using a hip new type of communication that resonates with the young ones.[47]

Vines are similar to GIFs, but are deliberately limited to a length of six seconds videos that loop continuously. Using the Vine app, you record by pushing a button. The app allows to pause and continue, making it possible to cut and paste several moments within those six seconds. One of the advantages over GIFs is that it has some form of measurement, as every video shows the number of times the video has been looped, giving some sense of quantity in viewership. The company was acquired by Twitter in 2012 and therefore allows to easily share videos on the tweeting platform as well as on Facebook. Six second videos are a challenge for creative minds inside companies, and some brands have already launched successful examples on how to use the platform. UK retailer ASOS encouraged buyers to record vines of them unboxing their delivery while using the hashtag #ASOSUnbox. The mundane act of opening an ugly brown box suddenly turned into a branded, shareable event. Popular cookie producer Oreos also launched the hashtag #SnackHacks on their Vine-account, showing fans of the milk & chocolate cookies six-second tutorials on how to get experimental with the snacks. For example, one of the Vines showed how you can mix milk and Oreos to create a 'cookie cube'.[48]

Meerkat and Periscope: ephemeral video

Meerkat achieved hype-status during the SXSW festival in 2015. Suddenly, live video streaming became the newest cool thing in town. This was only reinforced when the similar Twitter-owned service Periscope appeared on the scene. Both Meerkat and Periscope allow you to film with your phone and livestream it for free on social media. These 'Meerkasts' are more affordable because you only need your phone to film something instead of a team with camera equipment or a desktop. You can easily broadcast events or activities. There is a delay of around 20 seconds and you can schedule your show beforehand. Compared to other streaming services like Google Hangout the streams of Meerkat and Periscope are ephemeral. The person that launches the stream can download a copy but otherwise you can't rewind or replay it, which sort of takes away stage-fright and makes it more 'real'. The 'performers' are very authentic because the interaction is in real-time, they can't fake their personality in comparison to for example YouTubers. They are also very informal. You can just watch a stranger showing his view on holiday and your comments will appear on the screen. This creates a form of interaction that TV shows miss, because you get immediate reactions from the person on the screen.[49]

A lot of well-known people have jumped onto this trend. Katy Perry has an incredible following on Twitter, over 67 million. She was the first entertainer to use Periscope. To promote her concert movie Epix she filmed the event, streamed the pink carpet and encouraged a Q&A with the hashtag #PerryScope. TV show host Jimmy Fallon sometimes uses Meerkat to air show rehearsals, giving the fans of his Tonight Show some live behind-the-scenes footage.[50] Several brands have also seen possibilities for this new type of video streaming. Before the start of the New York International Auto Show in 2015, car companies revealed their newest models on Periscope and Meerkat. Different manufacturers including Jaguar, Toyota, Mercedes and Nissan provided followers with behind-the-scenes, live footage from the event as well as interviews with relevant people from the company. Red Bull has used Periscope to stream events and L'Oréal did for a product launch.[51]

The digital age also means that clever people try to work around the ephemeral element. Initiatives like Glow are popping up, making it possible to record livestreams so they can be watched later. The company launched MeerkatStreams.com and OnPersiscope.com, both sides providing stored content from the respective apps. With a plugin called Katch you can easily upload your stream to YouTube. More and more companies are trying to break the ephemerality.[52]

Snapchat: ephemeral messaging

The app Snapchat differentiates itself from social media platforms like Twitter and Facebook by its ephemeral characteristics. While the latter two are focused on their archival 'timeline' functionality which allows shared posts, photos or tweets to remain visible for as long as the platforms exist, Snapchat was designed to make shared content disappear as soon as it appears. Users can send self-destructing photos to their connected friends: directed at specific people, via 'stories' for 24 hours for everyone to see or in a chat area. When you send a 'snap' you can see if the person opened it, and the chat functionality also allows video chat when both persons push a button, creating an opportunity for a more intimate approach. To end the conversation you can just lift your finger off the button and it's gone.

Snapchat is not trying to be just another messaging service. Somehow it resembles real-world talks more than the usual chat or instant messaging application. When you talk to someone in person, your conversation does not get saved in some archive either. The only thing you can access is your own memory. The key is that the messages don't need to be permanent on this platform. Users can send everything that comes to mind. For instance, a quick 'good morning' or something you see during the day can immediately be uploaded onto a digital space with the same immediacy and fleetingness as talks in real life. Building on the hype and trying to provide more utility, Snapchat has also launched the ability to transfer money with a simple 'money text' called SnapCash. Monthly almost 200 million active users spend their short attention span on the app, daily sending over 700 million snaps that disappear almost instantly.[53]

According to a study by Sumpto, 67 per cent of US college students would like to receive promotions on Snapchat and 58 per cent would buy a product with coupons acquired on the platform. This type of communication and technology can disrupt markets like e-commerce. Ephemeral communication is becoming ephemeral commerce.[54]

Several brands have already tried out tactics on Snapchat. For their Valentine's Day campaign in 2015, Taco Bell used the Stories feature to send out several virtual Valentine's cards. These deliberately unprofessional-looking cards mostly contained wordplays or cheesy lines linked to the Taco brand, as well as a 'to' and 'from' so that followers could forward the snaps to friends or lovers. For example, one snap showed a nacho with the line: 'Nacho average valentine. To: From:'. Even though people could access these snaps multiple times because they were uploaded via the Stories feature, the little snippets still disappeared after 24 hours of high online buzz.[55]

Another food brand turned Snapchat into one of their most important channels for promotions and competitions. American leading online and

FIGURE 8.4   GrubHub sending out Snapchat coupons

SOURCE: PR News Social Media Summit with Taste of Tech. © KC Kee

mobile food company GrubHub started using the app in February 2014 and quickly utilized it to send out promo codes, challenges, giveaways or behind-the-scenes footage. For instance, from March 23 to March 27 2015, followers could participate in different challenges allowing them daily to try and win GrubHub-coupons worth $30. Similarly, a #SnapHunt was organized in 2014 with various discounts as leverage. One of the different challenges they've run so far was to find a GrubHub employee in the middle of a Where's Wally-styled image or simply a challenge to promote their Snapchat account in a creative way.[56]

So-called 'Snapchat takeovers' are another popular strategy for brands to get their fans involved. Every week, the account of Belgian radio station Studio Brussel is in the hands of one of the presenters, allowing them to give their own twisted views and experiences a showcase. But listeners also get the chance to shine. The months of May and June are a tough period for Belgian students because of college and school exams. During this period in 2015, Studio Brussel picked a different student each day and allowed him or her to register 24 hours in a random student's life. This resulted in some hilarious videos and photos, while the participants suddenly enjoyed a large audience to show their 'talents'.[57]

McDonald's closed a deal with Snapchat in 2015 to make use of branded so-called 'geofilters'. Originally, Snapchat only allowed regular users to use these filters. For instance, when taking a picture in Paris, the app automatically enables adding the location plus a sticker of a special place close by (eg the Eiffel Tower). McDonald's introduced similar stickers branded with their M-logo and drawn burgers. This meant customers could snap a picture of them inside a McDonald's and then use branded filters over their picture to send to friends, resulting in a very visual exposure for the fast-food chain.[58] For an example, see **http://uk.businessinsider.com/snapchat-wants-you-to-brand-your-posts-with-a-mcdonalds-filter-2015-6**

Interactivity to conquer FOMO

The 'fear of missing out' (FOMO) is high in the minds of Gen Zers, higher compared with the members of Generation Y.[59] This is showcased by the way they watch TV. The classic medium is still often used by and important to Gen Zers. 72 per cent of kids aged between 8 and 12 watch TV multiple times per day, while 77 per cent state they would miss television 'a lot' if the device was taken away from them.[60]

TV shows and programming need to be interactive, however, as Gen Zers want to be able to keep up to date with their friends or other people watching at the same time. These days, Gen Zers are able to multitask with at least five screens each day.[61] In our InSites survey about activities while watching TV, about 56 per cent of Gen Z kids declared to chat or text with friends and 42 per cent said they use social media. In one Nielsen study, 15 per cent of surveyed people declared that they enjoy television more when social media is made a part of the experience.[62] Awards shows like the Academy Awards and talent shows like *The Voice* have already embraced the 'live tweeting' of their viewers by often showing the official hashtag (eg #TheVoice) and tweets live on-screen. In 2015, Twitter started experimenting with their own dedicated 'TV Timelines', providing shows with a separate area inside the Twitter application so that viewers can immediately follow the latest updates from the show's accounts, media outlets talking about the show or actors playing in the series.[63] Similarly, so-called companion apps providing a full-blown second-screen experience are on the rise. In Belgium, commercial TV channel VIER launched a companion app for their game show

FIGURE 8.5   Gen Z's messaging activities while watching TV

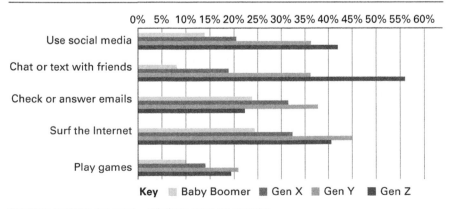

SOURCE: Joeri Van den Bergh – Who's Up NXT? presentation

'De Val Van 1 Miljoen' (The 1 Million Drop) that allowed users to play the game simultaneously with the on-screen participants. During live shows, the show showed statistics and high scores from the online players, ensuring a completely interactive way of watching the show. After just two episodes, over 12,000 users had already downloaded the app.[64]

Dreaming of a better world

Generation Z are realistic, but they are also dreamers striving to make their world better for them and for future generations. Only 6 per cent of Generation Z says that they're afraid of what the future will bring.[65] Global issues are very important to these Gen Zers, being brought up in an era of economic crisis, 'the war on terror' and debates about equality and diversity. The digital interconnectedness that features this generation plays a large part in this, as they have been able to see and experience people 'fighting the good fight' on the internet from a very young age. Take the Occupy Movement, for instance. This worldwide movement started in September 2011 with Occupy Wall Street, a widely mediatized protest in New York against social and economic inequality. In just over a month after the initial event, the movement had spread to 951 cities in 82 countries. Using websites and Twitter hashtags (#occupy) with catchy slogans ('We are the 99%'), the movement went completely viral, allowing young Gen Zers to come across these inspiring ideas and actions.[66]

FIGURE 8.6   World issues Generation Z would tackle first

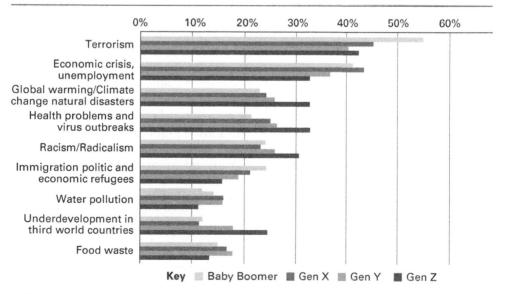

SOURCE: Joeri Van den Bergh – Who's Up NXT? presentation

According to studies, 60 per cent of Generation Zers want to 'change the world', while this was only the case for 39 per cent of Generation Y. When asked what issues they would tackle first if they could, Gen Z seems to care more about health issues (32 per cent), global warming (32 per cent), racism (30 per cent) and the Third World (24 per cent) than other generations. On top of their mind are still terrorism (42 per cent) and economic crisis (32 per cent) as well, but less so than previous generations. What's even more striking is that Gen Zers aren't just talking about what they would do, they are also already doing it. Almost one out of four Generation Zers claim to actively volunteer, trying to help various good causes.[67]

Equality and diversity

Generation Z is a very diverse generation. Predictions in the United States show that Gen Z will be the last generation with a 'Caucasian majority', meaning that they are the final stepping stone towards a pluralistic society, containing a broad spectrum of ethnicities. Similarly, Gen Zers have experienced increasingly blurred gender roles. With gay marriage becoming more and more common, Gen Zers are strong advocates of equal rights in terms of sexuality. Similarly, women are viewed as more empowered. While previous generations had gotten used to seeing the father as the main source of income in the family and the mother as the nurturer, recently these distinctions have become more vague for Gen Z. Their Gen X parents cared a whole lot about 'sharing responsibilities' between mum and dad, with Gen X mothers being less likely than other generations to say that their husband was properly involved in the upbringing of their children.[68]

In our research, 82 per cent of Gen Zers agreed that gay couples should be able to walk hand in hand on the street, compared to only 64 per cent with Generation Y. Similarly, over 60 per cent agreed that same-sex couples are capable of bringing up children the way traditional couples did. Another study by JWT Intelligence discovered that no less than 82 per cent of Gen Zers in the US and the UK say that they do not care about someone's sexual orientation, with 81 per cent declaring that they do not think a person is defined by their gender as much as before. As summarized by JWT: 'These issues have never been hypothetical for them.'[69]

When Australian actress Ruby Rose appeared in season 3 of the Netflix show *Orange is the New Black*, she started grabbing headlines as people championed her 'gender-neutral' look. The openly lesbian actress and model doesn't identify as either woman or man, and quickly became an example of gender neutrality. High-end department store Selfridges introduced a whole 'Agender' pop-up store, dedicated entirely to gender-neutral fashion.[70]

Female empowerment

Women in movies for youngsters are no longer portrayed as princesses in a classic 'damsel in distress' way (eg old Disney Cinderella or Sleeping Beauty).

Girls now more often than not take lead roles and rule the screen. In the highly successful *Frozen*, Elsa and Anna are the main focus, playing two sisters who overcome various difficulties in trying to keep their relationship intact. Katniss Everdeen from *The Hunger Games* franchise continuously conquers difficult situations with the goal of making society a better place, sort of reminiscent of everything that Generation Z stands for.[71]

A poll taken in 2009 with kids aged 8 to 17 about attraction to domains in STEM (Science, Technology, Engineering and Mathematics) revealed that only five per cent of the girls were interested in a future in engineering, versus 24 per cent of the boys. To conquer this imbalance, Debbie Sterling launched a Kickstarter campaign for a range of toys called GoldieBlox. Mascot 'Goldie' is a science-loving, engineering antitheses of Barbie, and the idea for this new toy role model came to Sterling as she got frustrated at the lack of women in her own chemical engineering classes at college. Toys and popular culture in the past often stereotyped with either the pretty girl that likes dolls and princesses (eg Barbie), or the more boring nerdy girl with glasses (eg Velma from Scooby Doo). Goldie looks like a normal, imperfect young girl but with an heightened interest in everything concerning science and engineering. The idea is similar to that of classic kids role model Bob the Builder, but targeted towards girls.[72] The first campaign video for the toy brand was put up on YouTube in 2013 and showed three young girls being bored by the usual 'pink' TV commercials. The ad then portrayed how the girls constructed a Rube Goldberg machine, turning their house into a 'massive, magical contraption'. The video ended with their tagline: 'Toys for future engineers'. The campaign was massively successful, with over 10 million views on the video streaming site.[73]

Always embraces being #LikeAGirl

In 2014 Procter & Gamble launched a highly resonating campaign towards female empowerment with their feminine protection brand Always. The campaign was called #LikeAGirl and pointed out that the phrase 'like a girl' has become too much of an insult, with for instance phrases such as 'throwing like a girl' and 'fighting like a girl' coming across as being a sign of weakness. Always' target was clear: turning this insulting tone into a compliment.[74]

In June 2014 the first phase of the campaign kicked off with a YouTube video. In the three-minute clip, people are asked to perform some actions 'like a girl'. For instance: 'Show me what it looks like to run like a girl?' Both the male and female participants then start acting out the stereotypical 'feminine' type of running, while for example complaining about their hair. Then, young girls get asked the same questions, and they start doing the reverse, normal type of running. One kid answers by saying: 'To me it means running as fast as you can.' The video then explains how this common 'insult' can result in low self-confidence for girls, and ends with the line:

'Let's make #LikeAGirl mean amazing things.'[75] This video was seen by over 80 million on the internet, and a shorter version was used by Always during the Super Bowl in 2015. In a survey conducted by Procter & Gamble after the video, 76 per cent of surveyed females and 59 per cent of surveyed males declared that they had changed their perception of saying 'like a girl'.[76]

A year later in June 2015, phase two started with a new video called 'Unstoppable' in which young girls are asked if they have ever been told that they can't do something 'because you are a girl'. According to a survey cited in the video, 72 per cent of girls feel that society limits them (puts them in boxes) in what they are allowed to do. The girls are then invited to take one of the cardboard boxes in the room, write on them what they had been told and then do whatever they want to 'break' through the boxes, metaphorically breaking through their imposed limits. In just two days the video exceeded 5 million views on YouTube.[77] Additionally, Always organized The Always #LikeAGirl Confidence Summit in New York City on July 7, which premiered the Unstoppable clip as well as a Confidence Teaching Curriculum to help young girls' confidence, created in collaboration with education experts and conference organizer TED. To top off the event, they also announced the signing of a real Generation Z ambassador for the whole #LikeAGirl campaign: Maisie Williams. The Z-actress born in 1997 rose to fame playing Arya Stark on the HBO show *Game of Thrones*, a character who herself is a prime example of an empowered girl.[78]

Love for world-improving brands

Generation Z is environmentally and socially conscious. Their well-developed online skills have made them more informed about what companies can do and are doing to make the world a better place.[79] 60 per cent would pick a brand if they knew that they are attempting at improving the world, while 77 per cent agree that 'doing good' and not just donating to charity should be a central part of business.[80] In a sense, this fits with research on consumers' relationships with brands. Academic research in the past found that when people have a relationship with a 'sincere' brand, it shows similarities to friendship, while relating with an 'exciting' brand portrays more similarities with short-term 'flings'. Therefore, to turn Gen Zers into more of a friend it's important that brands have a strong positioning concerning worldly issues, but they should also perform this positioning through actions.

'Buy one from us, we'll give one to someone in need': it's a rather simple model, one upon which TOMS and its founder Blake Mycoskie have built an empire. In 2006, TOMS started selling shoes. For every pair sold, the company donated a pair to a country in need of footwear. In less than 10 years the company has donated over 50 million pairs of shoes in 60 different countries.[81] Even though this idea resonated well with youngsters as well as non-profit organizations (the model won a prize for being an 'innovative enterprise solution to poverty'), it was not without its criticisms. Simply giving shoes to people in need might not fix the fundamental issues, and could in fact cause the local businesses to lose even more ground. Mycoskie acknowledged these issues and decided to extend the TOMS line in addition to starting the construction of a shoe manufacturing facility in Haiti in late 2013, providing a more direct fix (eg extra jobs) for the problems.[82] TOMS eyeglasses were introduced with a similar idea: for each pair bought, TOMS invested in eye surgeries and general eye care. According to the company this initiative has resulted in helping more than 360,000 people by giving them prescription glasses or performing vital surgery to clear their vision. In 2014 TOMS also launched a coffee line, with sales proceedings going directly to 'clean water' initiatives such as rainwater reservoirs and piping systems. The company provided 250,000 weeks of safe water.[83]

TOMS meanwhile has inspired other companies to take on similar ideas. In 2013, three Canadians launched 'Mealshare', an organization that partners with restaurants to turn meals into meals for those who need them the most. When you visit a restaurant from the partner list and order a Mealshare-branded item, the organization automatically donates a meal to someone in need. Restaurants that decide to partner need to provide the necessary funding for Mealshare at the end of every month. The Mealshare initiative has served over 250,000 meals in less than two years, using a network of almost 200 Canadian restaurants.[84]

Other companies embracing the 1-4-1 ('one for one') business model are for instance Warby Parker (glasses), Roma Boots (boots), Sir Richard's (condoms), The Munchery (meal delivery) and Soapbox Soaps (soap and vitamins). Even though the business model sometimes becomes subject to criticism, these companies are all definitely acting on their positioning.[85]

Gen Z entrepreneurs want to make it

The *New York Times* put it well when describing Generation Z: 'These children are so mature and they learn so fast, they might just be ready to take over by the time they're 22.' Their independence at a young age is remarkably high and they don't wait to go out and discover things on their own, as proved by the creation of a 'Generation Z Conference' at the American University in Washington.[86] In 2009 Swedish developer Markus 'Notch' Persson created Minecraft, an 'online builder game' dedicated to building things with pixelated blocks in a virtual world resembling the graphics of 80s arcade games, which of course are the type of games their Gen X parents grew up with.[87] Minecraft is a multiplayer game, relying on community assistance to give tips and get help while building larger structures. The game has no real specific goals and is expandable with various community-built 'mods' that extend gameplay capabilities. You can become an adventurer, a farmer, an explorer, an architect, and the Minecraft game-world is so vast that there is a large chance that you never play the same game as someone else. You have to pretty much figure out how things work by yourself or via the community that is spread all over the internet, from forums to dedicated subReddits. There are over 68 million videos uploaded on YouTube with tips, tricks and examples of impressive builds. For example, 'captainsparklez' is one of the most famous Minecraft players with a YouTube subscriber number of over 8 million.[88] This game basically is a great summary of typical Gen Z elements: DIY, endless possibilities to sculpture your own world and entirely community-based. Since 2009 it has sold over 70 million copies, with the number growing by over 10,000 each day and more than 100 million registered users.[89] Even the *Financial Times* has discovered that this game is no laughing stock, as they received the following 'complaint' from six-year-old Zorawar Bhangoo: 'Sir, Your big Minecraft picture on the front page of your Life & Arts section (July 4) is wrong. In Minecraft, smoke does not come out of chimneys and doors cannot be a light colour. Doors need four boxes at the top of them. Trees have to be round and not any other shape and you put the trees a rectangle shape [*sic*]. The clouds have to be 3D. You put the clouds upright. The roof of a house cannot be blue.'[90]

Generation Z is filled with achievers, striving to make a personal impact through their work. Gen Zers disapprove of the classic hierarchic model that still rules a lot of workplaces and put less importance on qualifications compared to having a network of people around you.[91] Compared with other Generation, the Zers desire to start their own business significantly more, while working for others is much less popular compared to their predecessors. In fact, 42 per cent of Gen Zers have made plans to actually start a business, with three per cent already actively running one. Above all, they feel ready and have started preparing for later professional life: 80 per cent of students in high school believe that they are more driven than colleagues, while over half are actively doing internships and gaining professional experience during high school, often advised by their parents.[92]

FIGURE 8.7   Example of a large Minecraft design

SOURCE: http://mashable.com/2013/02/13/amazing-minecraft-creations/

Jordan Casey: interview with a young Gen Z entrepreneur

Jordan Casey started programming apps aged 9 and three years later, with one of the games he developed, he had one of the best-selling game apps at the iTunes store. He has already started three companies and is now in the process of developing a new idea. Jordan, now 15, was interviewed by Niels Schillewaert, managing partner and co-founder of InSites at ESOMAR's global conference in Dublin in September 2015.

Niels: You're working on a new product. Tell us a little bit about it.

Jordan: A couple of months ago, I had this idea, it was called KidsCode. Basically, what I want to do with it is to combine gaming with programming. And use it to teach children how to program. So that's what I'm working on now. Similar to games on the internet, like Club Penguin, which is a game that inspired me to begin with programming and games like Minecraft, it would sort of be a multi-player game. As a kid, you log in, make your own character, with your friends, and explore this huge virtual world, but program that world to how you like it, using a visual programming language, like drag and drop and learn programming as you go on in the game. So what I want to do with it is teach the fundamentals of programming, collaborative skills, like getting the kids together, to work together, and show how you can be creative with programming.

Niels: So will kids walk away being a programmer, then? Or will they learn a specific technique?

Jordan: I hope it would inspire the next generation of programmers, because if everyone in the world started programming, like I did, I think we could have a really cool future. So I just want to inspire the next generation of programmers, show people how you can be creative with it, I see programming as an art form, really, expressing yourself, using interactive games and things like that. So I just want to show the people the fun side of it as well, how cool programming can be.

Niels: You're already talking about the next generation; that is so funny to me! You started when you were nine, is that something you've seen going down, are kids really starting to code before they even learn to read and write? As of what age will your game be played?

Jordan: With KidsCode I want to aim at the own demographic, because since I started so many kids have gone into programming. Since then

Continued...

Continued...

there's been a huge media pile-up of what kids can do. In Ireland we have this organization called CoderDojo, which pretty much is a free club where kids can go and learn programming with their friends. And so because of things like CoderDojo people have really started to see the potential of young people and what they can accomplish, if they are given the right support. So a lot of younger people are starting to program and I want to provide the support, with KidsCode, for them. So mainly we would be aiming at five-, six-year-olds, up to 12, 13.

Niels: So a year from now and then it's going to be launched. And say three years down the road, if you look at it now, when will you be satisfied, when will it be a success for you?

Jordan: I'd really like to get a million users, something like that, that would be really cool. I know it's a bit farfetched, but I think this has the potential to reach a million kids. I want to teach a million kids how to program. That's something I'm really passionate about, education and in particular technological education, getting kids into tech literacy, showing them the future, so to get a million kids, I'd be really satisfied.

Niels: Great goal! Teaching a million kids is business, but is there any financial drive to this?

Jordan: Yes, a bonus obviously would be to be making some money from it. So what most virtual worlds like this do, is like a subscription model, a 'freemium' type of model, all the games and apps do it nowadays; you have your free version, the kids sign up, play the game, but if they want bonus and extra, they pay €4 or €5 a month. So if you have a million kids paying that, that would be pretty cool. So I'd like to make some money from it as well.

Niels: Where do you get your inspiration? You could have immediately gone to developing the next game, what's the driver behind it?

Jordan: It comes back to my story a bit, me learning programming. When I started, I didn't really have the support there, I did it pretty much on my own, just reading books. What inspires me, is the potential to inspire others. Again, teaching a million kids via a program is something that drives me forward, and I have a lot of inspiration, like Minecraft, again, is a game that really inspired me. The guy who made it, his story inspired me. It made me think about creative things, like 'I want to be seen as the next Minecraft.' I want to inspire people, sort of like myself.

Bedroom influencers

Gen Zers still see adults (especially close ones) as inspirations, but increasingly the importance of peer influencers has become larger. YouTube and social media have made it possible to be influential from your bedroom. This trend already started with young, successful 'hoodie-CEO's' like Mark Zuckerberg (founded Facebook aged 20) and Pete Cashmore (created Mashable aged 19) and has crossed over into the realm of celebrities on YouTube, Instagram, Twitter and other social media. This has resulted in 76 per cent of Gen Zers wanting to turn their hobby into their job, using the internet as a way of making this reality.[93,94]

A report by Tesco Mobile found that 40 per cent of teens want to become a 'professional blogger', while another survey from Variety showed that the most influential people for surveyed teens were all 'YouTubers', with Hollywood celebs lagging behind. Gen Zers look up to 'celebrities' that could be their friends, therefore meaning that they trust these people when they promote a brand or a certain product.[95] Brands need to give influencers a form of creative freedom instead of simply co-creating an obvious advertisement, going from storytelling to 'storyliving'. As a brand you have to instigate an emotional connection with the influencer so they become so involved that they want to share it with their community. They have to empower and be enthusiastic about your brand.[96] To choose the influencer you do not only look at the number of followers they have but also how their audience matches your message, they have to be relevant. While more and more online stars are entering the Hollywood world, they are also gradually losing their appeal to Generation Z by becoming too 'Hollywood'. The industry will have to find a good balance so they don't destroy the close connections between influencers and followers.[97]

The Total Audience Report by Nielsen showed that the number of viewers of online video streams is growing with 60 per cent a month. Another study revealed that YouTube contains 63 per cent of all the video consumption around the world, generating one billion unique visitors per month who watch over six billion hours monthly.[98] PewDiePie arguably is one of the biggest YouTube-stars on the planet right now. So-called 'vloggers' like him document their life, their ideas, thoughts and activities (eg gaming) through videos on the internet, giving them a special personal connection with (mostly teenage) viewers. Felix Kjellberg, as PewDiePie is really called, reportedly earned over $7.4 million from his videos in 2014, and others are reaching the same type of stardom.[99] As a shy teen, Bethany Mota started her beauty and lifestyle channel on YouTube when she was 14 years old. Less than five years later she is an internet phenomenon with more than 10 million subscribers across her different channels. Bethany already launched different collections of her own clothing line in the popular store Aéropostale, starred in YouTube ads, was a guest judge in Project Runway and participated in 'Dancing With The Stars'.[100] Together with several other YouTubers in 2015 she also interviewed Barack Obama using questions that followers asked with the hashtag #YouTubeAsksObama. This was the sixth year that YouTube and the White House worked together. This way the White House could reach the younger generations who are otherwise hard to target because they are not as active on traditional media as other generations. The interview was live-streamed on YouTube and is still available as a video.[101] Bethany stimulates her viewers to recreate her DIY ideas by introducing a hashtag on Twitter and Instagram. The teens are part of a community and can share their work with their role-model. She also invested a stake in BeautyCon, a beauty convention that is evolving into a media brand because of its success.[102]

Toyota promoted the 2015 redesign of the Toyota Camry with the comedy duo Rhett & Link. The influencers tested the car by doing different kinds of challenging stunts like riding through a ring of fire. Toyota recorded this and subsequently used the videos as advertisements. The video had only 74.000 views on Toyota's channel, but due to the duo also giving a shout-out during six videos of their daily talk show 'Good Mythical Morning' it generated more than 10 million views. Instead of making people watch a traditional commercial, followers of Rhett & Link could see their favourite YouTubers talk and promote the new redesign.[103]

We are perfectly imperfect

You don't need to be perfect, being unique is the new perfect. Former America's Next Top Model contestant Winnie Harlow suffers from the rare skin condition vitiligo. Rather than being cast aside immediately, the fashion industry has embraced her. In September of 2014 clothing brand Ashish invited her to run the catwalk during the London Fashion Week, causing an outpour of support.[104] Similarly, women like Cara Delevingne, Jennifer Lawrence or Lena Dunham, in the past considered to be 'imperfect', have become icons for generation Z. In 2014, the hashtag #uglyselfie trended over all kinds of different social media encouraging people to take the most ridiculous, ugly-looking selfie.[105]

This appreciation of the imperfect also rings true for products. French supermarket Intermarché wanted to do something about the 300 million tons of fruit and vegetables that gets thrown away yearly. 57 per cent of the fruit and vegetable waste is because of the 'aesthetics', meaning that the looks were not up to the strict standards.

Intermarché wanted to embrace these 'inglorious fruits and vegetables' and turned them into 'wanted' items. A full-blown print, radio and film campaign was combined with in-store branding, a dedicated aisle in the stores, special labelling and separate spots on the receipt. To prove to people that the taste was not affected by the looks, they even provided sample soups made with the 'bad' fruit and vegetables. The initial campaign was launched in March 2014 in just one store, before Intermarché expanded it to all of its 1,800 French locations in October. Just during the first two days of the sale, over 1.2 tons of these fruits and vegetables were sold on average per store, while also resulting in an increase of store traffic by 24 per cent.

The responses from the customers were almost unanimously positive.[106] Intermarché's competitors Auchan and Monoprix decided to start similar campaigns, while initiatives have meanwhile crossed the border to Portugal, the UK and Canada.[107]

Failosophy

As a brand or company, Generation Z wants you to embrace mistakes. Being honest and authentic is more important than being without mistakes. For instance, Etsy was honoured by the 'Great Place To Work Institute' in 2013, but still published a report about some negatives that were discovered in a survey with their employees. The report, available to read for everyone, for example showed that a large number of Etsy's employees are unsure about their job and feel that they don't get enough feedback from higher-ranked managers. Etsy could have acted like many other companies do and kept this information strictly internal, risking a leak somewhere on the internet. Instead, they played the transparency card and showed that even though the company appears to be 'amazing' on the outside, there are still issues that need to be resolved.[108]

Originally started in Mexico in 2012, the 'FuckUp Nights' are an initiative to celebrate failure-stories by young entrepreneurs. Rather than disappearing into hiding, these events want to give businesses the opportunity to talk about their failures without judging, but rather as a means for others to learn from the made mistakes. Apart from the original events in Mexico, the FuckUp Nights concept has since spread to Argentina, Spain, Germany, the US, the Netherlands and many other countries and other conferences such as #Failcon are tapping into the same idea.[109]

At the end of 2014, LEGO launched the #keepbuilding campaign targeting young girls and their parents. 'I don't always want you to help me,' the girl says in the video addressing her parents. 'Do you know why? I want to figure it out on my own. Even when it doesn't turn out the way I want, I know it's not wrong. Because you taught me how to think. And how to dream. I'm about to make something that I know will make you proud.' Since LEGO's 2012 roll-out of the LEGO Friends line, with girl-specific colours and themes and a new range of appealing figures for role-play the brand is successfully attracting a female audience. 'We have always known that creating and constructing is as relevant for girls as it is for boys,' says Per Hjuler, SVP Innovation & Consumer Marketing LEGO Group in an interview with us. 'But not until the launch of LEGO Friends did we crack the code of how girls prefer to have this play type presented in terms of products, marketing and other forms of engagement.'[110] While boys tend to replicate what's on the box as fast as possible, girls follow a more personal and less rigid approach. To them, constructing is less competitive and all about creating their own environments. The stuff they create leaves room for imagination, self-expression and personal storytelling. The #keepbuilding campaign is a good reflection of this different motivation.[111]

'Just a logo' is not enough

'If it fits, it fits' seems to be the mantra followed by Generation Z. The functionality and quality reigns over the popularity of a certain brand. Therefore they are more likely to buy specific items they like from several brands, rather than staying loyal to a certain brand because it's 'their' brand. Brand loyalty, in other words, is on the low side.[112] It's hard to discover brands that are considered the 'favourites' of Gen Z. In terms of clothing, they have moved away from the Gen Y brands such as Abercrombie & Fitch or Hollister. In the spring of 2014, 19 per cent of Gen Zers declared that they had stopped wearing Abercrombie & Fitch while 16 per cent said the same about Hollister.[113] In a survey from JWT Intelligence, only 35 per cent of Gen Zers thought that not having the latest gadget equals to not being cool.

A great example of this is the trend towards 'athleisure' in fashion. Gen Zers love to dress themselves combining the functionality of real sportswear (eg yoga pants, running shoes) with 'normal' wear. This way they can 'actively chillax'. Maybe it doesn't look beautiful or perfect, but it's easy to wear and allows a lot of room for movement. A study by Piper Jaffray showed that the tendency for Gen Zers to wear denim went down to 12,7 per cent in the spring of 2014, while 'athleisure' had already overtaken this with 14,4 per cent. According to retail analysts, the sector of athleisure will see a growth of 24 per cent by 2020. H&M already invested in a special collection created by Alexander Wang in 2014, while retailer Topshop is collaborating with icon Beyoncé to create an entirely new 'athletic street-wear brand'. Gen Zers might not work out all the time, but they like looking as if they actually do.[114]

HOT TAKEAWAYS FOR COOL GEN Z BRAND BUILDERS

- Generation Z are the children of Gen X parents who rate inner-focused qualities such as 'independent' and 'hard-working' higher than Baby Boomer parents and outer-focused values such as 'honesty', 'trust' and 'ethical' lower.

- Gen Zers themselves find creativity and independence more important than respect.

- Generation Z gets more weekly allowance than previous youth generations and they spend their money more on games, hobbies and food.

- They also have a high influence on their parents' purchasing decisions.

- Generation Z is a 'snappy' generation with a shorter attention span and a more visual style of communicating (eg YouTube, Instagram, SnapChat).

- They adore (live) video content, short formats and ephemeral messaging and like to engage in interactive content creation themselves.

- Generation Z is dreaming of creating a better world and cares about the environment, racism, the third world and health.

- They are the most diverse youth generation ever and are raised in a world where LGBT rights, female empowerment and blurring gender roles has become more prominent.

- Brands should have a strong positioning concerning more worldly issues and live up to expectations by their actions rather than mere storytelling.

- Generation Z is eager to start up their own business and have a personal impact on society.

- They embrace imperfections in celebrities, products and life and understand that you learn from mistakes.

Conclusion

From our daily experience with both advertisers and youth, we know that the word 'cool' is as dangerous as it is useful in discussions on building brands that are appealing to Generation Y. The second you tell a Millennial you are cool, you can be very sure that, well, you are not. They decide themselves what's cool. It's not a characteristic you can deliberately plan or chase. You have to earn the status 'cool brand'. When you are capable of attaining this status, your brand's coolness will translate into buying preference and long-term loyalty. The new Gen Y consumers are connected, pragmatic, eclectic and honest. They don't want to feel constrained by time, place or choice. Above all Gen Y is a generation that values freedom. In this book, we have created the mnemonical CRUSH framework that might be helpful in protecting your brands from losing their relevancy for the new consumer generation. In other words: to stay hot.

The brand-building model, combining coolness, realness, uniqueness, self-identification with the brand and happiness, is based on years of interacting with Millennials through qualitative and quantitative research as well as the everyday creation of compelling content and brand solutions for them. The era of one-way communication is completely over. To stay hot, cool brands need to connect on a deep and individual emotional level with Generation Yers. They wear their heart on their sleeves. Cool brands make them happy. Youth will engage with brands that feel as close to them as their best friends. The metaphor of an engagement is actually very useful in visualizing the different steps youth marketers can consider in this branding process. Marketing and branding to the previous Generation X could be compared to an arranged marriage. Individual preferences were restrained by the generation's desire to belong to the predominant 'achievers' predilection. Image was important and Gen Xers were prepared to pay dowries to be seen with the right bride/brand.

You will probably expect that we will now compare Gen Y branding to the other extreme of speed dating... wrong. If you scratch the surface of what is commonly described as a cool and trendy phenomenon, the truth will reveal that the average duration between the initial meeting of a partner and accepting a marriage proposal for Gen Yers today is two years and 11 months. Between proposal and wedding, there's another two years and 3 months! For strategic brand management this means: if you don't want to surf on hypes and fads and want to avoid your brand's obsolescence, it takes a lot more branding efforts than just a speed date with these critical youngsters.

With Gen Y, you first need to deserve trust and affection. Successful Gen Y brands don't dictate or shout, but empower, engage and leave control in the hands of youth. The main difference between shouting and having a conversation is actually: listening. Those brands that are devoted to listening to the assertive voice of this generation will find their relationship gaining strength.

Generation Y has been dubbed 'the echo boomer generation', because of the big resemblance with its parents and the strong ties between child and parent. With Gen Yers – and Gen Xers will frown now – their parents' opinion is highly valued in every important choice they make. And it goes both ways. In this new cross-generational relationship, we see the tremendous influence Gen Y has on most of their parent consumption choices. A strong reason also for brands primarily targeting an older demo to understand the motivations of youngsters? Considering the boomerang and hotel mum and dad trend, as a youth marketer, you should never forget the parental voice.

In the first phase of traditional courtship, men might show off by sending love letters, poems and singing romantic songs. For a Gen Y brand, continuously bringing compelling content and cool utilities linked to the brand's unique vision is an important first step to be noticed and raise awareness. Content is youth's social currency and they talk about the brands they perceive as unique and buy brands they hear recommended by peers. Since youngsters are sceptical about a brand's uniqueness, it is only through consistent positioning in all details that you will manage to break through the clutter in a credible way and acquire their attention. To stay on youth's stimulus-oriented radar, brands need to adapt to changing tastes and offer variety and choice. You might think that Apple iPhone does the trick with just one model, but they are actually selling a cool tool to access an enormous daily updated variety of apps, and Apple has introduced five generations of the device in less than five years. Cool youth brands know how to develop this well-balanced area of tension between recognizable consistency and regular novelty and surprise. Your brand has to reward this triumph-craving generation's efforts in life and support their busy lifestyle.

Once your brand is able to catch Gen Y's interest, the next step is to enduringly confirm that you share the same interests. As with romance, it is by finding out what partners have in common that flirting moves to the next phase of bonding. Winning youth brands show us every day how their vision is related to the passions of the lifestyle groups they are targeting. Those brands that represent the identity aspects that youngsters want to accentuate and fit in with the aspired crowd behaviour will be able to establish a relationship. Self-identification with brands is by far the most important step in remaining a hot brand. Just like lovers often mirror their body language, great youth brands echo Gen Y's passion points. Yet, remember again that it's not about shouting you have the same passions. Youth should experience with their own eyes that you fit in with their lives. Act, don't tell. Deliver utility and value. Gen Y advertising needs to go from just communicating value to actually engage youngsters in creating the value together.

This brings us to the next step in the courtship: dating. Couples go out together for a meal, a party, a film or shopping. Brands have so many on- and offline touch points with their fan base. For this marketing-wise generation brands will have to deliver the same values and unique experience every single time they connect with consumers. For our emotional consumer generation, spending magic moments together with a brand will arouse feelings of happiness. When a dating couple engages in thrilling activities together, like a roller-coaster ride or rafting, psychologists have found that the excitement involved with the activity is transposed to the person they are with and their relationship. For brands this works in exactly the same way. Positive emotions evoked on brand-initiated or -endorsed events will strengthen the bond Gen Yers have with your brand. Brands should surpass the delivery of short-term pleasures and think of challenging gratifications that will leave a long-lasting impression. Just like a bit of role-playing or gaming can refresh a relationship, using gamification techniques can help to keep the variation oriented consumer generation on board.

One of the biggest fears of Gen Yers is to lead a boring life. They are addicted to excitement and will walk away the minute they are not surprised anymore. In an era with more divorces than marriages, there's one main breeding ground for long-term relationships: honesty and authenticity. After all, you can pretend you have a lot in common for a while. Or lovesickness sometimes makes you blind to reality. But in the long run, your true personality traits and behaviour will inevitably be revealed. Only Gen Y brands that don't imitate or fake their personality and stay true to their DNA will earn a sustainable place in the heart of this savvy generation.

This metaphor of courtship and relationship building is of course just another angle to look at the five strategic brand CRUSH dimensions we have developed for this book. When preparing the first edition of the book Mattias introduced me to Jörgen Andersson, who was working as Global Brand Director of H&M back then. He was probably one of the most inspiring people I have ever met. I was happy to meet him again when working on this second edition. Andersson has since moved on to manage the global brands of Esprit and Uniqlo, authentic brands that he has been trying to get back on Gen Y's radar. I would like to add this one quote from him in this conclusion:

> When you take something for granted, whether it's the love of your life or in business terms, it goes wrong. You get disconnected. Brands should stay connected to their personality and past and listen and stay in close contact with consumers and be prepared to adapt to evolutions. To make small changes to everything they are doing all the time. The minute you sit back and relax and think you're successful, there will be other brands surpassing you. Even if you're married to your wife for 30 years, the minute you stop caring about her dreams and ambitions, the minute you're not interested any more, you will lose her. Because of course some of her dreams will remain but some will change and when you don't feel your partner understands you and listens to you, you get bored and then it's very easy to find a new love somewhere because you are

open for distractions. A relationship between a company and a consumer is just like any other relationship. You need to be in a constant dialogue and be up to surprise and challenge each other to make it work over time. Continuously listening to your consumer is the difference between success and death of a company.

Jörgen Andersson

We wish you good luck in approaching this demanding new consumer market and keeping your brand alive and hot. Remember, the future of your company is depending on how strong your connection with these young adults will turn out to be. Addressing the needs and wants of this new consumer generation and adapting your strategies and tactics to fit their lives will be of a much higher importance for your brands than it was to understand Generation X. The size of the articulate Gen Y and Gen Z cohort is substantial. The influence of this generation on society, economics, politics and business will be comparable to the impact of their Baby Boomer parents in the past three decades. As Gen Yers and Gen Zers are only starting to enter job markets and creating households, you ain't seen nothing yet...

We hope you have enjoyed this book as a stirring source of strategic Gen Y & Z branding. Frequent updates will be available on the companion website and blog **www.howcoolbrandsstayhot.com**. It is also a good place to share your own experiences or campaigns and interact with the authors as well as other passionate youth brand builders. Both authors would love to hear your comments also via Twitter using **#coolbrands** or by following us via **@joeri_insites** and **@mattias_behrer**.

APPENDIX
A word from the research team

The CRUSH© study was fielded between 29 October 2009 and 3 December 2009. All questionnaires were completed online, and the research was conducted in Belgium, the Netherlands, France, Germany, Spain, Sweden and the UK. The total sample size was 6,994 respondents, of which 40 per cent (N = 2,820) were male and 60 per cent (N = 4,174) were female. The sample was composed of 2,474 respondents from the Talk to Change community, a market research panel maintained by InSites Consulting. Of the Talk to Change sample, 51 per cent (N = 1,259) were aged 14–29, while 49 per cent (N = 1,215) were aged 30–65. With the participation of MTV Europe, an additional 4,489 respondents were recruited by means of a pop-up that was shown on the MTV websites in the countries listed above. The pop-up directed interested website visitors to the online survey. Of the participants recruited through the MTV websites, 89 per cent (N = 3,987) were aged 14–29, while 11 per cent (N = 502) were 30+.

The CRUSH© branding model was tested by means of path analysis. Path analysis is a regression-based technique designed to test hypothesized directional relationships between variables. This is a complicated way of saying that path analysis can be used to evaluate theories about how different kinds of brand attitudes (in this case, the constructs in the CRUSH model) lead to overall evaluations of brand (in this case, Brand Leverage).

The model (see Figure A1.1) starts with the foundation of perceptions of the brand as cool, real, unique, self-brand identification (perceived overlap between one's own personality and the brand's personality) and of positive emotions engendered by thoughts of the brand. These five dimensions are all included as independent variables in two separate regression models, one explaining brand conversations, and one explaining brand image. The results from this first set of analyses indicate that seeing a brand as cool, real, unique and having greater identification with the brand and feeling more positive emotions when thinking about the brand, are associated with having more conversations about the brand as well as having a better image of the brand.

The second set of analyses consisted of a single regression analysis examining the joint impact of brand conversations, brand image and brand identification on brand leverage, which is defined as the overall strength of the brand in the consumer's mind. These three variables are all included as direct predictors of brand leverage because of their importance and indeed centrality to brand evaluation for the modern consumer. The results from

FIGURE A1.1   The CRUSH branding model

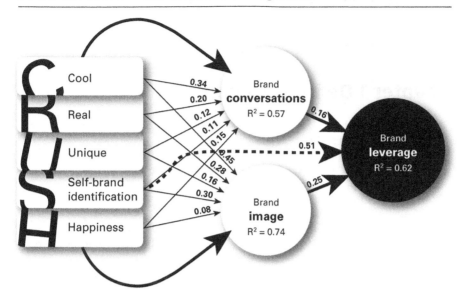

this analysis show that more conversations about the brand, a better image of the brand and greater identification with the brand are all associated with greater brand leverage, in other words: with a stronger brand.

The sum of these analyses provide support for the CRUSH© branding model that is the backbone of this book. By proposing a theoretical explanation of the ways in which strong brands are formed in consumers' minds, and then evaluating and testing the relationships between the hypothesized constructs and brand strength, this research provides marketers with a useful and validated framework to better understand key drivers of brand strength, especially among young consumers.

Michael Friedman, Niels Schillewaert and
Annelies Verhaeghe, ForwaR&D Lab, InSites Consulting
More information can be found on: **www.insites.eu**

REFERENCES

Chapter 1 Defining Generation Y

1 Di Falco A, Gibbs D, Corcoran A. *MTV generation V.2.* London: MTV Networks Europe; 2009

2 Doherty M. *Millennials could be your next growth opportunity* [Online]. 2 Apr 2010 [accessed 5 Apr 2010]; Available from: http://www.mediapost.com/publications/?fa=Articles.showArticle&art_aid=125415

3 Morales C. [Interview]. *eBay Europe.* 21 Jun 2012

4 Grealish H. [Interview]. *Diageo Brands.* 25 May 2012

5 Maartense J-J. [Interview]. *Eastpak (VF Corporation).* 3 Apr 2012

6 Urwin R. Generation Y. Attracting, engaging and leading a generation at work. *White paper series Drake International* 2006; 3(1): 1–20

7 Taylor P, Keeter S. *Millennials. A portrait of generation next. Confident. Connected. Open to change* [Online]. 24 Feb 2010 [accessed 28 Mar 2010]; Available from: http://www.pewresearch.org/millennials

8 Van den Bergh J, Pallini K. *Who's up Next? A cross-generational view on marketing and branding* [Research]. Ghent (Belgium): InSites Consulting; Apr 2015

9 Van den Broek M. *The truth about youth* [Online]. 15 Jun 2011 [accessed 23 Aug 2012]; Available from: http://www.howcoolbrandsstayhot.com/2011/06/15/the-truth-about-youth/

10 Taylor P, Keeter S. *Millennials. A portrait of generation next. Confident. Connected. Open to change* [Online]. 24 Feb 2010 [accessed 28 Mar 2010]; Available from: http://www.pewresearch.org/millennials

11 Bethencourt F. [Interview]. *PepsiCo.* 13 Apr 2012

12 Goodstein A. Interview with Neil Howe in *Ypulse Daily Update* [Online]. 18 Mar 2010 [accessed 28 Mar 2010]; Available from: http://www.ypulse.com/ypulse-interview-neil-howe-president-lifecourse-associates

13 Roy I. [Interview]. *BBC Worldwide.* 4 May 2012

14 Van den Bergh J, Pallini K. *Who's up Next? A cross-generational view on marketing and branding* [Research]. Ghent (Belgium): InSites Consulting; Apr 2015

15 Rosen LD. *Rewired: Understanding the iGeneration and the way they learn.* New York: Palgrave MacMillan; Apr 2010

16 Palley W. *April Trend Report examines the digital world of Gen Z* [Online]. 23 Apr 2012 [accessed 7 Aug 2012]; Available from: http://www.jwtintelligence.com/2012/04/april-trend-report-examines-digital-world-gen/

17 Potts M. *Make way for generation nice* [Online]. 15 Jun 2012 [accessed 9 Aug 2012]; Available from: http://www.mediapost.com/publications/article/175985/make-way-for-generation-nice.html

18 Heller L. *Move Over Millennials, Generation Z Is In Charge* [Online]. 14 Aug 2015 [accessed 18 Sep 2015]; Available from: www.forbes.com/sites/lauraheller/2015/08/14/move-over-millennials-generation-z-is-in-charge/

19 *What comes after generation Z? Introducing generation alpha* [Online]. 1 Aug 2014 [accessed 18 Sep 2015]; Available from: www.mccrindle.com.au/the-mccrindle-blog/what-comes-after-generation-z-introducing-generation-alpha

20 *Babiesborn from 2010 to form Generation Alpha* [Online]. 15 Nov 2009 [accessed 17 Sep 2015]; Available from: www.news.com.au/babies-born-from-2010-to-form-generation-alpha/story-e6frfl49-1225797766713

21 Urwin R. Generation Y. Attracting, engaging and leading a generation at work. *White paper series Drake International* 2006; 3(1): 1–20

22 Barton C, Fromm J, Egan C. *The Millennial Consumer. Debunking Stereotypes* [Online]. 16 Apr 2012 [accessed 21 Aug 2012]; Available from: http://www.brandchannel.com/images/papers/536_BCG_The_Millennial_Consumer_Apr_2012%20(3)_tcm80-103894.pdf

23 Taylor P, Keeter S. *Millennials. A portrait of generation next. Confident. Connected. Open to change* [Online]. 24 Feb 2010 [accessed 28 Mar 2010]; Available from: http://www.pewresearch.org/millennials

24 Verhaegen B. *18–30 in Belgium and Europe. The New Pragmatics*. Belgium: Presentation for VMA; 7 Nov 2006

25 Schupak HT. Teen survey. Courting the next wave of customers. *JCK* 2008 Mar:106

26 Rand N. The 'peace and plenty' generation: understanding teenagers' lives. *Advertising & Marketing to Children*. 2003 Oct–Dec: 45–52

27 Jayson S. *Many 'emerging adults' 18–29 are not there yet* [Online]. 30 Jul 2012 [accessed 21 Aug 2012]; Available from: http://www.usatoday.com/news/health/wellness/story/2012-07-30 Emerging-adults-18-29-still-attached-to-parents/56575404/1

28 Ypulse. *Helicopter VS free-range: the new great parenting debate.* [Online]. 25 Mar 2015 [accessed 21 May 2015]; Available from: https://www.ypulse.com/post/view/helicopter-vs-free-range-the-new-great-parenting-debate

29 Johnson D. *Households doubling up* [Online]. 13 Sep 2011 [accessed 7 Aug 2012]; Available from: http://blogs.census.gov/2011/09/13/households-doubling-up/

30 Newman, K. *The Accordion Family*: referenced in Smith N. *Why new grads are homeward bound* [Online]. 22 May 2012 [accessed 7 Aug 2012]; Available from: http://www.businessnewsdaily.com/2568-college-graduates-returning-home.html

31 Van den Bergh J. *Influential generation calls for more attention* [Online]. 8 Feb 2011 [accessed 7 Aug 2012]; Available from: http://www.howcoolbrandsstayhot.com/2011/02/08/influential-generation-calls-for-more-attention/

32 Giedd J, Blumenthal J, Jeffries NO, Castellanos F, Liu H, Zijdenbos A, *et al.* Brain development during childhood and adolescence: a longitudinal MRI study. *Nature Neuroscience* 1999; 2 (10): 861–63

33 Feinstein S. *Secrets of the teenage brain. Research-based strategies for reaching and teaching today's adolescents*. San Diego (CA): The Brain Store; 2004

34 Baird AA, Gruber SA, Fein DA, Maas LC, Steingard RJ, Renshaw PF, *et al.* Functional magnetic resonance imaging of facial affect recognition in children and adolescents. *Journal of the American Academy of Child and Adolescent Psychiatry* 1999; 38 (2): 195–99

35 Spear LP. The adolescent brain and the college drinker: biological basis of propensity to use and misuse alcohol. *Journal of Studies on Alcohol Supplement* 2000; 14: 71–81

36 Feinstein S. *Secrets of the teenage brain. Research-based strategies for reaching and teaching today's adolescents*. San Diego (CA): The Brain Store; 2004

37 Couch R. *Instagram users went #WithoutShoes this month and gave 265000 pairs to kids in need*. [Online]. 21 May 2015 [accessed 28 May 2015]; Available from: www.huffingtonpost.com/2015/05/21/toms-shoes-without-shoes-_n_7360312.html

38 Morgan N. *Blame My Brain. The amazing teenage brain revealed*. London: Russel Cobb; 2007

39 Morgan N. *Blame My Brain. The amazing teenage brain revealed*. London: Russel Cobb; 2007

40 Berman J. *Pepsi's latest ad campaign has little to do with soda*. [Online]. 11 Mar 2015 [accessed 28 May 2015]; Available from: www.huffingtonpost.com/2015/03/11/new-pepsi-challenge_n_6839230.html

41 Miller J. *Pepsi's new global campaign features a game of drone football*. [Online]. 1 May 2015 [accessed 28 May 2015]; Available from: www.fastcocreate.com/3045817/pepsis-new-global-campaign-features-a-game-of-drone-football

42 Ember S, Steel E. *The Pepsi challenge is returning, but this time for the social media generation*. [Online]. 11 Mar 2015 [accessed 28 May 2015]; Available from: www.nytimes.com/2015/03/11/business/media/the-pepsi-challenge-is-returning-but-this-time-for-the-social-media-generation.html?_r=1

43 Colette H. *O2 positions new mobile brand as exclusive club for 18–22-year-olds* [Online]. 16 Apr 2012 [accessed 7 Aug 2012]; Available from: http://www.jwtintelligence.com/2012/04/o2-positions-mobile-brand-exclusive-club-18-22-year-olds/

44 Twenge JM. *Generation Me. Why today's young Americans are more confident, assertive, entitled – and more miserable than ever before*. New York: Free Press; 2006

45 Yarrow K, O'Donnell J. *Gen BuY. How tweens, teens and twenty-somethings are revolutionizing retail*. San Francisco: Jossey-Bass; 2009

46 Penman S, McNeill LS. Spending their way to adulthood: consumption outside the nest. *Young Consumers* 2008; 9(3): 115–69

47 Loechner J. *Gen X and Millennials driving recovery* [Online]. 25 Mar 2010 [accessed 29 Mar 2010]; Available from: http://www.mediapost.com/publications/?fa=Articles.showArticle&art_aid=124696

48 Rose H. *A new F word for Millennials* [Online]. 2 May 2012 [accessed 7 Aug 2012]; Available from: http://www.howcoolbrandsstayhot.com/2012/05/02/a-new-f-word-for-millennials/

49 Van den Bergh J. *Two thirds of the USA youth believe 2012 will be better* [Online].15 Feb 2012 [accessed 7 Aug 2012]; Available from: http://www.howcoolbrandsstayhot.com/2012/02/15/two-thirds-of-the-usa-youth-believe-2012-will-be-better/

50 Bulea C. *Why don't gen Y women buy from you?* [Online]. 5 Aug 2011 [accessed 23 Aug 2012]; Available from: http://www.howcoolbrandsstayhot.com/2011/08/05/why-dont-gen-y-women-buy-from-you/

51 Van den Broek M. *Gen Y social shopping* [Online]. 22 Jul 2011 [accessed 23 Aug 2012]; Available from: http://www.howcoolbrandsstayhot.com/2011/07/22/gen-y-social-shopping/

52 Di Falco A, Gibbs D, Corcoran A. *MTV generation V.2*. London: MTV Networks Europe; 2009

53 Greene J. *How Nike's social network sells to runners* [Online]. 6 Nov 2008 [accessed 26 Mar 2010]; Available from: http://www.businessweek.com/print/ magazine/content/08_46/b4108074443945.htm

54 *Nike + FuelBand* [Online]. [accessed 21 Aug 2012]; Available from: http://nikeplus.nike.com/plus/products/fuelband

55 Christensen O. Changing attitudes of European Youth. *Advertising & Marketing to Children* 2002 Apr–Jun: 19–32

56 *Russian Standard Vodka: Russian Facebook Roulette* [Online]. May 2011 [accessed 8 Aug 2012]; Available from: http://adsoftheworld.com/media/online/ russian_standard_vodka_russian_facebook_roulette

57 Dover D. *A bad day for search engines: how news of Michael Jackson's death travelled across the web* [Online]. 26 Jun 2009 [accessed 27 Mar 2010]; Available from: http://www.seomoz.org/ blog/a-bad-day-for-search-engines-how-news-of-michael-jacksons-death- traveled-across-the-web

58 *Michael Jackson* [Online]. 6 Jul 2009 [accessed 27 Mar 2010]; Available from: http://infodisiac.com/blog/2009/07/michael-jackson/

59 Van Belleghem S, Van den Branden S. *Global social media study* [Research]. Ghent (Belgium): InSites Consulting; Mar 2010

60 Van den Bergh J, Thijs D. *Social media & Gen Y around the world study* [Research]. Ghent (Belgium): InSites Consulting; Aug 2012

61 Van den Bergh J. *Don't you wish your girlfriend was hot like me* [Online]. 19 May 2011 [accessed 23 Aug 2012]; Available from: http://www. howcoolbrandsstayhot.com/2011/05/19/dont-you-wish-your-girlfriend- was-hot-like-me/

62 Doherty M. *Millennials could be your next growth opportunity* [Online]. 2 Apr 2010 [accessed 5 Apr 2010]; Available from: http://www.mediapost.com/ publications/?fa=Articles.showArticle&art_aid=125415

63 Twenge JM. *Generation Me. Why today's young Americans are more confident, assertive, entitled – and more miserable than ever before.* New York: Free Press; 2006

64 Twenge JM, Campbell WK. *The Narcissism Epidemic. Living in the age of entitlement.* New York: Free Press; 2009

65 Halpern J. *Fame Junkies. The Hidden Truths Behind America's Favorite Addiction.* New York: Houghton Mifflin Company; 2007

66 Sandoval G. *Teen iPad destruction – 'what was the point of that?'* [Online]; 5 Apr 2010 [accessed 6 Apr 2010]; Available from: http://news.cnet.com/ 8301-31001_3-20001729-261.html

67 Niedzviecki H. *Hello I'm Special. How individuality became the new conformity.* San Francisco: City Lights; 2006

68 Halpern J. *Fame Junkies. The Hidden Truths Behind America's Favorite Addiction.* New York: Houghton Mifflin Company; 2007

69 Taylor P, Keeter S. *Millennials. A portrait of generation next. Confident. Connected. Open to change* [Online]. 24 Feb 2010 [accessed 28 Mar 2010]; Available from: http://www.pewresearch.org/millennials

70 Twenge JM. *Generation Me. Why today's young Americans are more confident, assertive, entitled – and more miserable than ever before.* New York: Free Press; 2006

71 Medeiros G, Walker C. *GenWorld. The new generation of global youth* [Research]. Chicago: Energy BBDO; 2005

72 Van den Bergh J, De Vuyst P. *Generation Y around the world* [Online]. 15 Feb 2012 [accessed 21 Aug 2012]; Available from: http://www.slideshare.net/ joerivandenbergh/generation-y-around-the-world-by-insites-consulting

73 Verhaegen B. *Generation health* [Online]; 12 Aug 2011 [accessed 21 Aug 2012]; Available from: http://www.howcoolbrandsstayhot.com/2011/08/12/ generation-health/

74 *The Pinterest phenomenon: Pinterest's users growth, statistics, usage trends, interesting facts.* [Online]. [accessed 21 Aug 2012]; Available from: http://www.vabsite.com/2012/02/pinterest-users-usage-trends-statistics.html

75 Indvik L. *Pinterest drives more traffic to blogs than Twitter* [Online]. 8 Mar 2012 [accessed 21 Aug 2012]; Available from: http://mashable. com/2012/03/08/pinterest-more-traffic-twitter-study/

76 Vasan P. *Pinterest reaches 100 million monthly users.* [Online]. 17 Sep 2015 [accessed 19 Sep 2015]; Available from: www.cnet.com/news/pinterest-reaches-100-million-monthly-users/

77 Bianchi L. OR Laurens B. *The world's first Pinterest campaign* [Online]. 27 Mar 2012 [accessed 21 Aug 2012]; Available from: http://www.viralblog.com/ social-media/kotex-launches-worlds-first-pinterest-campaign/

78 Van den Bergh J, De Ruyck T. *Brand authenticity study for Levi's Europe* [Research]; Ghent (Belgium): InSites Consulting; Nov 2008

79 Christensen O. Changing attitudes of European youth. *Advertising & Marketing to Children* 2002 Apr–Jun: 19–32

80 Van den Bergh J, De Ruyck T. *Brand authenticity study for Levi's Europe* [Research]; Ghent (Belgium): InSites Consulting; Nov 2008

81 Verbeurgt W. [Interview]. *MINI.* 14 Sep 2012

82 *Volunteer travel* [Online]. [accessed 23 Aug 2012]; Available from: http://en.wikipedia.org/wiki/Voluntourism

83 *Puma new shoe box by Yves Behar/Fuse project* [Online]. 14 Apr 2010 [accessed 21 Apr 2010]; Available from: http://www.designboom.com/ weblog/cat/8/view/9828/puma-new-shoe-box-by-yves-behar-fuse-project.html

84 Taylor P, Keeter S. *Millennials. A portrait of generation next. Confident. Connected. Open to change* [Online]. 24 Feb 2010 [accessed 28 Mar 2010]; Available from: http://www.pewresearch.org/millennials

85 Namiranian L. *Brand engagement. Teenagers and their brands in emerging markets.* ESOMAR World Research Paper, London; Sept 2006

86 Van den Bergh J. *What social & environmental brands mean for Generation Y* [Online]. 27 Jul 2011 [accessed 23 Aug 2012]; Available from: http://www.howcoolbrandsstayhot.com/2011/07/27/what-social-environmental-brands-mean-for-generation-y/

87 Rand N. The 'peace and plenty' generation: understanding teenagers' lives. *Advertising & Marketing to Children* 2003 Oct–Dec: 45–52

88 *Drought Draught: climate change beer from WWF.* [Online]. 13 Apr 2015 [accessed 22 May 2015]; Available from: www.adnews.com.au/campaigns/ drought-draught-climate-change-beer-from-wwf

89 Rose H. *Youthopia. A study of hopes and dreams.* London: Viacom Brand Solutions International; Nov 2010

90 Van den Bergh J, De Vuyst P. *Generation Y around the world* [Online]. 15 Feb 2012 [accessed 21 Aug 2012]; Available from: http://www.slideshare.net/ joerivandenbergh/generation-y-around-the-world-by-insites-consulting

91 Palmaerts T. *God is a designer* [Online]. 7 May 2012 [accessed 23 Aug 2012]; Available from: http://www.secondsight.nl/making-worlds/god-is-a-designer-2/

92 Fellinger C. [Interview]. *Beiersdorf*. 19 Mar 2012

93 Derycke L. *Social media access and personal devices are significant job criteria for Gen Y* [Online]. 9 Nov 2011 [accessed 21 Aug 2012]; Available from: http://www.howcoolbrandsstayhot.com/2011/11/09/social-media-access-personal-devices-significant-job-criteria-geny/

94 Corley T. [Interview]. *Abercrombie & Fitch*. 18 Apr 2012

95 Schawbel D. *Millennials vs. Baby Boomers: who would you rather hire?* [Online]. 29 Mar 2012 [accessed 21 Aug 2012]; Available from: http://moneyland.time.com/2012/03/29/millennials-vs-baby-boomers-who-would-you-rather-hire/

96 Nelis H, van Sark Y. *Puber brein, binnenstebuiten (Adolescent brain, inside out)*. Utrecht (The Netherlands), Antwerp (Belgium): Kosmos Uitgevers; 2009

97 Foehr UG. *Media multitasking among American youth: prevalence, predictors and pairings*. Menlo Park (CA): The Henry J. Kaiser Foundation; 2006 Dec: 1–36

98 Johnson S. *Everything Bad Is Good for You*. New York: Riverhead Books; 2005

99 De Bruyckere P, Smits B. *Is het nu Generatie X, Y of Einstein? (Is it generation X, Y or Einstein?)*. Mechelen (Belgium): Plantyn; 2009

100 Patel K. *MTV will have a 'Beavis and Butt-head' iPad App and much more* [Online]. 28 Mar 2010 [accessed 5 Apr 2010] Available from: http://www.businessinsider.com/mtv-will-have-a-bevis-and-butt-head-ipad-app-and-much-more-2010-3

101 McCrindle M. *Understanding Generation Y*. North Parramatta: Australia: The Australian Leadership Foundation; Dec 2001

102 Verhaegen B. *18–30 in Belgium and Europe. The New Pragmatics*. Belgium: Presentation for VMA; 7 Nov 2006

103 Binkley C. *Teen stores try texts as gr8 nu way to reach out* [Online]. 1 Aug 2012 [accessed 21 Aug 2012]; Available from: http://online.wsj.com/article/SB10000872396390444405804577561093050635960.html

104 Twenge JM. *Generation Me. Why today's young Americans are more confident, assertive, entitled – and more miserable than ever before*. New York: Free Press; 2006

105 Christensen O. Changing attitudes of European Youth. *Advertising & Marketing to Children* 2002 Apr–Jun: 19–32

106 Reisenwitz TH, Iyer R. Differences in generation X and generation Y: implications for the organization and marketers. *The Marketing Management Journal* 2009; 19(2): 91–103

Chapter 2 Developing a brand model for the new consumer

1 Dale R. *Tumour in the Whale*. A collection of modern myths. London: WH Allen; 1978

2 Snowden D, Stienstra J. *Stop asking questions. Understanding how consumers make sense of it all*. Proceedings of the ESOMAR Congress; 8 Sep 2007; Berlin (Germany)

3 Zaltman G. *How Customers Think. Essential insights into the mind of the market.* Boston, MA: Harvard Business School Press; 2003: 211–13
4 Cottrill G. [Interview] *Converse.* 29 Aug 2012
5 Hein K. *Teen talk is, like, totally branded* [Online]. 6 Aug 2007 [accessed 1 Apr 2010]; Available from: http://kellerfay.com/news/Brandweek_8_6_07.pdf
6 Van den Bergh J, Lagae M, Vandenbranden S. *MTV Cool brand awards study: emotions & conversations.* Ghent (Belgium): InSites Consulting, Jun 2010
7 Okazaki S. The tactical use of mobile marketing: how adolescents' social networking can best shape brand extensions. *Journal of Advertising* 2009 Mar; 49(1): 12–26
8 Claus D. *Conversation diary* [Research]. Ghent (Belgium): InSites Consulting; Feb 2010
9 Van den Bergh J, Lagae M, Vandenbranden S. *MTV Cool brand awards study: emotions & conversations.* Ghent (Belgium): InSites Consulting, Jun 2010
10 Jung P. [Interview]. *MasterCard International.* 13 Apr 2012
11 Cottrill G. [Interview] *Converse.* 29 Aug 2012
12 Van den Bergh J, Friedman M, Verhaeghe A, Schillewaert S. *Developing the CRUSH branding model.* Ghent (Belgium): InSites Consulting; 2010
13 Van den Bergh J. *Gen Y wants more than cool brands* [Online]. 21 Feb 2011 [accessed 1 Oct 2012]; Available from: http://www.howcoolbrandsstayhot.com/2011/02/21/gen-y-wants-more-than-cool-brands/
14 Friedman M, Schillewaert S, Ahearne, Lam S. *Brand leverage study* [Research]. InSites Consulting and Houston University; 2009
15 Andersson J. [Interview]. *Esprit.* 19 Mar 2012
16 Michils M. [Interview]. *Saatchi & Saatchi.* 1 Oct 2012

Chapter 3 What cool means to brands

1 Danesi M. *Cool. The Signs and Meanings of Adolescence.* Toronto: University of Toronto Press; 1994
2 Van den Bergh J, Claus D. *The meaning of cool.* Ghent (Belgium): InSites Consulting & MTV Networks; 2007
3 Coates D. *So very cool in more ways than one* [Online]. 12 Feb 2010 [accessed 14 Feb 2010]; Available from: www.Ypulse.com
4 Van den Bergh J, Claus D. *The cool sneaking formula.* Ghent (Belgium): InSites Consulting & MTV Networks; 2008
5 Van den Bergh J, Friedman M, Verhaeghe A, Schillewaert S. *Developing the CRUSH branding model.* Ghent (Belgium): InSites Consulting; 2010
6 Van den Bergh J, De Vuyst P. *Cool today, gone tomorrow by Generation Y around the world* [Online]. 30 May 2012 [accessed 30 Aug 2012]; Available from: http://www.slideshare.net/joerivandenbergh/cool-today-gone-tomorrow-by-generation-y-around-the-world
7 *Converse (shoe company)* [Online]. [accessed 29 Aug 2012]; Available from: http://en.wikipedia.org/wiki/Converse_(shoe_company)
8 Tschorn A. *Testing Converse's Chuck Taylor All Star II vs. the original* [Online]. 16 Aug 2015 [accessed 23 Sep 2015]; Available from: http://www.latimes.com/fashion/la-ig-converse-update-20150816-story.html
9 Cottrill G. [Interview] *Converse.* 29 Aug 2012

10 Klara R. *Converse's Street-Style Campaign Shows How People Rock Their Chucks Around the World*. [Online] 2 Mar 2015 [accessed 23 Sep 2015]; Available from: http://www.adweek.com/news/advertising-branding/converse-s-street-style-campaign-shows-how-people-rock-their-chucks-around-world-163189

11 Cottrill G. [Interview] *Converse*. 29 Aug 2012

12 MTV Networks Cool Brand Awards Research, conducted by InSites Consulting

13 Van den Bergh J, Claus D. *The cool sneaking formula*. Ghent (Belgium): InSites Consulting & MTV Networks; 2008

14 Maartense JJ. [Interview]. *Eastpak (VF Corporation)*. 3 Apr 2012

15 Nestle Waters. *The couch converter service by Vittel*. [Online]. 19 May 2015 [accessed 19 May 2015]; Available from: http://www.nestle-waters.com/media/featuredstories/the-couch-converter-service-by-vittel%C2%AE

16 Contagious I/O. *En garde for a driver dual*. [Online]. 16 Jan 2015 [accessed 21 May 2015]; Available from: https://www.contagious.io/articles/en-garde-for-a-driver-duel

17 Van Biesen J. [Interview] *VRT*. 24 Sep 2012

18 Claes P. [Interview] *VRT*. 24 Sep 2012

19 Parpis E. *Ideas that inspire: water boy* [Online]. 28 Jul 2008 [accessed 2 Sep 2012]; Available from: http://www.adweek.com/news/advertising-branding/ideas-inspire-water-boy-96445

20 Nancarrow C, Nancarrow P, Page J. An analysis of the concept of cool and its marketing implications. *Journal of Consumer Behaviour* 2002 Jun; 1(4): 311–22

21 Pathak S. *Luxury brands on Snapchat? Why Michael Kors is taking the plunge*. [Online]. 19 Feb 2015 [accessed 18 May 2015]; Available from: http://digiday.com/brands/michael-kors-snapchat/

22 Hutchings E. *Burberry Partners with Social App to live-stream Fashion Shows*. [Online]. 6 Feb 2015 [accessed 18 May 2015]; Available from: http://www.psfk.com/2015/02/burberry-line-social-app-livestream-fashion.html

23 Contagious I/O. *Top Trends*. [Online]. 18 Feb 2015 [accessed 18 May 2015]; Available from: https://www.contagious.io/articles/top-trends

24 Olson EM, Czaplewski AJ, Slater SF. Stay cool. *Marketing Management* 2005 Sep–Oct: 14–7

25 Kirsten Narula S. *The incredible staying power of the Oreo cookie*. [Online]. 13 Feb 2015 [accessed 26 May 2015]; Available from: http://qz.com/342782/the-incredible-staying-power-of-the-oreo-cookie/

26 Van den Bergh J, Claus D. *The meaning of cool*. Ghent (Belgium): InSites Consulting & MTV Networks; 2007

27 Elliott S. Sprite recast as spark in a bottle [Online]. *The New York Times*. 11 Feb 2010 [accessed 15 Feb 2010]; Available from: http://mediadecoder.blogs.nytimes.com/2010/02/11/sprite-recast-as-spark-in-a-bottle/?scp=1&sq=Sprite%20Recast&st=cse

28 Van den Bergh J. *10 rules of cool advertising* [Online]. 28 Feb 2011 [accessed 1 Sep 2012]; Available from: http://www.howcoolbrandsstayhot.com/2011/02/28/10-rules-of-cool-advertising/

29 Van den Bergh J, Lagae M. *Cool today, gone tomorrow? Generation Y and loyalty*. Ghent (Belgium): InSites Consulting & MTV Networks; 2009

30 Lawton M. *Scion sells the cool factor* [Online]. 6 Jul 2010 [accessed 2 Sep 2012]; Available from: http://www.thenextgreatgeneration.com/2010/07/scion-sells-cool-factor/

31 Ramsey J. *Volkswagen People's Project had produced 3 concepts* [Online]. 9
    May 2012 [accessed 2 Sep 2012]; Available from: http://www.autoblog.com/
    2012/05/09/volkswagens-peoples-car-project-in-china-has-produced-three-co/

32 Contagious I/O. *The mini fashion bar.* [Online]. 21 May 2015 [accessed 21
    May 2015]; Available from: https://www.contagious.io/articles/fashion

33 Van den Bergh J. *Get the vibe going for chewing gum* [Online]. 3 May 2011
    [accessed 2 Sep 2012]; Available from: http://www.howcoolbrandsstayhot.
    com/2011/05/03/get-the-vibe-going-for-chewing-gum/

34 Stephens C. *Powerade billboards let you get your sweat on.* [Online]. 3 Jun
    2015 [accessed 3 Jun 2015]; Available from: http://www.psfk.com/2015/06/
    miami-the-lab-miami-startup-incubator-wynwood-coworking-space.html

35 Hall K. *The big ideas behind the Nintendo Wii* [Online]. 16 Nov 2006
    [accessed 16 Feb 2010]; Available from: http://www.businessweek.com/
    technology/content/nov2006/tc20061116_750580.htm

36 Meeus R. Nintendo keert terug naar zijn roots (Nintendo returns to its roots).
    De Morgen 9 Dec 2011: 38

37 Meeus R. *Toys-to-life is big business in the videogame industry* [Online].
    27 Aug 2015 [accessed 29 Sep 2015]; Available from: http://www.demorgen.be/
    technologie/levend-speelgoed-bij-videogames-is-big-business-a2436889/

38 Van den Bergh J, Lagae M, De Vuyst P. *Branded solutions tracking* [Research].
    InSites Consulting for MTV Networks; 2010

39 GfK Data provided with permission of Procter & Gamble. Belgium:
    Nov–Dec 2009

40 Mortimer R. Bling bling branding with strictly no mention of 'cool'. *Brand
    Strategy.* 2002 Oct: 10–11

41 Nancarrow C, Nancarrow P, Page J. An analysis of the concept of cool and its
    marketing implications. *Journal of Consumer Behaviour* 2002 Jun; 1(4): 311–22

42 Gladwell M. *Annals of style. The coolhunt* [Online]. 17 Mar 1997 [accessed
    16 Feb 2010]; Available from: http://www.newyorker.com/
    archive/1997/03/17/1997_03_17_078_TNY_CARDS_000378002

43 Southgate N. Coolhunting with Aristotle. *International Journal of Market
    Research* 2003; 45(2): 167–89

44 Rogers EM. *Diffusion of Innovations.* New York: Free Press; 1962

45 Metcalfe B. *Metcalfe's law: a network becomes more valuable as it reaches
    more users* [Online]. 2 Oct 1995 [accessed 12 Aug 2010]; Available from:
    www.infoworld.com

46 Reed D. The law of the pack. *Harvard Business Review* 2001 Feb: 23–4

47 Domensino C. [Interview]. 27 Feb 2010

48 Van den Bergh J. *European MC DC survey* [Research]. InSites Consulting;
    summer 2009

49 Verhaeghe A. *Qualitative report for Johnnie Walker* [Research]. InSites
    Consulting with permission of Diageo Benelux; 2008

50 Martel A. [Interview]. Diageo Benelux; 22 Feb 2010

51 Gloor P, Cooper S. *Coolhunting. Chasing down the next big thing.* New York:
    AMACOM Books; 2007

52 Verhaeghe A, Schillewaert N, Van den Bergh J, Claes P, Ilustre G. *Crowd
    interpretation.* Are participants the researchers of the future? Proceedings of
    the ESOMAR congress 2011; Amsterdam (Netherlands); 18 Sep 2011

53 Van Dijk J. *MSc thesis: The effects of co-creation on consumers' brand and
    product perceptions* [Online]. 24 Jun 2012 [accessed 3 Sep 2012]; Available
    from: http://issuu.com/joycediscovers/docs/msc_thesis_joycevandijk_public

54 Gloor P, Cooper S. *Coolhunting. Chasing down the next big thing.* New York: AMACOM Books; 2007

55 Van Belleghem S, De Ruyck T. *From co-creation to collaboration.* [Paper]. Ghent (Belgium): InSites Consulting; 2012

56 Andersson J. [Interview]. *Esprit.* 19 Mar 2012

57 Burstein D. *How Lay's is tapping its audience for its next big chip idea* [Online]. 1 Aug 2012 [accessed 3 Sep 2012]; Available from: http://www.fastcocreate.com/ 1681333/how-lays-is-tapping-its-audience-for-its-next-big-chip-idea

58 *Cutting hair to cut prices for Chinese New Year* [Online]. 12 Apr 2012 [accessed 3 Sep 2012]; Available from: http://www.campaignbrief.com/ asia/2012/04/china-cut-hair-to-cut-prices-f.html

59 Kimmels M. [Interview]. *Heinz Continental Europe.* 18 Jun 2012

60 Ypulse. *Brands co-creating their futures with Millennials.* [Online]. 6 Nov 2014 [accessed 27 May 2015]; Available from: https://www.ypulse.com/post/view/ brands-co-creating-their-futures-with-millennials

61 The Unilever Foundry. [Online]. [accessed 27 May 2015]; Available from: http://foundry.unilever.com/

62 Rubin J. *Smells like teen spirit: inside the secretive world of Brandy Melville.* [Online]. 24 Sep 2014 [accessed 27 May 2015]; Available from: http://www.racked.com/2014/9/24/7575693/brandy-melville

63 Contagious I/O. *Titan of taco.* [Online]. 11 Mar 2015 [accessed 27 May 2015]; Available from: https://www.contagious.io/articles/titan-of-taco

64 Van Iterson M. [Interview]. *Heineken International.* 28 Spe 2015

65 VBSI. *Golden age of youth research challenges assumptions about the meaning of youth* [Online]. 10 Oct 2008 [accessed 17 Feb 2010]; Available from: http://www2.prnewswire.com/cgi-bin/stories.pl?ACCT=104&STORY=/ www/story/10-07-2008/0004899039&EDATE=

66 Noxon C. *Rejuvenile. Kickball, cartoons, cupcakes and the reinvention of American grown-up.* New York: Three Rivers Press; 2006

67 ESA [Online]. *Industry facts.* 2009 [accessed 17 Feb 2010]; Available from: www.theesa.com/facts

68 Higham W. *Old is the new young* [Online]. 17 Mar 2010 [accessed 3 May 2010]; Available from: http://www.adweek.com/aw/content_display/ community/columns/other-columns/e3iff897d5a72be7303195a70be8209cf9d

69 Noxon C. *The rejuvenile phenomenon from a to z* [Online]. 2010. [accessed 18 Feb 2010]; Available from: www.rejuvenile.com.

Chapter 4 The real thing: brand authenticity

1 *Don Draper's presentation for Kodak* [Online]. 16 Apr 2008 [accessed 23 Feb 2010]; Available from: http://blogs.amctv.com/mad-men/2008/04/don-drapers-kodak-presentation.php

2 Eng J. *Kirstin Chenoweth, Jon Cryer win first Emmys* [Online]. 20 Sept 2009 [accessed 23 Feb 2010]; Available from: http://www.tvguide.com

3 Rolling Stone. *'Mad Men' paid $250K for Beatles song* [Online]. 8 May 2012 [accessed 3 Sep 2012]; Available from: http://www.rollingstone.com/music/ news/mad-men-paid-250k-for-beatles-song-20120508

4   Kondolojy A. *Season five premier is most watched episode of 'Mad Men'
ever* [Online]. 26 Mar 2012 [accessed 3 Sep 2012]; Available from:
http://tvbythenumbers.zap2it.com/2012/03/26/season-five-premiere-is-most-
watched-mad-men-episode-ever/126048/

5   Our journal *Madipedia* [Online]. 9 Sept 2009 [accessed 23 Feb 2010];
Available from: http://www.madisonavenuejournal.com/2009/09/08/
our_journal_madipedia/

6   Satran R. *How did the Adidas Stan Smith become the ultimate fashion shoe?*
[Online]. 26 May 2015 [accessed 2 Oct 2015]; Available from: https://i-d.vice.com/
en_us/article/how-did-the-adidas-stan-smith-become-the-ultimate-fashion-shoe

7   Lasaleta JD, Sedikides C, Vohs KD. Nostalgia weakens the desire for money.
Journal of Consumer Research 2014 Oct; 1;41(3):713–729

8   Nudd T. *Expedia travels back in time to recreate your best throwback
Thursday photos* [Online]. 24 Jul 2014 [accessed 2 Oct 2015]; Available from:
http://www.adweek.com/adfreak/expedia-travels-back-time-recreate-your-best-
throwback-thursday-photos-159087

9   Dzieza J. *Facebook's new nostalgia feature is already bringing up painful
memories* [Online]. 2 Apr 2015 [accessed 2 Oct 2015]; Available from:
http://www.theverge.com/2015/4/2/8315897/facebook-on-this-day-nostalgia-
app-bringing-back-painful-memories

10 Beuker I. *Nike Turns Runner's Data Into 100,000 Personalized Videos*
[Online]. 19 Jan 2015 [accessed 2 Oct 2015]; Available from:
http://www.viralblog.com/community-marketing/nike-turns-runners-data-
100-000-personalized-videos/

11 Derbaix M, Decrop A. Authenticity in the performing arts: a foolish quest?
Advances in Consumer Research 2007; 34: 75–80

12 Millet K, Van den Bergh B, Pandelaere M. *First things first? The value of
originality.* Belgium: Faculty of Business and Economics of the KULeuven;
2008

13 Beverland MB. *Building Brand Authenticity. 7 habits of iconic brands.*
Basingstoke (UK): Palgrave Macmillan; 2009

14 Elber L. *Mad Men makes a splash bigger than its ratings* [Online]. 23 Oct 2008
[accessed 24 Feb 2010]; Available from: http://www.usatoday.com/life/television/
2008-10-23-2948376121_x.htm

15 *Sesame Street: Mad Men* [Online]. [accessed 24 Feb 2010]; Available from:
http://www.youtube.com/watch?v=YgvKCfZqxrQ&feature=fvst

16 Gilmore JH, Pine II BJ. *Authenticity. What consumers really want.* Boston
(MA): Harvard Business School Press; 2007

17 Van den Bergh J, De Ruyck T. *Authenticity for Gen Y.* [Research]. Ghent
(Belgium): InSites Consulting; 17 Feb 2009

18 Rose RL, Wood SL. Paradox and the consumption of authenticity through
reality television. *Journal of Consumer Research* 2005 Sep; 32: 284–96

19 Botterill J. Cowboys, outlaws and artists: the rhetoric of authenticity and
contemporary jeans and sneaker advertisements. *Journal of Consumer Culture*
2007; 7(105): 105–25

20 Peterson RA. In search of authenticity. *Journal of Management Studies* 2005
Jul; 42(5): 1083–98

21 Beverland MB. Crafting brand authenticity: the case of luxury wines. *Journal
of Management Studies* 2005 Jul; 42(5): 1003–29

22 Mol JM, Wijnberg NM. Competition, selection and rock and roll: the
economics of Payola and authenticity. *Journal of Economic Issues* 2007 Sep;
XLI(3): 701–14

23 *Truth In Advertising* [Online]. 9 June 2014 [accessed 29 June 2015];
Available from: https://www.contagious.io/articles/truth-in-advertising

24 *A dollar for your data* [Online]. 15 June 2014 [accessed 29 June 2015];
Available from: https://www.contagious.io/articles/buying-an-audience

25 *Truth In Advertising* [Online]. 9 June 2014 [accessed 29 June 2015];
Available from: https://www.contagious.io/articles/truth-in-advertising

26 Hall S. *Newcastle Brown Ale Hijacks Super Bowl With Hilarious
#BandOfBrands Stunt* [Online]. 28 January 2015 [accessed 29 June 2015];
Available from: http://marketingland.com/newcastle-brown-ale-hijacks-
super-bowl-hilarious-bandofbrands-stunt-115929

27 Botterill J. Cowboys, outlaws and artists: the rhetoric of authenticity and
contemporary jeans and sneaker advertisements. *Journal of Consumer Culture*
2007; 7(105): 105–25

28 Ransdell E. *The Nike story? Just tell it* [Online]. 31 Dec 1999 [accessed 3 Sep
2012]; Available from: http://www.fastcompany.com/38979/nike-story-just-tell-it

29 Beverland MB. *Building Brand Authenticity. 7 habits of iconic brands*.
Basingstoke (UK): Palgrave Macmillan; 2009

30 Janoff B. Off the wall and in the black. *Brandweek* 2006 9 Oct; 47(37):
40–61

31 Klinger M. *Jack O'Neill, 89, a surfing legend who endures* [Online]. 27 May
2012 [accessed 3 Sep 2012]; Available from: http://www.sfgate.com/sports/
article/Jack-O-Neill-89-a-surfing-legend-who-endures-3589127.php

32 *Taste with Tarquin* [Online]. 2014 [accessed 1 July 2015]; Available from:
http://tastewithtarquin.com/

33 *Always – Intimate Words* [Online]. 30 April 2015 [accessed 29 June 2015];
Available from: https://www.youtube.com/watch?v=741DJkJTnXQ

34 Nudd T. *Y&R Wins Media Grand Prix for App That Lets Women Call for
Help by Shaking Their Phones* [Online]. 24 June 2015 [accessed 1 July 2015];
Available from: http://www.adweek.com/news/advertising-branding/yr-wins-
media-grand-prix-app-lets-women-call-help-shaking-their-phones-165538

35 Beverland MB. *Building Brand Authenticity. 7 habits of iconic brands*.
Basingstoke (UK): Palgrave Macmillan; 2009

36 Gilmore JH, Pine II BJ. *Authenticity. What consumers really want*. Boston (MA):
Harvard Business School Press; 2007

37 Pandelaere M, Sampermans D, Verbruggen T. Various student dissertations
and research. Ghent (Belgium): Department of Marketing Ghent University;
2007–08

38 Pandelaere M, Millet K, Van den Bergh B. *Attitudinal effects of first exposure.*
[Working paper]. Ghent (Belgium): Faculty of Business and Economics,
University of Ghent; Nov 2008

39 Millet K, Van den Bergh B, Pandelaere M. *First things first? The value of
originality*. Leuven (Belgium): Faculty of Business and Economics Leuven
University; 2008

40 Gilmore JH, Pine II BJ. *Authenticity. What consumers really want*. Boston
(MA): Harvard Business School Press; 2007

41 Van den Bergh J, De Ruyck T, Van Kemseke D. *Even better than the real thing.
Understanding generation Y's definition of authenticity for the Levi's brand*.
Proceedings of the ESOMAR qualitative conference; Marrakech (Morocco);
16 Nov 2009

42 Fishman TC. Manufaketure. *New York Times Magazine* 9 Jan 2005: 40–44

43 *Foreign branding* [Online]. [accessed 25 Feb 2010]; Available from:
http://en.wikipedia.org/wiki/Foreign_branding

44 Campbell B. *What do hard rock, ice cream, and do-it-yourself furniture have in common?* [Online]. [accessed 25 Feb 2010]; Available from: http://www.clicknation.com/snoof/stuff/umlaut.pdf

45 Beverland MB, Lindgreen A, Vink MW. Projecting authenticity through advertising. Consumer judgments of advertisers' claims. *Journal of Advertising* 2008 Spring; 37(1): 5–15

46 Wagstaff K. *Why more brands should copy the New York Times Facebook timeline* [Online]. 29 Feb 2012 [accessed 4 Sep 2012]; Available from: http://techland.time.com/2012/02/29/why-more-brands-should-copy-the-new-york-times-facebook-timeline/

47 Ritson M. Want brand authenticity? Be authentic. *Marketing* 2008 14 May: 21

48 McCarthy M. *Ad of the day: Adidas comes out swinging in big new brand campaign.* [Online]. 13 Feb 2015 [accessed 27 May 2015]; Available from: http://www.adweek.com/news/advertising-branding/ad-day-adidas-comes-out-swinging-big-new-brand-campaign-162944

49 Johnson Lauren. *Top 10 branded videos: Adidas racks up 21 Million YouTube views in one week.* [Online]. 25 Feb 2015 [accessed 27 May 2015]; Available from: http://www.adweek.com/news/technology/top-10-branded-videos-adidas-racks-21-million-youtube-views-one-week-163145

50 *Natura Plant makes use of social networking to propagate* [Online]. 14 March 2013 [accessed 21 June 2015]; Available from: http://www.cosmeticosbr.com.br/ing/conteudo/noticias/noticia.asp?id=3272

51 Zhang M. *Taiwanese Coffee Machines Print Photos of Customers Onto Lattes* [Online]. 21 June 2013 [accessed 21 June 2015]; Available from: http://petapixel.com/2013/06/21/taiwanese-coffee-machines-prints-photos-of-customers-onto-lattes/

52 *Dogs 'Muttbomb' Celebrities to Boost Adoptions* [Online]. 12 March 2014 [accessed 2 July 2015]; Available from: http://www.nytimes.com/aponline/2014/03/12/us/ap-us-pets-muttbombing.html

53 Van den Bergh J, De Ruyck T. *Authenticity for Generation Y.* [Research]. Ghent (Belgium): InSites Consulting; 2008

54 Millet K, Van den Bergh B, Pandelaere M. *First things first? The value of originality.* Leuven (Belgium): Faculty of Business and Economics Leuven University; 2008

55 Rodriguez S. *Nokia caught faking Lumia 920 camera ad, issues apology* [Online]. 6 Sep 2012 [accessed 10 Sep 2012]; Available from: http://www.latimes.com/business/technology/la-fi-tn-nokia-fake-ad-20120906,0,323217,print.story

56 Hollister S. *Nokia's Pure View still photos also include fakes (update: Nokia confirms)* [Online]. 6 Sep 2012 [accessed 10 Sep 2012]; Available from: http://www.theverge.com/2012/9/6/3297878/nokias-pureview-still-photos-lso-include-fakes/in/3057769

57 Bethencourt F. [Interview]. *PepsiCo worldwide.* 13 Apr 2012

58 Murray R. *'Missed the mark': Bud Light admits latest branding is a mistake* [Online]. 29 April 2015 [accessed 23 June 2015]; Available from: http://www.msnbc.com/msnbc/missed-the-mark-bud-light-admits-latest-branding-mistake

59 Vagianos A. *Salvo Sports, Indonesian Clothing Company, Apologizes For Ridiculously Sexist Shirt Label* [Online]. 12 March 2015 [accessed 23 June 2015]; Available from: http://www.huffingtonpost.com/2015/03/11/salvo-sports-sexist-shirt-label-apology_n_6846856.html

60 Van den Bergh J, De Ruyck T. *Authenticity for Generation Y.* [Research]. Ghent (Belgium): InSites Consulting; 2008

61 Fellinger C. [Interview]. Beiersdorf; 19 Mar 2012

62 Van den Bergh J, Veris E, De Ruyck T, Sbarbaro S. *How to connect with urban Millennials* [Online]. 30 May 2012 [accessed 10 Sep 2012]; Available from: http://www.slideshare.net/joerivandenbergh/how-to-connect-with-urban-millennials-results-from-a-global-research-community

63 Krick C. [Interview]. *Crumpler*. 16 Apr 2012

64 Kimmels M. [Interview]. *Heinz Continental Europe*. 18 Jun 2012

65 Brown S, Kozinets RV, Sherry JF Jr. Teaching old brands new tricks: retro branding and the revival of brand meaning. *Journal of Marketing* 2003; 67(3): 19–33

66 Grealish H. [Interview]. *Diageo*. 25 May 2012

67 *The greenest leaflet campaign in the world* [Online]. 16 Jul 2011 [accessed 16 Apr 2012]; Available from: http://socialmediastories.net/the-greenest-leaflet-campaign-in-the-world

68 Blackshaw P. The six drivers of brand credibility. It's time to tell credible stories. *MM* 2008 May/June: 51–4

69 Phelvin P, Wallop H. *Innocent smoothies accused over environmental marketing* [Online]. 1 Aug 2008 [accessed 26 Feb 2010]; Available from: http://www.telegraph.co.uk/news/2484148/Innocent-Smoothies-accused-over-environmental-marketing.html

70 Sibun J. *Not such a smooth ride for Innocent* [Online]. 2 Aug 2008 [accessed 26 Feb 2010]; Available from: http://www.telegraph.co.uk/finance/newsbysector/retailandconsumer/2794173/Not-such-a-smooth-ride-for-Innocent.html

71 Northedge R. *Slaughter of the Innocent? Or is Coke the real deal?* [Online]. 1 2 Apr 2009 [accessed 26 Feb 2010]; Available from: http://www.independent.co.uk/news/business/analysis-and-features/slaughter-of-the-innocent-or-is-coke-the-real-deal-1667412.html

72 *Food With Integrity* [Online]. 2015 [accessed 21 June 2015]; Available from: https://chipotle.com/food-with-integrity

73 Giammona C, Shruti S. *Chipotle Has a Pork Problem* [Online]. 8 April 2015 [accessed 21 June 2015]; Available from: http://www.bloomberg.com/news/articles/2015-04-08/chipotle-s-carnitas-shortage-reflects-broader-supply-woes

74 Coyle E. *American Millennials' 7 Favorite Fast Food Brands* [Online]. 19 April 2014 [accessed 21 June 2015]; Available from: http://www.cheatsheet.com/life/american-millennials-7-favorite-fast-food-brands.html/

75 *The Scarecrow* [Online]. 11 September 2013 [accessed 21 June 2015]; Available from: https://www.youtube.com/watch?v=lUtnas5ScS

76 *Chipotle Celebrates 5th Anniversary of Cultivate Festival Series* [Online]. 12 February 2015 [accessed 21 June 2015]; Available from: http://ir.chipotle.com/mobile.view?c=194775&v=203&d=1&id=2016219

77 Kuburas M. *Chipotle to invest in more long-form web projects* [Online]. 4 June 2014 [accessed 21 June 2015]; Available from: http://streamdaily.tv/2014/06/04/chipotle-to-invest-in-more-long-form-web-projects/

78 *Essay Contest Offers Students Scholarships and a Chance to Have Their Writing Published on Chipotle Packaging* [Online]. 4 May 2015 [accessed 21 June 2015]; Available from: http://ir.chipotle.com/mobile.view?c=194775&v=203&d=1&id=2043417

79 Wahba P. *Chipotle co-CEO rips into fast-food rivals, slams their 'short-sighted' strategies* [Online]. 20 Oct 2014 [accessed 03 Oct 2015]; Available from: http://fortune.com/2014/10/20/chipotle-co-ceo-rips-into-fast-food-rivals-slams-their-short-sighted-strategies/

80 *Price of Water (Coca-Cola Company)* [Online]. 04 May 2015 [accessed 23 June 2015]; Available from: http://www.euronews.com/2015/05/04/price-of-water-coca-cola-company/

81 Van den Bergh J, De Ruyck T, Van Kemseke D. *Even better than the real thing. Understanding generation Y's definition of authenticity for the Levi's brand.* Proceedings of the ESOMAR qualitative conference; Marrakech (Morocco); 16 Nov 2009

Chapter 5 We all want unique brands

1 *Moonwalk (dance)* [Online]. [accessed 11 Apr 2010]; Available from: http://en.wikipedia.org/wiki/Moonwalk_(dance)

2 Trout J. *Differentiate or Die. Survival in our era of killer competition.* 2nd edn. Hoboken, NJ: John Wiley & Sons; 2008: 27–29

3 Mason M. *The Pirate's Dilemma. How youth culture is reinventing capitalism.* New York: Free Press; 2009: 704

4 Verbeurgt W. [Interview] *MINI.* 15 Sep 2012

5 Michelsen C. The truth about NPD. *Brand Strategy* 2008 May: 44–45

6 Rosso R. [Interview] *DIESEL*; 19 Jun 2012

7 Cullinane S. *The old new* [Online]. 21 Sep 2005 [accessed 16 Apr 2010]; Available from: http://news.bbc.co.uk/2/hi/uk_news/magazine/4265374.stm

8 Mason M. *The Pirate's Dilemma. How youth culture is reinventing capitalism.* New York: Free Press; May 2009: 70–71

9 Diaz J. *1960s Braun products hold the secrets to Apple's future* [Online]. 14 Jan 2008 [accessed 16 Apr 2010]; Available from: http://gizmodo.com/343641/1960s-braun-products-hold-the-secrets-to-apples-future

10 Bogusky AM, Winsor J. *Baked In. Creating products and businesses that market themselves.* Chicago, IL: Agate publishing; 2009: 116–17

11 Prigg M. *Sir Jonathan Ive: the iMan cometh* [Online]. 12 Mar 2012 [accessed 16 Jun 2012]; Available from: http://www.standard.co.uk/lifestyle/london-life/sir-jonathan-ive-the-iman-cometh-7562170.html

12 Twenge JM, Campbell WK. *The Narcissism Epidemic. Living in the age of entitlement.* New York: Free Press; 2009

13 Van den Bergh J, De Vuyst P. *Why I'm unique* [Online]. 26 Jun 2012 [accessed 16 Jul 2012]; Available from: http://www.slideshare.net/joerivandenbergh/why-im-unique-by-generation-y-around-the-world

14 Ciminillo JA. Elusive Gen Y demands edgier marketing. *Automative News* 2005 Apr; 79(6411): 28B

15 Kostecki E. *Brand extension to the youth and young adult markets.* Thesis submitted in fulfilment of the requirements for the degree of Bachelor of Science. LN Stern School of Business, New York University; May 2005: 43–49

16 Contagious I/O. *Spray-on Safety.* [Online]. 30 Mar 2015 [accessed 19 May 2015]; Available from: https://www.contagious.io/articles/spray-on-safe

17 *Volvo gives green light for 'shopping delivery to your car' service.* [Online]. 23 Apr 2015 [accessed 18 May 2015]; Available from: http://www.computing.co.uk/ctg/analysis/2405456/volvo-gives-green-light-for-shopping-delivery-to-your-car-service

18 *Tomorrowland Sells 360,000 Tickets in Under An Hour* [Online]. 15 February 2014 [accessed 18 June 2015]; Available from: http://www.billboard.com/articles/columns/code/5908407/tomorrowland-sells-360000-tickets-in-under-an-hour

19 Lemmens K. [Interview] *ID&T (Tomorrowland)*; 24 Apr 2012

20 *Inscribing Peace Message, Secretary-General Says 'Tomorrowland' Music Festival, One World Bridge Demonstrate Importance of Creativity in Building Safer World* [Online]. 27 May 2015 [accessed 18 June 2015]; Available from: http://www.un.org/press/en/2015/sgsm16795.doc.htm

21 Meadow M. *Tomorrowland brings authentic experience to Mexico & India* [Online]. 9 June 2015 [accessed 18 June 2015]; http://www.youredm.com/2015/06/09/tomorrowland-brings-authentic-experience-to-mexico-india/

22 Van den Bergh J, De Ruyck T, Van Kemseke D. *Even better than the real thing. Understanding generation Y's definition of authenticity for the Levi's brand.* Proceedings of the ESOMAR qualitative conference; Marrakech (Morocco); 16 Nov 2009

23 *Dan and Phil limited edition sim.* [Online]. [accessed 26 May 2015]; Available from: http://shop.ee.co.uk/campaigns/dan-and-phil

24 Ciambriello R. *Nike turns can't into can in its largest women's campaign ever.* [Online]. 14 Apr 2015 [accessed 28 May 2015]; Available from: http://www.adweek.com/adfreak/nike-turns-cant-can-its-largest-womens-campaign-ever-164059

25 Ballantyne R, Warren A, Nobbs K. The evolution of brand choice. *Brand Management* 2006 Jun; **13**(4/5): 339–52

26 MacMillan D. What's in a name? *Business Week* 2007 9 Jul: 18

27 *About Doodles* [Online]. [accessed 2 Jul 2012]; Available from: http://www.google.com/doodles/about

28 Day A. The right kit for the game. *Brand strategy* 2003 Nov: 28

29 *Absolut Unique. One of a kind. Millions of expressions* [Online]. [accessed 2 Jul 2012]; Available from: http://www.absolut.com/Unique/

30 Werner M. T. [Interview]. *KFC*. 3 Apr 2012

31 *KFC 'Brings Back' the Colonel, and even the word 'Fried', for 75th anniversary.* [Online]. 20 May 2015 [accessed 20 May 2015]; Available from: http://www.mediapost.com/publications/article/250270/kfc-brings-back-the-colonel-and-even-the-word.html

32 Nudd T. *Colonel Sanders just took over KFC's Twitter and he's amusingly terrible at it.* [Online]. 27 May 2015 [accessed 29 May 2015]; Available from: http://www.adweek.com/adfreak/colonel-sanders-just-took-over-kfcs-twitter-and-hes-amusingly-terrible-it-165022

33 Lindstrom M. *Buyology. How everything we believe about why we buy is wrong.* London: Random House Business Books; 2008

34 Jones CRM, Fazio RH. Associative strength and consumer choice behaviour. In: Haugtvedt CP, Herr PM, Kardes FR (eds). *Handbook of Consumer Psychology.* New York: Psychology Press; 2008: 437–59

35 Loewe EM. Wireless world. *Display & Design Ideas* 2007 Mar; **19**(3): 60–62

36 Westerik I. [Interview]. *Reckitt Benckiser (Durex).* 16 Apr 2012

37 Nosek BA, Banaji MR. The go/no-go association task. *Social Cognition* 2001; **19**(6): 625–64

38 Riesenbeck H, Perrey J. *Power Brands. Measuring, making, managing brand success.* Weinheim (Germany): Wiley-VCH; 2007: 41–42

39 Friedman M, Van den Bergh J, De Wulf K, Vantomme D. *Implicit measurement of brand distinctive assets for energy drinks* [Research]. Ghent (Belgium): InSites Consulting; April 2010

40 Lopis G. *Why Trader Joe's stands out from all the rest in the grocery business* [Online]. 5 Sep 2011 [accessed 10 Apr 2012]; Available from: http://www.forbes.com/sites/glennllopis/2011/09/05/why-trader-joes-stands-out-from-all-the-rest-in-the-grocery-business/

41 *Whole Foods Plans New Chain To Court Millennials.* [Online]. 8 May 2015 [accessed 18 May 2015]; Available from: http://www.huffingtonpost.com/2015/05/06/whole-foods-market-millen_n_7228384.html

42 Wu Y, Ardley B. Brand strategy and brand evolution: welcome to the world of the meme. *The Marketing Review* 2007; 7(3): 301–10

43 Bauerlein V. *Vitaminwater tries winking. New campaign hints at brand's repute in some circles as a hangover remedy* [Online]. 5 April 2010 [accessed 14 April 2010]; Available from: http://adage.com/globalnews/article?article_id=143166 http://online.wsj.com/article/SB10001424052702303450704575160280077022428.html?mod=googlenews_wsj

44 Madden N. *Coke launches Spritea to bolster brand among Chinese youth* [Online]. 7 Apr 2010 [accessed 14 Apr 2010]; Available from: http://adage.com/globalnews/article?article_id=143166

45 Dodes R. *Levi aims for high-end halo* [Online]. 14 Apr 2010 [accessed 14 Apr 2010]; Available from: http://online.wsj.com/article_email/SB20001424052702303695604575182252816707936-lMyQjAyMTAwMDEwNDExNDQyWj.html

46 Aaker DA, Joachimsthaler E. *Brand Leadership.* New York: The Free Press; 2000: 168–73

47 Wu Y, Ardley B. Brand strategy and brand evolution: welcome to the world of the meme. *The Marketing Review* 2007; 7(3): 301–10

48 *Tattoo* [Online]. [accessed 9 Mar 2010]; Available from: http://en.wikipedia.org/wiki/Tattoo

49 *Gang tattoos. Unique gang identifiers for street and prison gangs* [Online]. [accessed 9 Mar 2010]; Available from: http://www.gangsorus.com/tattoos.html

50 Thomas A. *Youth Online. Identity and literacy in the digital age.* New York: Peter Lang Publishing; 2007

51 Brown BB, Klute C. Friendships, cliques and crowds. In: Adams GR, Berzonsky MD (eds). *Blackwell Handbook of Adolescence.* Oxford (UK): Blackwell Publishing; 2003: 330–48

52 Bourdieu P. *Distinction. A social critique of the judgment of taste.* New York: Routledge; 1986

53 Thornton S. *Club Cultures. Music, media and subcultural capital.* Oxford: Blackwell Publishers; 1995

54 Maule A, Head N, Moroney L. *Consumers, trends and trendsetters. Do we speak to the sheep or the sheepdog?* Proceedings of the ESOMAR Worldwide Qualitative Research Conference; Cannes: France; Nov 2004

55 Poole T *Rolex, Skittles and the brands caught in world events* [Online]. 7 May 2015 [accessed 1 July 2015]; Available from: www.bbc.com/news/world-32622717

56 *Ikea toy wolf becomes Hong Kong protest symbol* [Online]. 10 December 2013 [accessed 1 July 2015]; Available from: www.bbc.com/news/world-asia-china-25314580

57 Delaney B. *Hipsters in firing line in 2010's culture war* [Online]. 6 November 2010 [accessed 3 July 2015]; Available from: www.smh.com.au/it-pro/hipsters-in-firing-line-in-2010s-culture-war-20101105-17hej

58 Berman J. *10 Great Cultural Contributions by 'Hipsters'* [Online]. 3 March 2011 [accessed 3 July 2015]; Available from: http://flavorwire.com/157024/10-great-cultural-contributions-by-hipsters/

59 Ferrier M. *The end of the hipster: how flat caps and beards stopped being so cool* [Online]. 21 June 2014 [accessed 3 July 2015]; Available from: www.theguardian.com/fashion/2014/jun/22/end-of-the-hipster-flat-caps-and-beards

60 Segran E. *The Fall of the Hipster Brand: Inside the Decline of American Apparel and Urban Outfitters* [Online]. 3 March 2015 [accessed 3 July 2015]; Available from: www.theguardian.com/fashion/2014/jun/22/end-of-the-hipster-flat-caps-and-beards

61 Van den Bergh J. *Subcultures and internet. Speech on Talkie Walkie Event, Ladda*; Ghent: Belgium; 22 Mar 2007

62 Beek J. *UKTribes*, Channel 4 Television; London: 2010

63 Taylor N. *Targeting tribes factsheet: creative approaches* [Online]. [accessed 19 Sep 2012]; Available from: http://www.uktribes.com

64 Wells T. *Chasing Youth Culture and Getting It Right: How your business can profit by tapping today's most powerful trendsetters and tastemakers.* Hoboken, NJ: John Wiley & Sons; Apr 2011

65 Van den Bergh J, Alders P, Boullaert A, Van Bijnen M. *Getting Close to Youth. Understanding Millennials' Themes of Life to Create Gen Y-Proof Brands.* Proceedings of the ESOMAR Qualitative Conference; Venice (Italy); 16–18 Nov 2014.

66 Kurz, Christian (2013). TV S.M.A.R.T. Anytime Anywhere, The evolution continues. Viacom InSights. [Online]; Available from: http://vimninsights.viacom.com/post/78442961166/

67 Chmielewski, DC. *MTV's 'Catfish' was top-tweeted TV show last week, SocialGuide says.* [Online] 29 Jul 2013. [accessed 08 Oct 2015]; Available from:http://articles.latimes.com/2013/jul/29/entertainment/la-et-ct-mtvs-catfish-the-tv-show-20130729

68 Huffington, A., (2013, 19 Feb.) *Millennials Come of Age as America's Most Stressed Generation* [Online] 19 Feb 2013 [accessed 08 Oct 2015]; Accessible from: www.huffingtonpost.com/arianna-huffington/millennials-stress_b_2718986.html

69 MTV Press (2013, 18 June). *New MTV Study Shows Sharp Differences Between Younger and Older Millennials* [Online] 18 Jun 2013 [accessed 08 Oct 2015] Available from: http://mtvpress.com/press/release/new_mtv_study_show_sharp_differences_between_younger_and_older_millennials

70 Van den Bergh, J. (2013) Youth Around The World Report, InSites Consulting.

71 Jung P. [Interview]. *MasterCard International*. 13 Apr 2012

72 Bethencourt F. [Interview]. *Pepsi*. 4 May 2012

73 elpoderdelasideas.com. *Kandia Dulce: The American Rom – Cannes Lions 2011* [Online]. 21 Jun 2011 [accessed 10 May 2012]; Available from: http://www.youtube.com/watch?v=HhRRi8iIL0o

74 Blanaru C. *Rom is trying to convince Romanians working abroad to come back home with a new campaign.* [Online] 28 Nov 2014 [accessed 19 May 2015]; Available from: www.adhugger.net/2014/11/28/rom-is-trying-to-convince-romanians-working-abroad-to-come-back-home-with-a-new-campaign/

75 Borreli L. The Future Of Healthy Eating? Generation Z More Likely To Eat Fresh, Home-Cooked Meals [Online]. 14 May 2014 [accessed 13 Jul 2015]; Available from: www.medicaldaily.com/future-healthy-eating-generation-z-more-likely-eat-fresh-home-cooked-meals-282524

76 Borreli L. The Future Of Healthy Eating? Generation Z More Likely To Eat Fresh, Home-Cooked Meals [Online]. 14 May 2014 [accessed 13 Jul 2015]; Available from: www.medicaldaily.com/future-healthy-eating-generation-z-more-likely-eat-fresh-home-cooked-meals-282524

77 Meet Generation Z: Forget Everything You Learned About Millennials [Online]. 17 Jun 2014 [accessed 8 Jul 2015]; Available from: www.slideshare.net/sparksandhoney/generation-z-final-june-17/1

78 About Etsy [Online]. [accessed 13 Jul 2015]; Available from: https://www.etsy.com/about/

79 Beese J. Etsy Collaborates With Brands to Curate Shopping Pages [Online]. 17 Sep 2013 [accessed 13 Jul 2015]; Available from: http://sproutsocial.com/insights/etsy-pages-brands/

80 Caap A. [Interview]. *Our/Vodka*.

81 Petridis A. *Youth subcultures: what are they now?* [Online]. 20 March 2014 [accessed 3 July 2015]; Available from: www.theguardian.com/culture/2014/mar/20/youth-subcultures-where-have-they-gone

82 Read P., Shah C., O'Brien LS., Woolcott J. 'Story of one's life and a tree of friends' – understanding millennials' information behavior in social networks. *Journal of Information Science* 2012 Oct; 38: 489-497

83 Roncero-Menendez S. *The Complete Guide to Tumblr Subcultures* [Online]. 13 November 2013 [accessed 3 July 2015]; Available from: http://mashable.com/2013/11/13/tumblr-subcultures/

84 *MagicTCG* [Online]. [accessed 3 July 2015]; Available from: https://www.reddit.com/r/magicTCG/

85 *Tumblr is so easy to use that it's hard to explain* [Online]. [accessed 3 July 2015]; Available from: www.tumblr.com

86 *GWI Social – Q1 2015* [Online]. 2015 [accessed 3 July 2015]; Available from: http://insight.globalwebindex.net/social-q1-2015

87 *A New Clique: Millennials and Internet Subculture* [Online]. 3 May 2014 [accessed 3 July 2015]; Available from: www.millennialmanifesto.literallydarling.com/new-clique-millennials-internet-subculture/

88 Amarca N. *Cyber Trends: 5 Subcultures Created on the Internet* [Online]. 11 March 2015 [accessed 3 July 2015]; Available from: www.highsnobiety.com/2015/03/11/internet-subcultures-health-goth-seapunk/

89 (1): Petridis A. *Youth subcultures: what are they now?* [Online]. 20 March 2014 [accessed 3 July 2015]; Available from: http://www.theguardian.com/culture/2014/mar/20/youth-subcultures-where-have-they-gone

Chapter 6 Self-identification with the brand

1 *Tattoo* [Online]. [accessed 9 Mar 2010]; Available from: http://en.wikipedia.org/wiki/Tattoo

2 *Gang tattoos. Unique gang identifiers for street and prison gangs* [Online]. [accessed 9 Mar 2010]; Available from: http://www.gangsorus.com/tattoos.html

3 Thomas A. *Youth Online. Identity and literacy in the digital age.* New York: Peter Lang Publishing; 2007

4 Brown BB, Klute C. Friendships, cliques and crowds. In: Adams GR, Berzonsky MD (eds). *Blackwell Handbook of Adolescence.* Oxford (UK): Blackwell Publishing; 2003: 330–48

5 Bourdieu P. *Distinction. A social critique of the judgment of taste.* New York: Routledge; 1986

6 Thornton S. *Club Cultures. Music, media and subcultural capital.* Oxford: Blackwell Publishers; 1995

7 Maule A, Head N, Moroney L. *Consumers, trends and trendsetters. Do we speak to the sheep or the sheepdog?* Proceedings of the ESOMAR Worldwide Qualitative Research Conference; Cannes: France; Nov 2004

8 Poole T. *Rolex, Skittles and the brands caught in world events* [Online]. 7 May 2015 [accessed 1 July 2015]; Available from: www.bbc.com/news/world-32622717

9 *Ikea toy wolf becomes Hong Kong protest symbol* [Online]. 10 December 2013 [accessed 1 July 2015]; Available from: www.bbc.com/news/world-asia-china-25314580

10 Delaney B. *Hipsters in firing line in 2010's culture war* [Online]. 6 November 2010 [accessed 3 July 2015]; Available from: www.smh.com.au/it-pro/hipsters-in-firing-line-in-2010s-culture-war-20101105-17hej

11 Berman J. *10 Great Cultural Contributions by 'Hipsters'* [Online]. 3 March 2011 [accessed 3 July 2015]; Available from: http://flavorwire.com/157024/10-great-cultural-contributions-by-hipsters/

12 Ferrier M. *The end of the hipster: how flat caps and beards stopped being so cool* [Online]. 21 June 2014 [accessed 3 July 2015]; Available from: www.theguardian.com/fashion/2014/jun/22/end-of-the-hipster-flat-caps-and-beards

13 Segran E. *The Fall of the Hipster Brand: Inside the Decline of American Apparel and Urban Outfitters* [Online]. 3 March 2015 [accessed 3 July 2015]; Available from: www.theguardian.com/fashion/2014/jun/22/end-of-the-hipster-flat-caps-and-beards

14 Van den Bergh J. *Subcultures and internet. Speech on Talkie Walkie Event, Ladda*; Ghent: Belgium; 22 Mar 2007

15 Beek J. *UKTribes*, Channel 4 Television; London: 2010

16 Taylor N. *Targeting tribes factsheet: creative approaches* [Online]. [accessed 19 Sep 2012]; Available from: http://www.uktribes.com

17 Wells T. *Chasing Youth Culture and Getting It Right: How your business can profit by tapping today's most powerful trendsetters and tastemakers.* Hoboken, NJ: John Wiley & Sons; Apr 2011

18 Van den Bergh J, Alders P, Boullaert A, Van Bijnen M. *Getting Close to Youth. Understanding Millennials' Themes of Life to Create Gen Y-Proof Brands.* Proceedings of the ESOMAR Qualitative Conference; Venice (Italy); 16–18 Nov 2014

19 Kurz, Christian (2013). TV S.M.A.R.T. Anytime Anywhere, The evolution continues. Viacom InSights. [Online]; Available from: http://vimninsights.viacom.com/post/78442961166/

20 Chmielewski, DC. *MTV's 'Catfish' was top-tweeted TV show last week, Social Guide says.* [Online] 29 Jul 2013. [accessed 08 Oct 2015]; Available from: http://articles.latimes.com/2013/jul/29/entertainment/la-et-ct-mtvs-catfish-the-tv-show-20130729

21 Huffington, A., (2013, 19 Feb.) *Millennials Come of Age as America's Most Stressed Generation* [Online] 19 Feb 2013 [accessed 08 Oct 2015]; Accessible from: www.huffingtonpost.com/arianna-huffington/millennials-stress_b_2718986.html

22 MTV Press (2013, 18 June). *New MTV Study Shows Sharp Differences Between Younger and Older Millennials* [Online] 18 Jun 2013 [accessed 08 Oct 2015] Available from: http://mtvpress.com/press/release/new_mtv_study_show_sharp_differences_between_younger_and_older_millennials

23 Van den Bergh, J. (2013) Youth Around The World Report, InSites Consulting.

24 Jung P. [Interview]. *MasterCard International.* 13 Apr 2012

25 Bethencourt F. [Interview]. *Pepsi.* 4 May 2012

26 elpoderdelasideas.com. *Kandia Dulce: The American Rom – Cannes Lions 2011* [Online]. 21 Jun 2011 [accessed 10 May 2012]; Available from: http://www.youtube.com/watch?v=HhRRi8iIL0o

27 Blanaru C. *Rom is trying to convince Romanians working abroad to come back home with a new campaign.* [Online] 28 Nov 2014 [accessed 19 May 2015]; Available from: www.adhugger.net/2014/11/28/rom-is-trying-to-convince-romanians-working-abroad-to-come-back-home-with-a-new-campaign/

28 Borreli L. The Future Of Healthy Eating? Generation Z More Likely To Eat Fresh, Home-Cooked Meals [Online]. 14 May 2014 [accessed 13 Jul 2015]; Available from: www.medicaldaily.com/future-healthy-eating-generation-z-more-likely-eat-fresh-home-cooked-meals-282524

29 Borreli L. The Future Of Healthy Eating? Generation Z More Likely To Eat Fresh, Home-Cooked Meals [Online]. 14 May 2014 [accessed 13 Jul 2015]; Available from: www.medicaldaily.com/future-healthy-eating-generation-z-more-likely-eat-fresh-home-cooked-meals-282524

30 Meet Generation Z: Forget Everything You Learned About Millennials [Online]. 17 Jun 2014 [accessed 8 Jul 2015]; Available from: www.slideshare.net/sparksandhoney/generation-z-final-june-17/1

31 About Etsy [Online]. [accessed 13 Jul 2015]; Available from: https://www.etsy.com/about/

32 Beese J. Etsy Collaborates With Brands to Curate Shopping Pages [Online]. 17 Sep 2013 [accessed 13 Jul 2015]; Available from: http://sproutsocial.com/insights/etsy-pages-brands/

33 Caap A. [Interview]. *Our/Vodka.*

34 Petridis A. *Youth subcultures: what are they now?* [Online]. 20 March 2014 [accessed 3 July 2015]; Available from: www.theguardian.com/culture/2014/mar/20/youth-subcultures-where-have-they-gone

35 Read P, Shah C, O'Brien LS, Woolcott J. 'Story of one's life and a tree of friends' – understanding millennials' information behavior in social networks. *Journal of Information Science* 2012 Oct; 38: 489–497

36 Roncero-Menendez S. *The Complete Guide to Tumblr Subcultures* [Online]. 13 November 2013 [accessed 3 July 2015]; Available from: http://mashable.com/2013/11/13/tumblr-subcultures/

37 *MagicTCG* [Online]. [accessed 3 July 2015]; Available from: https://www.reddit.com/r/magicTCG/

38 *Tumblr is so easy to use that it's hard to explain* [Online]. [accessed 3 July 2015]; Available from: www.tumblr.com

39 *GWI Social – Q1 2015* [Online]. 2015 [accessed 3 July 2015]; Available from: http://insight.globalwebindex.net/social-q1-2015

40 *A New Clique: Millennials and Internet Subculture* [Online]. 3 May 2014 [accessed 3 July 2015]; Available from: www.millennialmanifesto. literallydarling.com/new-clique-millennials-internet-subculture/
41 Amarca N. *Cyber Trends: 5 Subcultures Created on the Internet* [Online]. 11 March 2015 [accessed 3 July 2015]; Available from: www.highsnobiety. com/2015/03/11/internet-subcultures-health-goth-seapunk/
42 (1): Petridis A. *Youth subcultures: what are they now?* [Online]. 20 March 2014 [accessed 3 July 2015]; Available from: http://www.theguardian.com/ culture/2014/mar/20/youth-subcultures-where-have-they-gone

Chapter 7 Happiness: Gen Y's adoration for branded emotions

1 Emoticon [Online]. [accessed 7 Apr 2010]; Available from: http://en.wikipedia.org/ wiki/Emoticon
2 Haidt J. *The Happiness Hypothesis. Putting ancient wisdom and philosophy to the test of modern science*. London: Arrow Books; 2006
3 Maclean PD. Some psychiatric implications of physiological studies on frontotemporal portion of limbic system (visceral brain). *Electroencephalography and Clinical Neurophysiology* 1952; 4(4): 407–18
4 LeDoux J. *The Emotional Brain. The mysterious underpinnings of emotional life*. London: Phoenix; 1998
5 *Top Top: Yes sticks*. [Online]. [accessed 20 May 2015]; Available from: http://adsoftheworld.com/media/ambient/tip_top_yes_sticks
6 Gladwell M. *Blink: The power of thinking without thinking*. New York: Little Brown; 2005
7 Marcus G. *The Sentimental Citizen*. Pennsylvania: Pennsylvania State University Press; 2002
8 Fox E, Russo R, Georgiou GA. Anxiety modulates the degree of attentive resources required to process emotional faces. *Cognitive, Affective & Behavioural Neuroscience* 2005; 5(4): 396–404
9 LeDoux J. Emotion, memory and the brain. *Scientific American* 1994 June: 50–57
10 Rimé B, Finkenhauer C, Luminet O, Zech E, Philippot P. Social sharing of emotions: new evidence and new questions. In: Stroebe W, Hewstone M (eds). *European Review of Social Psychology* 1998; 3: 145–89. Chichester: Wiley and Sons
11 LeDoux J. Emotion, memory and the brain. *Scientific American* 1994 June; 50–57
12 Dobele A, Lindgreen A, Beverland M, Vanhamme J, Van Wijk R. Why pass on viral messages? Because they connect emotionally. *Business Horizons* 2007 1 Jul; 50: 291–304
13 Izard CE. Basic emotions, relations among emotions, and emotion-cognition relations. *Psychological Review* 1992; 99: 561–65
14 LeDoux J. Emotion, memory and the brain. *Scientific American* 1994 June; 50–57
15 Thomson M, MacInnis D, Whan Park C. The ties that bind: measuring the strength of consumers' emotional attachment to brands. *Journal of Consumer Psychology* 2005; 15(1): 77–91

16 Lindstrom M. *Brand Sense. Sensory secrets behind the stuff we buy.* 2nd edn. London: Kogan Page; 2010

17 Gobé M. *Emotional Branding. The new paradigm for connecting brands to people.* 2nd edn. New York: Allworth Press; 2009

18 Alexander S. *KFC to offer edible coffee cups* [Online]. 25 February 2015 [accessed 8 June 2015]; Available from: http://www.telegraph.co.uk/foodanddrink/foodanddrinknews/11434220/KFC-to-offer-edible-coffee-cups.html

19 Yarrow K, O'Donnell J. *Gen BuY. How tweens, teens and twenty-somethings are revolutionizing retail.* San Francisco: Jossey-Bass; 2009

20 Yarrow K, O'Donnell J. *Gen BuY. How tweens, teens and twenty-somethings are revolutionizing retail.* San Francisco: Jossey-Bass; 2009

21 Halperin S, Christman E. *Starbucks to Stop Selling CDs* [Online]. 15 February 2015 [accessed 8 June 2015]; Available from: http://www.billboard.com/articles/6479986/starbucks-stop-selling-music

22 *Starbucks and Spotify Redefine Retail Experience by Connecting Spotify Music Streaming Service Into World-Class Store and Digital Platform* [Online]. 18 May 2015 [accessed 8 June 2015]; Available from: http://www.businesswire.com/news/home/20150518006730/en/#.VXWtKmSqpBd

23 Yarrow K, O'Donnell J. *Gen BuY. How tweens, teens and twenty-somethings are revolutionizing retail.* San Francisco: Jossey-Bass; 2009

24 Gobé M. *Emotional Branding. The new paradigm for connecting brands to people.* 2nd edn. New York; Allworth Press; 2009

25 *Haptic advertising: A touch of science* [Online]. 25 March 2014 [accessed 16 June 2015]; Available from: http://www.eppi-online.com/2014/03/25/haptic-advertising-a-touch-of-science/

26 *Touching me, touching you* [Online]. 30 April 2015 [accessed 16 June 2015]; Available from: https://www.contagious.io/articles/touching-me-touching-you

27 Li A. *This Chair Will Hug You Each Time You Get a Facebook Birthday Wish* [Online]. 11 July 2013 [accessed 16 June 2015]; Available from: http://mashable.com/2013/07/11/facebook-birthday-wish-chair-hug/

28 Barns M. *Marketers take touchy route to engagement via haptic feedback* [Online]. 31 December 2015 [accessed 16 June 2015]; Available from: http://www.mobilemarketer.com/cms/news/software-technology/19457.html

29 *Innovation in every interaction* [Online]. 2015 [accessed 1 July 2015]; Available from: https://www.apple.com/watch/technology/

30 Dahl DW, Frankenberger KD, Manchanda R. Does it pay to shock? Reactions to shocking and nonshocking advertising content among university students. *Journal of Advertising Research* 2003; **43**(3): 268–80

31 De Pelsmacker P, Van den Bergh J. The communication effects of provocation in print advertising. *International Journal of Advertising* 1997; **15**(3): 203–21

32 Kim HS. Examination of emotional response to apparel brand advertisements. *Journal of Fashion Marketing and Management* 2000; **4**(4): 303–13

33 Bergin A. *American Apparel's back-to-school ads banned for being 'inappropriately sexualising'* [Online]. 3 September 2014 [accessed 8 June 2015]; Available from: http://fashion.telegraph.co.uk/article/TMG11072152/American-Apparels-back-to-school-ads-banned-for-being-inappropriately-sexualising.html

34 Berman T. *Dov Charney Fired From American Apparel, Again* [Online]. 16 December 2014 [accessed 22 June 2015]; Available from: http://gawker.com/dov-charney-fired-from-american-apparel-again-1671916642

35 Gallegos G.E. *American Apparel's New Call For Models Almost Makes Us Miss Dov Charney* [Online]. 24 March 2015 [accessed 22 June 2015]; Available from: http://laist.com/2015/03/24/american_apparel_casting_call_almos.php

36 *World Cup Marketing: How Allstate enables Fans to send 'Mala Suerte' to rival Teams* [Online]. 7 July 2014 [accessed 30 June 2015]; Available from: http://www.portada-online.com/2014/07/07/world-cup-marketing-how-allstate-enables-fans-to-send-mala-suerte-to-rival-teams/

37 Craig D. *Netflix or study? A guinea pig has your answer* [Online]. 6 May 2015 [accessed 9 June 2015]; Available from: http://www.phillyvoice.com/netflix-or-study-bunny-has-your-answer/

38 Romani S, Sadeh H, Dalli D. When the brand is bad, I'm mad! An exploration of negative emotions to brands. *Advances in Consumer Research* 2009; 36: 494–501

39 Trotman A, Davidson L, Warman M. *Apple says just nine people have complained about bent iPhones* [Online]. 25 September 2014 [accessed 9 June 2015]; Available from: http://www.telegraph.co.uk/technology/apple/11122342/Apple-says-just-nine-people-have-complained-about-bent-iPhones.html

40 *Neo-Nazi teenagers fight in British boxing's No 1 brand* [Online]. 9 Apr 2005 [accessed 11 Apr 2010]; Available from: http://www.timesonline.co.uk/tol/news/world/article379031.ece

41 Van den Berg S. *Branded youths* [Online]. 7 Feb 2005 [accessed 8 Apr 2010]; Available from: http://www.dailynews.co.za/index.php?fArticleId=2401151

42 *Neo-Nazi group calls for Thor Steinar boycott. On the wrong side of the right* [Online]. 27 May 2009 [accessed 8 Apr 2010]; Available from: http://www.spiegel.de/international/germany/0,1518,627114,00.html

43 *Greggs' Logo Nightmare Over As Google Comes To The Rescue* [Online]. 19 August 2014 [accessed 9 June 2015]; Available from: http://www.huffingtonpost.co.uk/2014/08/19/google-greggs-and-somethi_n_5690792.html

44 Khor S. *When A Bloomberg Writer Mentioned 'Watsons Malaysia' On Twitter, The Unthinkable Happened* [Online]. 16 February 2015 [accessed 10 June 2015]; Available from: http://says.com/my/news/when-a-bloomberg-writer-mentioned-watsons-malaysia-on-twitter-the-unthinkable-happened

45 Alves A. *Social media and brand hijacking* [Online]. 3 Sept 2008 [accessed 9 Apr 2010] Available from: http://www.asourceofinspiration.com/2008/09/03/social-media-and-brand-hijacking/

46 Thomas G. *Brand hijack: when unintended segments desire your brand* [Online]. [accessed 10 Apr 2010]; Available from: http://www.emorymi.com/thomas2.shtml

47 Vaughan A. *Lego ends Shell partnership following Greenpeace campaign* [Online]. 9 October 2014 [accessed 11 June 2015]; Available from: http://www.theguardian.com/environment/2014/oct/09/lego-ends-shell-partnership-following-greenpeace-campaign

48 Roberts D. *The pressure on FIFA sponsors is mounting* [Online]. 29 May 2015 [accessed 12 June 2015]; Available from: http://fortune.com/2015/05/29/fifa-sponsors-pressure-corruption-scandal/

49 Van den Bergh J, De Vuyst P. *Don't worry be happy* [Online]. 14 Mar 2012 [accessed 4 Sep 2012]; Available from: http://www.slideshare.net/joerivandenbergh/dont-worry-be-happy-results-from-an-international-youth-study-by-insites-consulting

50 Jung P. [Interview] *MasterCard International*. 13 Apr 2012

51 Bettingen JF, Luedicke MK. Can brands make us happy? A research framework for the study of brands and their effects on happiness. *Advances in Consumer Research* 2009; 36: 308–14

52 Haidt J. *The Happiness Hypothesis. Putting ancient wisdom and philosophy to the test of modern science.* London: Arrow Books; 2006

53 Kimmels M. [Interview] *Heinz Continental Europe.* 18 Jun 2012

54 *Nike's Most Wanted* [Online]. 11 August 2014 [accessed 17 June 2015]; Available from: http://news.nike.com/news/nike-s-most-wanted

55 Grealish H. [Interview]. *Diageo.* 25 May 2012

56 Smilansky S. *Experiential Marketing. A practical guide to interactive brand experiences.* London: Kogan Page; 2009

57 Wohlfeil M, Whelan S. Consumer motivations to participate in event-marketing strategies. *Journal of Marketing Management* 2006; 22: 643–69

58 Preston N. Do brands hit the right note with Gen Y? *B&T Magazine* 2008 11 Apr: 22–25

59 *Rock in Rio divulga balanço geral mega evento* [Online]. 4 Oct 2012 [accessed 28 Sep 2012]; Available from: http://www.jb.com.br/rock-in-rio-2011/noticias/2011/10/04/rock-in-rio-divulga-balanco-geral-de-mega-evento/

60 McIntyre H. *PayPal Uses Music Festivals to Push Mobile App* [Online]. 8 August 2014 [accessed 17 June 2015]; Available from: http://www.forbes.com/sites/hughmcintyre/2014/08/08/paypal-uses-music-festivals-to-push-mobile-app/

61 *BBVA Continental The concert no one was waiting for* [Online]. 22 May 2015 [accessed 17 June 2015]; Available from: https://www.youtube.com/watch?v=DFz8R0oto7c

62 McGonigal J. *Reality is Broken. Why games make us better and how they can change the world.* London: Penguin; 2011

63 Anderson S. *Just one more game… Angry Birds, Farmville and other hyperaddictive 'stupid games'* [Online]. 4 Apr 2012 [accessed 10 Sep 2012]; Available from: http://www.nytimes.com/2012/04/08/magazine/angry-birds-farmville-and-other-hyperaddictive-stupid-games.html

64 Herngaard A. *Impressive digital campaign: Magnum pleasure hunt* [Online]. 14 Apr 2011 [accessed 10 Sep 2012]; Available from: http://www.mindjumpers.com/blog/2011/04/magnum-pleasure-hunt/

65 James. *Magnum Pleasure Hunt 2: play across the globe* [Online]. 4 Mar 2012 [accessed 10 Sep 2012]; Available from: http://www.tracyandmatt.co.uk/blogs/index.php/magnum-pleasure-hunt-2-play-across-the-g

66 *Magnum: pleasure hunt across Amsterdam ARG* [Online]. 22 Apr 2012 [accessed 10 Sep 2012]; Available from: http://www.digitalbuzzblog.com/magnum-pleasure-hunt-across-amsterdam-arg/

67 White C. *McDonald's gaming billboard gives winners free food* [Online]. 5 Jun 2011 [accessed 10 Sep 2012]; Available from: http://mashable.com/2011/06/05/mcdonalds-interactive-billboard/

68 *The Chocolate Log. Cinnabon* [Online]. [accessed 3 Aug 2012]; Available from: http://thechocolatelog.tumblr.com/post/25291301073/russians-earn-their-treats-with-cinnabon-consumers

69 *Plan The Unexpected* [Online]. 4 April 2015 [accessed 16 June 2015]; Available from: http://180hb.com/en/projects/plan-the-unexpected.html

70 Yalcin YDM, Eren-Erdogmus I, Demir S. Using associations to create positive brand attitude for generation Y consumers: application in fashion retailing.

Suleyman Demirel University Turkey. *The Journal of Faculty of Economics and Administrative Sciences* 2009; **14**(2): 261–76

71 Niehm LS, Fiore AM, Jeong M, Kim HJ. Pop-up retail's acceptability as an innovative business strategy and enhancer of the consumer shopping experience. *Journal of Shopping Center Research* 2007; **1**(2): 1–30

72 Mikunda C. *Brand Lands, Hot Spots and Cool Spaces. Welcome to the third place and the total marketing experience.* London: Kogan Page; 2007

73 Pathak S. *Target Builds Life-Size 'Dollhouse' Inside Grand Central* [Online]. 6 May 2013 [accessed 21 June 2015]; Available from: http://adage.com/article/media/target-builds-life-size-dollhouse-inside-grand-central/241289/

74 O'Loughlin S. *How Target Became The Big Brand On Campus* [Online]. 7 May 2014 [accessed 21 June 2015]; Available from: http://www.eventmarketer.com/article/grand-ex-2014/

75 Milnes H. *Target makes art out of products in pop-up store* [Online]. 30 March 2015 [accessed 21 June 2015]; Available from: http://digiday.com/brands/target-makes-art-products-pop-store/

76 *These Virtual Outdoor Pop-Up Shops Open Only at 'Magic Hours' Before Sunrise and Sunset* [Online]. 19 March 2015 [accessed 23 June 2015]; Available from: http://creativity-online.com/work/peak-performance-magic-hour-popup-shops/39927

77 Bondolowski C, Hendriksen D. [Interviews] *The Coca-Cola Company.* 30 Apr and 4 May 2010

78 Dodd K. Coca-Cola. Case study. *Contagious Magazine* 2012 3Q; 32

79 *Coca-Cola Small World Machines Bringing India & Pakistan Together* [Online]. 19 May 2013 [accessed 23 June 2015]; Available from: https://www.youtube.com/watch?v=ts_4vOUDImE

80 *Happiness Arcade Case Study* [Online]. 2014 [accessed 23 June 2015]; Available from: http://grey.com/apac/work/key/happiness-arcade/id/1472/

81 *Watch: Finns Share a White Christmas with Singaporeans* [Online]. 23 December 2014 [accessed 1 July 2015]; Available from: http://www.coca-colacompany.com/holidays/holiday-videos/watch-finns-share-a-white-christmas-with-singaporeans

82 *Happiness From The Skies: Watch Coke Drones Refresh Guest Works In Singapore* [Online]. 12 May 2014 [accessed 23 June 2015]; Available from: http://www.coca-colacompany.com/stories/happiness-from-the-skies-watch-coke-drones-refresh-guest-workers-in-singapore

83 Lum R. *Coca-Cola Phone Booth Turns Bottle Caps Into Currency* [Online]. 12 May 2014 [accessed 23 June 2015]; Available from: http://www.creativeguerrillamarketing.com/guerrilla-marketing/coca-cola-phone-booth-turns-bottle-caps-currency/

84 *Coca-Cola Taking Home Happiness #WishUponACoke* [Online]. 27 January 2015 [accessed 23 June 2015]; Available from: https://www.youtube.com/watch?v=6s5r-GHU0BU

85 *#WishUponACoke: Dreams Come True for Ex-pat Workers in UAE* [Online]. 3 April 2015 [accessed 23 June 2015]; Available from: http://www.coca-colacompany.com/stories/wishuponacoke-dreams-come-true-for-expat-workers-in-uae

Chapter 8 Generation Z

1   Generation Z – The New Kids on the Block Have Arrived [Online]. 10 Jan 2015 [accessed 6 Jul 2015]. Available from: http://www.happen.com/generation-z-the-new-kids-on-the-block-have-arrived/

2   Bearne S. Forget millennials, brands need to win over Generation Z [Online] 22 May 2015 [accessed 6 Jul 2015]. Available from: http://www.marketingmagazine.co.uk/article/1348169/forget-millennials-brands-need-win-generation-z

3   Generation Z – The New Kids on the Block Have Arrived [Online]. 10 Jan 2015 [accessed 6 Jul 2015]. Available from: http://www.happen.com/generation-z-the-new-kids-on-the-block-have-arrived/

4   Wood S. Generation Z as Consumers: Trends and Innovation [Online] Jan 2013 [accessed 6 Jul 2015]. Available from: http://iei.ncsu.edu/wp-content/uploads/2013/01/GenZConsumers.pdf

5   The First Generation Of The Twenty-First Century [Online]. 2014 [accessed 6 Jul 2015]. Available from: http://magid.com/sites/default/files/pdf/MagidPluralistGenerationWhitepaper.pdf

6   Consumers of tomorrow insights and observations about generation z [Online]. 18 Sep 2011 [accessed 8 Jul 2015]. Available from: http://www.slideshare.net/johnyvo/consumers-of-tomorrow-insights-and-observations-about-generation-z

7   The First Generation Of The Twenty-First Century [Online]. 2014 [accessed 6 Jul 2015]. Available from: http://magid.com/sites/default/files/pdf/MagidPluralistGenerationWhitepaper.pdf

8   The First Generation Of The Twenty-First Century [Online]. 2014 [accessed 6 Jul 2015]. Available from: http://magid.com/sites/default/files/pdf/MagidPluralistGenerationWhitepaper.pdf

9   Peterson H. Generation Z Is A Complete Nightmare For Retailers [Online]. 27 Jun 2014 [accessed 13 Jul 2015]. Available from: http://www.businessinsider.com/generation-z-is-retailers-nightmare-2014-6

10 Bernstein R. Move Over Millenials – Here Comes Gen Z [Online]. 21 Jan 2015 [accessed 6 Jul 2015]. Available from: http://adage.com/article/cmo-strategy/move-millennials-gen-z/296577/

11 Holloway D, Green L, Livingstone S. Zero to eight. Young children and their internet use. London: EU Kids Online. 2013

12 Consumers of Tomorrow [Online]. Nov 2011 [accessed 8 Jul 2015]. Available from: https://docs.google.com/file/d/0Bz_fwcHqLV4xRVV1czg3VjBwdE0

13 Consumers of tomorrow insights and observations about generation z [Online]. 18 Sep 2011 [accessed 8 Jul 2015]. Available from: http://www.slideshare.net/johnyvo/consumers-of-tomorrow-insights-and-observations-about-generation-z

14 Hjuler P. [Interview]. *The LEGO Group*. 6 Oct 2015

15 JWT: Generation Z – Executive Summary [Online]. 12 May 2015 [accessed 6 Jul 2015]. Available from: http://www.slideshare.net/jwtintelligence/jwt-generation-z-48070734

16 Generation Z – The New Kids on the Block Have Arrived [Online]. 10 Jan 2015 [accessed 6 Jul 2015]. Available from: http://www.happen.com/generation-z-the-new-kids-on-the-block-have-arrived/

17 Toland B. Generation Z values tech toys over salary. [Newspaper].14 Nov 2011. *Pittsburgh Post-Gazette*

18 Williams KC., Page RA. Marketing to the generations. *Journal of Behavioral Studies in Business* 2011. 33: 1–17

19 White MC. American Families Increasingly Let Kids Make Buying Decisions [Online]. 11 Apr 2013 [accessed 7 July 2015]. Available from: http://business.time.com/2013/04/11/american-families-increasingly-let-kids-make-buying-decisions/

20 Goodkind N. Why car companies are targeting your kids [Online].22 Dec 2014 [accessed 7 Jul 2015]. Available from: http://finance.yahoo.com/news/ford-targeting-youth-born-after-1993-080111141.html

21 The Force: Volkswagen commercial [Online]. 2 Feb 2011 [accessed 7 Jul 2015]. Available from: https://www.youtube.com/watch?v=R55e-uHQna0

22 The Muppets Toyota Highlander No Room for Boring Song commercial [Online]. 30 January 2014 [accessed 7 Jul 2015]. Available from: https://www.youtube.com/watch?v=pDTfKS0CQhQ

23 Consumers of Tomorrow [Online]. Nov 2011 [accessed 8 Jul 2015]. Available from: https://docs.google.com/file/d/0Bz_fwcHqLV4xRVV1czg3VjBwdE0

24 Wood S. Generation Z as Consumers: Trends and Innovation [Online] Jan 2013 [accessed 6 Jul 2015]. Available from: http://iei.ncsu.edu/wp-content/uploads/2013/01/GenZConsumers.pdf

25 Baxter E. Cyber intimidation and the art of bullying [Online]. 19 Nov 2007 [accessed 6 Jul 2015]. Available from: http://www.smh.com.au/news/technology/the-new-art-of-bullying/2007/11/18/1195321595404.html

26 Tulgan B. Meet Generation Z: The second generation within the giant 'Millennial' cohort [Online]. Oct 2013 [accessed 6 July 2015]. Available from: http://rainmakerthinking.com/assets/uploads/2013/10/Gen-Z-Whitepaper.pdf

27 Williams KC., Page RA. Marketing to the generations. *Journal of Behavioral Studies in Business* 2011. 33: 1–17

28 Lane S. Beyond Millennials: How to Reach Generation Z [Online].20 Aug 2014 [accessed 7 Jul 2015]. Available from: http://mashable.com/2014/08/20/generation-z-marketing/

29 Sydell L. How Vine Settled On 6 Seconds [Online]. 20 Aug 2013 [accessed 7 Jul 2015]. Available from: http://www.npr.org/sections/alltechconsidered/2013/08/20/213846816/how-vine-settled-on-6-seconds

30 Family: Unskippable – GEICO Extended Cut [Online]. 27 Feb 2015 [accessed 7 Jul 2015]. Available from: https://www.youtube.com/watch?v=pvcj9xptNOQ

31 Nicholas D, Rowlands I, Clark D, Williams P. Google Generation II: web behaviour experiments with the BBC. Aslib Proceedings: New Information Perspectives 2011. 631: pp. 28–45

32 The future of e-commerce: Generation Z [Online]. [accessed 8 Jul 2015]. Available from: http://www.keepitusable.com/blog/?tag=generation-z

33 Meet Generation Z: Forget Everything You Learned About Millennials [Online]. 17 Jun 2014 [accessed 8 Jul 2015]. Available from: http://www.slideshare.net/sparksandhoney/generation-z-final-june-17/1

34 Wood S. Generation Z as Consumers: Trends and Innovation [Online] Jan 2013 [accessed 6 Jul 2015]. Available from: http://iei.ncsu.edu/wp-content/uploads/2013/01/GenZConsumers.pdf

35 Meet Dom: the Virtual Voice Ordering Assistant for Domino's Pizza [Online]. 6 Oct 2014 [accessed 8 Jul 2015]. Available from: http://www.prnewswire.com/news-releases/meet-dom-the-virtual-voice-ordering-assistant-for-dominos-pizza-278235881.html

36 Perez S. Starbucks Mobile Ordering Expands To More States, Now Live In Over 4,000 Stores [Online]. 16 Jun 2015 [accessed 8 Jul 2015]. Available from: http://techcrunch.com/2015/06/16/starbucks-mobile-ordering-expands-to-21-more-states-now-live-in-over-4000-stores/

37 KFC launches ordering app [Online]. 9 Jan 2014 [accessed 8 Jul 2015]. Available from: https://www.insideretail.com.au/blog/2014/01/09/kfc-launches-ordering-app/

38 A new way to shop: Love it. Find it. Hold it. [Online]. [accessed 8 Jul 2015]. Available from: http://www.gap.com/products/reserve-in-store.jsp

39 Edwards T. 2015 will see the rise of dark social. [Online]. 21 January 2015 [accessed 10 June 2015]. Available from: http://www.mediapost.com/publications/article/242124/2015-will-see-the-rise-of-dark-social.html?print

40 Shields M. Tweens Love YouTube, Even Though it's Not For Kids [Online]. 1 Dec 2014 [accessed 9 Jul 2015]. Available from: http://blogs.wsj.com/cmo/2014/12/01/tweens-love-youtube-even-though-its-not-for-kids/

41 Kemp N. Five marketing lessons from Generation YouTube [Online]. 3 Mar 2015 [accessed 18 May 2015]. Available from: http://www.marketingmagazine.co.uk/article/1335724/five-marketing-lessons-generation-youtube

42 *The Complete History of Instagram* [Online]. 3 Jan 2014 [accessed 6 Oct 2015]. Available from: http://wersm.com/the-complete-history-of-instagram/

43 Bliss ML. Is food the new status symbol? [Online]. 10 Oct 2014 [Accessed 6 Oct 2015]. Available from: http://www.mediapost.com/publications/article/235941/is-food-the-new-status-symbol.html

44 Durdin M, Hudson J, Gray M, Scott T, Taylor-Laird J. The near and far future of emoji. [Online]. 22 Apr 2015 [accessed 20 May 2015]. Available from: http://www.hopesandfears.com/hopes/future/technology/168949-the-future-of-emoji

45 Sternbergh A. Smile, you're speaking emoji. The rapid evolution of a wordless tongue. [Online]. 16 Nov 2014 [accessed 26 May 2015]. Available from: http://nymag.com/daily/intelligencer/2014/11/emojis-rapid-evolution.html

46 Petronzio M. Saving endangered animals, one emoji at a time. [Online]. 12 May 2015 [accessed 26 May 2015]. Available from: http://mashable.com/2015/05/12/emoji-tweet-endangered-animals/

47 Greenberg K. Toyota touts manufacturing with 'Gifony'. [Online]. 31 Mar 2015 [accessed 11 Jun 2015]. Available from: http://www.mediapost.com/publications/article/246812/toyota-touts-manufacturing-with-gifony.html

48 Examples of Content Marketing with Vine that you can do, too [Online]. 29 Jan 2014 [accessed 8 Jul 2015]. Available from: https://blog.kissmetrics.com/content-marketing-with-vine/

49 Elgan M. Understanding the Meerkat live-streaming magic. [Online] 14 Mar 2015 [accessed 11 Jun 2015]. Available from: http://www.computerworld.com/article/2896228/understanding-the-meerkat-live-streaming-magic.html

50 Reilly D. How early adopters are using Meerkat and Periscope. [Online]. 27 Apr 2015 [accessed 10 Jun 2015]. Available from: http://fortune.com/2015/04/27/periscope-meerkat-apps/

51 Dua T. 4 new cars unveiled on Meerkat and Periscope at New York's auto show. [Online]. 3 Apr 2015 [accessed 10 Jun 2015]. Available from: http://digiday.com/brands/4-new-cars-unveiled-meerkat-periscope-new-yorks-auto-show/

52 Blattberg E. So much for ephemeral: Meerkat videos get some staying power. [Online] 1 May 2015 [accessed 11 Jun 2015]. Available from: http://digiday.com/social/much-ephemeral-meerkat-videos-get-staying-power/

53 Shontell A. Snapchat is a lot bigger than people realize and it could be nearing 200 million active users. [Online]. 3 Jan 2015 [accessed 10 Jun 2015]. Available from: http://uk.businessinsider.com/snapchats-monthly-active-users-may-be-nearing-200-million-2014-12?r=US

54 Khaleejesque Magazine. Bahbahani H. Ephemeral messaging: a trend that won't disappear. [Online]. Jan 2015 [accessed 10 Jun 2015]. Available from: http://startupq8.com/2015/01/25/ephemeral-messaging-a-trend-that-wont-disappear/

55 Smith A. 5 Ways Brands Are Using Snapchat For Marketing and Promotion [Online]. [accessed 8 Jul 2015]. Available from: http://www.reelseo.com/brands-snapchat-marketing/

56 March Makes Us Crazy! Win $30 In #SnapMadness! [Online]. 23 Mar 2015 [accessed 9 Jul 2015]. Available from: http://blog.grubhub.com/grublife/march-snapmadness-2015/

57 Studenten nemen Snapchat van Studio Brussel over [Online]. 15 Jun 2015 [accessed 9 Jul 2015]. Available from: http://stubru.be/fokdeblok0/studentenne mensnapchatvanstudiobrusselover

58 McAlone N. Snapchat just turned its popular geofilters into ad units, and McDonald's is already on board [Online]. 17 Jun 2015 [accessed 9 Jul 2015]. Available from: http://uk.businessinsider.com/snapchat-wants-you-to-brand-your-posts-with-a-mcdonalds-filter-2015-6

59 Peterson H. Millennials Are Old News – Here's Everything You Should Know About Generation Z [Online]. 25 Jun 2014 [accessed 8 Jul 2015]. Available from: http://www.businessinsider.com/generation-z-spending-habits-2014-6

60 GEN Z: Digital In Their DNA [Online]. Apr 2012 [accessed 8 Jul 2015]. Available from: http://www.slideshare.net/fullscreen/jwtintelligence/f-external-genz041812-12653599/1

61 Peterson H. Millennials Are Old News – Here's Everything You Should Know About Generation Z [Online]. 25 Jun 2014 [accessed 8 Jul 2015]. Available from: http://www.businessinsider.com/generation-z-spending-habits-2014-6

62 Ulanoff L. Twitter experiments with 'TV Timelines' [Online]. 13 Mar 2015 [accessed 8 Jul 2015]. Available from: http://mashable.com/2015/03/12/twitter-experiment-tv-timelines/

63 Ulanoff L. Twitter experiments with 'TV Timelines' [Online]. 13 Mar 2015 [accessed 8 Jul 2015]. Available from: http://mashable.com/2015/03/12/twitter-experiment-tv-timelines/

64 VIER ook online en op sociale media graag gezien [Online]. 12 Sep 2013 [accessed 8 Jul 2015]. Available from: http://walkietalkie.prezly.com/vier-ook-online-en-op-sociale-media-graag-gezien

65 Generation Z: Rebels With A Cause [Online]. 28 May 2013 [accessed 9 Jul 2015]. Available from: http://www.forbes.com/sites/onmarketing/2013/05/28/generation-z-rebels-with-a-cause/

66 Adam K. Occupy Wall Street protest go global [Online]. 15 Oct 2011 [accessed 9 Jul 2015]. Available from: https://www.washingtonpost.com/world/europe/occupy-wall-street-protests-go-global/2011/10/15/gIQAp7kimL_story.html

67 Peterson H. Millennials Are Old News – Here's Everything You Should Know About Generation Z [Online]. 25 Jun 2014 [accessed 8 Jul 2015]. Available from: http://www.businessinsider.com/generation-z-spending-habits-2014-6

68 The First Generation Of The Twenty-First Century [Online]. 2014 [accessed 6 Jul 2015]. Available from: http://magid.com/sites/default/files/pdf/MagidPluralistGenerationWhitepaper.pdf

69 Laughlin S. Data Point: Generation Z and gender [Online]. 20 May 2015 [accessed 9 Jul 2015]. Available from: http://www.jwtintelligence.com/2015/05/generation-z-gender/#axzz3c0WQjVrW

70 Tsjeng Z. Inside Selfridges' radical, gender-neutral department store [Online]. Apr 2015 [accessed 9 Jul 2015]. Available from: http://www.dazeddigital.com/fashion/article/24088/1/inside-selfridges-radical-gender-neutral-department-store

71 Generation Z: Rebels With A Cause [Online]. 28 May 2013 [accessed 9 Jul 2015]. Available from: http://www.forbes.com/sites/onmarketing/2013/05/28/generation-z-rebels-with-a-cause/

72 Dockterman E. The War on Pink: GoldieBlox Toys Ignite Debate Over What's Good For Girls [Online]. 2 Feb 2014 [accessed 9 Jul 2015]. Available from: http://time.com/3281/goldie-blox-pink-aisle-debate/

73 GoldieBlox & Rube Goldberg 'Princess Machine' [Online]. 26 Nov 2013 [accessed 9 Jul 2015]. Available from: https://www.youtube.com/watch?v=IIGyVa5Xftw

74 #LikeAGirl Inspires Girls Everywhere [Online]. 26 Jun 2014 [accessed 9 Jul 2015]. Available from: http://news.pg.com/blog/always/likeagirl-inspires-girls-everywhere

75 Always #LikeAGirl [Online]. 26 Jun 2014 [accessed 9 Jul 2015]. Available from: https://www.youtube.com/watch?v=XjJQBjWYDTs

76 Hugely Popular 'Like a Girl' Campaign From Always Will Return as a Super Bowl Ad [Online]. 29 Jan 2015 [accessed 9 Jul 2015]. Available from: http://www.adweek.com/news/advertising-branding/hugely-popular-girl-campaign-always-will-return-sunday-super-bowl-ad-162619

77 Always #LikeAGirl – Unstoppable [Online]. 7 Jul 2015 [accessed 9 Jul 2015]. Available from: https://www.youtube.com/watch?t=49&v=VhB3l1gCz2E

78 Always #LikeAGirl – Confidence Summit announcing partnership with TED [Online]. 7 Jul 2015 [accessed 9 Jul 2015]. Available from: https://www.youtube.com/watch?v=pSkwHLnHpzI

79 Consumers of tomorrow insights and observations about generation z [Online]. 18 Sep 2011 [accessed 8 Jul 2015]. Available from: http://www.slideshare.net/johnyvo/consumers-of-tomorrow-insights-and- observations-about-generation-z

80 Always #LikeAGirl – Confidence Summit announcing partnership with TED [Online]. 7 Jul 2015 [accessed 9 Jul 2015]. Available from: https://www.youtube.com/watch?v=pSkwHLnHpzI

81 The One-for-one Business Model: Avoiding Unintended Consequences [Online]. 16 Feb 2015 [accessed 10 Jul 2015]. Available from: http:// knowledge.wharton.upenn.edu/article/one-one-business-model-social-impact-avoiding-unintended-consequences/

82 Townsend J. C. A Better Way To 'Buy One, Give One' [Online]. 10 Aug 2014 [accessed 10 Jul 2015]. Available from: http://www.forbes.com/sites/ashoka/2014/10/08/a-better-way-to-buy-one-give-one/

83 Strom S. Turning Coffee Into Water to Expand Business Model [Online]. 11 Mar 2014 [accessed 10 Jul 2015]. Available from: http://www.nytimes.com/2014/03/12/business/turning-coffee-into-water-to-expand-a-one-for-one-business-model.html

84 Townsend J. C. A Better Way To 'Buy One, Give One' [Online]. 10 Aug 2014 [accessed 10 Jul 2015]. Available from: http://www.forbes.com/sites/ashoka/2014/10/08/a-better-way-to-buy-one-give-one/

85 The One-for-one Business Model: Avoiding Unintended Consequences [Online]. 16 Feb 2015 [accessed 10 Jul 2015]. Available from: http:// knowledge.wharton.upenn.edu/article/one-one-business-model-social- impact-avoiding-unintended-consequences/

86 Levit A. Make Way for Generation Z [Online]. 28 Mar 2015 [accessed 10 Jul 2015]. Available from: http://www.nytimes.com/2015/03/29/jobs/make-way-for-generation-z.html

87 What Minecraft Teaches Us About Gen Z [Online]. Feb 2015 [accessed 10 Jul 2015]. Available from: http://xyzuniversity.com/2014/02/what-minecraft-teaches-us-about-gen-z/

88 CaptainSparklez [Online]. [accessed 13 Jul 2015]. Available from: https://www.youtube.com/user/CaptainSparklez

89 Ashworth A. What Recruitment Can Learn from Minecraft and Gen Z #TechTuesday [Online]. [accessed 10 Jul 2015]. Available from: http://theundercoverrecruiter.com/recruitment-minecraft-gen-z/

90 A 6-year-old totally owned the Financial Times over a 'Minecraft' error [Online]. 12 Jul 2015 [accessed 13 Jul 2015]. Available from: http://fusion.net/story/165400/a-6-year-old-totally-owned-the-financial-times-over-a-minecraft-error/

91 Benhamou L. Everything you need to know about Generation Z [Online]. 12 Feb 2015 [accessed 10 Jul 2015]. Available from: http://uk.businessinsider.com/afp-generation-z-born-in-the-digital-age-2015-2?r=US

92 Schawbel D. 39 Of The Most Interesting Facts About Generation Z [Online]. 17 Jul 2014 [accessed 10 Jul 2015]. Available from: http://danschawbel.com/blog/39-of-the-most-interesting-facts-about-generation-z/

93 Lane S. Beyond Millennials: How to Reach Generation Z [Online].20 Aug 2014 [accessed 7 Jul 2015]. Available from: http://mashable.com/2014/08/20/generation-z-marketing/

94 Marchetti TJ. 3 fundamental ways Generation Z differs from Millennials [Online]. 21 Jul 2014 [accessed 10 Jul 2015]. Available from: http://www.imediaconnection.com/content/37005.asp#tz7c5EKTq3lkRZ8r.99

95 Ault S. Survey: YouTube stars more popular than mainstream celebs among US teens. [Online]. 5 Aug 2014 [accessed 8 Jun 2015]. Available from: http://variety.com/2014/digital/news/survey-youtube-stars-more-popular-than-mainstream-celebs-among-u-s-teens-1201275245/

96 Identica. Born on the web. [Online]. 10 Apr 2015 [accessed 8 Jun 2015]. Available from: http://www.identica.co.uk/born-web/#sthash.Ryd71P45.dpbs

97 Russel M. What Gen Z stars mean for the entertainment and advertising industry. [Online]. 19 Aug 2014 [accessed 8 Jun 2015]. Available from: http://www.visiblemeasures.com/2014/08/19/what-gen-z-youtube-stars-mean-for-the-entertainment-and-advertising-industries

98 Nielsen. The total audience report December 2014. [Online]. Dec 2014 [accessed 12 Jun 2015]. Available from: http://www.nielsen.com/content/dam/corporate/us/en/reports-downloads/2014%20Reports/total-audience-report-december-2014.pdf

99 Baysinger T. PewDiePie Fires Back at 'Haters' Over the $7.4 Million He Made on YouTube. [Online]. 9 Jul 2015 [accessed 10 Jul 2015]. Available from: http://www.adweek.com/news/television/pewdiepie-fires-back-haters-over-74-million-he-made-youtube-165820

100 Castillo M. Bethany Mota: great content creators focus on their viewers, not on stardom. [Online]. 13 Nov 2014 [accessed 9 Jun 2015]. Available from: http://www.adweek.com/news/technology/bethany-mota-admits-she-wasnt-dancer-dancing-stars-161416

101 Castillo M. Why President Obama agreed to be interviewed by YouTubers. [Online]. 23 Jan 2015 [accessed 9 Jun 2015]. Available from: http://www.adweek.com/news/technology/why-president-obama-agreed-be-interviewed-youtubers-162530

102 Castillo M. Bethany Mota: great content creators focus on their viewers, not on stardom. [Online]. 13 Nov 2014 [accessed 9 Jun 2015]. Available from: http://www.adweek.com/news/technology/bethany-mota-admits-she-wasnt-dancer-dancing-stars-161416

103 Johnson L. How Brands and YouTube Stars Are Hooking Up to Reach Millions of Millennials [Online]. 27 Apr 2015 [accessed 10 Jul 2015]. Available from: http://www.adweek.com/news-gallery/technology/how-brands-and- youtube-stars-are-hooking-reach-millions-millennials-164316

104 Moss R. How Winnie Harlow, Who Has Vitiligo, Challenged All Perceptions About Beauty At London Fashion Week [Online]. 17 Sep 2014 [accessed 13 Jul 2015]. Available from: http://www.huffingtonpost.co.uk/2014/09/17/winnie-harlow-london-fashion-week-ashish_n_5834686.html

105 Manrodt A. The Ugly Selfie Trend: How Funny Pics Are Turning Social Media on Its Head [Online]. 24 Mar 2014 [accessed 13 Jul 2015]. Available from: http://www.teenvogue.com/story/ugly-selfies

106 Intermarche – Inglorious Fruits and Vegetables [Online]. 2014 [accessed 13 Jul 2015]. Available from: https://vimeo.com/98441820

107 Godoy M. In Europe, Ugly Sells In The Produce Aisle [Online]. 9 Dec 2014 [accessed 13 Jul 2015]. Available from: http://www.npr.org/sections/thesalt/2014/12/09/369613561/in-europe-ugly-sells-in-the-produce-aisle

108 Crafting Culture [Online]. 8 Dec 2014 [accessed 13 Jul 2015]. Available from: https://www.contagious.io/articles/crafting-culture

109 What Is Fuckup Nights? [Online]. [accessed 13 Jul 2015]. Available from: http://www.fuckupnights.com/

110 Hjuler P. [Interview]. *The LEGO Group*. 6 Oct 2015

111 Klara R. Lego's Consistency Has Been the Key to Success [Online]. 15 Apr 2013 [accessed 8 Oct 2015]. Available from: http://www.adweek.com/news/advertising-branding/legos-consistency-has-been-key-its-success-148553

112 Lane S. Beyond Millennials: How to Reach Generation Z [Online].20 Aug 2014 [accessed 7 Jul 2015]. Available from: http://mashable.com/2014/08/20/generation-z-marketing/

113 Taking Stock With Teens – Spring 2014 [Online]. 2014 [accessed 13 Jul 2015]. Available from: http://www.piperjaffray.com/3col.aspx?id=3045

114 Cochrane L. Athleisure: Beyoncé + Topshop = surefire style trend [Online]. 1 Jan 2015 [accessed 13 Jul 2015]. Available from: http://www.theguardian.com/fashion/2015/jan/01/athleisure-beyonce-topshop-style-trend-gym-ready-gear

INDEX

Note: Page numbers in *italic* indicate figures or tables.

CPSIA information can be obtained at www.ICGtesting.com
Printed in the USA
BVOW06s1030040816

457948BV00007B/16/P